W9-CBB-656

Student Edition

British
LITERATURE

ENCOURAGING THOUGHTFUL CHRISTIANS TO BE WORLD CHANGERS

By James P. Stobaugh

Copyright © 2005, James P. Stobaugh

All rights reserved.
Printed in the United States of America

10-Digit ISBN: 0805458948
13-Digit ISBN: 9780805458947

Published by Broadman & Holman Publishers
Nashville, Tennessee

DEWEY: 820
SUBHD: BRITISH LITERATURE

Unless otherwise noted, scripture text is from The Holy Bible, *Holman Christian Standard Bible* ®, Copyright © 1999, 2000, 2001, 2002, 2003 by Holman Bible Publishers. Other "Credits, Permissions, and Sources" are listed at the back of the book.

No part of this book may be reproduced in any form or by any means, unless it is stated otherwise, without written permission from the publisher, Broadman & Holman Publishers, 127 Ninth Avenue, North, Nashville, TN 37234-0115 or broadmanholman.com.

Cover and interior design by Paul T. Gant, Art & Design — Nashville, TN

1 2 3 4 5   09 08 07 06 05

This Book is gratefully dedicated to
Karen
and
our four children:
Rachel, Jessica, Timothy, and Peter.

He has given us a ministry of reconciliation . . .
2 Corinthians 5:18

Students, to you 'tis given to scan the heights
Above, to traverse the ethereal space,
And mark the systems of revolving worlds.
Still more, ye sons of science ye receive
The blissful news by messengers from heav'n,
How Jesus blood for your redemption flows . . .

—Phillis Wheatley

ACKNOWLEDGMENTS

From the Broadman and Holman Home Education Division, I wish to thank Sheila Moss, whose editorial assistance and encouragement have been greatly appreciated; Matt Stewart, whose vision and perseverance have made this project possible; and Paul Gant and Mark Grover for their work with graphics and the DVD. Likewise, I thank my four children and my distance learning students who so graciously allowed me to use their essays. Finally, and most of all, I want to thank my best friend and lifelong editor, my wife, Karen. "Come, let us glorify the Lord and praise His name forever . . . ." (Psalm 34:3)

Contents

*Readings are provided in the text.

Preface

INTRODUCTION

British Literature is a rhetoric level course. There are two distinctives of rhetoric level courses: they are content driven and they presume higher-level thinking. In most cases, you will be reading in excess of 200 pages per week. Therefore, to ease your weekly schedule throughout the school year, most of this material should be read the summer before you begin this course.

In any event, you will need to read the whole book/literary work before the week's lesson begins. Sometimes this is not a very lengthy assignment (e.g., reading Queen Elizabeth's poetry, Lesson 5). In other cases it will take you more than a week to read the assigned text (e.g., *MacBeth*, Lesson 6 or *Frankenstein*, Lesson 23).

If you have worked through the *Skills for Literary Analysis* and *Skills for Rhetoric* courses in this series, you already know how to accomplish elementary literary criticism. If you have not worked through the introductory courses and you are concerned, don't be. You will be reviewed on how to do literary analysis as the course progresses. Literary analysis questions are the most often asked questions in the study of literature, and in this course, analysis type questions are divided into three main categories: Critical Thinking, Biblical Application, and Enrichment.

In *Merriam Webster's Collegiate Dictionary* (10th ed., 1993), *literature* is defined as "writings in prose or verse: especially having excellence of form or expression and expressing ideas of permanent or universal interest."

The person who examines, interprets, and analyzes literature is a *critic*. That is your job. A critic is a guide to the reader, not a prophet or a therapist. While it is the critic's right to express his preferences, and even his privilege to influence others, it is not his job to tell the reader what to like or not like. However, the critic is a helper, a guide helping the reader better understand the author's intention and art. In fact, the critic is concerned about the structure, sound, and meaning of the literary piece. These structures are described as genres: *narrative prose*, *essays*, *poetry*, and *drama*.

Literary analysis or criticism is a way to talk about literature. It is a way to understand literature better so that you can tell others about it. If you really want to understand something, you need to have a common language with everyone else. If you were talking about football, for instance, you would need to know about certain terminology and use it when describing the game. How lost you would be without knowing what a tackle is! Or how could you enjoy watching the game without knowing what the referee means when he shouts, "First and Ten!"

Literary analysis employs *a common language* to take apart and to discuss literary pieces. You will learn that language with its literary terms as this course progresses over the year. A list of literary terms is found in the glossary at the end of this book.

You will be asked to participate in higher-level thinking and problem-solving. Saying, "I don't know" or "I can't think" or "I don't know how to do it" isn't problem solving!

Typically, you and your teachers/parents will decide on required essays for the lessons, choosing two or three essays per week. Remember to follow the writing suggestions in the appendices as you write the essays.

STUDENT ROLES AND RESPONSIBILITIES:

1. Read the assigned, whole literary piece before the first classroom assignment. You will need to read ahead: you cannot wait until two days before an assignment is due to read the material. At the end of each lesson, the Suggested Weekly Implementation boxes will prompt you concerning future assignments, but you will need to make sure you do the work in a timely way. In addition to the information in the Suggested Implementation box at the end of each lesson, you will be prompted at the beginning of each lesson in a text memo box.

Your teacher/parent may try to help you occasionally with more difficult readings by providing unabridged book tape copies of the assigned text.

2. Read and discuss the guide question concerning future reading found in the text box on and at the end of each lesson. For example, the guide questions at the end of Lesson 1, concerning Lesson 2, are "What does the word *worldview* mean? What is your worldview? What worldviews do you encounter in the world around you?" These questions will guide you as you review (because you should have already *read*) the next reading assignments.

3. Discuss with your parent/educator the background material.

4. Discuss with your parent/educator the assigned questions. The highlighted term is defined in simple language and illustrated by a readable example. If you need more information, access other composition handbooks.

5. Complete all assigned activities that teachers and students decide upon, choosing from three essay types:
Critical Thinking
Biblical Application
Enrichment

> Sample Text Box:
> **Analyze** "The Seafarer," Author Unknown; Beowulf, Author Unknown.
> **Reading Ahead:** *An Ecclesiastical History of the English People,* Venerable Bede.
> **Guide Questions:** How does Bede's view of history differ from contemporary views? What does the word "worldview" mean? What is your worldview? What worldviews do you encounter in the world around you?

You will be writing two to three 1-2 page essays/week, depending on the level of accomplishment you and your parent/educator decide upon. To experience the optimum from the course, you should be willing to write from all essay types—including the Enrichment essays. After you and your parent/educator decide on the *required* essays, I recommend that you at least *outline* and/or *discuss* the remaining essays. Outline strategies are found in the Appendix at the back of this book.

Complete literary reviews. You will be assigned particular works to read during this course; however, as time allows, read books from the enclosed list (See Appendix). You should read most of the books on the enclosed supplemental book list before you graduate from high school. After reading a literary work, for this course or for any other reason, you should complete a literary review (See Appendix) as a record of your high school reading. The supplemental book list is not meant to be exhaustive but is intended as a guide to good reading. Reading 35-50 pages per night (or 200 pages per week), including the reading for this course, is a good plan to strengthen your reading protocol.

7. Create 3x5 vocabulary cards.
Part of the reason for reading so many challenging literary works is for you to increase your functional vocabulary. Your best means of increasing vocabulary is through reading a vast amount of classical, well-written literary works. I could give you 15 new words to learn every week, but studies show that most of you would forget those words within 24 hours. While reading literary works, you should harvest as many unknown words as you can. *You should use five new words in each essay you write.*

Then most conspicuous, when great things of small,/Useful of hurtful, rosperous of *adverse*/We can create . . .

Harmful, Evil Adj., Adversity is Noun The <u>adverse</u> effects of smoking are great.

Front   Back

When you meet a new word, do your best to figure out the word in context; check your guess by looking in the dictionary; write a sentence with the word in it.

Use the illustration above to formulate your vocabulary cards of new words.

8. Write in a prayer journal. If you don't have a prayer journal, try using the prayer journal template in the appendix. Make 25-50 copies of this page and put it in a notebook. As often as you can—hopefully daily—fill out one of these sheets on a biblical passage. You will find a sample format in the Appendices.

NOTE: Used along with the Biblical Application Questions, commitment to the daily process of Prayer Journaling could lead to a separate elective credit course. Be sure to discuss this option with your parent/educator.

9. Begin the final project. See appendix for more specific instructions.

Your **Final Portfolio** should include corrected essays, literary reviews, writing journal, vocabulary cards, pictures from field trips, and other pertinent material (See Lesson 35 for more details).

SUGGESTED WEEKLY IMPLEMENTATION SCHEDULE

If you follow this schedule, you will get all your work done in a timely way.

SUGGESTED
Weekly *Implementation*

DAY 1	DAY 2	DAY 3	DAY 4	DAY 5
Prayer journal. Review the required reading(s) before the assigned lesson begins. Teacher may want to discuss assigned reading(s) with students. Teacher and students will decide on required essays for this lesson, choosing two or three essays. The rest of the essays can be outlined, answered with shorter answers, or skipped. Review all readings for Assigned Lesson.	**Prayer journal.** Review reading(s) from next lesson. Outline essays due at the end of the week. Per teacher instructions, students may answer orally in a group setting some of the essays that are not assigned as formal essays.	**Prayer journal.** Write rough drafts of all assigned essays. The teacher and/or a peer evaluator may correct rough drafts.	**Prayer journal.** Rewrite corrected copies of essays due tomorrow.	**Prayer journal.** Essays are due. Take Lesson 1 test. Reading ahead: This will give you a reminder of what to be reading ahead for future lessons. Guide: These questions will guide your thinking and study for the next lesson.

NOTE: Remember to read ahead the requisite literary material for this course; many students read the required literature *during the summer* before the course begins.

SCOPE AND SEQUENCE
BRITISH LITERATURE

LESSON	PERIOD/WORLDVIEW AUTHORS/ TEXTS
1	*Anglo-Saxon Age (Part 1)* **Author Unknown**, "The Seafarer."* **Author Unknown**, *Beowulf*.
2	*Anglo-Saxon Age (Part 2)* **Venerable Bede**, *The Ecclesiastical History of the English People*. Worldviews
3	*Middle Ages (Part 1)* **Author Unknown** (Scottish folk ballads), "Bonny Barbara Allan,"* Author Unknown; "Get Up and Bar the Door."* **Geoffrey Chaucer**, "The Prologue,"* "The Pardoner's Tale," and "The Nun Priest's Tale," in *The Canterbury Tales*.
4	*Middle Ages (Part 2)* **Author Unknown**, *Sir Gawain and The Green Knight*.
5	*Elizabethan Age (Part 1)* **Queen Elizabeth**, (1533-1603) "On Monsieur's Departure,"* "The Doubt of Future Woes,"* "Speech to the Troops at Tilbury."* **Isabella Whitney**, "The Admonition by the Author to all Young Gentlewomen: And to all other Maids being in Love."* **Edmund Spenser**, *The Fairie Queene*, "Sonnet 26,"* and "Sonnet 75,"* from *Amoretti*. **Christopher Marlowe**, "The Passionate Shepherd to His Love."* **Sir Walter Raleigh**, "The Nymph's Reply to the Shepherd." **William Shakespeare**, "Sonnet 116,"* "Sonnet 18,"* "Sonnet 29,"*, "Sonnet 55,"* "Sonnet 73."*
6	*Elizabethan Age (Part 2)* **William Shakespeare**, *Macbeth*.
7	*Elizabethan Age (Part 3)* **Elizabeth Cary** *The Tragedy of Mariam The Faire Queen of Jewry."* **Ben Jonson**, "On My First Son,"* "The Noble Nature,"* "To the Memory of My Beloved Master, William Shakespeare,"* "A Farewell to the World."* **Francis Bacon**, *Essays*.
8	*Elizabethan Age (Part 4)* **Christopher Marlowe**, *Dr. Faustus* **Mary Sidney Herbert**, Countess of Pembroke "To the Thrice-Sacred Queen Elizabeth," "Psalm 58."* The English Bible

*Readings are provided in the text.

*Readings are provided in the text.

	Robert Burns, "A Man's a Man for A' That,"* "O, My Luve Is Like A Red, Red Rose,"* "Till 'a the seas gang dry,"* "To a Mouse."* **William Blake.** "How Sweet I Roam'd From Field to Field,"* "And Did Those Feet in Ancient Time,"* "The Clod and the Pebble,"* "The Lamb,"* "The Tyger."*
21	*Nineteenth Century (Part 1)* **Helen Maria Williams,** "A Song."* **William Wordsworth,** "London 1802,"* "A Slumber did my Spirit Seal,"* "To the Cuckoo,"* "To a Sky Lark,"* "Composed upon Westminster Bridge, September 3, 1802,"* "Strange Fits of Passion Have I Known,"* "The Tables Turned," "Lines Written in Early Spring."* **Dorothy Wordsworth,** from *The Grasmere Journals.**
22	*Nineteenth Century (Part 2)* **Mary Wollstonecraft,** *A Vindication of the Rights of Woman.* **Lord Byron,** "Don Juan,"* "The Prisoner of Chillon,"* "She Walks in Beauty."* **Samuel Taylor Coleridge,** "Kubla Khan"* and "The Rime of the Ancient Mariner." **Percy Bysshe Shelley,** "Ozymandias*" and "To a Skylark,"* **John Keats,** "Bright Star,"* "Ode on a Grecian Urn,"* "Ode to a Nightingale,"* "Posthuma."*
23	*Nineteenth Century (Part 3)* **Charlotte Brontë,** *Jane Eyre.* **Mary Shelley,** *Frankenstein.*
24	*Nineteenth Century (Part 4)* **Charles Dickens,** *A Tale of Two Cities.*
25	*Nineteenth Century (Part 5)* **Jane Austen,** *Pride and Prejudice.*
26	*Nineteenth Century (Part 6)* **Robert Louis Stevenson,** *Dr. Jekyll and Mr. Hyde*
27	*Nineteenth Century (Part 7)* **Mary Elizabeth Coleridge,** "The Witch."* **John Henry Newman** "The Idea of a University."* **Alfred Lord Tennyson,** "Break, Break, Break,"* "The Charge of the Light Brigade," "Ulysses," "Crossing the Bar."* **Robert Browning,** "Prospice," "The Lost Leader," "My Last Duchess Ferrara."* **Elizabeth Barrett,** "Sonnet XIV,"* "Sonnet I,"* "Sonnet XLIII."*
28	*Nineteenth Century (Part 8)* **Thomas Hardy,** *The Mayor of Casterbridge.*
29	*Twentieth Century (Part 1)* **Joseph Conrad,** *Lord Jim.*
30	*Twentieth Century (Part 2)*

*Readings are provided in the text.

		Stevie Smith (Florence Margaret Smith), "Not Waving but Drowning."*
		Katherine Mansfield, "Miss Brill."*
		James Joyce, "Araby"*
		Oscar Wilde, "The Selfish Giant."*
		Saki (H. H. Munro), "The Bag."*
		Rudyard Kipling, "Without Benefit of Clergy."*
		D. H. Lawrence, "Rocking Horse Winner."*
31		*Twentieth Century (Part 3)*
		Dorothy L. Sayers, "Are Women Human?" "The Human-Not-Quite Human"
		A. E. Housman, "Terence, This is Stupid Stuff," "Loveliest of Trees," and "Be Still my Soul."
		Wilfred Owen, "Greater Love."*
		Rupert Brooke, "The Fish."*
		George McCrae, "In Flanders Fields."*
		William Butler Yeats, "An Irish Airman Foresees His Death," "When You are Old," "The Second Coming," "The White Swans at Coole," and "Byzantium."
32		*Twentieth Century (Part 4)*
		C. S. Lewis, *Mere Christianity.*
33		*Twentieth Century (Part 5)*
		J.R.R. Tolkien, *The Lord of the Rings.*
34		*Twentieth Century (Part 6)*
		T.S. Eliot, *Murder in the Cathedral.*
35		*Final Portfolio*
		Student: Written and Oral Presentation

*Readings are provided in the text.

Audio presentations of most of the readings in the book may be obtained from Blackstoneaudio.com

British Literature Reading List

Additional texts, not included within the study, needed for this program:

Beowulf by author unknown

The Ecclesiastical History of the English People by Venerable Bede

"The Pardoner's Tale" and "The Nun's Priest's Tale" from Canterbury Tales by Geoffrey Chaucer

Sir Gawain and the Green Knight by author unknown

The Fairie Queene by Edmund Spenser

Macbeth by William Shakespeare

Dr. Faustus by Christopher Marlowe

"Holy Sonnet XIV" by John Donne
"Silex" by Henry Vaughan
Paradise Lost by John Milton
"An Essay of Dramatic Poesy" by John Dryden
Eveline or *Cecilia* by Frances Burney d'Arblay
Robinson Crusoe by Daniel Defoe
Gulliver's Travels by Jonathan Swift
The Vicar of Wakefield by Oliver Goldsmith
The Rivals by Richard Brimsley Sheridan
"The Rime of the Ancient Mariner" by Samuel Taylor Coleridge
Jane Eyre by Charlotte Brontë
Frankenstein by Mary Shelley
A Tale of Two Cities by Charles Dickens
Pride and Prejudice by Jane Austen
Dr. Jekyll and Mr. Hyde by Robert Lewis Stevenson
"The Witch" by Mary Elizabeth Coleridge
The Mayor of Casterbridge by Thomas Hardy
Lord Jim by Joseph Conrad
Are Women Human? And The Human-Not-Quite Human by Dorothy Sayers
"Terence, This is Stupid Stuff," "Loveliest of Trees," and "Be Still my Soul" by A. E. Housman
"An Irish Airman Foresees His Death," "When You are Old," "The Second Coming," "The White Swans at Coole," and "Bazantium" by William Butler Yeats
Mere Christianity by C. S. Lewis
The Lord of the Rings by J.R.R.Tolkien
Murder in the Cathedral by T.S. Eliot

My prayer for you is

"For this reason I bow my knees before the Father from whom every family in heaven and on earth is named. I pray that He may grant you, according to the riches of His glory, to be strengthened with power through His Spirit in the inner man, and that the Messiah may dwell in your hearts through faith. I pray that you, being rooted and firmly established in love, may be able to comprehend with all the saints what is the length and width, height and depth of God's love, and to know the Messiah's love that surpasses knowledge, so you may be filled with all the fullness of God. Now to Him who is able to do above and beyond all that we ask or think —according to the power that works in you—to Him be glory in the church and in Christ Jesus to all generations, forever and ever. Amen."
(Ephs. 3:14-21)

James Stobaugh

From the Editor

Developing appropriate curricula for a specific audience is a major and intricate endeavor. Doing so for the homeschool and Christian communities is perhaps even more difficult: homeschool approaches, methodology, and content are as diverse as traditional educational trends have ever dared to be. Homeschooling is complex—from unschooling to the Classical approach, there are a myriad of opinions of what to teach, when to teach it, and how to teach it to whom at what age and at what level of development. Perhaps you struggle with choices between a *whole-book* approach to literature study or a more traditional and inclusive canon. Perhaps you are still wading through a myriad of questions associated with homeschooling teenagers. However, perhaps your decision is final and you merely need a solid literature-and-writing-based English curriculum. Keep reading.

In one-year literature/writing-based courses, including all the quality literature that has ever been published is impossible—there is simply too much good literature and not enough space to include it; neither is there time enough to read it all. Regrettably, many selections of quality literature have not been included in this course—not because they are unworthy, but because they all cannot fit into the designated framework. The author and I have done our best to include whole-book or whole-work selections from the major genres of literature (prose, poetry, and drama). In the *Literary Analysis, Rhetoric*, and *American, British*, and *World Literature* courses in this series, literary selections incorporate many ethnicities from both male and female writers. We believe our selections inform the purpose of the curricula: *Encouraging Thoughtful Christians to be World Changers.*

According to a well-known author, homeschool conference speaker, and long-time homeschooling mom, two of the greatest needs in the homeschool community reside in curricula for high school and for special needs. These English curricula consider those needs; they were conceived in prayer, deliberated through educational experience, and nurtured with inspiration. We are providing unique five-year curricula for required English studies for the multifarious Christian community. Canonical and Classical literature is emphasized; students are meticulously guided through carefully honed steps of *critical thinking, biblical challenge for spiritual growth*, and even additional *enrichment* motivators. A major key to the successful completion of these courses falls in the statements, "Teachers and students will decide on required essays for this lesson, choosing two or three essays. All other essays may be outlined, discussed, or omitted." These statements, repeated in every lesson, allow tremendous flexibility for various levels of student maturity and interests. Since each lesson may offer 10-15 essays, choosing essays each week is vital.

In any literature course offered to Christian audiences there will be differences in opinions regarding acceptable and appropriate content, authors, poets, and playwrights. Some educators may object to specific works or specific authors, poets, or playwrights included in these curricula *even though we have been very conscientious with selections*. For that reason we highly encourage educators and students to confab—choose units according to students' maturity, ability, age, sensitivity, interests, educational intentions, and according to family goals. Educators decide how much they want to shelter their students or to sanction certain works or authors, poets, and playwrights.

On a broader note, our goal in this series is to provide parent educators and Christian schools with educationally sound, rigorous literature courses that equip students

1. to think critically about their world and their participation in it;

2. to write their thoughts, primarily through essays;

3. to articulate their thoughts through small group discussions with peers, families, broader communities, and through occasional formal speeches;

4. to enhance vocabulary through reading and studying quality literature;

5. to converse about the major worldviews of authors of literature, past and present;

6. to develop and refine their own worldviews through participating in biblical application and Christian principles in weekly studies.

Additionally, we provide educators with an instructional CD in the back of each teacher edition. Narrated by the author, the CD is designed to provide extra commentary on the unit studies.

Ideally, students will complete these entire curricula; however, parent educators and teachers are free to choose literary selections that best fit their goals with students. Regardless of the choices, I pray that students come away from studying *Skills for Literary Analysis, Skills for Rhetoric, American Literature, British Literature*, and *World Literature* not only highly educated but also equipped to participate in and contribute to their earthly home while preparing for their heavenly home.

Enjoy!
Sheila Moss

Introduction

I am profoundly enthusiastic about the future. Not only do I trust in our Mighty God, I am greatly encouraged by what I see in this generation. God is doing great things in the midst of students.

There is much need in our physical world. In his seminal work *The Dust of Death* (Downers Grove, Illinois: Intervarsity Press, 1973), social critic Os Guinness prophetically argues that "western culture is marked . . . by a distinct slowing of momentum . . . a decline in purposefulness. . . . Guinness implies that ideals and traditions that have been central to American civilization are losing their compelling cultural authority. In short, there is no corpus of universally accepted morality that Americans follow. As Dallas Willard in *The Divine Conspiracy* (San Francisco: HarperCollins Publishers, 1997) states, ". . . there is no recognized moral knowledge upon which projects of fostering moral development could be based."

In his poem "The Second Coming" William Butler Yeats writes

The best lack all conviction, while the worst
Are full of passionate intensity
Turning and turning in the widening gyre;
The falcon cannot hear the falconer.

In the beginning of the twenty-first century, America is spinning out of control. She is stretching her wings adventurously but is drifting farther away from her God. America is in trouble. How do we know?

You are America's first generation to grow up when wholesale murder is legal; the first generation to access 130 channels and at the same time to access almost nothing of value. In 1993 in their book *The Day America Told the Truth* (NY: Simon & Schuster Publishers, Inc.), James Patterson and Peter Kim warned that 87% of Americans do not believe that the Ten Commandments should be obeyed and 91% of them tell at least one lie a day. Unfortunately, I doubt things are any better today than they were over 10 years ago. The challenge, the bad news, is that this is a time when outrage is dead. Whatever needs to be done, you and your friends are probably going to have to do it.

I think the good news is that we are turning a corner. I believe that in the near future Americans will be looking to places of stability and strength for direction. Besides, by default, those people whose lives are in reasonably good shape, who have some reason to live beyond the next paycheck, will have an almost inexorable appeal. Those who walk in the Light will draw others into the very-same Light. My prayer is that these curricula will help you walk in the Light in a modest way.

I believe that God is raising a mighty generation at the very time that many twenty-first century Americans are searching for truth—at the very time they are hungry for things of the Lord. You will be the culture-creators of the next century. You are a special generation, a special people.

Young people, I strongly believe that you are the generation God has called *for such a time as this* to bring a Spirit-inspired revival. God is stirring the water again at the beginning of this century. He is offering a new beginning for a new nation. I believe you are the personification of that new beginning.

You are part of one of the most critical generations in the history of Western culture. Indeed, only Augustine's generation comes close in importance to your generation. In both cases—today and during the life of Augustine, Bishop of Hippo—civilizations were in decline. Young Augustine lived through the decline of the Roman world; you are living through the decline of American cultural superiority. Even though the barbarians conquered Rome, the Christians conquered the barbarians.

Similar to Anne Bradstreet and other young Puritans who settled in 1630 Boston, you will need to replace this old, reprobate culture with a new God-centered, God-breathed society, or our nation may not survive another century.

While I was a graduate student at Harvard University in the mid-1970s, I attended a chapel service where the presenter self-righteously proclaimed that we Harvard students were the next generation of culture creators. Indeed. Perhaps he was right—look at the moral mess my generation created!

Evangelical scholars Nathan Hatch and George Marsden argue, and I think persuasively, that you young people will be the next generation of elites: important politicians, inspired playwrights, and presidents of Fortune 500 companies.

I profoundly believe and fervently hope that you young people will also be the new elite of culture creators. I define "elitism" as the ability and propensity of an individual or a group to assume leadership and culture-creation in a given society. In his essay "Blessed Are the History-Makers," theologian Walter Bruggemann reminds us that culture is created and history is made by those who are radically committed to obeying God at all costs.

Will you be counted among those who are radically committed—being smart, but above all, loving, worshipping, and being obedient to the Word of God? In your generation and for the first time in 300 years of American cultural history, the marriage of smart minds and born-again hearts is becoming visible. This combination is potent indeed and has revolutionary implications for twenty-first century cultural America. Now, as in the Puritan era, a spirit-filled elite with all its ramifications is exciting to behold.

This book is dedicated to the ambitious goal of preparing you to be a twenty-first century world changer for the Christ whom John Milton in *Paradise Lost* called "the countenance too severe to be beheld." (VI, 825)

James Stobaugh

LESSON 1

ANGLO SAXON AGE *(Part 1)*

Anglo-Saxon Literature

BACKGROUND

It was in A.D. 449 that the Jutes, from Denmark, invaded land previously conquered by the Romans and earlier by the Britons, Celts, and Druids. Following the Jutes came the Angles and Saxons. The origins of the Anglo-Saxon people are obscure. Scholars believe that they inhabited southern Sweden, the Danish peninsula, and northern Germany (between the Ems River on the west, the Oder River on the east, and the Harz Mountains on the south). The Anglo-Saxons created an English civilization that lasted until 1066 A.D., when William the Conqueror, from Normandy, France, conquered England at the Battle of Hastings. Who were the Anglo-Saxons? They were a Germanic people who loved epic legends and stories about the sea. They loved a good fight but also had a highly developed feeling for beauty. The Anglo-Saxons loved to describe rippling brooks and stunning sunsets. They dominated England's culture for almost a century.

Analyze: "The Seafarer," Author Unknown; *Beowulf*, Author Unknown.

Reading Ahead: *An Ecclesiastical History of the English* People, Venerable Bede.

Review: "Bonny Barbara Allan," Author Unknown; "Get Up and Bar the Door," Author Unknown (Scottish folk ballads); "The Prologue," "The Pardoner's Tale," and "The Nun's Priest's Tale," in *The Canterbury Tales*, Geoffrey Chaucer (Lesson 3). In what ways were the English middle ages, so called dark ages, full of light?

Guide Question: How does Bede's view of history differ from contemporary views? What does the word "worldview" mean? What is your worldview? What worldviews do you encounter in the world around you? In what ways were the English middle ages, so-called Dark Ages, full of light?

The Seafarer

Author unknown

BACKGROUND

"True is the tale that I tell of my travels . . ." is the beginning of one of the oldest pieces of literature in the English language (although one would not recognize the language—it is closer to contemporary German). "The Seafarer," however, written by an unknown Anglo-Saxon, is quite contemporary in its magnitude of feeling. It is an elegy. Elegies are common in Old English poems. They lament the loss of worldly goods, glory, or human companionship. A contemporary elegy, for instance, might be a story-song performed by the contemporary Christian musician

> A *motif* is a recurring literary theme. It assumes a central part of the literary piece.

Carmen. One Anglo-Saxon poem, "The Wanderer," is narrated by a man, deprived of lord and kinsmen, whose journeys lead him to the realization that there is stability and hope only in the afterlife. "The Seafarer" is similar, but its *journey motif* more explicitly symbolizes the speaker's spiritual yearnings. In this sense it is Judeo-Christian: Moses and the Children of Israel wander in the wilderness, too. The journey motif is common in Western literature.

The Seafarer

This tale is true, and mine. It tells
How the sea took me, swept me back
And forth in sorrow and fear and pain,
Showed me suffering in a hundred ships,
In a thousand ports, and in me. It tells
Of smashing surf when I sweated in the cold
Of an anxious watch, perched in the bow
As it dashed under cliffs. My feet were cast
In icy bands, bound with frost,
With frozen chains, and hardship groaned
Around my heart. Hunger tore
At my sea-weary soul. No man sheltered
On the quiet fairness of earth can feel

how wretched I was, drifting through winter
On an ice-cold sea, whirled in sorrow,
Alone in a world blown clear of love,
Hung with icicles. The hail storms flew.
The only sound was the roaring sea,
the freezing waves. The song of the swan
Might serve for pleasure, the cry of the sea-fowl,
The death-noise of birds instead of laughter,
The mewing of gulls instead of mead.
Storms beat on the rocky cliffs and were echoed
By icy-feathered terns and the eagle's screams;
No kinsmen could offer comfort there,
To a soul left drowning in desolation.
And who could believe, knowing but
The passion of cities,
    swelled proud with
    wine
And no taste of misfor-
    tune, how often,
    how wearily
I put myself back on the
    paths of the sea.
Night would blacken; it
    would snow from

In the Old Testament, Moses and the children of Israel wander in the wilderness, but they are not lost. God is leading them.

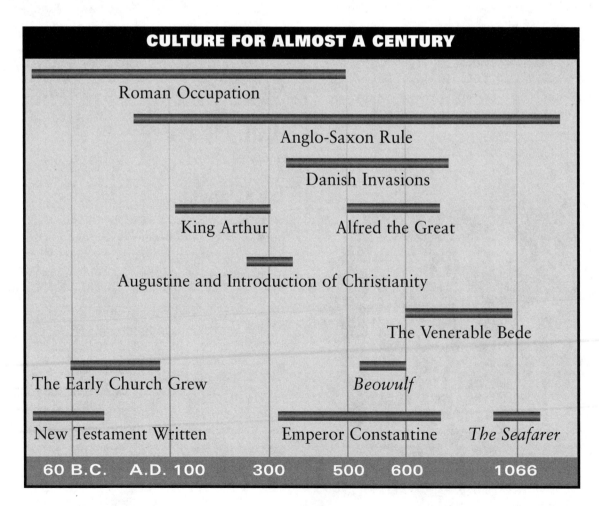

CULTURE FOR ALMOST A CENTURY

Roman Occupation
Anglo-Saxon Rule
Danish Invasions
King Arthur   Alfred the Great
Augustine and Introduction of Christianity
The Venerable Bede
The Early Church Grew   *Beowulf*
New Testament Written   Emperor Constantine   *The Seafarer*

60 B.C.   A.D. 100   300   500   600   1066

the north.
Frost bound the earth and hail would fall,
The coldest seeds. And how my heart
Would begin to beat, knowing once more
The salt waves tossing and the towering sea!
The time for journeys would come and my soul
Called me eagerly out, sent me over
The horizon, seeking foreigner's homes.
But there isn't a man on earth so proud,
So born to greatness, so bold with his youth,
Grown so brave, or so graced by God,
That he feels no fear as the sails unfurl,
Wondering what Fate has willed and will do.
No harps ring in his heart, no rewards,
No passion for women, no worldly pleasures,
Nothing, only the ocean's heave;
But longing wraps itself around him.
Orchards blossom, the towns bloom,
Fields grow lovely as the world springs fresh,
And all these admonish that willing mind
Leaping to journeys, always set
In thoughts traveling on a quickening tide.
So summer's sentinel,
    the cuckoo, sings
In his murmuring
    voice, and our
    hearts mourn
As he urges. Who
    could understand,
In ignorant ease, what
    we others suffer
As the paths of exile
    stretch endlessly
    on?

> Anglo-Saxon poetry was spoken before it was written. Poems were memorized by *scops* who wandered around the countryside chanting their poems in castles and mead halls.

And yet my heart wanders away,
My soul roams with the sea, the whales'
Home, wandering to the widest corners
Of the world, returning ravenous with desire,
Flying solitary, screaming, exciting me
To the open ocean, breaking oaths
On the curve of a wave.
Thus the joys of God
Are fervent with life, where life itself
Fades quickly into the earth. The wealth
Of the world neither reaches to Heaven nor remains.
No man has ever faced the dawn
Certain which of Fate's three threats
Would fall: illness, or age, or an enemy's
Sword, snatching the life from his soul.
The praise the living pour on the dead
Flowers from reputation: plant

An earthly life of profit reaped
Even from hatred and rancor, of bravery
Flung in the devil's face, and death
Can only bring you earthly praise
And a song to celebrate a place
with the angels, life eternally blessed
In the hosts of Heaven.
The days are gone
When the kingdoms of earth flourished in glory;
Now there are no rulers, no emperors,
No givers of gold, as once there were,
When wonderful things were worked among them
And they lived in lordly magnificence.
Those powers have vanished, those pleasures are
    dead.
The weakest survives and the world continues,
Kept spinning by toil. All glory is tarnished.
The world's honor ages and shrinks,
Bent like the men who mold it. Their faces
Blanch as time advances, their beards
Wither and they mourn the memory of friends.
The sons of princes, sown in the dust.
The soul stripped of its flesh knows nothing
Of sweetness or sour, feels no pain,
Bends neither its hand nor its brain. A brother
Opens his palms and pours down gold
On his kinsmen's grave, strewing his coffin
With treasures intended for Heaven, but nothing
Golden shakes the wrath of God
For a soul overflowing with sin, and nothing
Hidden on earth rises to Heaven.
We all fear God. He turns the earth,
He set it swinging firmly in space,
Gave life to the world and light to the sky.
Death leaps at the fools who forget their God.
He who lives humbly has angels from Heaven
To carry him courage and strength and belief.
A man must conquer pride, not kill it,
Be firm with his fellows, chaste for himself,

> If few Anglo-Saxon poems can be dated accurately, still fewer can be attributed to particular poets. The most important author from whom a considerable body of work survives is Cynewulf, who wove his writings into the epilogues of four poems. Aside from his name, little is known of him; he probably lived in the ninth century in Mercia.

Treat all the world as the world deserves,
With love or with hate but never with harm,
Though an enemy seek to scorch him in hell,
Or set the flames of a funeral pyre
Under his lord. Fate is stronger
And God mightier than any man's mind.
Our thoughts should turn to where our home is,
Consider the ways of coming there,
Then strive for sure permission for us
To rise to that eternal joy,
That life born in the love of God
And the hope of Heaven. Praise the Holy
Grace of Him who honored us,
Eternal, unchanging creator of earth. Amen.
(http://is2.dal.ca/~caowen/startp.htm)

CRITICAL THINKING

Answer all questions in essay form. A formal essay should include an outline with thesis statement or question, rough draft, revised drafts, and final copy.

A. Anglo-Saxons love meter and rhythm. What are the meter and rhythm of this narrative poem? Meter is the pattern of accented syllables in a writing. For instance, notice how this phrase is accented: This is/ the day/ that God/ has made/.

B. Who are the two speakers presented in this epic poem?

C. *Alliteration* (repetition of consonant sounds) is an important part of Anglo-Saxon poetry. Find several examples in "The Seafarer" and discuss how this technique affects the author's meaning. Answer this question in a one-page expository essay. An expository essay exposes or reveals information about a subject.

D. Define the word *kenning*. Find several examples of this literary technique in "The Seafarer."

E. Is this poem a dialogue between two speakers or a monologue in a speaker's own mind? Support your answers with passages from the text.

There is no extant, original copy of *Beowulf*. This first great English epic is known only from a single eleventh-century manuscript, which was badly damaged by fire in 1731. Transcriptions made in the late eighteenth century show that many hundreds of words and letters then visible along the charred edges subsequently crumbled away.

BIBLICAL APPLICATION

A. Some scholars think this poem's oral tradition is much older than its present written form. In fact, they argue that the Christian additions to the poem are later redactions. Write a one-page essay describing how the poem might have sounded before its Christian influences.

B. Moses, led by the Holy Spirit, writes the first five books of the Old Testament. No doubt, Moses records stories that he heard through oral stories and traditions. Obviously, Moses is not present when God created the world. Realizing that the Word of God is inerrant and inspired, identify several *narrative stories* that exist in the Old Testament. Identify the main characters, the conflict in the story, and when the climax occurs. Imagine these stories being told around the campfires (as in Joshua 4).

ENRICHMENT

Find a contemporary song or ballad about the sea and compare it in content, in theme, and in style with "The Seafarer." Write your answer in essay form.

Beowulf
Author unknown

BACKGROUND

Beowulf, the oldest of the famous Old English long poems, was written over twelve centuries ago by a native of West Mercia, the West Midlands of England today. The long narrative poem was probably performed orally by the poet before a "live" audience—like the contemporary Tonight Show—and in that sense the story had to be embellished and full of action or the author would quickly lose his audience. Most scholars, therefore, conclude that Beowulf was recited from memory by a *scop*, a traveling entertainer who went from court to court, singing songs and telling stories; eventually, *Beowulf* was written down at the request of a king who wanted to hear it again.

Imagine that you are a scop. As you read the poem, try to picture yourself in the banquet hall of a large castle, eating and drinking with your friends. You, the court entertainer—much like a stand-up comedian—begin telling your story. Your audience is full of food and mead, and they will demand a lively presentation. Your presence in the hall means that you're probably a

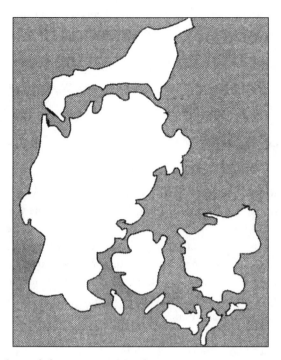

member of the aristocratic class.

As you will discover, *Beowulf* gives us little information about the life of the average person in Anglo-Saxon society; instead, it concerns itself exclusively with life in the court and on the battlefield. Like "The Seafarer," the English in this ancient narrative poem would have appeared much different from contemporary English.

Because there were sounds in Old English (A.D. 600–1100) that were not thought to be represented by the Roman alphabet, Old English used *runic characters* for those sounds. The runes were "asc" (pronounced "ash") (æ), "eth" (x), "thorn" (p), and "wen" (looks similar to a "p" but with a smaller curved bow). Here is the first line and a half from the first leaf of the manuscript of *Beowulf*, followed by a translation into modern English:

HWÆT WE GARDE / na in geardagum _eodcyninga
Lo! we [have heard] about the might of the Spear-
   Danes' kings in the early days. . . .

The following are more examples of Old English:

Nu sculon herigean
Now we must praise

A *foil* is a character used by the author to reveal important characteristics about the protagonist (main character) and to further the action surrounding the protagonist.

ece Drihten
eternal Lord

Scolde Grendel thonen
Should Grendel thence

In Anglo-Saxon culture, order is valued above everything else. The real threat to Beowulf's world is that Grendel brings disorder.

Wiste the geornor
Knew he more surely

(*Norton Anthology of English Literature*, W.W. Norton & Co. 2001, pp. 23-94)
(www.Georgetown.edu/faculty/irvinem/english016/beowulf/beowulf)

Can you recognize any Old English words? Read the Old English phrases aloud.

Beowulf is the most famous and no doubt the greatest literary work that we have inherited from the Anglo-Saxons. This epic poem is a Christian poem—at least in the form we have it; however, there are clearly some pagan elements; notice the Anglo-Saxon concept of Wyrd, or fate. It dominates the poem and in many cases seems to be a stronger influence than God Himself. As you read this poem, find examples of how fate has a ubiquitous presence.

CRITICAL THINKING

A. Anglo-Saxon poetry makes frequent use of *figurative language*, especially *similes*. Define simile and find examples in this poem.

B. Because there are three major battle scenes in the poem, some scholars believe that *Beowulf* was composed by three different authors. Others claim that the sections that take place in Denmark and the sections that occur after Beowulf returns to Geatland were the work of different authors. However, the majority of scholars agree that because of the unified structure of the poem, with its combination of historical information in the flow of the main narrative, it was most likely composed by one person. What do you think? Analyze *Beowulf* and decide if you think one, two, three, or more authors wrote this poem. Defend your answer in a two-page essay.

C. Hrothgar, Unferth, and Wiglaf function as literary foils to the main character, Beowulf. Defend this statement in a two-page expository essay. Offer copious examples from the text.

D. Brave, dependable, loyal, and strong, Beowulf is the quintessential hero. Find evidence from the text to support this description. Given the above description, compare Beowulf to a modern media hero/heroine.

BIBLICAL APPLICATION

A. *Beowulf* takes a serious look at the problem of evil. Evaluate the veracity of this early view of evil in light of the Word of God.

B. Compare the hero Beowulf with Jesus Christ. In your essay, give frequent references to the text and to Scripture.

C. Like the devil, to whom he's often compared, Grendel is an extreme example of evil and corruption. He possesses no human feelings except hatred and bitterness toward mankind. Unlike human beings who can contain elements of good and evil, however, there's no way Grendel can ever be converted to goodness. As much as he stands for a symbol of evil, he also represents disorder and chaos—a projection of what was most frightening to the Anglo-Saxon mind. An early nineteenth-century German philosopher named Friedrich Nietzsche had a similar view. His fundamental contention was that traditional values (represented primarily by Christianity) had lost their power in the lives of individuals. He expressed this in his proclamation "God is dead." This loss, he argued, led to the chaos described earlier in *Beowulf*. He was convinced that Judeo-Christian values represented a "slave morality," a morality created by weak individuals who encouraged such behavior because the behavior served their selfish interests. Nietzsche claimed that new values could be created to replace the traditional ones, and his discussion of the possibility led to his concept of the overman or superman. What do you think? In a two-page essay, agree or disagree with Nietzsche.

ENRICHMENT

A. Psychoanalysis (a way of treating emotional disorders by encouraging conscious discussions of traumatic problems with another person) is the therapy of choice for many Americans. While there are some very good things in psychoanalysis, as Dr. Karl Menninger argues, some psychoanalysis in the hands of some non-Christian analysts invites its participants to ignore evil and sin which are counted merely as emotional disorders. What happens to a culture that minimizes the importance of evil? Can a person really be healed if he is living in sin?

B. John Gardner rewrote the *Beowulf* epic in his book *Grendel* (New York: Vintage, 1989). Gardner writes this modern version of *Beowulf* from Grendel's mother's perspective. Compare it to the earlier version.

FINAL PORTFOLIO

Correct and rewrite all essays and place them in your Final Portfolio.

SUGGESTED
Weekly *Implementation*

DAY 1	DAY 2	DAY 3	DAY 4	DAY 5
Prayer journal.	**Prayer journal.**	**Prayer journal.**	**Prayer journal.**	**Prayer journal.**
Review the required reading(s) *before* the assigned lesson begins.	Review reading(s) from the next lesson.	Write rough drafts of all assigned essays.	Rewrite corrected copies of essays due tomorrow.	Essays are due.
Teacher may want to discuss assigned reading(s) with students.	Outline essays due at the end of the week.	Teacher and/or a peer evaluator may correct rough drafts.		Take Lesson 1 test.
Teacher and students will discuss required essays for this lesson, choosing two or three essays.	Per teacher instructions, students may answer orally in a group setting some of the essays that are not assigned as formal essays.			Reading ahead: Review *An Ecclesiastical History of the English People,* Venerable Bede
The rest of the essays can be outlined, answered with shorter answers, or skipped.				Guide: How does Bede's view of history differ from contemporary views? What does the word "worldview" mean? What is your worldview? What worldviews do you encounter in the world around you?
Review all readings for Lesson 1.				

LESSON 2

ANGLO-SAXON AGE *(Part 2)*; WORLDVIEW FORMATION AND DISCERNMENT

The Ecclesiastical History of the English People

The Venerable Bede

BACKGROUND

The earliest and most important writer of English prose was the Venerable Bede, a contemporary of the author of *Beowulf*. Bede, Anglo-Saxon theologian, historian, and chronologist, is best known today for his *Historia ecclesiastica gentis Anglorum* (*Ecclesiastical History of the English People*), a source vital to the history of the Anglo-Saxon people's conversion to Christianity. A brilliant man and a devoted Christian, Bede (also spelled Baeda, or Beda; 672/673–735), wrote the first extant English history. Many students will find reading the entire History difficult. Those who persevere, however, will be blessed by the gentle, committed Christian who understood history better than many know.

CRITICAL THINKING

A. As a literary genre, prose originates with men like the Venerable Bede. What advantages and disadvantages does prose offer when compared to poetry? In what ways would a poem "The Poet Caedmon" differ from the prose "The Poet Caedmon?"

B. Write a three-page ballad/poem about a significant adult in your life. Then, rewrite the same piece in prose. Which do you like better? Why?

BIBLICAL APPLICATION

A. Caedmon was "a certain brother, particularly remarkable for the grace of God." Bede presents an image of a Christian brother all of us would do well to emulate. Compare and contrast Caedmon to Jesus Christ, to King David (another poet), and to Paul.

B. Bede was a devoted Christian. To him, the super-

Analyze: *An Ecclesiastical History of the English People*, Venerable Bede; articulate your own worldview as you evaluate the veracity of other worldviews.

Reading Ahead: "Bonny Barbara Allan," Author Unknown; "Get Up and Bar the Door," Author Unknown (Scottish folk ballads); "The Prologue," "The Pardoner's Tale," and "The Nun's Priest's Tale," in *The Canterbury Tales*, Geoffrey Chaucer.

Guide Question: In what ways were the English middle ages (called Dark Ages) full of light?

natural was common and everyday. To many people in the twenty-first century, however, the supernatural does not exist. What do you think?

C. Read Philippians 3:1-13. When is loss gain? When we surrender our control and our search for security in tangible things, we discover that trusting in God and God's design is ultimately more satisfying. As a historian, Bede understood and firmly believed that human history was always reconstructed from evidence. Bede understood, and modern historians understand, that history cannot be re-created—only reinterpreted. However, Paul is telling us, and Bede understood, that salvation is

Caedmon (fl. 658–680), the first Old English Christian poet, is known from Bede's *Ecclesiastical History of the English People*, which tells how Caedmon, an illiterate herdsman, retired in shame from company one night because he could not comply with the demand made from each guest to sing. Then in a dream a stranger appeared, commanding him to sing of "the beginning of things," and the herdsman found himself uttering "verses which he had never heard."

out of history, that it is really something new. Something is created that was not here before: a new birth that is worth more than all the knowledge, money, or prestige in the world. What do you want more than anything else in the whole world? To win the World Cup? To be rich? Handsome? To receive a full academic or athletic scholarship to Yale or Harvard or Vanderbilt? What does Paul and the poet Caedmon tell you is of inestimable worth? Write a two-page essay that answers these questions.

D. In the winter of 1976, I was sitting in a drafty Harvard Yard building listening to Dr. Williams lecture on a miracle described by the Venerable Bede. Williams was notorious for his criticism of miracles—supernatural hocus-pocus, he called it. However, Professor Williams was sick and needed a miracle. He knew it, too. As he lectured on the Venerable Bede, he reached a point in his lecture where he paused and looked out the window at Widener Library. We all sat and waited. "You know," he finally said, still looking out the frosted window, "I used to laugh at people who believed in miracles." In good nature, we all laughed with him. "But, now, it's not funny. I need a miracle. I have cancer. And now, laugh at me too, because now I believe in miracles, too." Funny, isn't it? We find it easier to believe in a miracle when things are bad. For many of us, the greatest miracle was the day Christ came into our hearts. The Venerable Bede thought miracles were a natural part of history. Bede was not afraid to admit that he, himself, needed a miracle. Are you willing to admit to Him that you need a miracle? Write a one-page expository essay describing a miracle you need in your life.

ENRICHMENT

A. The Venerable Bede lived when England was in great transition from the Celtic and Briton post-Roman world to the world of the Angles, Saxons, and Jutes—a difficult time to be alive. As you read *The Ecclesiastical History of the English People*, find evidence to support this transition theme.

B. At the start of the third millennium since the birth of Jesus, many Christians feel that the world as we know it is disappearing. Some people call this era "The Postmodern Age." The Postmodern Age is dominated by anxiety, irrationalism, and helplessness. In such a world, consciousness is adrift,

unable to anchor itself to any universal ground of justice, truth, or reason. Consciousness itself is thus "decentered": no longer an agent of action in the world, but a function through which impersonal forces pass and intersect (Patricia Waugh, in Gene Edward Veith Jr., *Postmodern Times: A Christian Guide to Contemporary Thought and Culture*, p. 45).

To Bede, eighth-century England ravished by invading barbarians must have also felt like the Postmodern Era. Using the text to support your answer, agree or disagree with this statement in a 2 page essay.

Worldviews

BACKGROUND

If you are a committed Christian believer, you will be challenged to analyze the worldviews of individuals and institutions around you. You are inextricably tied to your culture, but that does not mean you can't be *in* this culture but not *of* this culture. Furthermore, you will be asked to explain your own worldview and to defend that worldview against all sorts of assaults. It is important that you pause and examine several worldviews that you will encounter. You also need to be able to articulate your own worldview.

Throughout this course and your educational career, you will be challenged to analyze the worldviews of many writers. You will be asked to articulate your own worldview and to defend that worldview against all sorts of assaults. William Bradford, for instance, has a worldview that is radically different from many writers you have read but which is probably similar to yours. What is Bradford's worldview? His worldview is obviously Christian Theism. For now, though, it is important that you examine several worldviews that you will encounter in literature and the arts. Afterwards, you will be able to articulate your own worldview.

What is a "worldview?" A worldview is a way that

Articulate your own worldview as you evaluate the veracity of other worldviews.

Reading ahead: *Religious* Affections, Edwards.

Guide Question: Why was Jonathan Edwards so effective in his preaching during the 18th century?

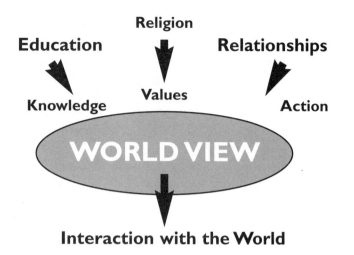

Education　　**Religion**　　**Relationships**

Knowledge　　**Values**　　**Action**

WORLD VIEW

Interaction with the World

a person understands, relates to, and responds from a philosophical position that he embraces as his own. Worldview is a framework that ties everything together, that allows us to understand society, the world, and our place in it. A worldview helps us to make the critical decisions which will shape our future. A worldview colors all our decisions and all our artistic creations. In the first *Star Wars* movie (1977) for instance, Luke Skywalker clearly values a Judeo-Christian code of ethics. That does not mean that he is a believing Christian–indeed he is not–but he does uphold and fight for a moral world. Darth Vader, on the other hand, represents chaos and amoral behavior. He does whatever it takes to advance the Emperor's agenda, regardless of who he hurts or what rule he breaks. It is important that you learn to articulate your worldview so that you will be ready to discern other worldviews later.

From studying Greek history we know that there are basically two worldview roots: One originates from Aristotle and argues that the empirical world is primary. Thus, if one wants to advance knowledge, one has to learn more about the world. Another root originates with Plato who argues that the unseen world is primary. In Plato's case that meant that if one wished to understand the world, one studied the gods. In our case, we agree with Plato to the extent that we believe God–who cannot be seen or measured–is in fact more real than the world.

Both Plato and Aristotle were impacted by Socrates. Socrates was one of the most influential but mysterious figures in Western philosophy. He wrote nothing, yet he had a profound influence on someone who did: Plato. Plato carefully recorded most of his dialogues. Unlike earlier philosophers, Socrates' main concern was with ethics. There was nothing remotely pragmatic about Socrates who was the consummate idealist. Until his day, philosophers invested most of their time explaining the natural world. In fact, the natural world often intruded into the abstract world of ideas and reality. Socrates kept both worlds completely separate. To Socrates, the natural laws governing the rotation of the earth were merely uninteresting speculation of no earthly good. Socrates was more interested in such meaty concepts as "virtue" and "justice." Taking issue with the Sophists, Socrates believed that ethics, specifically virtue, must be learned and practiced like any trade. One was not born virtuous; one developed virtue as he would a good habit. Virtue could be practiced only by experts. There was, then, nothing pragmatic about the pursuit of virtue. It was systematic; it was intentional. Virtue was acquired and maintained by open and free dialogue. For the first time, the importance of human language was advanced by a philosopher (to reappear at the end of the 20th century in Post-modern philosophy).

There was no more important philosopher in Western culture than Socrates' disciple, Plato. Plato, like Socrates, regarded ethics as the highest branch of knowledge. He stressed the intellectual basis of virtue, identifying virtue with wisdom. Plato believed that the world was made of *forms* (such as a rock) and *ideas* (such as virtue). The ability of human beings to appreciate forms made a person virtuous. Knowledge came from the gods; opinion was from man. Virtuous activity, then, was dependent upon knowledge of the forms.

To Plato, knowledge and virtue were inseparable. To Aristotle, they were unconnected. Aristotle was not on a search for absolute truth. He was not even certain it existed. Truth, beauty, and goodness were to be observed and quantified from human behavior and the senses, but they were not the legal tender of the land. Goodness in particular was not an absolute, and in Aristotle's opinion it was much abused. Goodness was an average between two absolutes. Aristotle said that mankind should strike a balance between passion and temperance, between extremes of all sorts. He said that good people should seek the "Golden Mean" defined as a course of life that was never extreme. Finally, while Plato argued that reality lay in knowledge of the gods, Aristotle argued that reality lay in empirical, measurable knowledge. To Aristotle, reality was tied to purpose and to action. For these reasons, Aristotle, became known as the father of modern science. His most enduring impact occurred in the area of metaphysics—philosophical speculation about the nature, substance, and structure of reality. It is not physics concerned with the visible or natural world. Metaphysics is concerned with explaining the non-physical world. Aristotle advanced the discussion about God, the human soul, and the nature of space and time. What makes this particularly interesting is Aristotle's penchant for delving into the metaphysical by talking about the gods in human terms. He said, "All men by nature desire to know," and it is by the senses that the gods were known–or not. Faith had nothing to do with it. In other words, Aristotle, for the first time, discussed the gods as if they were quantified entities. He spoke about them as if they were not present. The Hebrews had done this earlier (Genesis 3), but Aristotle was probably not aware of Moses' text. While some Christian thinkers such as Augustine and Aquinas employed Aristotelian logic in their discussions about God, they never speculated about His existence as Aristotle did. They only used Aristotle's techniques to understand more about Him.

From Aristotle vs. Plato a panoply of worldviews evolved in four main epochs.

The following are characteristics of each epoch:

Classical Theism	Pernicious gods involved in human affairs
Christian Theism	Loving God involved in human affairs
Modernism	Faith in science
Post-Modernism	Faith in experience; suspicious of science

Most of you have not heard of this particular worldview paradigm. It is called a cultural worldview paradigm (as contrasted to a socio-political paradigm). Both are useful. Both are accurate. However, most Americans obtain their worldviews from culture, not from scholarship and education.

While socio-political descriptions of worldviews are completely accurate, they are not used by American universities or the media at all. When have you heard the word "Cosmic Humanist" used on television? In a movie? Very few people use this terminology in the real world. Therefore, if Christians wish to be involved in apologetics, they must use a language that the unsaved can understand. Chesterton once lamented that

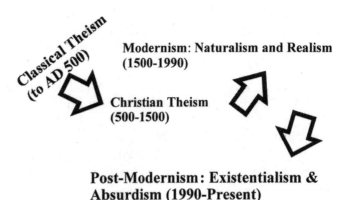

Evangelical Christians are like Americans who visit France. He generalized that Americans, by and large, speak their words slower, articulate their words more carefully, and speak fewer words to complete a thought. However, what they should do, Chesterton argues, is to speak French in France! If we believers want the world to hear us, we need to relate to their language.

The four epochs above manifested seven basic worldviews. The worldviews are best discerned through works of art and of literature. The worldview of an artist/writer is a reflection of how the author expresses his views on such essential issues as *God*, *Man*, and *Morality*. The following seven worldviews are found in art and literature:

Christian Theism: God is personally involved with humankind. Theism argues that the universe is a purposive, divinely created entity. It argues that all human life is sacred and all persons are of equal dignity. They are, in other words, created in the image of God. History is linear and moves toward a final goal. Nature is controlled by God and is an orderly system. Humanity is neither the center of nature nor the universe, but is the steward of creation. Righteousness will triumph in a decisive conquest of evil. This is the only viable worldview until the Renaissance. Examples: Homer, Virgil, C. S. Lewis, A. J. Cronin, Tolkien.

Deism: God *was* present but is no longer present. The world is like a clock wound up by God many years ago, but He is now absent. The clock (i.e., the world) is present; God is absent. Still, though, Deism embraced a Judeo-Christian morality. God's absence, for instance, in no way mitigated His importance to original creation. He was also omnipotent, but not omniscient.

His absence was His decision. He was in no way forced to be absent from the world. He chose to assume that role so that Socratic empiricism and rationalism could reign as sovereign king. Examples: Ben Franklin, Thomas Jefferson.

Romanticism: Once Americans distanced themselves from the self-revealing God of the Old and New Testaments, they could not resist making further concessions to subjectivity. Romanticism, and its American version, Transcendentalism, posited that God was nature, and "it" was good. The more natural things were, the better. Nature was inherently good. Nature alone was the ultimate reality. In other words, nature was the Romantic god. Man was essentially a complex animal, too complex to be controlled by absolute, codified truth (as one would find in the Bible). Human intuition replaced the Holy Spirit. Depending upon the demands on individual lives, truth and good were relative and changing. Romanticism, however, like Deism, had not completely abandoned Judeo-Christian morality. Truth and the good, although changing, were nonetheless relatively durable. Examples: James Fenimore Cooper, Goethe.

Naturalism: If God exists, He is pretty wimpish. Only the laws of nature have any force. God is either uninterested or downright mean. All life, including human life, was transient. Its final destination was death. Truth and good, therefore, were also transient. Examples: Joseph Conrad, Stephen Crane.

Realism: Akin to Naturalism is Realism. Reality is, to a Realist, a world with no purpose, no meaning, no order. Realism insists that personality has no ultimate status in the universe but is logically inconsistent when it affirms an ethically imperative social agenda congruent with universal human rights and dignity. Realism throws around such terms as "dignity" and "human rights" and "power." What Realists mean, however, is that these concepts are real when they fulfill a social agenda that enhances human dominance over the uni-

> Modern people conclude that history really has no meaning. . . . The biblical view is that history had a beginning and will have an end and that both the beginning and the end are in God's hands.

versal. Thus, Realism believes in a world where bad things happen all the time to good people. Why not? There is no God, no ontological controlling force for good. The world is a place where the only reality is that which we can experience, but it must be experience that we can measure or replicate. Certainly, pain and misery fit that category. If an experience is a unique occurrence (Example: a miracle) it is not real. Examples: Ernest Hemingway, F. Scott Fitzgerald.

Absurdism: A modern movement where there is neither a god, nor any reason to have one. Everything is disorganized, anarchy rules. There is a complete abandonment of explaining the cosmos and therefore an abandonment of being in relationship with the deity. It is not that Absurdists are unsure about who creates everything or is in control of everything. Absurdists simply do not care one way or the other. Examples: John Barth, Kurt Vonnegut, Jr.

Existentialism: The submergence of God in overwhelming data and in experience is the first step toward putting God out to die. Truth is open to debate. Everything is relative. Existentialism is a very pessimistic view. Examples: Albert Camus, Franz Kafka, and Jean Paul Sartre.

Culture Wars: The Battle for Truth

GREEK MYTHOLOGY

The Greeks introduced the idea that the universe is orderly, that man's senses are valid and, as a consequence, that man's proper purpose is to live his own life to the fullest.

Ionian School
(500 B.C.)
The Ionian fascination with the physical world anticipated later discussions in Western philosophy.

The Phythagoreans
(530 B.C.)
Phythagoras was the first philosopher to require some standard of behavior from his followers. One can imagine what a novel and important step this was–that a religion would require a commitment from its adherents.

The Eleatic School
(500 B.C.)
The Eleatic School argued that reality was indivisible and endless.

The Pluralists
(500 B.C.)
With no outside force in place, by chance the universe evolved from chaos to structure, and vice versa, in an eternal cycle.

The Sophists
(500 B.C.)
Ethical rules needed to be followed only when it was to one's practical advantage to do so. Goodness, morality, and ethics were a reflection of culture rather than vice versa.

Socrates
(469-399 B.C.)
For the first time, the importance of human language was advanced by a philosopher. Plato stressed the intellectual basis of virtue, identifying virtue with wisdom.

Plato
(428 B.C.-?)
"Love" to Plato was a "form" from which virtue flowed.

Aristotle
(350 B.C.-?)
Aristotle was the first agnostic. Aristotle argued that reality lay in empirical, measurable knowledge. Aristotle, for the first time discussed the gods as if they were quantified entities. He spoke about them as if they were not present.

Cynicism
(350 B.C.)
For the first time, philosophers began to talk about the individual in earnest, as if he were a subject to be studied.

Skepticism
(300 B. C.)
Skepticism maintained that human beings could know nothing of the real nature of things, and that consequently the wise person would give up trying to know anything.

Epicurianism
(300 B. C.)
The aim of human life, Epicurus claimed, was to achieve maximum pleasure with the least effort and risk.

Stoicism
(300 B.C.)
Stoicism celebrated the human spirit and became the measuring rod against which all social and religious institutions were measured.

Neoplatonism
(A.D. 50)
Neoplatonism dared to speak of a religious experience as a philosophical phenomenon

Augustine
(A.D. 354-430)
Augustine effectively articulated a theology and worldview for the Church as it journeyed into the inhospitable, post-Christian, barbarian era.

Scholasticism
(A.D. 1100-1300)
Scholasticism, with varying degrees of success, attempted to use natural human reason—in particular, the philosophy and science of Aristotle—to understand the metaphysical content of Christian revelation.

Erasmus
(1466-1536)
Erasmus, for the first time, discussed things like happiness as being centered in the self or personhood of the man or woman. Happiness was based on some narcissistic notions of self-love.

Michel de Montaigne
(1533-1592)
Montaigne reintroduced Greek skepticism to Western culture.

Frances Bacon
(1561-1626)
Bacon advanced vigorously the idea that reasoning must triumph over theology.

Thomas Hobbes
(1588-1679)
Hobbes was one of the first modern Western thinkers to provide a secular justification for political power.

Rene Descartes
(1596-1650)
After Descartes, mankind replaced God as the center of the universe in the midst of many. This was an ominous moment in Western culture.

Benedictus de Spinoza
(1732-1677)
Spinoza argued that human morality arose from self-interest.

John Locke
(1632-1704)
Locke believed in reasoning and common sense, rather than in metaphysics.

G. W. Leibniz
(1646-1716)
Leibniz believed in a God who created a world separate from His sovereignty.

George Berkeley
(1685-1753)
Berkeley called "intuition" the voice of God to mankind.

David Hume
(1711-1726)
Hume, for the first time in Western history, seriously suggested that there was no necessary connection between cause and effect.

Immanuel Kant
(1724-1804)
Kant argued that reality was experience. If one could not experience something with his senses, then it was not real.

Jean Jacques Rousseau
(1712-1778)
Rousseau advocated one of the first "back-to-nature" movements.

William Godwin
(1756-1836)
The notion that there were individual rights, or a codex of governing laws, was anathema to Godwin.

Soren Kierkegaard
(1813-1855)
Kierkegaard explained life in terms of logical necessity, which became a means of avoiding choice and responsibility.

G. W. F. Hegel
(1770-1831)
Truth had no application if there were not opposites warring for its reality.

Karl Marx
(1818-1883)
To the Hegelian Marx, Christianity was a fairy tale created to placate weak people.

Pierre Joseph Proudon
(1809-1865)

Proudon instituted the last serious philosophical attempt to undermine the human will as a determining factor in human decision-making.

Arthur Schopenhauer
(1788-1860)
The human will, with all its chauvinism and narcissism, was the most powerful human impulse.

Herbert Spencer
(1820-1903)
Spencer argued that in biological sciences and in the social sciences the fittest and the strongest survived.

Frederich Nietzsche
(1844-1890)
Nietzsche believed that the collapse of the religious impulse has left a huge vacuum. The history of modern times is in great part the history of how that vacuum is filled.

Martin Heidegger
(1889-1976)
The meaning of the world must be discovered outside human experience.

Jean Paul Sartre
(1905-1980)
People exist in a world of their own making.

Simone De Beauvoir
(1906-1986)
Beauvoir was an advocate of "free love" and completely rejected the biblical understanding of marriage, which she saw as an oppressive institution.

John Dewey
(1859-1952)
Truth to Dewey was a reflection of circumstances and contingencies.

Bertrand Russell
(1872-1970)
If an actual event could not be quantified or repeated, then it was not real.

John Stuart Mill
(1806-1873)
To Mill, the individual and his needs were paramount.

Max Weber
(1864-1920)
The notion that God was pleased with hard work and frugal living assured a healthy maturation of society.

Ludwig Wittgenstein
(1889-1951)

If a person could not speak it, it was not real.

Richard Rorty
(1931-)

Truth to Rorty is what we all agree is truth, and what we agree is truth is more a reflection of circumstances than any absolute or objective reality outside mankind's experience.

Alfred North Whitehead
(1861-1947)

The agnostic Whitehead believed in God—if a decidedly anemic God.

Jacques Derrida
(1930-)

Derrida argued that most of us merely play language games. Every utterance is a move in a language game.

Jean Baudrillard
(1929-)

Reality to Baudrillard is not necessarily defined by human language: it is defined by the public media.

Jurgen Habermas
(1929-)

Habermas has resurrected the works of Plato and other metaphysicists and has taken philosophy away from language and communication and has taken it back to a discussion of rationality.

Viktor E. Frankl
(1905-1997)

Man was the result of a purposeless and materialistic process that did not have him in mind.

WORLDVIEW REVIEW

Christian Theism Christian Theism advances a worldview that there is an omnipotent God who has authored an inspired, authoritative work called the Bible, upon whose precepts mankind should base its society.

Deism. Deism advances a worldview that accepts the notion that there is an authoritative, inspired source from which mankind should base its society (i.e., the Bible). Likewise the Deist is certain that there was once an omnipotent God. However, once the world was created, that same omnipotent God chose to absent Himself from His creation. The world, then, is like a clock. It was once created by an intelligent process. However, now the creator is absent, leaving mankind on its own to figure out how the clock works and to go on living.

Romanticism. A natural companion to Deism was Rationalism. Rationalism (e.g., John Locke's philosophy) invited the Deist to see mankind as a "chalkboard" on which was written experience that ultimately created a personality. Thus, Rationalists/Deists were fond of speaking of "unalienable rights" or "common sense." The Romantic (in America the Romantic would be called "the Transcendentalist") took issue with Deism and Theism. To the Romantic, Nature was God. Nature—an undefined indigenous, omnipotent presence—was very good. Original sin was man's separation from Nature. In fact, the degree to which mankind returned to Nature would determine his goodness and effectiveness. Thus, a man like Henry David Thoreau lived a year on Walden Pond so that he could find his God. In *Deerslayer* by James Fenimore Cooper, the protagonist is safe while he is on a lake separated from evil mankind. Only when he participates in human society is he in trouble. The Romantic was naturally suspicious of Theism because Theism appeared to be dogmatic and close-minded. The Romantics had confessions, but they had no dogma. Deism also bothered the Romantics. Romanticism emphasized the subjective; Deism emphasized the objective. In the Romantic novel *Frankenstein*, the Deist/Rationalist Dr. Frankenstein creates a monster. Dr. Frankenstein, with disastrous results, turns his back on the subjective and tries to use science to create life.

Naturalism. Naturalism was inclined to agree with Romanticism's criticism of Theism and Deism but did not believe in a benevolent Nature. In fact, Nature, to the Naturalist, was malevolent, mischievous, and unpredictable. Mankind, as it were, lost control of the universe and the person who had control did not really care much for his creation. Theism of course was absurd. How could any sane person who experienced World War I believe in a loving, living God? Deism was equally wrong. God was not absent—he was present in an unpredictable, at times evil way. Romanticism was on the right track but terribly naive. God and His creation were certainly not "good" in any sense of the word. Nature was evil. Naturalism embraced a concept of fate not dissimilar to that held by the Greeks. In Homer's *Iliad*, for instance, the characters were subject to uncontrolled fate and pernicious gods and goddesses who inflicted terrible and good things on mankind with no apparent design or reason. No, to the Naturalist, God was at best absent or wimpish; at worst, he was malevolent.

Realism. Realism was philosophically akin to Naturalism. In a sense, Naturalism was a natural companion to Realism. Realism was different from Naturalism in degree, not in substance. Realism argued that if people were honest, they would admit that God was not present at all. If there were anything worth embracing, it was reality. Realism advanced an in-your-face view of life. Realists prided themselves in "telling it like it is." They entered the cosmic arena and let the chips fall where they might. They shared the same criticisms of views that the Naturalists held.

Absurdism. Absurdism certainly believed that Realism was on track. Where Realism erred, however, was its propensity to see meaning in life. Mind you, the meaning was tied to things one could see and feel–not in things that were abstract or immutable–but the Realist still sought some meaning in this life. The Absurdist abandoned all hope of finding meaning in life and embraced a sort of nihilism. The Absurdist was convinced that everything was meaningless and absurd. The subjectivity of a Romantic was appealing to the Absurdist. However, even that implied that something was transcendent–a desire–and the Absurdist would have nothing to do with that. Billy Pilgrim, a protagonist in one of the Absurdist Kurt Vonnegut, Jr.'s novels, became "unhinged from time" and "wandered around in the cosmos." Things without meaning happen to him whose life had no meaning. Everything was absurd.

Existentialism. Existentialism stepped outside the debate of meaning altogether. Existentialists argued that the quest was futile. The only thing that mattered was subjective feeling. "Experience" was a God at whose feet the Existentialist worshiped. Romanticism was on the right track in that it invited mankind to explore subjectivity. Where it erred was when it refused to give up the deity. Naturalism was an anomaly. It was too busy arguing with the cosmos to see that reality was

in human desire not in providence. The degree to which mankind was to discover and experience these desires determined the degree to which people participated in the divine.

CRITICAL THINKING

In a two-page essay, compare the worldviews of each of the following statements.

People are the same as animals—just smarter.

So God created man in His own image, in the image of God. Gatsby believed . . . tomorrow we will run faster, stretch out our arms farther . . . And one fine morning—So we beat on, boats against the current, borne back ceaselessly into the past (Fitzgerald, *The Great Gatsby*, Charles Scribner's Sons, 1925, p. 182)

For mere improvement is not redemption . . . God became man to turn creatures into sons: not simply to produce better men of the old kind but to produce a new kind of man (Lewis, *Mere Christianity*, A Touchstone Book, 1980, p. 183)

Life is futile.

All my friends do it, so it must be ok.

FINAL PORTFOLIO

Correct and rewrite all essays and place them in your Final Portfolio.

Contemporary Worldviews

Life is what happens to you when you're busy making other plans.–Yoko Ono

I don't think any of us really know why we are here.–Ray Charles

Animal liberation will come!–Ingrid Newkirk

If we had no other purpose in life, it would be good enough simply to goose people once in a while.–Garrison Keillor

The meaning of life is felt through relationship–Jonas Salk

To fulfill the purpose of life is to ignite the spark of divinity in us and give meaning to our lives.–Michael Jackson

Just chill out.–Ice-T.

SUGGESTED
Weekly *Implementation*

DAY 1	DAY 2	DAY 3	DAY 4	DAY 5
Prayer journal.	**Prayer journal.**	**Prayer journal.**	**Prayer journal.**	**Prayer journal.**
Review the required reading(s) *before* the assigned lesson begins.	Review reading(s) from next lesson.	Write rough drafts of all assigned essays.	Rewrite corrected copies of essays due tomorrow.	Essays are due.
Teacher may want to discuss assigned reading(s) with students.	Outline essays due at the end of the week.	The teacher and/or a peer evaluator may correct rough drafts.		Take Lesson 2 test.
Teacher and students will decide on required essays for this lesson, choosing two or three essays.	Per teacher instructions, students may answer orally in a group setting some of the essays that are not assigned as formal essays.			Reading ahead: "Bonny Barbara Allan," Author Unknown; "Get Up and Bar the Door," Author Unknown (Scottish folk ballads); "The Prologue," "The Pardoner's Tale," and "The Nun's Priest's Tale," in *The Canterbury Tales*, Geoffrey Chaucer.
The rest of the essays can be outlined, answered with shorter answers, or skipped.				Guide: In what ways were the English middle ages (called The Dark Ages) full of light?
Review all readings for Lesson 2.				

Middle English Literature

BACKGROUND

The Middle Ages were not "dark," as many characterize them. They were a time of heightened religious sensitivity. Most medieval Englishmen were more conscious of their eternal state than their present one, and with no wonder. Many of them would only live forty years—most women even died by age thirty-five. This hard time was graced by great writers. The Middle Ages was a time of proliferation, though not necessarily refinement, for short narratives. The short tale became an important means of diversion and amusement. From the Dark Ages (A.D. 500) to the Renaissance (1500), Englishmen adopted short fiction for their own purposes.

EARLY BALLADS

The ballads of early England and Scotland were some of the earliest indigenous poems of Norman English lit-

Analyze: the following literary works: "Bonny Barbara Allan," author unknown; "Get Up and Bar the Door," author unknown (Scottish folk ballads); "The Prologue," "The Pardoner's Tale," and "The Nun's Priest's Tale," in *The Canterbury Tales*, Geoffrey Chaucer.

Reading Ahead: *Sir Gawain and the Green Knight*, Author Unknown. (pronunciation: Ga' win)

Guide Question: What sort of hero is Sir Gawain?

erature (i.e., French Normandy poems brought by William the Conqueror). The old folk ballads were meant to be sung. They were the popular songs of their day. Unrequited love and revenge were the most common themes in these ballads. It was common in medieval England to sing stories in song called *ballads*. Ballads were either stories composed for the occasion out of a repertoire of traditional motifs or phrases, or they were stories preserved by memory and handed down orally. As an oral art, the ballad did not need to be written down to be performed or preserved; in any case, many of the carriers of the ballad tradition were illiterate and could not read a written ballad. The precise date of a ballad, therefore, or even any particular version of a ballad, is almost impossible to determine. Historical ballads would seem on the surface to be easily datable, but their origins were usually quite uncertain. The ballad could have arisen long after the events it described.

Bonny Barbara Allan

Author unknown

It was in and about the Martinmas time,
When the green leaves were a falling,
That Sir John Græme in the West Country,
Fell in love with Barbara Allan.
He sent his man down through the town,
To the place where she was dwelling:

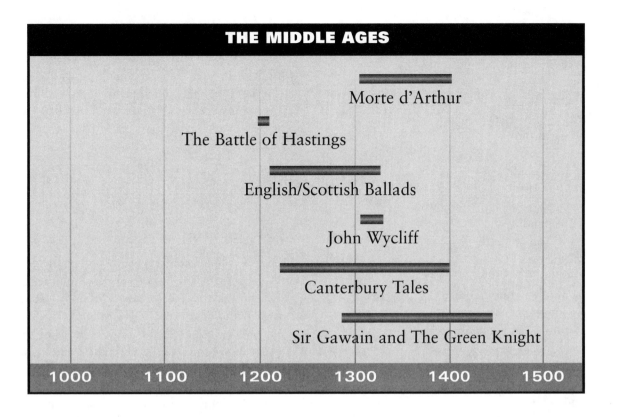

THE MIDDLE AGES

Morte d'Arthur

The Battle of Hastings

English/Scottish Ballads

John Wycliff

Canterbury Tales

Sir Gawain and The Green Knight

1000   1100   1200   1300   1400   1500

"O haste and come to my master dear,
Gin ye be Barbara Allan."

O hooly, hooly rose she up,
To the place where he was lying,
And when she drew the curtain by,
"Young man, I think you're dying."

"O it's I'm sick, and very, very sick,
And 'tis a' for Barbara Allan:"
"O the better for me ye's never be,
Tho your heart's blood were a spilling.

"O dinna ye mind, young man," said she,
"When ye was in the tavern a drinking,
That ye made the healths gae round and round,
And slighted Barbara Allan?"

He turned his face unto the wall,
And death was with him dealing:
"Adieu, adieu, my dear friends all,
And be kind to Barbara Allan."

And slowly, slowly raise she up,
And slowly, slowly left him,
And sighing said, she coud not stay,
Since death of life had reft him.

She had not gane a mile but twa,
When she heard the dead-bell ringing,
And every jow that the dead-bell gied,
It cry'd, Woe to Barbara Allan!

"O mother, mother, make my bed!
O make it saft and narrow!
Since my love died for me to-day,
I'll die for him to-morrow."
(www.bartleby.com)

Get Up and Bar the Door
Author unknown

It fell about the Martinmas time,
And a gay time it was then,
When our good wife got puddings to make,
And she's boild them in the pan.

The wind sae cauld blew south and north,
And blew into the floor;
Quoth our goodman to our goodwife,
"Gae out and bar the door."

"My hand is in my hussyfskap,
Goodman, as ye may see;
An it shoud nae be barrd this hundred year,
It's no be barrd for me."

They made a paction tween them twa,
They made it firm and sure,
That the first word whaeer shoud speak,
Shoud rise and bar the door.

Then by there came two gentlemen,
At twelve o'clock at night,
And they could neither see house nor hall,
Nor coal nor candle-light.

"Now whether is this a rich man's house,
Or whether is it a poor?"
But neer a word wad ane o them speak,
For barring of the door.

And first they ate the white puddings,
And then they ate the black;
Tho muckle thought the goodwife to hersel,
Yet neer a word she spake.

Then said the one unto the other,
"Here, man, tak ye my knife;
Do ye tak aff the auld man's beard,
And I'll kiss the goodwife."

"But there's nae water in the house,
And what shall we do than?"
"What ails thee at the pudding-broo,
That boils into the pan?"

O up then started our goodman,
An angry man was he:
"Will ye kiss my wife before my een,
And scad me wi pudding-bree?"

Then up and started our goodwife,
Gied three skips on the floor:
"Goodman, you've spoken the foremost word,
Get up and bar the door."
(http://www.bartleby.com/40/20.htm)

CRITICAL THINKING

A. Evaluate this observation: ballads were normally written in dramatic fashion with only slight attention paid to characterization, theme, or setting. Support your arguments with passages from the text.

B. Create an original ballad based on a tragic incident that has occurred within the last few years. Use the same rhyme (iambic) as the old ballads.

BIBLICAL APPLICATION

Compare early English/Scottish folk ballads with the biblical story of Samson. Compare and contrast theme, characterization, plot development, and setting. Then rewrite the story of Samson in ballad (i.e., iambic poetic) form.

The Canterbury Tales
Geoffrey Chaucer

BACKGROUND

Geoffrey Chaucer lived at the end of the Middle Ages. He was born into a prosperous middle class family rather than a noble or peasant family. Chaucer was a soldier, diplomat, and royal official. His most famous work was *The Canterbury Tales*, a series of short stories. The setting for *The Canterbury Tales* was centered on pilgrims traveling to Canterbury, England, the cultic center of British Catholicism. Each pilgrim was to tell two stories on the way and two as he returned. Chaucer died before he could finish all the stories, but the stories he completed are the best picture of life in fourteenth-century England that we have.

Most people in English society during Chaucer's time viewed the world in a similar way. People believed that, behind the frustration of the day-to-day world, God was in control. Chaucer's society could feel, at least much of the time, a sense of security about the world, knowing that it was following a divine plan. The reason Chaucer so vehemently disliked people like the Monk and the Friar, for instance, was that they hypocritically violated the fragile unity of this feudal society.

Chaucer's world was a world in transition. A middle class was budding within British society. Still entrenched, however, was a noble and ecclesiological class that was resistant to all change. These groups engendered different values, represented in the medieval world by two structures: the class system and the church. People believed both setups were established by God, and each went unchallenged.

CRITICAL THINKING

A. Compare this selection from "The Prologue to the Canterbury Tales" with the Anglo-Saxon Old English of *Beowulf*:

Here bygynneth the Book of the Tales of Canterbury.
  Here begins the Book of Canterbury Tales.
Whan that Aprill with his shoures soote
  When April with his showers sweet
The droghte of March hath perced to the roote
  The drought of March has pierced to the root,
And bathed every veyne in swich licour
  And flooded every (plant) vein with such liquor
Of which vertu engendred is the flour;
  Of which its strength creates the flower,
What Zephirus eek with his sweete breeth
  When Zephyr [the west wind] also with his pleas-
  ant breath
Inspired hath in every holt and heet
  Has brought to life in every small woods and
  heath
The tendred croppes, and the yonge sonne

  The tender shoots, and the young sun
Hath in the Ram his halfe cours y-ronne:
  Has in the Ram [sign of zodiac for spring] his half
  course run:
And smale fowles maken melodye
  And small birds make melody
That slepen al the night with open ye—
  That sleep all night with open eye—
So priketh hem Nature in hir corages—
  So Nature pierces them in their spirits—
Thanne longen folk to goon on pilgrimages . . .
  Then folks long to go on pilgrimages . . .
(Paul McCormick, et al., *Adventures in English
  Literature*, NY: Harcourt, Brace, Jovanovich, Inc,.
  1973, p.36)

Memorize this portion of "The Prologue" given above and then translate it into modern English.

B. How do Chaucer's descriptions of the outside appearance, such as the dress and physical attributes of the pilgrims, reveal their inner nature?
C. Which of the pilgrims does Chaucer most admire? Why?
D. Chaucer is describing a type of person more than an individual. Explain.

BIBLICAL APPLICATION

A. Research the state of English religion during Chaucer's day. As a guide, analyze the way he described the Monk, the Parson, and other church officials in his prologue.
B. The journey is a powerful motif in Chaucer's *Canterbury Tales* and in the Bible. The call of Abraham to Palestine, the wilderness wanderings, and the road to Emmaus are only a few instances of journeys in the Bible. Can you think of others? What advantages does this setting offer an author?

ENRICHMENT

A. In "The Pardoner's Tale" the Pardoner, who is a hypocrite and a disreputable character if ever there were one, goes on a moral rampage against the very crimes he himself commits. Ironically, the Pardoner is the very personification of the sins he condemns. How does Chaucer use irony to make his point? To Chaucer hypocrisy is the worst sin anyone can commit. Why?
B. "The Nun's Priest's Tale" is a "beast fable" in which animals behave like human beings. Create a beast fable illustrating an important truism.
C. Compare the themes of "The Nun's Priest's Tale" to the themes of *Beowulf*.

CRITICAL THINKING

A. "The Pardoner's Tale" is an almost perfect short

> *Irony* is a way of writing that depends on a difference between what is obviously true and what is real. There are three kinds: In *verbal irony* a writer or character says one thing and does another. In *dramatic irony* a reader or audience perceives a character's foibles. In *irony of situation* there is a difference between purpose and result.

story. What makes a great short story? Compare this short story to another short story you have read.

B. A famous publisher has retained you to illustrate a new comic book version of "The Pardoner's Tale." You must begin by drawing the most important five scenes in the short story. Which scenes would you choose? Why?

FINAL PORTFOLIO

Correct and rewrite all essays and place them in your Final Portfolio.

SUGGESTED
Weekly *Implementation*

DAY 1	DAY 2	DAY 3	DAY 4	DAY 5
Prayer journal. Review required reading(s) *before* the assigned lesson begins. Teacher may want to discuss assigned reading(s) with students. Teacher and students will decide on required essays for this lesson, choosing two or three essays. The rest of the essays can be outlined, answered with shorter answers, or skipped. Review all readings for Lesson 3.	**Prayer journal.** Review reading(s) from next lesson. Student should outline essays, including a thesis statement/question due at the end of the week. Per teacher instructions, students may answer orally in a group setting some of the essays that are not assigned as formal essays.	**Prayer journal.** Write rough drafts of all assigned essays. The teacher and/or a peer evaluator may correct rough drafts.	**Prayer journal.** Rewrite corrected copies of essays due tomorrow.	**Prayer journal.** Essays are due. Take Lesson 3 test. Reading ahead: Review *Sir Gawain and The Green Knight*, author unknown. Guide: What sort of hero is Sir Gawain?

LESSON 4

MIDDLE AGES *(Part 2)*

Sir Gawain and the Green Knight

Author unknown

BACKGROUND

No one knows the authorship of *Sir Gawain and the Green Knight*. We do know that he was a contemporary of Geoffrey Chaucer—although his alliterative style would have been considered barbaric to Chaucer. *Sir Gawain and the Green Knight* (ca. 1360–1400) is a Middle English alliterative romance written by an anonymous West Midlands poet also credited with *The Pearl*, *Patience*, and *Purity* or Cleanness. The protagonist, Sir Gawain, survives two tests: a challenge to behead the fearsome

Analyze: *Sir Gawain and The Green Knight*, author unknown.

Reading Ahead: "On Monsieur's Departure," "The Doubt of Future Foes," Speech to the Troops at Tilbury, Queen Elizabeth; *The Fairie Queene*, Edmund Spenser; "Sonnet 26," and "Sonnet 75," from *Amoretti*, by Edmund Spenser; "The Passionate Shepherd to His Love," Christopher Marlowe; "The Nymph's Reply to the Shepherd," Sir Walter Raleigh; "The Admonition by the Author to all Young Gentlewomen: And to all other Maids being in Love," Isabella Whitney; "Sonnet 18," "Sonnet 29," "Sonnet 55," "Sonnet 73," and "Sonnet 116," William Shakespeare.

Guide Question: What themes continue to surface in Elizabethan poetry?

Green Knight (he alone of King Arthur's knights accepts the challenge), and a temptation to commit adultery with the wife of Lord Bertilak—in reality the Green Knight—in whose castle he stays en route to the chapel. Critics have long complimented the intricate and well-written poetry and the superb portrait of Gawain, an ideal knight who remains fallibly human.

CRITICAL THINKING

A. Sir Gawain combines two universally popular and immutable (i.e., unchangeable) plots: a martial arts contest and

> An *archetype* is a type or style prevalent in several places.

a temptation scene with a beautiful woman. Identify both of these plots in the text and discuss their development. Give copious references from the text.

B. Give characterizations of the Green Knight and Sir Gawain. What archetypes do they typify?

BIBLICAL APPLICATION

The poem is both a satire of manners and at the same time a reverent and profoundly Christian celebration of Judeo-Christian characteristics. Find evidence from the text to support these two arguments.

ENRICHMENT

A. The decapitation of the Green Knight has its origins in pagan English culture. Explain.

B. Research the life of Robin Hood. Was he a real historical figure? Read *The Merry Adventures of Robin Hood,* by Howard Pyle. How historically accurate is Pyle's version?

FINAL PORTFOLIO

Correct and rewrite all essays and place them in your Final Portfolio.

SUGGESTED
Weekly *Implementation*

DAY 1	DAY 2	DAY 3	DAY 4	DAY 5
Prayer journal. Review required reading(s) *before* the assigned lesson begins. Teacher may want to discuss assigned reading(s) with students. Teacher and students will decide on required essays for this lesson, choosing two or three essays. The rest of the essays can be outlined, answered with shorter answers, or skipped. Review all readings for Lesson 4.	**Prayer journal.** Review reading(s) from next lesson. Outline essays, including thesis statement, due at the end of the week. Per teacher instructions students may answer orally in a group setting some of the essays that are not assigned as formal essays.	**Prayer journal.** Write rough drafts of all assigned essays. The teacher and/or a peer evaluator may correct rough drafts.	**Prayer journal.** Rewrite corrected copies of essays due tomorrow.	**Prayer journal.** Essays are due. Take Lesson 4 test. Review *The Fairie Queen*, Edmund Spenser; "Sonnet 26," and "Sonnet 75," from *Amoretti*, by Edmund Spenser; "The Passionate Shepherd to His Love," Christopher Marlowe; "The Nymph's Reply to the Shepherd," Sir Walter Raleigh; "The Admonition by the Author to all Young Gentlewomen: And to all other Maids being in Love," Isabella Whitney; "Sonnet 18," "Sonnet 29," "Sonnet 55," "Sonnet 73," and "Sonnet 116," William Shakespeare Guide: What themes continue to surface in Elizabethan poetry?

Elizabethan Age

BACKGROUND

The Elizabethan Age is named after Queen Elizabeth, daughter of Henry VIII and one of the most important English monarchs. This era is marked by advances on almost all intellectual fronts: science, art, and drama. The Elizabethan Age is the English version of the European Renaissance. The *sonnet,* a poem of fourteen lines perfected in Italy in the fourteenth century, is a grand marker of this age. Elizabethan love sonnets celebrate beauty: especially female beauty. The Elizabethan love sonnet is the first love song in English literature.

QUEEN ELIZABETH I

Queen Elizabeth I (1533-1603) is perhaps England's greatest monarch, ruling from 1558 until her death in 1603. She oversaw England's victory over the Spanish Armada and the rise of the British Empire. In fact, her name was applied to the whole era—called the Elizabethan Age.

Analyze: "On Monsieur's Departure," "The Doubt of Future Woes," Elizabeth I's "Speech to the Troops at Tilbury," Queen Elizabeth; Sonnets 26 and 75, from *Amoretti,* by Edmund Spenser; "The Passionate Shepherd to His Love," Christopher Marlowe; "The Nymph's Reply to the Shepherd," Sir Walter Raleigh; "The Admonition by the Author to all Young Gentlewomen: And to all other Maids being in Love," Isabella Whitney; Sonnets 18 and 73, William Shakespeare.

Reading Ahead: *Macbeth,* William Shakespeare.

Guide Question: Is Macbeth an evil man or a pawn in the hands of an evil woman?

CRITICAL THINKING

A. Evaluate the personal touch, both for a monarch and a sixteenth century poet, of Queen Elizabeth's poetry.
B. Was Elizabeth writing this poetry for a large audience?

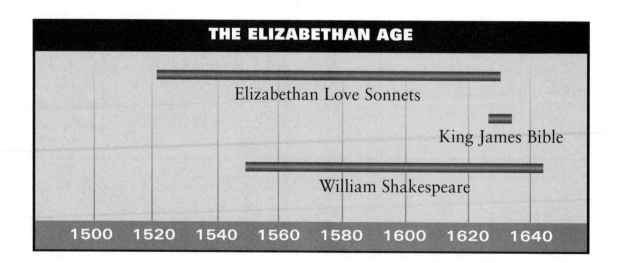

THE ELIZABETHAN AGE

Elizabethan Love Sonnets

King James Bible

William Shakespeare

| 1500 | 1520 | 1540 | 1560 | 1580 | 1600 | 1620 | 1640 |

C. What does Elizabeth's speech to the troops at Tilbury accomplish?

On Monsieur's Departure

I grieve and dare not show my discontent,
I love and yet am forced to seem to hate,
I do, yet dare not say I ever meant,
I seem stark mute but inwardly do prate.
I am and not, I freeze and yet am burned.
Since from myself another self I turned.

My care is like my shadow in the sun,
Follows me flying, flies when I pursue it,
Stands and lies by me, doth what I have done.
His too familiar care doth make me rue it.
No means I find to rid him from my breast,
Till by the end of things it be supprest.

Some gentler passion slide into my mind,
For I am soft and made of melting snow;
Or be more cruel, love, and so be kind.
Let me or float or sink, be high or low.
Or let me live with some more sweet content,
Or die and so forget what love ere meant.
(*The Norton Anthology of Literature by Women: The Traditions in English*, W.W. Norton & Co., 1996, pp. 28-29)

The Doubt of Future Foes

The doubt of future foes exiles my present joy,
And wit me warns to shun such snares as threaten
    mine annoy;
For falsehood now doth flow, and subjects' faith doth
    ebb,
Which should not be if reason ruled or wisdom
    weaved the web.
But clouds of joys untried do cloak aspiring minds,
Which turn to rain of late repent by course of changed
    winds.
The top of hope supposed the root upreared shall be,
And fruitless all their grafted guile, as shortly ye shall
    see.
The dazzled eyes with pride, which great ambition
    blinds,
Shall be unsealed by worthy wights whose foresight
    falsehood finds.
The daughter of debate that discord aye doth sow

Shall reap no gain where former rule still peace hath
    taught to know.
No foreign banished wight shall anchor in this port;
Our realm brooks not seditious sects, let them else-
    where resort.

My rusty sword through rest shall first his edge
    employ
To poll their tops that seek such change or gape for
    future joy.

        (*Norton Anthology*)

Elizabeth I's Speech to the Troops at Tilbury

This famous speech was given by Elizabeth I in 1588 as England prepared for an invasion by King Philip of Spain and his powerful Armada.

My loving people,

We have been persuaded by some that are careful of our safety, to take heed how we commit our selves to armed multitudes, for fear of treachery; but I assure you I do not desire to live to distrust my faithful and loving people. Let tyrants fear, I have always so behaved myself that, under God, I have placed my chiefest strength and safeguard in the loyal hearts and good-will of my subjects; and therefore I am come amongst you, as you see, at this time, not for my recreation and disport, but being resolved, in the midst and heat of the battle, to live and die amongst you all; to lay down for my God, and for my kingdom, and my people, my honour and my blood, even in the dust. I know I have the body but of a weak and feeble woman; but I have the heart and stomach of a king, and of a king of England too, and think foul scorn that Parma or Spain, or any prince of Europe, should dare to invade the borders of my realm; to which rather than any dishonour shall grow by me, I myself will take up arms, I myself will be your general, judge, and rewarder of every one of your virtues in the field. I know already, for your forwardness you have deserved rewards and crowns; and We do assure you in the word of a prince, they shall be duly paid you. In the mean time, my lieutenant general shall be in my stead, than whom never prince commanded a more noble or worthy subject; not doubting but by your obedience to my general, by your concord in the camp, and your valour in the field, we shall shortly have a famous victory over those enemies of my God, of my kingdom, and of my people.

(*Norton Anthology;* http://www.nationalcenter.org/ElizabethITilbury.html)

CRITICAL THINKING QUESTION

Write a three-page *definition essay* on Elizabethan England (refer to *Skills for Rhetoric* if you need review on writing a definition essay).

The Fairie Queene

Edmund Spenser

BACKGROUND

Edmund Spenser was born around 1552 in London, England. He began writing poetry in his early 20s and was at Queen Elizabeth's court. He was a life-long admirer of Queen Elizabeth. His first major work, *The Shepheardes Calender*, was published in 1579 and met with critical success; within a year he was at work on his greatest and longest work, *The Faerie Queene*, the longest narrative poem in the English language. Composing this poem occupied him for most of his life. Spenser intended to write 12 books of *The Faerie Queene* but actually completed about one-half. Each Book of *The Faerie Queene* concerns the story of a knight, representing a particular Christian virtue that he must represent at the court of the Faerie Queene.

CRITICAL THINKING

A. In what sense is *The Fairie Queene* an allegory?

B. Read Sonnet 26 and Sonnet 75 from Edmund Spenser's *Amoretti*. (Middle English spelling is retained). What is the rhyme scheme of these two sonnets? What effect does the rhyme scheme have on the reader?

Sonnet 26

Sweet is the Rose, but growes vpon a brere;
Sweet is the Iunipere, but sharpe his bough;
sweet is the Eglantine, but pricketh nere;
sweet is the firbloome, but his braunches rough
Sweet is the Cypresse, but his rynd is tough,
sweet is the nut, but bitter is his pill;
sweet is the broome-flowre, but yet sowre enough;
and sweet is Moly, but his root is ill.
So euery sweet with soure is tempred still,
that maketh it be coueted the more:
for easie things that may be got at will,
most sorts of men doe set but little store.
Why then should I accoumpt of little paine,
that endlesse pleasure shall vnto me gaine.
(Hugh MaClean, ed., *Edmund Spenser's Poetry*,
    W.W.Norton and Co., 1982, p. 491)

Sonnet 75

One day I wrote her name vpon the strand,
but came the waues and washed it away:
agayne I wrote it with a second hand,
but came the tyde, and made my paynes his pray.
Vayne man, sayd she, that doest in vaine assay,
a mortall thing so to immortalize,
for I my selue shall lyke to this decay,
and eek my name bee wyped out lykewize.
Not so, (quod I) let baser things deuize,
to dy in dust, but you shall liue by fame:
my verse your vertues rare shall eternize,
and in the heuens wryte your glorious name.
Where whenas death shall all the world subdew,
our loue shall liue, and later life renew.
(Hugh MaClean, ed., *Edmund Spenser's Poetry*,
    W.W.Norton and Co., 1982, p. 491)

C. What is the theme of Sonnet 26?
D. Sonnet 75 has a Christian theme. Explain.
E. Compare and contrast "The Passionate Shepherd to His Love," by Christopher Marlowe with "The Nymph's Reply to the Shepherd," a copycat version by Sir Walter Raleigh.

The Passionate Shepherd to His Love

Come live with me and be my Love,
And we will all the pleasures prove
That hills and valleys, dales and field,
Or woods or steepy mountain yields.

And we will sit upon the rocks
And see the shepherds feed their flocks,
By shallow rivers, to whose falls
Melodious birds sing madrigals.

And I will make thee beds of roses
And a thousand fragrant posies,
A cap of flowers, and a kirtle
Embroider'd all with leaves of myrtle.

A gown made of the finest wool,
Which from our pretty lambs we pull,
Fair _ined slippers for the cold,
With buckles of the purest gold.

A belt of straw and ivy buds
With coral clasps and amber studs:
And if these pleasures may thee move,
Come live with me and be my Love.

SUGGESTED
Weekly *Implementation*

DAY 1	DAY 2	DAY 3	DAY 4	DAY 5
Prayer journal.	**Prayer journal.**	**Prayer journal.**	**Prayer journal.**	**Prayer journal.**
Review required reading(s) *before* the assigned lesson begins. Teacher may want to discuss assigned reading(s) with students. Teacher and students will decide on required essays for this lesson, choosing two or three essays. The rest of the essays can be outlined, answered with shorter answers, or skipped. Review all readings for Lesson 4.	Review reading(s) from next lesson. Outline essays, including thesis statement, due at the end of the week. Per teacher instructions students may answer orally in a group setting some of the essays that are not assigned as formal essays.	Write rough drafts of all assigned essays. The teacher and/or a peer evaluator may correct rough drafts.	Rewrite corrected copies of essays due tomorrow.	Essays are due. Take Lesson 4 test. Review *The Fairie Queen*, Edmund Spenser; "Sonnet 26," and "Sonnet 75," from *Amoretti*, by Edmund Spenser; "The Passionate Shepherd to His Love," Christopher Marlowe; "The Nymph's Reply to the Shepherd," Sir Walter Raleigh; "The Admonition by the Author to all Young Gentle-women: And to all other Maids being in Love," Isabella Whitney; "Sonnet 18," "Sonnet 29," "Sonnet 55," "Sonnet 73," and "Sonnet 116," William Shakespeare Guide: What themes continue to surface in Elizabethan poetry?

LESSON 5
ELIZABETHAN AGE *(Part 1)*

Elizabethan Age

BACKGROUND

The Elizabethan Age is named after Queen Elizabeth, daughter of Henry VIII and one of the most important English monarchs. This era is marked by advances on almost all intellectual fronts: science, art, and drama. The Elizabethan Age is the English version of the European Renaissance. The *sonnet,* a poem of fourteen lines perfected in Italy in the fourteenth century, is a grand marker of this age. Elizabethan love sonnets celebrate beauty: especially female beauty. The Elizabethan love sonnet is the first love song in English literature.

QUEEN ELIZABETH I

Queen Elizabeth I (1533-1603) is perhaps England's greatest monarch, ruling from 1558 until her death in 1603. She oversaw England's victory over the Spanish Armada and the rise of the British Empire. In fact, her name was applied to the whole era–called the Elizabethan Age.

Analyze: "On Monsieur's Departure," "The Doubt of Future Woes," Elizabeth I's "Speech to the Troops at Tilbury," Queen Elizabeth; Sonnets 26 and 75, from *Amoretti,* by Edmund Spenser; "The Passionate Shepherd to His Love," Christopher Marlowe; "The Nymph's Reply to the Shepherd," Sir Walter Raleigh; "The Admonition by the Author to all Young Gentlewomen: And to all other Maids being in Love," Isabella Whitney; Sonnets 18 and 73, William Shakespeare.

Reading Ahead: *Macbeth,* William Shakespeare.

Guide Question: Is Macbeth an evil man or a pawn in the hands of an evil woman?

CRITICAL THINKING

A. Evaluate the personal touch, both for a monarch and a sixteenth century poet, of Queen Elizabeth's poetry.
B. Was Elizabeth writing this poetry for a large audience?

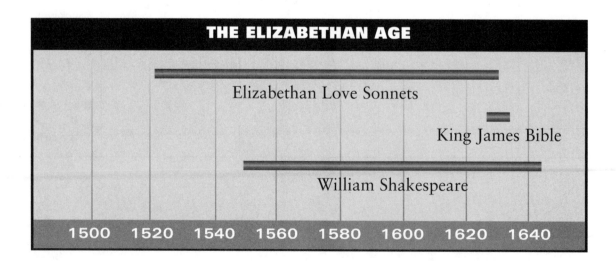

THE ELIZABETHAN AGE

Elizabethan Love Sonnets

King James Bible

William Shakespeare

| 1500 | 1520 | 1540 | 1560 | 1580 | 1600 | 1620 | 1640 |

How to Read Poetry

Read a poem with a pencil in your hand. Are there any words you do not understand? What is the meter/rhythm? Are any words repeated?

Carefully consider the poem's title. What does it promise? Does it invite you to read the poem?

First read through the poem silently and then aloud. Memorize as much of it as you can. Then, try singing it: sing the poem's words to a popular tune or make up a tune.

What is the theme of the poem?

What sort of poem is it? Narrative poem? Sonnet? Psalm?

What is the poem's basic situation? What is going on in it? Who is talking? To whom? Under what circumstances? Where? About what? Why?

One way to see the action in a poem is to list all its verbs. What do they tell you about the poem?

Is the poem built on a comparison or an analogy? If so, how is the comparison or the analogy appropriate? How are the two things alike? How different?

What mood is evoked in the poem? How is the mood accomplished?

What sort of literary techniques are used? Why?

What would the poem sound like if you paraphrased it?

The silver dishes for thy meat
As precious as the gods do eat,
Shall on an ivory table be
Prepared each day for thee and me.

The shepherd swains shall dance and sing
For thy delight each May-morning:
If these delights thy mind may move,
Then live with me and be my Love.

The Nymph's Reply to the Shepherd

If all the world and love were young,
And truth in every shepherd's tongue,
These pretty pleasures might me move
To live with thee and be thy Love.

But Time drives flocks from field to fold;
When rivers rage and rocks grow cold;
And Philomel becometh dumb;
The rest complains of cares to come.

The flowers do fade, and wanton fields
To wayward Winter reckoning yields:
A honey tongue, a heart of gall,
Is fancy's spring, but sorrow's fall.

Thy gowns, thy shoes, thy beds of roses,
Thy cap, thy kirtle, and thy posies,
Soon break, soon wither—soon forgotten,
In folly ripe, in reason rotten.

Thy belt of straw and ivy-buds,
Thy coral clasps and amber studs,—
All these in me no means can move
To come to thee and be thy Love.

But could youth last, and love still breed,
Had joys no date, nor age no need,
Then these delights my mind might move
To live with thee and be thy Love. (John Wain, ed.,
    The Oxford Anthology of English Poetry, Oxford U.
    Press, 1990, p. 67)
http://www.shakespeares-sonnets.com/Spenser1.htm

F. Read several poems by Sir Philip Sidney. Compare poems by Sidney and Spenser. In your two-page essay, consider each poet's theme, metaphors, tone, and biblical application.

To Sleep
Sir Philip Sidney

Come, Sleep; O Sleep! the certain knot of peace,
The baiting-place of wit, the balm of woe,
The poor man's wealth, the prisoner's release,
Th' indifferent judge between the high and low;
With shield of proof, shield me from out the prease
Of those fierce darts Despair at me doth throw:
O make in me those civil wars to cease;
I will good tribute pay, if thou do so.
Take thou of me smooth pillows, sweetest bed,
A chamber deaf to noise and blind to light,
A rosy garland and a weary head:
And if these things, as being thine by right,
    Move not thy heavy grace, thou shalt in me,
    Livelier than elsewhere, Stella's image see.
(http://swww.love-
    poems.me.uk/sydney_sir_philip_sleep.htm)

G. Read "Love's Farewell," by Michael Drayton; "To Sleep," by Samuel Daniel; and "When to Her Lute Corinna Sings," by Thomas Campion. Discuss how each poet uses *figurative language* to increase the effectiveness of each poem.

Love's Farewell
Michael Drayton
http://www.bartleby.com/40/70.html

Since there's no help, come let us kiss and part, —
Nay I have done, you get no more of me;
And I am glad, yea, glad with all my heart,
That thus so cleanly I myself can free;
Shake hands for ever, cancel all our vows,
And when we meet at any time again,
Be it not seen in either of our brows
That we one jot of former love retain.
Now at the last gasp of love's latest breath,
When his pulse failing, passion speechless lies,
When faith is kneeling by his bed of death,
And innocence is closing up his eyes,
Now if thou would'st, when all have given him over,
From death to life thou might'st him yet decover!

To Sleep
Samuel Daniel
http://www.bartleby.com/40/67.html

Care Charmer Sleep, son of the sable Night,
Brother to Death, in silent darkness born,
Relieve my languish, and restore the light;
With dark forgetting of my care return.
And let the day be time enough to mourn
The shipwreck of my illadventured youth:
Let waking eyes suffice to wail their scorn,
Without the torment of the night's untruth.
Cease, dreams, the images of day-desires,
To model forth the passions of the morrow;
Never let rising Sun approve you liars,
To add more grief to aggravate my sorrow:
Still let me sleep, embracing clouds in vain,
And never wake to feel the day's disdain.

When to Her Lute Corinna Sings
Thomas Campion
http://www.bartleby.com/40/142.html

When to her lute Corinna sings,
Her voice revives the leaden strings,
And doth in highest notes appear,
As any challenged echo clear;
But when she doth of mourning speak,
E'en with her sighs, the strings do break,

And as her lute doth live or die,
Led by her passion, so must I:
For when of pleasure she doth sing,
My thoughts enjoy a sudden spring,
But if she doth of sorrow speak,
E'en from my heart the strings do break.

H. Analyze "Love's Farewell," "To Sleep," and "When to Her Lute Corinna Sings" giving attention to the theme of mutability. Compare the views of these poets with Solomon's views in the Book of Ecclesiastes.

I. Compare and contrast Elizabethan love sonnets with modern love songs.

Isabella Whitney

Isabella Whitney (1540-1580?) was the first English woman to publish a collection of original poetry. Unlike many other female—and male—poets of the day, Whitney was not a noblewoman but was of the middle class. Because of this, relatively little is known about her life. However, since many of her poems occur in London, most scholars think that she lived there. Whitney's most ambitious work, *The Author . . . Maketh*

Her Will and Testament, depicts daily life in urban six-
teenth-century England. Her signature, *Is. W.*, was a
daring gesture in her day as was her courage in presenting the viewpoint of Elizabethan women.

CRITICAL THINKING

Discover the metaphors and viewpoint in Whitney's
poem. What warnings or advice does she offer?

The Admonition by the Author to all
Young Gentlewomen: And to all other
Maids being in Love

Ye Virgins, ye from Cupid's tents
do bear away the foil,
Whose hearts as yet with raging love
most painfully do boil.
To you I speak: for you be they
that good advice do lack:
Oh, if I could good counsell get,
my tongue should not be slack.
But such as I can give, I will
here in few words express,
Which, if you do observe, it will
some of your care redress.
Beware of fair and painted talk,
beware of flattering tongues:
The Mermaids do pretend no good
for all their pleasant songs.
Some use the tears of crocodiles,
contrary to their heart:
And if they cannot always weep,
they wet their cheeks by art.
Ovid, within his Art of Love,
doth teach them this same knack
To wet their hand and touch their eyes,
so oft as tears they lack.
Why have ye such deceit in store?
have you such crafty wile?
Less craft than this, God knows, would soon
us simple souls beguile.
And will ye not leave off? but still
delude us in this wise?
Sith it is so, we trust we shall
take heed to fained lies.
Trust not a man at the first sight
but try him well before:
I wish all maids within their breasts
to keep this thing in store.
For trial shall declare his truth
and show what he doth think,

Whether he be a lover true,
or do intend to shrink.
If Scilla had not trust too much
before that she did try,
She could not have been clean forsake
when she for help did cry.
Or if she had had good advice,
Nisus had lived long:
How durst she trust a stranger and
do her dear father wrong.
King Nisus had a hair by fate,
which hair, while he did kepe,
He never should be overcome,
neither on land nor deep.
The stranger that the daughter lou'd
did war against the King
And always sought how that he might
them in subjection bring.
This Scylla stole away the hair,
for to obtain her will,
And gave it to the stranger that
did straight her father kill.
Then she, who thought her self most sure
to have her whole desire,
Was clean reject and left behind
when he did home retire.
Or if such falsehood had been once
unto Oenone known,
About the fields of Ida wood,
Paris had walkt alone.
Or if Demophoon's deceit
to Phillis had been told,
She had not been transformed so,
as Poets tell of old.
Hero did try Leander's truth
before that she did trust:
Therefore she found him unto her
both constant, true, and just.
For he always did swim the sea
when stars in sky did glide
Till he was drowned by the way
near hand unto the side.
She scrat her face, she tare her hair
(it grieveth me to tell)
When she did know the end of him
that she did love so well.
But like Leander there be few,
therefore in time take heed
And always try before ye trust,
so shall you better speed.
The little fish that careless is

A *metaphor* is a figure of speech in which two unlike symbols or words are compared but in which no word of comparison (such as *like* or *as*) is used.

within the water clear,
How glad is he, when he doth see,
a bait for to appear.
He thinks his hap right good to be,
that he the same could spy,
And so the simple fool doth trust
too much before he try.
O little fish, what hap hadst thou?
to have such spiteful fate,
To come into one's cruel hands
out of so happy state?
Thou didst suspect no harm when thou
upon the bait didst look:
O that thou hadst had Linceus' eyes
for to have seen the hook.
Then hadst thou with thy pretty mates
been playing in the streams
Whereas sir Phoebus daily doth
shew forth his golden beams.
But sith thy fortune is so ill
to end thy life on shore,
Of this thy most unhappy end
I mind to speak no more.
But of thy fellow's chance that late
such pretty shift did make,
That he from fishers' hook did sprit
before he could him take,
And now he pries on euery bait,
suspecting still that prick
(for to lie hid in every thing)
wherewith the fishers strick,
And since the fish that reason lacks
once warnèd doth beware,
Why should not we take heed to that
that turneth us to care?
And I who was deceived late
by one's unfaithful tears
Trust now for to beware, if that
I live this hundreth years.
(http://eir.library.utoronto.ca/rpo/display/poem2952.ht
    ml)

Queen Elizabeth

BIBLICAL APPLICATION

Read the Song of Solomon and compare those love lyrics with examples written by English poets.

CRITICAL THINKING

A. Define (in the glossary) the literary term *hyperbole* and show how Shakespeare utilizes this type of metaphor effectively in Sonnet 55 to describe his beloved.

B. *Personification* is a special type of metaphor. It is a special figure of speech in which something nonhuman is given human qualities. Find examples of *personification* in Sonnets 18 and 55. Next, in an essay, discuss why Shakespeare used these images to communicate with his reader. What other choices did he have?

BIBLICAL APPLICATION

A. Compare and contrast the *metaphorical language* in Sonnets 18 and 55 and the Song of Solomon.

B. Find as many metaphors for God as you can in the Scriptures. Which one(s) do you like best? Why?

ENRICHMENT

A. Research English paintings of Anthony Van Dyck and compare his themes to the themes we see represented in Elizabethan literature. Themes among artistic mediums are often replicated.

How to Read Poetry

Read a poem with a pencil in your hand. Are there any words you do not understand? What is the meter/rhythm? Are any words repeated?

Carefully consider the poem's title. What does it promise? Does it invite you to read the poem?

First read through the poem silently and then aloud. Memorize as much of it as you can. Then, try singing it: sing the poem's words to a popular tune or make up a tune.

What is the theme of the poem?

What sort of poem is it? Narrative poem? Sonnet? Psalm?

What is the poem's basic situation? What is going on in it? Who is talking? To whom? Under what circumstances? Where? About what? Why?

One way to see the action in a poem is to list all its verbs. What do they tell you about the poem?

Is the poem built on a comparison or an analogy? If so, how is the comparison or the analogy appropriate? How are the two things alike? How different?

What mood is evoked in the poem? How is the mood accomplished?

What sort of literary techniques are used? Why?

What would the poem sound like if you paraphrased it?

The silver dishes for thy meat
As precious as the gods do eat,
Shall on an ivory table be
Prepared each day for thee and me.

The shepherd swains shall dance and sing
For thy delight each May-morning:
If these delights thy mind may move,
Then live with me and be my Love.

The Nymph's Reply to the Shepherd

If all the world and love were young,
And truth in every shepherd's tongue,
These pretty pleasures might me move
To live with thee and be thy Love.

But Time drives flocks from field to fold;
When rivers rage and rocks grow cold;
And Philomel becometh dumb;
The rest complains of cares to come.

The flowers do fade, and wanton fields
To wayward Winter reckoning yields:
A honey tongue, a heart of gall,
Is fancy's spring, but sorrow's fall.

Thy gowns, thy shoes, thy beds of roses,
Thy cap, thy kirtle, and thy posies,
Soon break, soon wither—soon forgotten,
In folly ripe, in reason rotten.

Thy belt of straw and ivy-buds,
Thy coral clasps and amber studs,—
All these in me no means can move
To come to thee and be thy Love.

But could youth last, and love still breed,
Had joys no date, nor age no need,
Then these delights my mind might move
To live with thee and be thy Love. (John Wain, ed.,
The Oxford Anthology of English Poetry, Oxford U.
Press, 1990, p. 67)
http://www.shakespeares-sonnets.com/Spenser1.htm

F. Read several poems by Sir Philip Sidney. Compare poems by Sidney and Spenser. In your two-page essay, consider each poet's theme, metaphors, tone, and biblical application.

To Sleep
Sir Philip Sidney

Come, Sleep; O Sleep! the certain knot of peace,
The baiting-place of wit, the balm of woe,
The poor man's wealth, the prisoner's release,
Th' indifferent judge between the high and low;
With shield of proof, shield me from out the prease
Of those fierce darts Despair at me doth throw:
O make in me those civil wars to cease;
I will good tribute pay, if thou do so.
Take thou of me smooth pillows, sweetest bed,
A chamber deaf to noise and blind to light,
A rosy garland and a weary head:
And if these things, as being thine by right,
    Move not thy heavy grace, thou shalt in me,
    Livelier than elsewhere, Stella's image see.
(http://swww.love-
    poems.me.uk/sydney_sir_philip_sleep.htm)

G. Read "Love's Farewell," by Michael Drayton; "To Sleep," by Samuel Daniel; and "When to Her Lute Corinna Sings," by Thomas Campion. Discuss how each poet uses *figurative language* to increase the effectiveness of each poem.

Love's Farewell
Michael Drayton
http://www.bartleby.com/40/70.html

Since there's no help, come let us kiss and part, —
Nay I have done, you get no more of me;
And I am glad, yea, glad with all my heart,
That thus so cleanly I myself can free;
Shake hands for ever, cancel all our vows,
And when we meet at any time again,
Be it not seen in either of our brows
That we one jot of former love retain.
Now at the last gasp of love's latest breath,
When his pulse failing, passion speechless lies,
When faith is kneeling by his bed of death,
And innocence is closing up his eyes,
Now if thou would'st, when all have given him over,
From death to life thou might'st him yet decover!

To Sleep
Samuel Daniel
http://www.bartleby.com/40/67.html

Care Charmer Sleep, son of the sable Night,
Brother to Death, in silent darkness born,
Relieve my languish, and restore the light;
With dark forgetting of my care return.
And let the day be time enough to mourn
The shipwreck of my illadventured youth:
Let waking eyes suffice to wail their scorn,
Without the torment of the night's untruth.
Cease, dreams, the images of day-desires,
To model forth the passions of the morrow;
Never let rising Sun approve you liars,
To add more grief to aggravate my sorrow:
Still let me sleep, embracing clouds in vain,
And never wake to feel the day's disdain.

When to Her Lute Corinna Sings
Thomas Campion
http://www.bartleby.com/40/142.html

When to her lute Corinna sings,
Her voice revives the leaden strings,
And doth in highest notes appear,
As any challenged echo clear;
But when she doth of mourning speak,
E'en with her sighs, the strings do break,

And as her lute doth live or die,
Led by her passion, so must I:
For when of pleasure she doth sing,
My thoughts enjoy a sudden spring,
But if she doth of sorrow speak,
E'en from my heart the strings do break.

H. Analyze "Love's Farewell," "To Sleep," and "When to Her Lute Corinna Sings" giving attention to the theme of mutability. Compare the views of these poets with Solomon's views in the Book of Ecclesiastes.

I. Compare and contrast Elizabethan love sonnets with modern love songs.

Isabella Whitney

Isabella Whitney (1540-1580?) was the first English woman to publish a collection of original poetry. Unlike many other female—and male—poets of the day, Whitney was not a noblewoman but was of the middle class. Because of this, relatively little is known about her life. However, since many of her poems occur in London, most scholars think that she lived there. Whitney's most ambitious work, *The Author . . . Maketh*

B. Read Sonnets 73, 29, and 116 and compare them with Sonnets 18 and 55.

Sonnet 116

Let me not to the marriage of true minds
Admit impediments. Love is not love
Which alters when it alteration finds,
Or bends with the remover to remove:
O no! it is an ever-fixèd mark
That looks on tempests, and is never shaken;
It is the star to every wandering bark,
Whose worth's unknown, although his height be
    taken.
Love's not Time's fool, though rosy lips and cheeks
Within his bending sickle's compass come;
Love alters not with his brief hours and weeks,
But bears it out ev'n to the edge of doom:
    If this be error, and upon me proved,
    I never writ, nor no man ever loved.
(http://www.bartleby.com/40/134.html)

Sonnet 18

http://www.classicreader.com/read.php/sid.1/bookid.10
    62/sec.1/

Shall I compare thee to a summer's day?
Thou art more lovely and more temperate;
Rough winds do shake the darling buds of May,
And summer's lease hath all too short a date:
Sometime too hot the eye of heaven shines,
And often is his gold complexion dimm'd:
And every fair from fair sometime declines,
By chance, or nature's changing course, untrimm'd.
But thy eternal summer shall not fade,
Nor lose possession of that fair thou owest;
Nor shall Death brag thou wanderest in his shade
When in eternal lines to time thou growest.
So long as men can breathe, or eyes can see,
So long lives this, and this gives life to thee.

Sonnet 29

http://www.classicreader.com/read.php/sid.5/bookid.10
    62/sec.2/

Shakespeare

When in disgrace with fortune and men's eyes
I all alone beweep my outcast state,
And trouble deaf heaven with my bootless cries,
And look upon myself, and curse my fate;
Wishing me like to one more rich in hope,
Featured like him, like him with friends possest,
Desiring this man's art, and that man's scope,
With what I most enjoy contented least;
Yet in these thoughts myself almost despising,
Haply I think on thee—and then my state,
Like to the lark at break of day arising
From sullen earth, sings hymns at heaven's gate;
For thy sweet love remember'd, such wealth
brings
That then I scorn to change my state with kings.

Sonnet 55

http://www.classicreader.com/read.php/sid.5/bookid.10
    62/sec.3/

Not marble, nor the gilded monuments
Of princes, shall outlive this powerful rhyme;
But you shall shine more bright in these contents
Than unswept stone, besmear'd with sluttish time.
When wasteful war shall statues overturn,
And broils root out the work of masonry,
Nor Mars his sword nor war's quick fire shall burn
The living record of your memory.
'Gainst death and all-oblivious enmity
Shall you pace forth; your praise shall still find room
Even in the eyes of all posterity
That wear this world out to the ending doom.
So, till the judgment that yourself arise,
You live in this, and dwell in lovers' eyes.

When presenting a *dramatic monologue* (in this case a poem), read the poem through and mark the words you wish to emphasize. Intonation, tone, pronunciation, and pauses all affect the meaning of the poem.

Sonnet 73

http://www.classicreader.com/read.php/sid.5/bookid.10
62/sec.4/

That time of year thou may'st in me behold
When yellow leaves, or none, or few, do hang
Upon those boughs which shake against the cold,
Bare ruin'd choirs, where late the sweet birds sang:
In me thou see'st the twilight of such day
As after sunset fadeth in the west,
Which by and by black night doth take away,
Death's second self, that seals up all in rest:
In me thou seest the glowing of such fire,
That on the ashes of his youth doth lie
As the deathbed whereon it must expire,
Consumed with that which it was nourish'd by:
This thou perceiv'st, which makes thy love more strong,
To love that well which thou must leave ere long.

FINAL PORTFOLIO

Correct and rewrite all essays and place them in your Final Portfolio.

SUGGESTED

Weekly *Implementation*

DAY 1	DAY 2	DAY 3	DAY 4	DAY 5
Prayer journal.	**Prayer journal.**	**Prayer journal.**	**Prayer journal.**	**Prayer journal.**
Review the required reading(s) *before* the assigned lesson begins. Teacher may want to discuss assigned reading(s) with students. Teacher and students will decide on required essays for this lesson, choosing two or three essays. The rest of the essays can be outlined, answered with shorter answers, or skipped. Review all readings for Lesson 5.	Review reading(s) from next lesson. Outline essays due at the end of the week. Per teacher instructions, students may answer orally in a group setting some of the essays that are not assigned as formal essays.	Write rough drafts of all assigned essays. The teacher and/peer evaluator may correct rough drafts.	Rewrite corrected copies of essays due tomorrow.	Essays are due. Take Lesson 5 test. Reading ahead: Review *Macbeth*, William Shakespeare. Guide Question: Is Macbeth an evil man or a pawn in the hands of an evil woman?

LESSON 6

ELIZABETHAN AGE *(Part 2)*

Macbeth, Act I

William Shakespeare

Macbeth, one of Shakespeare's best tragedies, is the story of how a man's debility first brought him puissance, and then destruction. We meet one of the greatest heroes in Western literature—Banquo—and one of the most diabolical villains—Lady Macbeth—whose chicanery would rival the most malevolent Walt Disney miscreant. The story is based on historical fact: *Holinshed's Chronicles* recounts a similar story of Scottish treachery.

CRITICAL THINKING

A. What is the literary purpose of the witches in Scene 1? Why begin the play in this way?

B. Already in Act I, Scenes 1–3, we have glimpses into the character and heart of Lady Macbeth. Write a characterization of Lady Macbeth.

C. Watch Macbeth develop as a character throughout this play. Write a five-page essay comparing Macbeth to King Saul. Use generous evidence from

Shakespeare

Analyze: *Macbeth*, William Shakespeare.

Reading Ahead: *The Tragedy of Mariam, the Faire Queene of Jewry,* Elizabeth Cary; Review "To the Memory of My Beloved Master, William Shakespeare," "The Noble Nature," "Farewell to the World," Ben Jonson; *Essays*, Francis Bacon.

Guide Question: What themes are prevalent in the late Elizabethan Age?

the play and from Scripture to support your argument.

D. In Act I, Scene 3, lines 126–140, Shakespeare discusses fate. Compare this view to the understanding of fate advanced in *Beowulf*. What does the Bible have to say about fate?

BIBLICAL APPLICATION

A. As intimated above, Macbeth is a King Saul figure. There are numerous examples in Scripture where heroes self-destruct: King Saul, King Ahab, Judas, and Samson, among others. Why? Is there an inherent flaw in the character of the above Macbeth-type characters? Or, are they basically good people whose environment/circumstances force them to be bad?

B. Compare Lady Macbeth to Jezebel.

Macbeth, Act II

CRITICAL THINKING

A. What is the setting in this tragedy? How important

Characterization is a technique that a writer employs to reveal his character to his audience. How do we meet the main character? Do we see into his mind? What do others think of him?

is the setting to the development of the plot? Would the play be as interesting and effective if it were staged in the South Bronx, circa 1960? Why or why not?

B. How does Shakespeare use Macbeth's "dagger soliloquy" in Act II, Scene 1, lines 33–64, to build suspense? What does this scene tell us about the character of Macbeth?

C. In what ways is the porter's knocking on the King's door in Act II, Scene 3, comic relief?

BIBLICAL APPLICATION

A. Many modern theologians have tried to make Judas Iscariot a victim rather than a perpetrator of evil (e.g., the rock opera *Jesus Christ Superstar*). Is he really a victim or the perpetrator of one of the greatest crimes? Is Macbeth a murderer, the weak instrument of his diabolical wife, or the true villain? Defend your answer from the text and from Scripture.

B. The problem of evil in Western thought is a real one. The problem of evil arises (1) from the loss of a sense of God's presence in the face of evil or suffering and (2) from an apparent conflict between the language used to describe God (e.g., all powerful, all good, and all wise) and that used to describe the world as being characterized by evil and suffering. The solution proffered by the Book of Job is that of evoking such a sense of awe around the created universe that, discovering in this way a renewed sense of God's omniscience and omnipotence, one accepts both evil and good and contents himself verbally by acknowledging a final incomprehensibility. The issue is God's omnipotence vs. God's impotence, God's sovereignty vs. God's incompetence. Do Job's conclusions satisfy you? Why or why not?

Macbeth, Act III

CRITICAL THINKING

A. Dramatic irony is found in *Macbeth*. For instance,

> The *setting* of a literary piece is both the time and place in which a plot unfolds. When writing an essay on the setting, ask yourself how important this particular setting is to the story.

> *Dramatic irony* is a literary device whereby a character inadvertently speaks the truth, foreshadowing tragic events of which he is unaware.

he was sure that he would be very happy after he killed Duncan. Of course, he was not happy at all. In Scene 1 find several instances of dramatic irony.

B. Describe the declining relationship between Macbeth and Lady Macbeth. Why is this occurring?

C. One of the unanswered questions of this play is the appearance of the third murderer in Scene 3. Some scholars insist that he is a messenger from Macbeth. Others argue he is Macbeth, and others claim that he is a friend who helps Fleance escape. What do you think? Defend your answer from the text.

D. Identify points of rising action, the climax, and the denouement of this play.

BIBLICAL APPLICATION

Banquo is one of the most tragic figures in this play. He is loyal, innocent, and loving. However, Macbeth and Lady Macbeth know that he must die. Why? In a two-page essay, compare and contrast him to Jonathan, son of Saul and good friend to David.

Macbeth, Acts IV and V

CRITICAL THINKING

A. In a literary sense, why is it necessary for Shakespeare to have Macbeth murder Macduff's family? What is happening to our protagonist?

B. In Act V, Scene 1, Lady Macbeth relives events in her sleepwalking sequence. She broods over three events. What are they? Which one disturbs her the most?

C. Write an essay explaining the theme of this play.

D. In an *expository essay*, analyze Macbeth's final words on the meaning of life in Act V, Scene 5.

E. Every character in *Macbeth* has flaws. Analyze the flaws in each character and explain in your

> A good *plot* has a purpose; it grows naturally out of events; and it is related to the main idea in the story.

judgment why or why not each character received his just punishment/reward.

F. *Macbeth* has both a dramatic and a narrative portion. Distinguish between these two elements and discuss how they are developed.

G. Why would a director omit Act III, Scene 5 from a modern version of this play?

FINAL PORTFOLIO

Correct and rewrite all essays and place them in your Final Portfolio.

> *Theme:* A belief about life expressed in a prose, poem, or play. A theme is usually subtly presented in the literary piece. A theme should not be confused with a moral. A *moral* is a lesson to apply in living one's life. A theme is a comment on life.

SUGGESTED
Weekly *Implementation*

DAY 1	DAY 2	DAY 3	DAY 4	DAY 5
Prayer journal.	**Prayer journal.**	**Prayer journal.**	**Prayer journal.**	**Prayer journal.**
Review required reading(s) *before* the assigned lesson begins.	Review reading(s) from next lesson.	Write rough drafts of all assigned essays.	Rewrite corrected copies of essays due tomorrow.	Essays are due.
Teacher may want to discuss assigned reading(s) with students.	Outline essays due at the end of the week.	The teacher and/or a peer evaluator may correct rough drafts.		Take Lesson 6 test.
Teacher and students will decide on required essays for this lesson, choosing two or three essays.	Per teacher instructions, students may answer orally in a group setting some of the essays that are not assigned as formal essays.			Reading ahead: Review "To the Memory of My Beloved Master, William Shakespeare," "The Noble Nature," "Farewell to the World," Ben Jonson; Essays, Francis Bacon.
The rest of the essays can be outlined, answered with shorter answers, or skipped.				Guide: What themes are prevalent in the late Elizabethan Age?
Review all readings for Lesson 6.				

Elizabeth Cary

Elizabeth Cary (1585-1639) was born the daughter of Sir Laurence and Lady Elizabeth Tanfield. Even in her youth, it was obvious that she was an extraordinarily gifted writer. In 1602, Elizabeth married Sir Henry Cary in what was no doubt a marriage arranged by her parents. Nonetheless, Elizabeth apparently was quite fond of her husband in spite of their religious preferences. Sir Henry was a fervent Protestant; Elizabeth was a closet Catholic. This religious tension hurt her relationship with the Elizabethan court and is evident in her writings.

Lady Elizabeth Cary's most famous work was *The Tragedy of Mariam*, written around 1602-1604 but not published until 1613. It was the first play by an Englishwoman ever to be published. Cary bases her play on the biblical story of evil King Herod and his wife Mariam. Many feel that she based it on the Jewish historian Josephus' *Antiquities of the Jews*.

CRITICAL THINKING

Elaborate on and evaluate the tragedy that Miriam experiences in this play.

BIBLICAL APPLICATION

In what way is this play a Christian moral drama?

The Tragedy of Mariam, the Faire Queene of Jewry

From Act 3, Scene 3

(On the Duties of a Wife)

CHORUS: "Tis not enough for one that is a wife
To keep her spotless from an act of ill:
But from suspicion she should free her life,
And bare herself of power as well as will.
'Tis not so glorious for her to be free.

> **Analyze:** *The Tragedy of Mariam, the Faire Queene of Jewry,* Elizabeth Cary; "To the Memory of My Beloved Master, William Shakespeare," "The Noble Nature," "Farewell to the World," Ben Jonson; *Essays,* Francis Bacon.
>
> **Reading Ahead:** *Dr. Faustus,* Christopher Marlowe; "To the Thrice-Sacred Queen Elizabeth," "Psalm 58," Mary Sidney Herbert; Portions of *The King James Bible.*
>
> **Guide Question:** As you read *Dr. Faustus,* contrast the ending of Marlowe's play with the ending of Goethe's *Faust.* Breaking the stereotype for women writers—Mary Sidney Herbert.

As by her proper self restrained to be.
When she hath spacious ground to walk upon,
Why on the ridge should she desire to go?
It is no glory to forbear alone
Those things that may her honor overthrow.
But 'tis thankworthy if she will not take
All lawful liberties for honor's sake.
That wife her hand against her fame cloth rear,
That more than to her lord alone will give
A private word to any second ear,
And though she may with reputation live,
Yet though most chaste, she doth her glory blot,
And wounds her honor, though she kills it not.
When to their husbands they themselves do bind,
Do they not wholly give themselves away?
Or give they but their body, not their mind,
Reserving that, though best, for others' prey?
No sure, their thoughts no more can be their own,
And therefore should to none but one be known.
Then she usurps upon another's right,
That seeks to be by public language graced:
And though her thoughts reflect with purest light,
Her mind if not peculiar is not chaste.
For in a wife it is no worse to find,
A common body than a common mind.
And every mind, though free from thought of ill,

That out of glory seeks a worth to show,
When any's ears but one therewith they fill,
Doth in a sort her pureness overthrow.
Now Mariam had (but that to this she bent)
Been free from fear, as well as innocent.
(*Nortons Anthology Literature by Women*, W.W.Norton &
    Co., 1996, pp.49-51)
(http://athena.english.vt.edu/~jmooney/renmats/cary.ht
    m)

Ben Jonson

BACKGROUND

His contemporaries characterized Ben Jonson as "a great
lover and praiser of himself, a
contemner and scorner of others." He gave evidence of his
narcissism by publishing his collected works in 1616—an
unprecedented event. However,
he had reason to boast.
Jonson—a friend of Shake-
speare, Marlowe, Raleigh,
Bacon, and John Donne—was a great writer in his
own right. Many think he was the greatest English
writer of the Elizabethan period.

CRITICAL THINKING

A. Write a two-page biographical essay outlining Ben
   Jonson's life.
B. Read "To the Memory of My Beloved Master,
   William Shakespeare." Based on Johnson's charac-
   terization of William Shakespeare, write an essay
   outlining the reasons why Jonson admires
   Shakespeare so much.
C. The poems "The Noble Nature" and "Farewell to
   the World" both concern the theme of mutability.
   Explain what mutability is and find evidence from
   all three poems.

On My First Son

http://eir.library.utoronto.ca/rpo/display/poem1105.ht
    ml

Farewell, thou child of my right hand, and joy;
My sin was too much hope of thee, lov'd boy.
Seven years tho' wert lent to me, and I thee pay,
Exacted by thy fate, on the just day.

O, could I lose all father now! For why
Will man lament the state he should envy?
To have so soon 'scap'd world's and flesh's rage,
And if no other misery, yet age?
Rest in soft peace, and, ask'd, say, "Here doth lie
Ben Jonson his best piece of poetry."
For whose sake henceforth all his vows be such,
As what he loves may never like too much.

The Noble Nature

http://www.bartleby.com/40/152.htm

It is not growing like a tree
In bulk, doth make Man better be;
Or standing long an oak, three hundred year,
To fall a log at last, dry, bald, and sere:
A lily of a day
Is fairer far in May,
Although it fall and die that night—
It was the plant and flower of Light
In small proportions we just beauties see;
And in short measures life may perfect be.

To the Memory of My Beloved Master,
Mr. William Shakespeare,
and What He Hath Left Us

http://www.luminarium.org/sevenlit/jonson/benshake.h
    tm

To draw no envy, Shakespeare, on thy name,
Am I thus ample to thy book and fame;
While I confess thy writings to be such
As neither man nor Muse can praise too much.
'Tis true, and all men's suffrage. But these ways
Were not the paths I meant unto thy praise;
For seeliest Ignorance on these may light,
Which, when it sounds at best, but echoes right;
Or blind Affection, which doth ne'er advance
The truth, but gropes and urgeth all by chance;
Or crafty Malice might pretend this praise,
And think to ruin where it seem'd to raise.
These are as some infamous bawd or whore
Should praise a matron. What could hurt her more?
But thou art proof against them, and, indeed,
Above the ill-fortune of them, or the need.
I, therefore, will begin. Soul of the age!
The applause, delight, the wonder of our stage,
My Shakespeare, rise! I will not lodge thee by
Chaucer, or Spenser, or bid Beaumont lie
A little further, to make thee a room:

Thou art a monument without a tomb,
And art alive still, while thy book doth live,
And we have wits to read, and praise to give.
That I not mix thee so, my brain excuses;
I mean, with great but disproportion'd Muses.
For, if I thought my judgment were of years,
I should commit thee, surely, with thy peers.
And tell how far thou didst our Lyly outshine,
Or sporting Kyd, or Marlowe's mighty line.
And though thou hadst small Latin and less Greek,
From thence, to honour thee, I would not seek
For names; but call forth thund'ring Aeschylus,
Euripides, and Sophocles to us,
Paccuvius, Accius, him of Cordova dead
To life again, to hear thy buskin tread
And shake a stage; or when thy socks were on,
Leave thee alone, for the comparison
Of all that insolent Greece or haughty Rome
Sent forth; or since did from their ashes come.
Triumph, my Britain! Thou hast one to show
To whom all scenes of Europe homage owe.
He was not of an age, but for all time!
And all the Muses still were in their prime,
When, like Apollo, he came forth to warm
Our ears, or, like a Mercury, to charm.
Nature herself was proud of his designs,
And joy'd to wear the dressing of his lines,
Which were so richly spun, and woven so fit
As, since, she will vouchsafe no other wit.
The merry Greek, tart Aristophanes,
Neat Terence, witty Plautus, now not please;
But antiquated and deserted lie,
As they were not of Nature's family.
Yet must I not give Nature all! Thy art,
My gentle Shakespeare, must enjoy a part.
For though the Poet's matter Nature be
His art doth give the fashion. And that he
Who casts to write a living line, must sweat
(Such as thine are), and strike the second heat
Upon the Muses' anvil, turn the same
(And himself with it), that he thinks to frame;
Or for the laurel he may gain a scorn!
For a good Poet's made as well as born;
And such wert thou! Look how the father's face
Lives in his issue; even so, the race
Of Shakespeare's mind and manners brightly shines
In his well-turnèd and true-filèd lines;
In each of which he seems to shake a lance
As brandish'd at the eyes of Ignorance.
Sweet Swan of Avon! what a sight it were
To see thee in our water yet appear,

And make those flights upon the banks of Thames
That so did take Eliza, and our James!
But stay, I see thee in the hemisphere
Advanc'd, and made a constellation there!
Shine forth, thou star of poets, and with rage
Or influence, chide, or cheer the drooping stage;
Which since thy flight from hence hath mourn'd like
      night,
And despairs day, but for thy volume's light.

A Farewell to the World

http://www.bartleby.com/40/154.html

False world, good night! since thou hast brought
That hour upon my morn of age;
Henceforth I quit thee from my thought,
My part is ended on thy stage.

Yes, threaten, do. Alas! I fear
As little as I hope from thee:
I know thou canst not show nor bear
More hatred than thou hast to me.

My tender, first, and simple years
Thou didst abuse and then betray;
Since stir'd'st up jealousies and fears,
When all the causes were away.

Then in a soil hast planted me
Where breathe the basest of thy fools;
Where envious arts professèd be,
And pride and ignorance the schools;

Where nothing is examined, weigh'd,
But as 'tis rumour'd, so believed;
Where every freedom is betray'd,
And every goodness tax'd or grieved.

But what we're born for, we must bear:
Our frail condition it is such
That what to all may happen here,
If 't chance to me, I must not grutch.

Else I my state should much mistake
To harbour a divided thought
From all my kind—that, for my sake,
There should a miracle be wrought.

No, I do know that I was born
To age, misfortune, sickness, grief:
But I will bear these with that scorn
As shall not need thy false relief.

Nor for my peace will I go far,
As wanderers do, that still do roam;
But make my strengths, such as they are,
Here in my bosom, and at home.
(www.bartleby.com)

BIBLICAL APPLICATION

What is the tone of "On My First Son"? In this poem Jonson reflects on the untimely death of his son. What is his conclusion? What is the fate of his son? Does the Bible agree or disagree with Jonson's understanding of death?

ENRICHMENT

The following are obituaries:

Timothy Steven, an old and respected citizen of East Rhyefield Township, Indiana County, died last Friday about four o'clock. . . . Mr. Steven leaves but two children . . . He was a member of the Methodist Church for many years and believed with firm conviction in the rewards promised to those who are faithful Christians. . . . He had a large acquaintance and was universally respected by all who knew him. (an 1887 obituary)

Ronald Dennish, 57, formerly of Jonnestown, died—at Roger Hospital. . . . was a local musician for many years, [and an] Army veteran. . . . Arrangements by Hensal Funeral Home. (a 1996 obituary)

Compare and contrast these two obituaries. What do they tell you about the way values have changed over the past hundred years?

Essays
Francis Bacon

BACKGROUND

Was Francis Bacon a Medieval man or a modern man? Bacon represents in broad relief the tensions of Elizabethan England. . . . He was both a scientist (most agree a "second-rate" scientist), a writer, and a philosopher. Philosophically, Bacon sought to purge the mind of what he called "idols," or a disposition to error. These came from human nature ("idols of the tribe"), from individual temperament and experience ("idols of the cave"), from language ("idols of the marketplace"), and from false philosophies ("idols of the theater"). Of ear-

lier philosophers, he particularly criticized Aristotle. Within the writings of Plato, Bacon found a kindred spirit. Aristotle, with his propensity toward celebration of the human spirit over the power of the cosmology, greatly offended Bacon. As you read *Essays*, find evidence of these tensions.

CRITICAL THINKING

A. Bacon's writing "Of Wisdom for a Man's Self" is an essay. Many consider Francis Bacon to be the "father of the English essay." An essay is a piece of prose that expresses a personal point of view. The formal essay is usually pedantic and impersonal in tone. The informal essay is relaxed and conversational in tone and can even be whimsical. As you read Bacon's *Essays* (1597), identify examples of both essay styles.

B. Bacon wrote in Latin more than he did in English, which caused his English style to be an unnatural, informal style. Find evidence of this style in "Of Wisdom for a Man's Self."

Bacon's Essay:

An ant is a wise creature for itself, but it is a shrewd thing in an orchard or garden. And certainly men that are great lovers of themselves waste the public. Divide with reason between self-love and society; and be so true to thyself, as thou be not false to others; specially to thy king and country. It is a poor centre of a man's actions, himself. It is right earth. For that only stands fast upon his own centre; whereas all things that have affinity with the heavens move upon the centre of another, which they benefit. The referring of all to a man's self is more tolerable in a sovereign prince; because themselves are not only themselves but their good and evil is at the peril of the public fortune. But it is a desperate evil in a servant to a prince, or a citizen in a republic. For whatsoever affairs pass such a man's hands, he crooketh them to his own ends; which must needs be often eccentric to the ends of his master or state. Therefore let princes, or states, choose such servants as have not this mark; except they mean their service should be made but the accessory. That which maketh the effect more pernicious is that all proportion is lost. It were disproportion enough for the servant's good to be preferred before the master's; but yet it is a greater extreme, when a little good of the servant shall carry things against a great good of the master's. And yet that is the case of bad officers, treasurers, ambassadors, generals, and other false and corrupt servants; which set a bias upon their bowl, of their own petty ends and envies, to the overthrow of their master's great and important affairs. And for the most part, the good such servants receive is after the model of their own fortune; but the hurt they sell for that good is after the model of their master's fortune. And certainly it is the nature of extreme self-lovers, as they will set an house on fire, and it were but to roast their eggs; and yet these men many times hold credit with their masters, because their study is but to please them and profit themselves; and for either respect they will abandon the good of their affairs. Wisdom for a man's self is, in many branches thereof, a depraved thing. It is the wisdom of rats, that will be sure to leave a house somewhat before it fall. It is the wisdom of the fox, that thrusts out the badger, who digged and made room for him. It is the wisdom of crocodiles, that shed tears when they could devour. But that which is specially to be noted is, that those which (as Cicero says of Pompey) are sui amantes, sine rivali [lovers of themselves without a rival] are many times unfortunate. And whereas they have all their times sacrificed to themselves, they become in the end themselves sacrifices to the inconstancy of fortune, whose wings they sought by their self-wisdom to have pinioned. (Harvard Classics, http://www.bartleby.com/3/1/23.html)

BIBLICAL APPLICATION

Most of us today are quite comfortable in talking about ourselves. Indeed, having "an identity crisis" is rather common. In Francis Bacon's day, it was unusual to talk about oneself so much, but Bacon does so with reckless abandon. Using *Essays* as a guide, write a two-page essay outlining several conclusions about the human self that Bacon advances. Do they line up with Scripture?

ENRICHMENT

In a famous treason trial Francis Bacon testified against his friend the Earl of Essex who subsequently was convicted. Many of his friends condemned Bacon as being a poor friend. Find evidence in *Essays* that supports/refutes how Bacon's testimony is consistent with his worldview.

FINAL PORTFOLIO

Correct and rewrite all essays and place them in your Final Portfolio.

SUGGESTED
Weekly *Implementation*

DAY 1	DAY 2	DAY 3	DAY 4	DAY 5
Prayer journal. Review required reading(s) *before* the assigned lesson begins. Teacher may want to discuss assigned reading(s) with students. Teacher and students will decide on required essays for this lesson, choosing two or three essays. The rest of the essays can be outlined, answered with shorter answers, or skipped. Review all readings for Lesson 7.	**Prayer journal.** Review reading(s) from next lesson. Outline essays due at the end of the week. Per teacher instructions, students may answer orally in a group setting some of the essays that are not assigned as formal essays.	**Prayer journal.** Write rough drafts of all assigned essays. The teacher and/or a peer evaluator may correct rough drafts.	**Prayer journal.** Rewrite corrected copies of essays due tomorrow.	**Prayer journal.** Essays are due. Take Lesson 7 test. Reading Ahead: Review *Dr. Faustus*, Christopher Marlowe; King James Bible. Guide: As you read Dr. Faustus, contrast the ending of Marlowe's play with the ending of Goethe's Faust.

LESSON 8
ELIZABETHAN AGE (Part 4)

Dr. Faustus
Christopher Marlowe

BACKGROUND

Christopher Marlowe's life tragically ended in 1593 when he was twenty-nine, yet in his short life, Marlowe became one of the preeminent Elizabethan dramatists—even considering he was a contemporary of William Shakespeare! When he began to write, English drama was crude and uninspiring. Marlowe, and then Shakespeare, transformed English drama into the most inspiring example of its genre in Western civilization.

CRITICAL THINKING

A. Analyze the plot of *Dr. Faustus*. In your answer, identify the rising action, climax, and falling action. How effective is Marlowe in building suspense?

B. How does Marlowe make Mephistophilis appear malevolent? In a strange way, Mephistophilis is quite charming. Agree or disagree.

ENRICHMENT

A. Contrast the ending of Dr. Faustus, by Christopher Marlowe, with Faust, by Johann Wolfgang von Goethe (who died in 1832).

B. What purpose does the chorus serve in this play? Next, compare the chorus in this play with the chorus in Oedipus Rex, by Sophocles.

Mary Sidney Herbert

Mary Sidney Herbert, Countess of Pembroke (1563-1621) was the first English woman to achieve a significant literary reputation. Unlike most early modern women writers, she never apologizes for, or even mentions, her role as a

Analyze: *Dr. Faustus*, Christopher Marlowe; "To the Thrice-Sacred Queen Elizabeth," "Psalm 58," Mary Sidney Herbert; King James Bible.

Reading Ahead: "An Excuse for So Much Writ upon My Verses," Margaret Cavendish; "Go and Catch a Falling Star," "Holy Sonnet IX," "Holy Sonnet XIV," and "Meditation XVII," John Donne.

Guide Question: In what ways does Donne's conversion affect his poetry?

woman writer. She was inspired by her poet brother Philip Sidney (although many think her poems better than her brother's). Her *Psalmes* influenced seventeenth-century writers including George Herbert and John Donne.

To the Thrice-Sacred Queen Elizabeth

1

Even now that care which on thy crown attends
And with thy happy greatness daily grows
Tells me, thrice-sacred Queen, my muse offends,
And of respect to thee the line out goes.
One instant will or willing can she lose
I say not reading, but receiving rhymes,
On whom in chief dependeth to dispose
What Europe acts in these most active times?

2

Yet dare I so, as humbleness may dare,
Cherish some hope they shall acceptance find;
Now weighing less thy state, lighter thy care,
But knowing more thy grace, abler thy mind.
What heavenly powers thee highest throne assigned,
Assigned thee goodness suiting that degree,
And by thy strength thy burthen so designed,
To others toil is exercise to thee.

3

Cares though still great, cannot be greatest still,
Business must ebb, though leisure never flow;
Then these the posts of duty and goodwill
Shall press to offer what their senders owe.

Which once in two, now in one subject go,
The poorer left, the richer rest away,
Who better might (O might, ah word of woe)
Have given for me what I for him defray.

4

How can I name whom sighing signs extend,
And not unstop my tears eternal spring?
But he did warp, I weaved this web to end;
The stuff not ours, our work no curious thing,
Wherein yet well we thought the Psalmist King
How English denizened, though Hebrew born.
Would to thy music undispleased sing,
Oft having worse, without repining worn;

5

And I the cloth in both our names present, A livery
    robe to be bestowed by thee;
Small parcel of the undischarged rent,
From which no pains nor payments can us free.
And yet enough to cause our neighbors see
We will our best, though scanted in our will;
And those nigh fields where sown they favors be
Unwealthy do, not else unworthy till.

6

For in our work what bring we but thine own?
What English is, by many names is thine,
There humble laurels in thy shadows grown
To garland others would themselves repine.
Thy breast the cabinet, thy seat the shrine,
Where muses hang their vowed memories;
Where wit, where art, where all that is divine
Conceived best, and best defended lies.

7

Which if men did not (as they do) confess,
And wronging worlds would otherwise consent,
Yet here who minds so meet a patroness
For authors' state or writings' argument?
A King should only to a Queen be sent;
God's loved choice unto his chosen love;
Devotion to devotion's president;
What all applaud, to her whom none reprove.

8

And who sees ought, but sees how justly square
His haughty ditties to thy glorious days?
How well beseeming thee his triumphs are?
His hope, his zeal, his prayer, plaint, and praise,
Needless thy person to their height to raise;
Less need to bend them down to thy degree;
Some holy garments each good soul assays,
Some sorting all, all sort to none but thee.

9

For even thy rule is painted in his reign;

Both clear in right; both nigh by wrong oppressed;
And each at length (man crossing God in vain)
Possessed of place, and each in peace possessed.
Proud Philistines did interrupt his rest,
The foes of heaven no less have been thy foes;
He with great conquest, thou with greater blessed;
Thou sure to win, and he secure to lose.
10 Thus hand in hand with him thy glories walk;
But who can trace them where alone they go?
Of thee who hemispheres on honor talk,
And lands and seas thy trophies jointly show.
The very winds did on thy party blow,
And rocks in arms thy foemen eft defy.
But soft, my muse, thy pitch is earthly love;
Forbear this heaven where only eagles fly.

11

Kings on a Queen enforced their states to lay,
Mainlands for empire waiting on an isle;
Men drawn by worth a woman to obey;
One moving all, herself unmoved the while;
Truth's restitution, vanity exile,
Wealth sprung of want, war held without annoy?
Let subject be of some inspired style,
Till then the object of her subjects' joy.

12

Thy utmost can but offer to her sight
Her handmaids' task, which most her will endears;
And pray unto thy pains life from that light
Which lively light some, court and kingdom cheers,
What wish she may (far past her living peers
And rival still to Judah's faithful king)
In more than he and more triumphant years,
Sing what God doth, and do what men may sing.
[1599]
(*Norton Anthology Literature by Women*, p. 30;
    http://athena.english.vt.edu/~jmooney/renmats/pe
    mbrk.htm)

Psalm 58

And call ye this to utter what is just
You that of justice hold the sovereign throne?
And call ye this, to yield, O sons of dust,
To wronged brethren every man his own?
O no! It is your long malicious will
Now to the world to make by practice known
With whose oppression you the balance fill:
Just to yourselves, indifferent else to none.
But what could they, who even in birth declined
From truth and right to lies and injuries?
To show the venom of their cankered mind
The adder's image scarcely can suffice;

Nay, scarce the aspic may with them contend,
On whom the charmer all in vain applies
His skillful'st spells, aye missing of his end, While she,
        self-deaf and unaffected, lies.
Lord, crack their teeth! Lord, crush these lions' jaws!
So let them sink as water in the sand.
When deadly bow their aiming fury draws,
Shiver the shaft ere past the shooter's hand.
So make them melt as the dishoused snail,
Or as the embryo whose vital band
Breaks ere it holds, and formless eyes do fail
To see the sun, though brought to lightful land.
O let their brood, a brood of springing thorns,
Be by untimely rooting overthrown;
Ere bushes waxed, they push with pricking horns,
As fruits yet green are oft by tempest blown.
The good with gladness this revenge shall see
And bathe his feet in blood of wicked one
While all shall say, "The just rewarded be;
There is a God that carves to each his own."
[1599]
(*Norton Anthology Literature by Women*, p. 33;
        (http://athena.english.vt.edu/~jmooney/renmats/pe
        mbrk.htm)

CRITICAL THINKING

Until recently many scholars refused to take seventeenth century female poets seriously. They believed
that women only wrote letters, and the occasional private devotional meditation. Discuss how Lady
Pembroke breaks that stereotype.

BIBLICAL APPLICATION

Discuss the purpose of Lady Pembroke's poem "Psalm
58." What are the purposes of meditative psalms?

The English Bible
King James Version

BACKGROUND

The world as we know it is deeply indebted to the
Bible. In fact, it is fair to say that the foundations of
modern Western culture evolved from its pages. For
over one thousand years, the Bible has influenced the
greatest English writers. As you remember, the first

> An *epic* is a long narrative poem that tells of the exploits and adventures of one or more great heroes. An epic often promotes the ideals and values of a nation.

Anglo-Saxon singer/writer Caedmon sang the stories of
the Bible in his histories. The total effect of the Bible on
later generations is incalculable. No part of our lives
remains untouched by the Bible. But in its original ver-
sions, Greek and Hebrew, and in its early translations,
such as Latin, most Englishmen could not read the
Bible. This was tolerable in pre-Reformation England
because Catholicism jealously reserved its Scripture for
the clergy alone. But, with the Reformation and its
emphasis on the priesthood of all believers, the Bible
needed to be read by all. It surprised no one, then,
when King James I, in 1604, asked 54 scholars to translate the Bible into the King's English. The world has
never been the same. The great Christian scholar Dr.
Bruce Metzger, professor emeritus of Princeton
Theological Seminary, chairman of the translation committee for the New Revised Standard Version (1990)
writes:

> *I read it (the Bible) and I am inspired by the inspired
> words of the writers. I also find it interesting as literature. It is
> productive for life, for the church, for the individual believer. I
> thank God that I am still able to study its passages. As long as
> I am able, I want to follow a motto that is found in a 1734 edi-
> tion of the Greek New Testament: "Apply yourself totally to the
> text; apply the text totally to yourself."* (In *Christian History*,
> issue 43, vol. 13, no. 3. (p. 40)

CRITICAL THINKING

Find examples of the following types of literature in the
Bible: lyric poetry, the song, the ballad, the ode, the
elegy, meditation poetry, monodies, dramatic lyrics, rit-
ual lyrics, lyric idyll, rhetoric, epistolary literature, wisdom literature, the riddle, the proverb, prophetic
literature, symbolic prophecy, dramatic prophecy, the
doom song, and the rhapsody. Consult the dictionary if
you do not know these terms.

FINAL PROJECT

Correct and rewrite all essays and place them in your
Final Portfolio.

SUGGESTED
Weekly *Implementation*

DAY 1	DAY 2	DAY 3	DAY 4	DAY 5
Prayer journal.	**Prayer journal.**	**Prayer journal.**	**Prayer journal.**	**Prayer journal.**
Review required reading(s) *before* the assigned lesson begins.	Review reading(s) from next lesson.	Write rough drafts of all assigned essays.	Rewrite corrected copies of essays due tomorrow.	Essays are due.
Teacher may want to discuss assigned reading(s) with students.	Outline essays due at the end of the week.	The teacher and/or a peer evaluator may correct rough drafts.		Take Lesson 8 test.
<u>Teacher and students will decide on required essays for this lesson, choosing two or three essays.</u>	Per teacher instructions, students may answer orally in a group setting some of the essays that are not assigned as formal essays.			Reading Ahead: "An Excuse for So Much Writ upon My Verses," Margaret Cavendish; "Go and Catch a Falling Star," "Holy Sonnet IX," "Holy Sonnet XIV," and "Meditation XVII," John Donne.
<u>The rest of the essays can be outlined, answered with shorter answers, or skipped.</u>				Guide: In what ways does Donne's conversion affect his poetry?
Review all readings for Lesson 8.				

Margaret Lucas Cavendish

Duchess of Newcastle

Margaret Lucas Cavendish (1623-1673), Duchess of Newcastle, was a Royalist during the English Civil War. She met and married William Cavendish, a leader of the Royalist forces and thirty years her senior. They lived on the Continent during the reign of Cromwell. At a time when it was considered bold for women to produce even the tamest of compositions, "the crazy duchess" tried to combine Metaphysical poetry with scientific speculation, philosophical meditation with fanciful fantasizing." (*Norton Anthology Literature by Women*, p. 93). Like her American contemporary Anne Bradstreet, Lady Cavendish loved to write about ordinary subjects. She even speculated on the meaning of femininity, exhibiting the "unusually sophisticated acknowledgment of the complex problems posed by woman's cultural situation." Both Cavendish and Bradstreet expressed the "anxieties authorship instilled." Cavendish was the first aristocratic woman in England continually to remind her readers that she is a woman and that she writes about issues from a woman's perspective.

An Excuse for So Much Writ upon My Verses

Condemne me not for making such a coyle
About my Book, alas it is my Childe.
Just like a Bird, when her Young are in Nest,
Goes in, and out, and hops and takes no Rest;
But when their Young are fledg'd, their heads out
    peep,
Lord what a chirping does the Old one keep.
So I, for feare my Strengthlesse Childe should fall
Against a doore, or stoole, aloud I call,
Bid have a care of such a dangerous place:

Analyze: "An Excuse for So Much Writ upon My Verses," Margaret Cavendish; "Go and Catch a Falling Star," "Holy Sonnet IX," "Holy Sonnet XIV," and "Meditation XVII," John Donne.

Reading Ahead: "To My Excellent Lucasia, on our friendship. 7th July 65," Katherine Philips; "To Lucasta, on Going to the Wars," Richard Lovelace; "The Collar," George Herbert; "The Retreat," Henry Vaughn; "To the Virgins to Make Much of Time," Robert Herrick; "Bermudas" and "To His Coy Mistress," Andrew Marvell.

Guide Question: What do you think about the theme of mutability?

Thus write I much, to hinder all disgrace.
(*Norton Anthology of Literature by Women*, p. 94)

CRITICAL THINKING

In a two-page essay discover the information Lady Cavendish offers for "so much writ upon my verses."

John Donne

BACKGROUND

In the seventeenth century English history took a rather maverick direction and produced some of the

greatest literary, philosophical, and theological movements in human history. This century belongs to three great Johns: John Donne, John Milton, and John Dryden. What a dynamic trio! At the same time and in its quiet way, England experienced the equivalent of the French

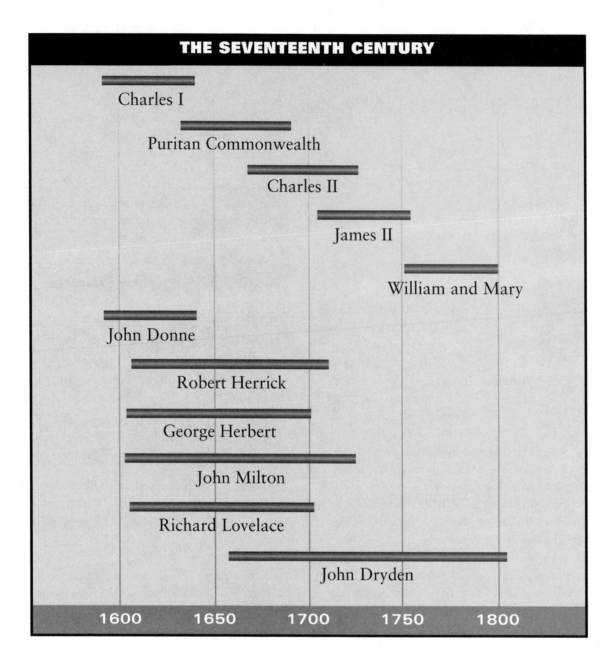

THE SEVENTEENTH CENTURY

Charles I

Puritan Commonwealth

Charles II

James II

William and Mary

John Donne

Robert Herrick

George Herbert

John Milton

Richard Lovelace

John Dryden

1600   1650   1700   1750   1800

Revolution—without the bloodshed and chaos. In the middle of this century, the English rebelled against their king Charles I (1625–49) and executed him. During this period, too, England saw the triumph of one of the truly great cultural worldviews in human history: Puritanism. Enjoy this great literature!

CRITICAL THINKING

A. Donne wrote refreshingly new poetry. His literary style is peculiarly his own, especially in the songs and sonnets. Almost every poem has a unique stanza pattern—never used before and never repeated. These stanzas are often nicely adjusted to the rhetoric of the units they form. Moreover, the

rhythm of the lines has little of the clichés so abundantly exemplified by English poetry during Donne's youth and maturity. The exceptionally easygoing movement of "Go and Catch a Falling Star" serves to underscore its simplicity and honesty.

Go and Catch a Falling Star

Go and catch a falling star,	a
Get with child a mandrake root,	b
Tell me where all past years are,	a
Or who cleft the devil's foot,	b
Teach me to hear mermaids singing,	c
Or to keep off envy's stinging,	c
And find	d

What wind	d
Serves to advance an honest mind.	d

If thou be'st born to strange sights,	d
Things invisible to see,	e
Ride ten thousand days and nights	f
Till age snow white hairs on thee;	e
Thou, when thou return'st, wilt tell me	f
All strange wonders that befell thee,	f
And swear	g
Nowhere	g
Lives a woman true, and fair.	g

If thou find'st one, let me know;	h
Such a pilgrimage were sweet.	i
Yet do not; I would not go	h
Though at next door we might meet.	j
Though at next door we might meet.	j
And last till you write your letter.	k
Yet she	l
Will be,	l
False, ere I come, to two or three.	l

(www.bartleby.com/40/169.html)

In a three-page essay, compare and contrast John Donne's style to earlier Elizabethan writers like William Shakespeare, Ben Jonson, and Edmund Spenser. Discuss theme, tone, rhyme, meter, and subject matter.

B. Including John Donne in this curriculum was a difficult decision. Donne, like Chaucer, wrote absolutely inspired poetry/prose. On the other hand, there are certain works that go beyond good taste and literature and wander into vulgarity. Today, with all the sexual temptations that surround us, it is vital that the Christian discern the difference between art and trash. The Bible has a great deal to say about the arts, and it also gives a detailed description of a particular artist and his ministry. Bezalel appears to be Moses' minister of the arts. His grandfather Hur held up Moses' arms during the battle with the Amalekites and obviously was one of Moses' trusted aides (Exodus 17:8-13; 24:14). Read about Bezalel in Exodus 31:1-11. In a two-page essay, list several criteria that separate art from junk. Be careful to defend your answer.

BIBLICAL APPLICATION

Holy Sonnet X

Death, be not proud, though some have called thee
Mighty and dreadful, for thou art not so;
For those whom thou think'st thou dost overthrow,
Die not, poor Death, nor yet canst thou kill me.
From rest and sleep, which but thy pictures be,
Much pleasure; then from thee much more must flow,
And soonest our best men with thee do go,
Rest of their bones, and soul's delivery.
Thou art slave to fate, chance, kings, and desperate
      men,
And dost with poison, war, and sickness dwell;
And poppy or charms can make us sleep as well
And better than thy stroke; why swell'st thou then?
One short sleep past, we wake eternally,
And death shall be no more; Death, thou shalt die.
(http://www.netpoets.com/classic/poems/022033.htm)

A. Identify the Christian themes in "Holy Sonnet X."
B. How does Donne use personification to enhance the effect of this poem?
C. Compare and contrast the theme of death in this poem and in the Book of Job.
D. How does "Holy Sonnet XIV" reflect some of the same language in the Book of Jeremiah?
E. Paraphrase this poem. How would you characterize John Donne's view of life? Why do you or do you not consider it theistic?

ENRICHMENT

A. Write a definition essay on the salient features of seventeenth-century England. Criteria that make up a definition essay include: it defines what a thing is and what it is not; for instance, seventeenth-century England would address such issues as the rise of the global British Empire, the rise of the novel, and the early beginnings of industrialization. Slavery abolition is not yet a big issue in British society.
B. Draw parallels between what was happening in seventeenth-century England and what was happening at the same time in the American colonies.
C. Write a report on seventeenth-century China.
D. Imagine you are a sixteen-year-old living in London, around 1650. Describe your life in great detail.
E. "Meditation XVII" is one of a number of short essays that Donne wrote while recovering from a

serious illness. In what ways is it a Christian document?

Meditation XVII

No man is an island entire of itself; every man is a piece of the continent, a part of the main. If a clod be washed away by the sea, Europe is the less, as well as if a man or of thy friend's or of thine own were. Any man's death diminishes me, because I am involved in mankind, and therefore never send to know for whom the bell tolls; it tolls for thee. . . . If a man carry treasure in bullion or in a wedge of gold and have none coined into current money, his treasure will not defray him as he travels. Tribulation is treasure in the nature of it, but it is not current money in the use of it, except we get nearer and nearer our home, heaven, by it. Another man may be sick too, and sick to death, and this affliction may lie in his bowels as gold in a mine and be of no use to him; but his bell that tells me of his affliction digs out and applies that gold to me, if by this consideration of another's danger I take mine own into contemplation, and so secure myself by making my recourse to my God, who is our only security.

(http://www.online-literature.com/donne/409)

F. "Meditation XVII" achieves both unity and diversity by stating a single theme and giving several variations of that theme. In a two-page essay, give examples of how Donne accomplishes unity and diversity.

G. Read Ernest Hemingway's *For Whom the Bell Tolls*. Does Hemingway employ a similar theme to Donne's?

> *Definition* is a method of analysis, as logical as possible, in which the subject is located in a general class and then distinguished from all other members of that class. Students, therefore, will need to analyze the seventeenth century in light of other epochs of British history as well as what was occurring in other parts of the world.

H. Pretend that you work for a major publisher. Your boss asks you, "Should John Donne's works be republished? Is his work relevant to the twentieth century? Why, or why not?"

I. Love is an emotion almost as old as humanity itself, and its pursuit has been defined in many ways throughout the ages. Perhaps the most vivid of these feelings is documented in love poetry, through which each era of a society can be analyzed according to its principles and values, and subsequently, relationships between men and women. The writings of seventeenth-century poet John Donne reveal the integrity of his love as a force of nature and as a passion for his God. Compare and contrast views of love in our culture with those in the seventeenth century.

FINAL PORTFOLIO

Correct and rewrite all essays and place them in your Final Portfolio.

SUGGESTED
Weekly *Implementation*

DAY 1	DAY 2	DAY 3	DAY 4	DAY 5
Prayer journal.	**Prayer journal.**	**Prayer journal.**	**Prayer journal.**	**Prayer journal.**
Review required reading(s) *before* the assigned lesson begins.	Review reading(s) from next lesson.	Write rough drafts of all assigned essays.	Rewrite corrected copies of essays due tomorrow.	Essays are due.
Teacher may want to discuss assigned reading(s) with students.	Outline essays due at the end of the week.	The teacher and/or a peer evaluator may correct rough drafts.		Take Lesson 9 test.
Teacher and students will decide on required essays for this lesson, choosing two or three essays.	Per teacher instructions, students may answer orally in a group setting some of the essays that are not assigned as formal essays.			Reading Ahead: "To My Excellent Lucasia, on our friendship. 7th July 65," Katherine Philips; "To Lucasta, on Going to the Wars," Richard Lovelace; "The Collar," George Herbert; "The Retreat," Henry Vaughn; "To the Virgins to Make Much of Time," Robert Herrick; "Bermudas" and "To His Coy Mistress," Andrew Marvell.
The rest of the essays can be outlined, answered with shorter answers, or skipped.				
Review all readings for Lesson 9.				Guide: What do you think of the theme of mutability?

LESSON 10

SEVENTEENTH CENTURY *(Part 2)*

Katherine Philips

Katherine Fowler was born on New Year's Day, 1631-1667 in London, England. Her father, John Fowler, was a Presbyterian merchant. Katherine was married to fifty-four-year old James Philips. She was a Royalist; he supported Oliver Cromwell. This difference in their views is recorded in Katherine's poetry. Katherine was the first English poet to participate openly in intellectual gatherings and clubs where she shared her own works and critiqued others.

To My Excellent Lucasia, on our friendship.
7th July 65

I did not live untill this time
Crown'd my felicity,
When I could say without a crime
I am not Thine, but Thee.
This Carkasse breath'd and walk'd and slept,
So that the world believ'd
There was a soule the motions kept;
But they were all deceiv'd.
For as a watch by art is wound
To motions such was mine:
But never had Orinda found
A Soule till she found thine;
Which now inspires, cures and supply's,
And guides my darken'd brest:
For thou art all that I can prize,
My Joy, my Life, my rest.
No Bridegroomes nor crown'd conqu'rour's mirth
To mine compar'd can be:
They have but pieces of this Earth
I've all the World in thee.
Then let our flames still light and shine
(And no bold feare controule)
As innocent as our designs
Immortall as our Soule.
(*Norton Anthology of Literature by Women*, p. 103)

Analyze: "To My Excellent Lucasia, on our friendship. 7th July 65," Katherine Philips; "To Lucasta, on Going to the Wars," Richard Lovelace; "The Collar," George Herbert; "The Retreat," Henry Vaughn; "To the Virgins to Make Much of Time," Robert Herrick; "Bermudas" and "To His Coy Mistress," Andrew Marvell.

Reading Ahead: Review "O Nightingale, How Soon Hath Time," "To A Virtuous Young Lady," "When I Consider How My Light Is Spent," "L'Allegro," and "Il Penseroso," John Milton.

Guide Question: Contrast the poetry of John Milton with other Metaphysical poets.

CRITICAL THINKING

In a two-page essay, analyze the primary metaphor that Lady Philips explores in this poem and how this metaphor enhances the poem.

Richard Lovelace

BACKGROUND

In 1618 Richard Lovelace was born into an old and wealthy English family. He was the first-born son of Sir William Lovelace. His dad, Sir Lovelace, had served in the Low Countries (i. e., the Netherlands) against the Spanish and was killed in action in 1627. Lovelace barely knew his father, but his death nonetheless greatly affected him. He was educated at Charterhouse School and at Gloucester Hall, Oxford. He was handsome, witty, and much admired by his peers. He was a classic cavalier, a supporter of King Charles I and Queen Henrietta Maria. Lovelace took part in the King's military expeditions to Scotland in 1639–40. After the failure of the campaign, he withdrew to his estates in Kent, where he remained until 1642. In April 1642 Lovelace presented a Royalist petition to Parliament favoring the restoration of the Anglican bishops who had been excluded from the Long Parliament. He joined the royalist side in the English Civil War and found himself on the losing side when Cromwell, political leader of Puritanism, assumed power. Lovelace was imprisoned in Westminster Gatehouse from April 30 to June 21, 1642. While in prison, Lovelace wrote "To Althea, from Prison," which includes the famous words: "Stone walls do not a prison make, / Nor iron bars a cage." Lovelace died in poverty in 1658.

CRITICAL THINKING

Lovelace often uses a metaphor called *personification* in his poetry. Identify its usage in "Lucasta" and discuss how it enhances the following poem:

To Lucasta, on Going to the Wars

Tell me not, (Sweet,) I am unkind,
That from the nunnery
Of thy chaste breast and quiet mind
To war and arms I fly.

True, a new mistress now I chase,
The first foe in the field;
And with a stronger faith embrace
A sword, a horse, a shield.

Yet this inconstancy is such
As you too shall adore;
I could not love thee, (Dear,) so much,
Lov'd I not Honour more.
(http://www.bartleby.com/40/237.html)

ENRICHMENT

Write a two-page essay on the English Civil War.

George Herbert

George Herbert was born in Montgomery, Wales, on April 3, 1593, the fifth son of Richard and Magdalen Newport Herbert. After his father's death in 1596, he and his six brothers and three sisters were reared by their godly mother. John Donne described Herbert's mother: "Her house was a court in the conversation of the best." Herbert was led to the Lord and into the priesthood by his mother. By the time of his death in 1633 Herbert was one of the best-known poets in England.

The Collar

I struck the board, and cried, "No more!
I will abroad.
What! shall I ever sigh and pine?
My lines and life are free; free as the road,
Loose as the wind, as large as store.
Shall I be still in suit?
Have I no harvest but a thorn
To let me blood, and not restore
What I have lost with cordial fruit?
Sure there was wine
Before my sighs did dry it; there was corn
Before my tears did drown it.
Is the year only lost to me?
Have I no bays to crown it?
No flowers, no garlands gay? all blasted?
All wasted?
Not so, my heart; but there is fruit,
And thou hast hands.
Recover all thy sigh-blown age
On double pleasures; leave thy cold dispute
Of what is fit and not; forsake thy cage,
Thy rope of sands,
Which petty thoughts have made, and made to thee
Good cable, to enforce and draw,
And be thy law,
While thou didst wink and wouldst not see.
Away! take heed;
I will abroad.

Call in thy death's-head there; tie up thy fears;
He that forbears
To suit and serve his need
Deserves his load."
But as I rav'd, and grew more fierce and wilde
At every word,
Me thoughts I heard one calling, "Child";
And I replied, "My Lord."
(http://www.bartleby.com/40/221.html)

CRITICAL THINKING

A. "The Collar" illustrates the main features of Herbert's poetry: symbolic writing and the use of the metaphysical conceit. Give several examples of this literary device in "The Collar." In a two-page essay explain how this literary technique enhances Herbert's poem.
B. Why is the title of this poem appropriate?
C. "The Collar" is a poem that suggests a fracas between man and God. How does this struggle end? Identify the "I" and the "Thou." Why does Herbert use words like "thorn," "blood," and "wine" in lines 7–10? Answer these questions in a cogent, two-page essay.

BIBLICAL APPLICATION

Contrast the themes presented in "The Collar" with those presented in the biblical Book of Job.

Henry Vaughan

Vaughan, a Christian believer, wrote much inspired religious poetry reminiscent of George Herbert's writings. Vaughan's poetry, full of metaphysical conceits, invites the reader to a serious reflection of his faith in Christ.

Metaphysical conceit is a special metaphor. It points out an unusual parallel between what are usually highly dissimilar elements. John Donne loved to use the metaphysical conceit. An example would be his comparison of his and his wife's soul to the two points of a compass, forever joined even though forced apart.

CRITICAL THINKING

A. Read the poem "The Retreat." Why do you think Vaughan calls his poem "The Retreat"?

The Retreat

Happy those early days! when I
Shin'd in my angel-infancy.
Before I understood this place
Appoint'd for my second race,
Or taught my soul to fancy ought
But a white, celestial thought,
When yet I had not walk'd above
A mile, or two, from my first love,
And looking back (at that short space,)
Could see a glimpse of his bright face;
When on some gild'd cloud or flower
My gazing soul would dwell an hour,
And in those weaker glories spy
Some shadows of eternity;
Before I taught my tongue to wound
My conscience with a sinful sound,
Or had the black art to dispense
A sev'ral sin to ev'ry sense,
But felt through all this fleshly dress
Bright shoots of everlastingness.

O how I long to travel back
And tread again that ancient track!
That I might once more reach that plain,
Where first I left my glorious train,
From whence th'enlightened spirit sees
That shady city of palm trees;
But (ah!) my soul with too much stay
Is drunk, and staggers in the way.
Some men a forward motion love,
But I by backward steps would move,
And when this dust falls to the urn
In that state I came return.
(http://www.bartleby.com/40/226.html)

B. Identify metaphysical conceits in "The Retreat." How do they affect the meaning of the poem?

BIBLICAL APPLICATION

What is the theological vision of "Silex"?

Robert Herrick

BACKGROUND

Robert Herrick was one of the best poets of the seventeenth century. Herrick, an Anglican minister, was assigned to the country. At first he hated country life; eventually, though, he learned to love it. In the seclusion of country life, he wrote some of his best work. Of the fourteen hundred poems in the volume, the following poem is the only one Herrick would ever publish.

To The Virgins to Make Much of Time

Gather ye rosebuds while ye may,
Old Time is still a-flying:
And this same flower that smiles today
Tomorrow will be dying.

The glorious lamp of heaven, the Sun,
The higher he's a-getting
The sooner will his race be run,
And nearer he's to setting.

That age is best which is the first,
When youth and blood are warmer;
But being spent, the worse, and worst
Times, still succeed the former.

Then be not coy, but use your time;
And while ye may, go marry:
For having lost but once your prime,
You may forever tarry.
(http://www.bartleby.com/40/209.html)

CRITICAL THINKING

The main theme of "To the Virgins, to Make Much of Time" concerns mutability and is part of a tradition called "carpe diem" (pluck the day). Using the text of this poem, defend this argument.

BIBLICAL APPLICATION

A. A born-again Christian friend of mine relates a story that has a shocking application to contemporary American youth. Once, while involved in a discussion at his college, this twenty-year-old friend of mine shared quite by accident that he was a virgin, that he had intentionally avoided premarital sexual activity. This was a rarity in this secular university. He was the laughingstock of his class. My friend remained silent. Finally, after everyone had had his laugh, my friend quietly retorted, "I could be like any of you by this time tomorrow. You can never be like me as long as you live." What does the Bible say about premarital sex? What would you, as a believer, say to Herrick's "virgin"? Would you advise her "to make much of time"? If you do, what would be your reasons?

B. "Making the most of time" is a common seventeenth-century theme that also has contemporary application: "you only go around once, you know. Grab life with all the gusto you can!" Offer biblical evidence to negate this viewpoint.

ENRICHMENT

Read several poems by George Herrick including "The Argument of His Book," "To Daffodils," "To Dianeme," "To Violets," and "Corinna's Going A-Maying." Identify two or three common themes exhibited by these poems and discuss the different ways that Herrick presents his themes.

Andrew Marvell

BACKGROUND

Born in 1621, Andrew Marvell was a preacher's kid who represents the enigma that existed in the English

Civil War literary scene. On one hand Marvell had clear Royalist sympathies, but he also served as a tutor at a country estate of one of Cromwell's strongest supporters. He wrote more prose than poetry, but most critics agree that his poetry was far superior. He died in 1678.

CRITICAL THINKING

A. Describe the structure of "Bermudas." How is it divided? Why? Defend your answers from the poem.

Bermudas

Where the remote Bermudas ride

In th' ocean's bosom unespy'd,
From a small boat, that row'd along,
The list'ning winds receiv'd this song:

"What should we do but sing his praise
That led us through the wat'ry maze
Unto an isle so long unknown,
And yet far kinder than our own?
Where he the huge sea-monsters wracks,
That lift the deep upon their backs,
He lands us on a grassy stage,
Safe from the storm's and prelates' rage.
He gave us this eternal spring
Which here enamels everything,
And sends the fowls to us in care,
On daily visits through the air.
He hangs in shades the orange bright,
Like golden lamps in a green night;
And does in the pomegranates close
Jewels more rich than Ormus shows.
He makes the figs our mouths to meet
And throws the melons at our feet,
But apples plants of such a price,
No tree could ever bear them twice.
With cedars, chosen by his hand,
From Lebanon, he stores the land,
And makes the hollow seas that roar
Proclaim the ambergris on shore.
He cast (of which we rather boast)
The Gospel's pearl upon our coast,
And in these rocks for us did frame
A temple, where to sound his name.
Oh let our voice his praise exalt,
Till it arrive at heaven's vault;
Which thence (perhaps) rebounding, may
Echo beyond the Mexico Bay."

Thus sung they in the English boat
An holy and a cheerful note,
And all the way, to guide their chime,
With falling oars they kept the time.
(http://bartleby.com/40/225.html)

B. Compare "Coy Mistress" with Marlowe's "The
Passionate Shepherd to His Love."

To His Coy Mistress

Had we but world enough, and time,
This coyness, Lady, were no crime.
We would sit down and think which way
To walk, and pass our long love's day;

Thou by the Indian Ganges' side
Shouldst rubies find; I by the tide
Of Humber would complain. I would
Love you ten years before the Flood;
And you should, if you please, refuse
Till the conversion of the Jews.
My vegetable love should grow
Vaster than empires, and more slow.
An hundred years should go to praise
Thine eyes, and on thy forehead gaze;
Two hundred to adore each breast,
But thirty thousand to the rest;
An age at least to every part,
And the last age should show your heart.
For, Lady, you deserve this state,
Nor would I love at lower rate.
But at my back I always hear
Time's winged chariot hurrying near;
And yonder all before us lie
Deserts of vast eternity.
Thy beauty shall no more be found,
Nor, in thy marble vault, shall sound
My echoing song; then worms shall try
That long preserv'd virginity,
And your quaint honour turn to dust,
And into ashes all my lust.
The grave's a fine and private place,
But none I think do there embrace.
Now therefore, while the youthful hue
Sits on thy skin like morning dew,
And while thy willing soul transpires
At every pore with instant fires,
Now let us sport us while we may;
And now, like am'rous birds of prey,
Rather at once our time devour,
Than languish in his slow-chapp'd power.
Let us roll all our strength, and all
Our sweetness, up into one ball;
And tear our pleasures with rough strife
Thorough the iron gates of life.
Thus, though we cannot make our sun
Stand still, yet we will make him run!
(http://eir.library.utoronto.ca/rpo/display/poem1386.ht
   ml)

FINAL PROJECT

Correct and rewrite all essays and place them in your
Final Portfolio.

SUGGESTED
Weekly *Implementation*

DAY 1	DAY 2	DAY 3	DAY 4	DAY 5
Prayer journal. Review required reading(s) *before* the assigned lesson begins. Teacher may want to discuss assigned reading(s) with students. <u>Teacher and students will decide on required essays for this lesson, choosing two or three essays.</u> <u>The rest of the essays can be outlined, answered with shorter answers, or skipped.</u> Review all readings for Lesson 10.	**Prayer journal.** Review reading(s) from next lesson. Outline essays due at the end of the week. Per teacher instructions, students may answer orally in a group setting some of the essays that are not assigned as formal essays.	**Prayer journal.** Write rough drafts of all assigned essays. The teacher and/or a peer evaluator may correct rough drafts.	**Prayer journal.** Rewrite corrected copies of essays due tomorrow.	**Prayer journal.** Essays are due. Take Lesson 10 test. Reading Ahead: Review "O Nightingale, How Soon Hath Time," "To A Virtuous Young Lady," "When I Consider How My Light Is Spent," "L'Allegro," and "Il Penseroso," John Milton. Guide: Contrast the poetry of John Milton with other Metaphysical poets.

John Milton

BACKGROUND

Analyze: "O Nightingale," "How Soon Hath Time," "To A Virtuous Young Lady," "When I Consider How My Light Is Spent," "L'Allegro," and "Il Penseroso," John Milton.

Reading Ahead: Review *Paradise Lost*, John Milton.

Guide Question: What sort of villain is the devil in Milton's *Paradise Lost*?

The English poet John Milton is one of the major figures of Western literature. His Christian epic *Paradise Lost* assures his stature as the finest non-dramatic poet of the Renaissance, the worthy successor to Homer, Virgil, Dante, and Tasso.

Some authors struggle to receive family approval. Not John Milton. He was born on December 9, 1608, into a prosperous London family that recognized and encouraged his remarkable writing gifts. His father, an accomplished musician, provided private tutors and sent him to Saint Paul's School in London so that even before he matriculated (1625) at Cambridge University, Milton was proficient in Latin, Greek, and Hebrew.

Milton's published works included a brief tribute to Shakespeare. In 1645, during the English Civil War, he published *Poems of Mr. John Milton*. The volume was largely ignored, although it contained the extraordinary "L'Allegro" and "Il Penseroso." In 1649, during the trial of Charles I, Milton wrote *Of the Tenure of Kings and Magistrates*, a republican argument that monarchs can rule only with their subjects' consent. He then became secretary to the Council of State under Oliver Cromwell and was entrusted with writing in Latin a defense of the execution of the king, *Eikonoklastes* (*The Image Breakers*, 1649). That proved to be the last major writing project he undertook before he went blind. In 1652 he became completely blind and was tempted, as he confessed in the moving sonnet "When I Consider How My Light Is Spent," to despair of ever accomplishing his life's work. However, the best was yet to come. *Paradise Lost*, published in 1667, stands with Chaucer's *The Canterbury Tales* and Spenser's *The Faerie Queene* as the greatest of English-language epics. It was followed four years later by *Paradise Regained*, a "brief epic" that dramatizes the fall of man and the triumph of Jesus Christ over the devil. With *Paradise Lost*, this work holds out the possibility of recovering a "paradise within" by faith in Jesus Christ.

In his last work published in his lifetime, *Samson Agonistes*, Milton recast a biblical folktale into classical tragic form, bestowing on the figure of Samson a moral stature that dignifies his violent revenge on the Philistines. He died, probably of complications arising from gout, on November 8, 1674. Milton remains one of the greatest saints and writers of the seventeenth century.

CRITICAL THINKING

A. Paraphrase "O Nightingale" in your own words.

B. Milton stayed closer to Italian models for the sonnet than did his predecessors Spenser and Shakespeare. "O Nightingale" rhymes abba, abba, cdcdcd. Milton scholars remind us that he does not encourage us to pause but moves through the poem in a prose-like fashion. His sonnets roll to conclusions that seem irresistible.

Agree or disagree with this description of "O Nightingale" and use copious examples from the text to support your answer.

O Nightingale

O nightingale that on yon bloomy spray
Warbl'st at eve, when all the woods are still,
Thou with fresh hope the lover's heart dost fill,
While the jolly hours lead on propitious May.
Thy liquid notes that close the eye of day,
First heard before the shallow cuckoo's bill,
Portend success in love. O, if Jove's will
Have linked that amorous power to thy soft lay,
Now timely sing, ere the rude bird of hate
Foretell my hopeless doom, in some grove nigh;
As thou from year to year hast sung too late
For my relief, yet hadst no reason why.
Whether the Muse or Love call thee his mate,
Both them I serve, and of their train am I.
(www.bartleby.com/4/203.html)

C. "When I Consider How My Light Is Spent" and "On His Blindness" are reflective poems in which Milton conceptualizes the tragedy that his blindness has brought to him. Yet, in his final analysis, there is reason for hope. What is this hope?

D. Compare John Milton's poems with John Donne's poem (especially "Sonnet IX").

BIBLICAL APPLICATION

A. Milton's poems are full of biblical references and motifs. Find examples of these references in this lesson's poems and other poems by Milton.

B. Compare and contrast "How Soon Hath Time" and "To a Virtuous Young Woman" with Marvell's "To His Coy Mistress." Which poem(s) advances a biblical view? Defend your answer from the text and Scripture.

How Soon Hath Time

How soon hath Time, the subtle thief of youth,
Stol'n on his wing my three-and-twentieth year!
My hasting days fly on with full career,
But my late spring no bud or blossom shew'th.
Perhaps my semblance might deceive the truth
That I to manhood am arriv'd so near;
And inward ripeness doth much less appear,
That some more timely-happy spirits endu'th.
Yet it be less or more, or soon or slow,
It shall be still in strictest measure ev'n
To that same lot, however mean or high,
Toward which Time leads me, and the will of Heav'n:
All is, if I have grace to use it so
As ever in my great Task-Master's eye.
(www.bartleby.com/4/111.html)

To a Virtuous Young Lady

Lady! that in the prime of earliest youth
Wisely hath shunned the broad way and the green,
And with those few art eminently seen
That labour up the hill of heavenly Truth;
The better part with Mary and with Ruth
Chosen thou hast; and they that overween,
And at thy growing virtues fret their spleen,
No anger find in thee, but pity and ruth.
Thy care is fixed, and zealously attends
To fill thy odorous lamp with deeds of light,
And hope that reaps not shame. Therefore be sure
Thou, when the Bridegroom with his feastful friends
Passes to bliss at the mid-hour of night,
Hast gained thy entrance, Virgin wise and pure.
(www.bartleby.com/4/302.html)

When I Consider How My Light Is Spent

When I consider how my light is spent
Ere half my days in this dark world and wide,
And that one talent which is death to hide
Lodged with me useless, though my soul more bent
To serve therewith my Maker, and present
My true account, lest he returning chide,"
Doth God exact day-labor, light denied?"
I fondly ask. But Patience, to prevent
That murmur, soon replies: "God doth not need
Either man's work or his own gifts: who best
Bear his mild yoke, they serve him best. His state
Is kingly; thousands at his bidding speed
And post over land and ocean without repose:
They also serve who only stand and wait."
(www.bartleby.com/4/313.html)

ENRICHMENT

A. John Milton is considered by many critics to be a transitional poet. Find evidence of Elizabethan-style poetry as well as new Puritan influences in his works. Milton also used copious references to classical literature. Find samples of these references.

B. Analyze Milton's stylistic tendencies as manifested in the poems you have read thus far and consider why he chose a certain style. In your essay, tell why he chose one style in one poem and another style in another poem. Discuss how his poetic style evolved over the course of his life.

C. Many literary critics argue that "L'Allegro" and "Il Penseroso" are rewrites of Milton's academic assignments at Cambridge University. "The cheerful man" ("L'Allegro") and "the thoughtful man"

("Il Penseroso") appeal to a *melancholy* mood. What does Milton mean by melancholy?

D. The first ten lines of "L'Allegro" evidence a popular metaphorical technique called *personification*. Give evidence of this from "L'Allegro" and show how Milton uses this technique to make his point.

E. Compare and contrast "L'Allegro," lines 1–24, and "Il Penseroso," lines 1–36. What similar themes are explored?

F. Compare and contrast "L'Allegro" and "Il Penseroso":

	"L'Allegro"	"Il Penseroso"
Characterization		
Setting		
Nature		
References to arts		
Rhyme scheme		

L'Allegro

Hence loathèd Melancholy
Of Cerberus and blackest midnight born,
In Stygian Cave forlorn
'Mongst horrid shapes, and shreiks, and sights unholy.
Find out som uncouth cell,
Where brooding darknes spreads his jealous wings,
And the night-Raven sings;
There, under Ebon shades, and low-brow'd Rocks,
As ragged as thy Locks,
In dark Cimmerian desert ever dwell.
But com thou Goddes fair and free,
In Heav'n ycleap'd Euphrosyne,
And by men, heart-easing Mirth,
Whom lovely Venus, at a birth
With two sister Graces more
To Ivy-crownèd Bacchus bore;
Or whether (as som Sager sing)
The frolick Wind that breathes the Spring,
Zephir with Aurora playing,
As he met her once a Maying,
There on Beds of Violets blew,
And fresh-blown Roses washt in dew,
Fill'd her with thee a daughter fair,
So bucksom, blith, and debonair.
Haste thee nymph, and bring with thee
Jest and youthful Jollity,
Quips and Cranks, and wanton Wiles,
Nods, and Becks, and Wreathèd Smiles,

Such as hang on Hebe's cheek,
And love to live in dimple sleek;
Sport that wrincled Care derides,
And Laughter holding both his sides.
Com, and trip it as ye go
On the light fantastick toe,
And in thy right hand lead with thee,
The Mountain Nymph, sweet Liberty;
And if I give thee honour due,
Mirth, admit me of thy cruel
To live with her, and live with thee,
In unreprovèd pleasures free;
To hear the Lark begin his flight,
And singing startle the dull night,
From his watch-towre in the skies,
Till the dappled dawn doth rise;
Then to com in spight of sorrow,
And at my window bid good morrow,
Through the Sweet-Briar, or the Vine,
Or the twisted Eglantine.
While the Cock with lively din,
Scatters the rear of darknes thin,
And to the stack, or the Barn dore,
Stoutly struts his Dames before,
Oft list'ning how the Hounds and horn
Chearly rouse the slumbring morn,
From the side of som Hoar Hill,
Through the high wood echoing shrill.
Som time walking not unseen
By Hedge-row Elms, on Hillocks green,
Right against the Eastern gate,
Wher the great Sun begins his state,
Rob'd in flames, and Amber light,
The clouds in thousand Liveries dight.
While the Plowman neer at hand,
Whistles ore the Furrow'd Land,
And the Milkmaid singeth blithe,
And the Mower whets his sithe,
And every Shepherd tells his tale
Under the Hawthorn in the dale.
Streit mine eye hath caught new pleasures
Whilst the Lantskip round it measures,
Russet Lawns, and Fallows Gray,
Where the nibling flocks do stray,
Mountains on whose barren brest
The labouring clouds do often rest:
Meadows trim with Daisies pide,
Shallow Brooks, and Rivers wide.
Towers, and Battlements it sees
Boosom'd high in tufted Trees,
Wher perhaps som beauty lies,

The Cynosure of neighbouring eyes.
Hard by, a Cottage chimney smokes,
From betwixt two agèd Okes,
Where Corydon and Thyrsis met,
Are at their savory dinner set
Of Hearbs, and other Country Messes,
Which the neat-handed Phillis dresses;
And then in haste her Bowre she leaves,
With Thestylis to bind the Sheaves;
Or if the earlier season lead
To the tann'd Haycock in the Mead,
Som times with secure delight
The up-land Hamlets will invite,
When the merry Bells ring round,
And the jocond rebecks sound
To many a youth, and many a maid,
Dancing in the Chequer'd shade;
And young and old com forth to play
On a Sunshine Holyday,
Till the live-long day-light fail,
Then to the Spicy Nut-brown Ale,
With stories told of many a feat,
How Faery Mab the junkets eat,
She was pincht, and pull'd the sed,
And he by Friars Lanthorn led
Tells how the drudging Goblin swet,
To ern his Cream-bowle duly set,
When in one night, ere glimps of morn,
His shadowy Flale hath thresh'd the Corn
That ten day-labourers could not end,
Then lies him down the Lubbar Fend,
And stretch'd out all the Chimney's length,
Basks at the fire his hairy strength;
And Crop-full out of dores he flings,
Ere the first Cock his Mattin rings.
Thus don the Tales, to bed they creep,
By whispering Windes soon lull'd asleep.
Towred Cities please us then,
And the busie humm of men,
Where throngs of Knights and Barons bold,
In weeds of Peace high triumphs hold,
With store of Ladies, whose bright eies
Rain influence, and judge the prise
Of Wit, or Arms, while both contend
To win her Grace, whom all commend.
There let Hymen oft appear
In Saffron robe, with Taper clear,
And pomp, and feast, and revelry,
With mask, and antique Pageantry,
Such sights as youthfull Poets dream
On Summer eeves by haunted stream.

Then to the well-trod stage anon,
If Jonsons learnèd Sock be on,
Or sweetest Shakespear fancies childe,
Warble his native Wood-notes wilde,
And ever against eating Cares,
Lap me in soft Lydian Aires,
Married to immortal verse
Such as the meeting soul may pierce
In notes, with many a winding bout
Of linckèd sweetnes long drawn out,
With wanton heed, and giddy cunning,
The melting voice through mazes running;
Untwisting all the chains that ty
The hidden soul of harmony.
That Orpheus self may heave his head
From golden slumber on a bed
Of heapt Elysian flowres, and hear
Such streins as would have won the ear
Of Pluto, to have quite set free
His half regain'd Eurydice.
These delights, if thou canst give,
Mirth with thee, I mean to live.
(www.bartleby.com/4/313.html)

Il Penseroso

HENCE vain deluding joyes,
The brood of folly without father bred,
How little you bested,
Or fill the fixèd mind with all your toyes;
Dwell in som idle brain,
And fancies fond with gaudy shapes possess,
As thick and numberless
As the gay motes that people the Sun Beams,
Or likest hovering dreams
The fickle Pensioners of Morpheus train.
But hail thou Goddes, sage and holy,
Hail divinest Melancholy,
Whose Saintly visage is too bright
To hit the Sense of human sight;
And therefore to our weaker view,
Ore laid with black staid Wisdoms hue.
Black, but such as in esteem,
Prince Memnons sister might beseem,
Or that Starr'd Ethiope Queen that strove
To set her beauties praise above
The Sea Nymphs, and their powers offended.
Yet thou art higher far descended,
Thee bright-hair'd Vesta long of yore,
To solitary Saturn bore;
His daughter she (in Saturns raign,
Such mixture was not held a stain)

Oft in glimmering Bowres, and glades
He met her, and in secret shades
Of woody Ida's inmost grove,
Whilst yet there was no fear of Jove.
Com pensive Nun, devout and pure,
Sober, stedfast, and demure,
All in a robe of darkest grain,
Flowing with majestick train,
And sable stole of Cipres Lawn,
Over thy decent shoulders drawn.
Com, but keep thy wonted state,
With ev'n step, and musing gate,
And looks commercing with the skies,
Thy rapt soul sitting in thine eyes:
There held in holy passion still,
Forget thy self to Marble, till
With a sad Leaden downward cast,
Thou fix them on the earth as fast.
And joyn with thee calm Peace, and Quiet,
Spare Fast, that oft with gods doth diet,
And hears the Muses in a ring,
Ay round about Joves Altar sing.
And adde to these retirèd Leasure,
That in trim Gardens takes his pleasure;
But first, and chiefest, with thee bring,
Him that yon soars on golden wing,
Guiding the fiery-wheelèd throne,
The Cherub Contemplation,
And the mute Silence hist along,
'Less Philomel will daign a Song,
In her sweetest, saddest plight,
Smoothing the rugged brow of night,
While Cynthia checks her Dragon yoke,
Gently o're th'accustom'd Oke;
Sweet Bird that shunn'st the noise of folly,
Most musical, most melancholy!
Thee Chauntress oft the Woods among,
I woo to hear thy even-Song;
And missing thee, I walk unseen
On the dry smooth-shaven Green.
To behold the wandring Moon,
Riding neer her highest noon,
Like one that had bin led astray
Through the Heav'ns wide pathles way;
And oft, as if her head she bow'd,
Stooping through a fleecy cloud.
Oft on a Plat of rising ground,
I hear the far-off Curfeu sound,
Over som wide-water'd shoar,
Swinging slow with sullen roar;
Or if the Ayr will not permit,

Som still removèd place will fit,
Where glowing Embers through the room
Teach light to counterfeit a gloom,
Far from all resort of mirth,
Save the Cricket on the hearth,
Or the bellman's drowsie charm,
To bless the dores from nightly harm:
Or let my Lamp at midnight hour,
Be seen in som high lonely Towr,
Where I may oft out-watch the Bear,
With thrice great Hermes, or unsphear
The spirit of Plato to unfold
What Worlds, or what vast Regions hold
The immortal mind that hath forsook
Her mansion in this fleshly nook:
And of those Dææmons that are found
In fire, air, flood, or under ground,
Whose power hath a true consent
With Planet, or with Element.
Som time let Gorgeous Tragedy
In Scepter'd Pall com sweeping by,
Presenting Thebs, or Pelops line,
Or the tale of Troy divine.
Or what (though rare) of later age,
Ennoblèd hath the Buskind stage.
But, O sad Virgin, that thy power
Might raise Musæus from his bower
Or bid the soul of Orpheus sing
Such notes as warbled to the string,
Drew Iron tears down Pluto's cheek,
And made Hell grant what Love did seek.
Or call up him that left half told
The story of Cambuscan bold,
Of Camball, and of Algarsife,
And who had Canace to wife,
That own'd the vertuous Ring and Glass,
And of the wondrous Hors of Brass,
On which the Tartar King did ride;
And if ought els, great Bards beside,
In sage and solemn tunes have sung,
Of Turneys and of Trophies hung;
Of Forests, and inchantments drear,
Where more is meant then meets the ear.
Thus night oft see me in thy pale career,
Till civil-suited Morn appeer,
Not trickt and frounc't as she was wont,
With the Attick Boy to hunt,
But Cherchef't in a comly Cloud,
While rocking Winds are Piping loud,
Or usher'd with a shower still,
When the gust hath blown his fill,

Ending on the russling Leaves,
With minute drops from off the Eaves.
And when the Sun begins to fling
His flaring beams, me Goddes bring
To archèd walks of twilight groves,
And shadows brown that Sylvan loves,
Of Pine, or monumental Oake,
Where the rude Ax with heavèd stroke,
Was never heard the Nymphs to daunt,
Or fright them from their hallow'd haunt.
There in close covert by som Brook,
Where no profaner eye may look,
Hide me from Day's garish eie,
While the Bee with Honied thie,
That at her flowry work doth sing,
And the Waters murmuring
With such consort as they keep,
Entice the dewy-feather'd Sleep;
And let som strange mysterious dream,
Wave at his Wings in Airy stream,
Of lively portrature display'd,
Softly on my eye-lids laid.
And as I wake, sweet musick breath
Above, about, or underneath,
Sent by som spirit to mortals good,
Or th'unseen Genius of the Wood.

But let my due feet never fail,
To walk the studious Cloysters pale,

And love the high embowèd Roof,
With antick Pillars massy proof,
And storied Windows richly dight,
Casting a dimm religious light.
There let the pealing Organ blow,
To the full voic'd Quire below,
In Service high, and Anthems cleer,
As may with sweetnes, through mine ear,
Dissolve me into extasies,
And bring all Heav'n before mine eyes.
And may at last my weary age
Find out the peacefull hermitage,
The Hairy Gown and Mossy Cell,
Where I may sit and rightly spell
Of every Star that Heav'n doth shew,
And every Herb that sips the dew;
Till old experience do attain
To somthing like Prophetic strain.
These pleasures Melancholy give,
And I with thee will choose to live.
(www.bartleby.com/4/202.html)

FINAL PORTFOLIO

Correct and rewrite all essays and place them in your Final Portfolio.

SUGGESTED
Weekly *Implementation*

DAY 1	DAY 2	DAY 3	DAY 4	DAY 5
Prayer journal.	**Prayer journal.**	**Prayer journal.**	**Prayer journal.**	**Prayer journal.**
Review the required reading(s) *before* the assigned lesson begins.	Review reading(s) from next lesson.	Write rough drafts of all assigned essays.	Rewrite corrected copies of essays due tomorrow.	Essays are due.
Teacher may want to discuss assigned reading(s) with students.	Outline essays due at the end of the week.	The teacher and/or a peer evaluator may correct rough drafts.		Take Lesson 11 test.
Teacher and students will decide on required essays for this lesson, choosing two or three essays.	Per teacher instructions, students may answer orally in a group setting some of the essays that are not assigned as formal essays.			Reading Ahead: Review *Paradise Lost*, John Milton.
The rest of the essays can be outlined, answered with shorter answers, or skipped.				Guide: What sort of villain is the devil in Milton's *Paradise Lost*?
Review all readings for Lesson 11.				

Paradise Lost

John Milton

CRITICAL THINKING

A. Paraphrase the following memorable passages from *Paradise Lost*:

Of Man's first disobedience, and the fruit
Of that forbidden tree whose mortal taste
Brought death into the world, and all our woe.
    (Book I, line 1)

A mind not to be chang'd by place or time.
The mind is its own place, and in itself
Can make a heaven of Hell, a Hell of heaven.
    (Book I, line 253)

Here we may reign secure; and in my choice
To reign is worth ambition, though in Hell:
Better to reign in Hell than serve in heaven.

> **Analyze:** *Paradise Lost*, John Milton.
>
> **Reading Ahead:** "Upon Being Contented with a Little," Anne Killigrew; Review "Of Dramatic Poesy" and "A Song for St. Cecilia's Day, 1687," John Dryden.
>
> **Guide Question:** Identify ways that Dryden was a trend-setter for his generation.

    (Book I, line 261)

For who would lose,
Though full of pain this intellectual being,
Those thoughts that wander through eternity,
To perish rather, swallow'd up and lost
In the wide womb of uncreated night?
    (Book II, line 146)

B. Find ten words Milton used that would not be used today and explain what they mean.

C. The clue to Adam's character is his relationship to

> I am, however, of opinion, that no just Heroic Poem ever was or can be made, from whence one great Moral may be deduced. That which reigns in Milton, is the most universal and most useful that can be imagined: It is in short this, That Obedience to the Will of God makes Men happy, and that Disobedience makes them miserable. This is visibly the Moral of the principal Fable, which turns upon Adam and Eve, who continued in Paradise, while they kept the Command that was given them, and were driven out of it as soon as they transgressed. This is likewise the Moral of the principal episode, which shews us how an innumerable Multitude of Angels fell from their State of Bliss, and were cast into Hell upon their Disobedience. (Joseph Addison and Richard Steele, *The Spectator*, 3 May 1712)

Eve. It ought to be his relationship to God, but it isn't—and that fact causes Adam's fall. Discuss the way Milton develops Adam as one of the main characters in his epic poem.

D. Who is the protagonist? Offer textual evidence to defend your argument.

BIBLICAL APPLICATION

A. As you read *Paradise Lost*, find parallels with the Book of Genesis in the Bible.

B. John Milton reclaimed for seventeenth-century society the fear of hell. Hell, today, may be a lost phenomenon. Hell is separation from God. Search for contemporary Christian teachers or teachings that emphasize hell.

C. Using a good concordance and commentary, research what the Bible says about Satan.

ENRICHMENT

A. In spite of the loss of paradise, this epic poem ends in tremendous optimism. How?

B. Read *Paradise Regained* and compare it to *Paradise Lost*. Why would John Milton choose the Temptation—and not the Garden of Gethsemane crisis—as the greatest threat Jesus faced? Argue your answer in a two-page essay.

C. Research the way children were presented in seventeenth-century art and literature.

FINAL PORTFOLIO

Correct and rewrite all essays and place them in your Final Portfolio.

SUGGESTED
Weekly *Implementation*

DAY 1	DAY 2	DAY 3	DAY 4	DAY 5
Prayer journal.	Prayer journal.	Prayer journal.	Prayer journal.	Prayer journal.
Review the required reading(s) *before* the assigned lesson begins.	Review reading(s) from next lesson.	Write rough drafts of all assigned essays.	Rewrite corrected copies of essays due tomorrow.	Essays are due.
Teacher may want to discuss assigned reading(s) with students.	Outline essays due at the end of the week.	The teacher and/or a peer evaluator may correct rough drafts.		Take Lesson 12 test.
Teacher and students will decide on required essays for this lesson, choosing two or three.	Per teacher instructions, students may answer orally in a group setting some of the essays that are not assigned as formal essays.			Reading Ahead: "Upon Being Contented with a Little," Anne Killigrew; "Of Dramatic Poesy" and "A Song for St. Cecilia's Day, 1687," John Dryden.
The rest of the essays can be outlined, answered with shorter answers, or skipped.				Guide: Identify ways that Dryden was a trend-setter for his generation.
Review all readings for Lesson 12.				

SEVENTEENTH CENTURY (Part 5)

Anne Killigrew

In many ways Anne Killigrew (c.1660-1685) is a mystery—we know very little about her life. All we really know about her is what other people wrote, since she wrote nothing autobiographical. We do know, however, that she was a great writer. John Dryden, for instance, another author in this lesson, highly esteemed her. Killigrew was the subject of Dryden's famous elegy, *To the Pious Memory of the Accomplished Young Lady Mrs. Anne Killigrew* (1686). According to *Norton's Anthology of Literature by Women*, Anne was "raised in an atmosphere where female talent was encouraged. . . . Dryden defined her as a modern equivalent of the famous Greek woman poet Sappho. . . . The hazards of female authorship were not insignificant, even in an age when women intellectuals were beginning to gain some strength." (p. 163)

Upon Being Contented with a Little

We deem them moderate, but Enough implore,
What barely will suffice, and ask no more:
Who say, (O Jove) a competency give,
Neither in Luxury, or Want we'd live.
But what is that, which these Enough do call?
If both the Indies unto some should fall,
Such Wealth would yet Enough but onely be,
And what they'd term not Want, or Luxury.
Among the Suits, O Jove, my humbler take;
A little give, I that Enough will make.
(http://www.poemhunter.com/p/m/poem.asp?poet=4&
poem=689

CRITICAL THINKING

Contrast the tone and theme of Killigrew's poem with other seventeenth-century poems.

John Dryden

BACKGROUND

John Dryden called himself Neander, the "new man," in his "Essay of Dramatic Poesy" (1668) and implied

Analyze: "Upon Being Contented with a Little," Anne Killigrew; "Of Dramatic Poesy" and "A Song for St. Cecilia's Day, 1687," John Dryden.

Reading Ahead: *Evelina* or *Cecilia*, Frances Burney; *Robinson Crusoe*, Daniel Defoe.

Guide Question: Is Robinson Crusoe a Christian believer?

that he was a spokesman for the concerns of his generation and the embodiment of its tastes. He was the Bob Dylan of his generation, setting the trend for a generation of poets and essayists. He specialized in comedy, heroic tragedy, and verse satire—genres that his contemporaries and later readers have defined as representative of the Restoration period. His writings had considerable influence on Alexander Pope and others. In a real sense Dryden determined the course of literary history for the next generation.

CRITICAL THINKING

A. Using "An Essay of Dramatic Poesy," recapitulate Dryden's opinions of the writings of Ben Jonson and William Shakespeare.
B. "A Song for St. Cecilia's Day" is an ode. What is an ode and why is this poem an ode?

A Song for St. Cecilia's Day

Stanza 1
From harmony, from Heav'nly harmony
This universal frame began.
When Nature underneath a heap
Of jarring atoms lay,

And could not heave her head,
The tuneful voice was heard from high,
Arise ye more than dead.
Then cold, and hot, and moist, and dry,
In order to their stations leap,
And music's pow'r obey.
From harmony, from Heav'nly harmony
This universal frame began:
From harmony to harmony
Through all the compass of the notes it ran,
The diapason closing full in man.

Stanza 2
What passion cannot music raise and quell!
When Jubal struck the corded shell,
His list'ning brethren stood around
And wond'ring, on their faces fell
To worship that celestial sound:
Less than a god they thought there could not dwell
Within the hollow of that shell
That spoke so sweetly and so well.
What passion cannot music raise and quell!

Stanza 3
The trumpet's loud clangor
Excites us to arms
With shrill notes of anger
And mortal alarms.
The double double double beat
Of the thund'ring drum
Cries, hark the foes come;
Charge, charge, 'tis too late to retreat.

Stanza 4
The soft complaining flute
In dying notes discovers
The woes of hopeless lovers,
Whose dirge is whisper'd by the warbling lute.

Stanza 5
Sharp violins proclaim
Their jealous pangs, and desperation,
Fury, frantic indignation,
Depth of pains and height of passion,
For the fair, disdainful dame.

Stanza 6
But oh! what art can teach
What human voice can reach

The sacred organ's praise?
Notes inspiring holy love,
Notes that wing their Heav'nly ways
To mend the choirs above.

Stanza 7
Orpheus could lead the savage race;
And trees unrooted left their place;
Sequacious of the lyre:
But bright Cecilia rais'd the wonder high'r;
When to her organ, vocal breath was giv'n,
An angel heard, and straight appear'd
Mistaking earth for Heav'n.
(www.bartleby.com/40/264.html)

Grand Chorus

As from the pow'r of sacred lays
The spheres began to move,
And sung the great Creator's praise
To all the bless'd above;
So when the last and dreadful hour
This crumbling pageant shall devour,
The trumpet shall be heard on high,
The dead shall live, the living die,
And music shall untune the sky.
(www.bartleby.com)

C. In Stanza 5 Dryden uses a literary technique called *antithesis*: the juxtaposition of two contrasting words, thoughts, and phrases. Find other examples of antithesis in this poem.

D. What is the rhyme scheme of this poem?

BIBLICAL APPLICATION

A. By the end of the seventeenth century, English society had already moved a long way from the godly principles of Puritanism. Ahead was the nihilism of the eighteenth century. Meditate on Daniel 5 as an example of a declining society.

B. In what ways does contemporary American society mirror a similar decline?

FINAL PORTFOLIO

Correct and rewrite all essays and place them in your Final Portfolio.

SUGGESTED
Weekly *Implementation*

DAY 1	DAY 2	DAY 3	DAY 4	DAY 5
Prayer journal.	**Prayer journal.**	**Prayer journal.**	**Prayer journal.**	**Prayer journal.**
Review required reading(s) *before* the assigned lesson begins.	Review reading(s) from next lesson.	Write rough drafts of all assigned essays.	Rewrite corrected copies of essays due tomorrow.	Essays are due.
Teacher may want to discuss assigned reading(s) with students.	Outline essays due at the end of the week.	The teacher and/or a peer evaluator may correct rough drafts.		Take Lesson 13 test.
<u>Teacher and students will decide on required essays for this lesson, choosing two or three essays.</u>	Per teacher instructions, students may answer orally in a group setting some of the essays that are not assigned as formal essays.			Reading Ahead: *Evelina* or *Cecilia*, Frances Burney d'Arblay; *Robinson Crusoe*, Daniel Defoe.
<u>The rest of the essays can be outlined, answered with shorter answers, or skipped.</u>				Guide: Is Robinson Crusoe a Christian believer?
Review all readings for Lesson 13.				

EIGHTEENTH CENTURY *(Part 1)*

Frances Burney d'Arblay

BACKGROUND

Frances Burney d'Arblay (1752-1840) created a new genre in the English novel, chronicled events ranging from George III's mad crisis to the aftermath of Waterloo, and wrote comedies that were as excellent as any written in the 18th century. Her first novel, *Evelina*, was published anonymously in 1778. It was written in secret and in a disguised hand because publishers were familiar with her handwriting. *Evelina* "explored the social development of a heroine who proves herself worthy of her well-born suitor." (*Norton Anthology of Literature by Women*, p. 242). *Evelina*, was a new school of fiction in English, one in which women in society were portrayed in realistic, contemporary circumstances— the novel of manners. "She conveyed the manners and morals of polite society with a relish for the ridiculous and a respect for the conventional that explain why Jane Austin found both the theme and the title of *Pride and Prejudice* in the concluding chapter of *Cecilia* (p. 242). Burney was the first woman to make the writing of novels a respectable endeavor. Her second novel, *Cecilia*, published in 1782, was an even greater critical success.

CRITICAL THINKING

A. Read *Cecilia* or *Evelina* and compare it/them to novels by Daniel Defoe.
B. In a two-page essay explore the difficulties women faced as they attempted writing and publication. Support your exploration with commentary about specific female authors, poets, or dramatists.

Robinson Crusoe

Daniel Defoe

BACKGROUND

The 18th century in English literature has been called the Augustan Age (the most famous Roman emperor

> **Analyze:** *Evelina* or *Celicia*, Frances Burney d'Arblay; *Robinson Crusoe*, Daniel Defoe.
>
> **Reading Ahead:** "London's Summer Morning," Mary Darby Robinson; "The Rape of The Lock," Alexander Pope.
>
> **Guide Question:** How does Pope develop satire?

was named Augustus), the Neoclassical (Greek Revival) Age, the Age of Reason (Enlightenment), and the Victorian Age. The 18th century introduced a new genre—the novel. The middle-aged printer Samuel Richardson introduced the novel and achieved fame with the long novel *Pamela; or, Virtue Rewarded*, followed by the even longer *Clarissa Harlowe* (1747-48). This new writing phenomenon was the newest thing in British literature since Spenser's *Faerie Queene*. Richardson's subjects—like many 18th century protagonists—were always women, quite unlike modern novels. Their temptations, tragedies, and triumphs were told in the form of letters, depicting society's attitude and opinion of women. Laurence Sterne, too, introduced the maudlin romance. *The Life and Opinions of Tristram Shandy, Gentleman* (1760-67) was a colorful medley of autobiographical details and cynical reflections on life. Sterne was the Jeannette Oake of his day. In comparison with Richardson and Sterne, Henry Fielding, Tobias Smollett, and Oliver Goldsmith were straightforward storytellers whose novels seem routine, almost modern. Fielding's greatest novel, *Tom Jones* (1749), gave an exciting and frequently hilarious, almost ribald, account of a young man's maturation. Goldsmith's *The Vicar of Wakefield*, immensely popular in its day, depicted the victory of domestic virtue over fashionable vice and therefore appeared a little contrived to modern readers, but the easy simplicity of its prose style enchanted his 18th-century public. All these Victorian novels hold a plethora of vocabulary words that every reader needs to absorb.

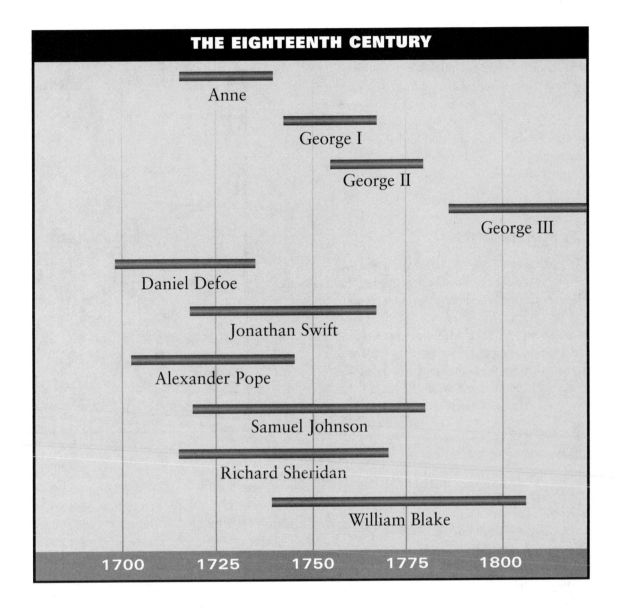

THE EIGHTEENTH CENTURY

Anne

George I

George II

George III

Daniel Defoe

Jonathan Swift

Alexander Pope

Samuel Johnson

Richard Sheridan

William Blake

1700   1725   1750   1775   1800

Daniel Defoe

BACKGROUND

Daniel Defoe was born in London in 1660, probably in September, third child and first son of James and Mary Defoe. Defoe's father hoped son Daniel would become  a minister, but Daniel wasn't interested. Defoe's family was part of the dissenting English church. Being a very bright student Defoe did well in school. In 1684 he joined the army of the Duke of Monmouth, who was attempting to take the throne from James II. When the rebellion failed, Defoe and many other troops were forced into semi-exile. He traveled around the continent for three years, writing very dangerous, very anti-government pamphlets. In 1701, he wrote a poem called *The True-Born Englishman* which became the best-selling poem of the time. The first volume of *Robinson Crusoe* was published April 25, 1719, and it was a big success, especially among ordinary people. In fact, Defoe was the first Clancy of his age! Since that one worked so well, Defoe published *Moll Flanders* in 1722. He died April 24, 1731.

CRITICAL THINKING

A. Defoe chose to disobey his godly parents and become a writer instead of a pastor. Some feel that, while he was a talented writer, his rebellious spirit haunted him all his life. Study Defoe's life and argue this statement.

B. James II, the pretender, was king for a very short time before he was removed because he was a Catholic (Catholics were not allowed to be king). Thus, England had a bloodless revolution. Contrast England's revolution with the bloody French revolution. Examine the following paradigm to determine why this revolution happened and then write a *report* comparing the bloodless English revolution with the French Revolution.

BIBLICAL APPLICATION

A. Eventually Friday has a conversion experience that separates him from servitude with his master. Do you think that the conversion experience is genuine? Why or why not?

B. To Defoe *conversion* would be differently understood from our definition. For instance, the *altar call* came into existence during the Finney Revivals of the 1820's. What did Defoe mean when he stated that Friday was converted to Christianity?

ENRICHMENT

A. The complete title of Defoe's novel is *The Life and Strange Surprizing Adventures of Robinson Crusoe, of York, Mariner: Who lived Eight and Twenty Years, all alone in an uninhabited Island on the Coast of America, near the Mouth of the Great River of Oroonoque; Having been cast on Shore by Shipwreck, wherein all the Men perished but himself. With An Account how he was at last as strangely deliver'd by Pyrates.* He also wrote *The Farther Adventures of Robinson Crusoe* (1719) and *Serious Reflections during the Life and Surprising*

pa. 28

Adventures of Robinson Crusoe (1720). Today these novels would be considered sequels. Can you find examples in contemporary American art or literature where the sequels were not equal to the original work?

B. Some critics remind the reader that in the passage that describes Crusoe's first encounter with Friday, Crusoe immediately suppresses the language and culture of the other, by authoritatively giving him a new name, and at the same time, a new language and a new (Western) concept of time. In what way

	Man	**God**	**Happiness/Government**	**Bible**
Voltaire				
Rousseau				
Locke				
Diderot				
Christian Reformers				

was Robinson Crusoe a typical seventeenth century Englishman?

FINAL PORTFOLIO

Correct and rewrite all essays and place them in your Final Portfolio.

SUGGESTED
Weekly *Implementation*

DAY 1	DAY 2	DAY 3	DAY 4	DAY 5
Prayer journal.	Prayer journal.	**Prayer journal.**	**Prayer journal.**	**Prayer journal.**
Review required reading(s) *before* the assigned lesson begins.	Review reading(s) from next lesson.	Write rough drafts of all assigned essays.	Rewrite corrected copies of essays due tomorrow.	Essays are due.
Teacher may want to discuss assigned reading(s) with students.	Outline essays due at the end of the week.	The teacher and/or a peer evaluator may correct rough drafts.		Take Lesson 14 test.
Teacher and students will decide on required essays for this lesson, choosing two or three essays.	Per teacher instructions, students may answer orally in a group setting some of the essays that are not assigned as formal essays.			Reading Ahead: "London's Summer Morning," Mary Darby Robinson; "The Rape of The Lock," Alexander Pope.
The rest of the essays can be outlined, answered with shorter answers, or skipped.				Guide: How does Pope develop his satire?
Review all readings for Lesson 14.				

LESSON 15

EIGHTEENTH CENTURY *(Part 2)*

Mary Darby Robinson

BACKGROUND

Mary Darby Robinson (1758-1800), whose life was marked by hardship and heartbreak, was nonetheless one of the greatest poets, playwrights, and actresses of the eighteenth century. Her first published work, *Poems*, received little critical support and made little money—and Mary and her husband needed money. They were in debtor's prison. Mary Robinson continued to write, dedicating "Captivity, A Poem" and "Celadon and Lydia, A Tale" (1777) to the Duchess of Devonshire. After 15 months in prison, Thomas Robinson finally negotiated their release. Having given up the theater when she married, Mary returned in hopes of supporting her family by acting. To increasing acclaim, she continued to act for the next four seasons. Robinson moved in "intellectual circles that included Wordsworth, Coleridge, Mary Wollstonecraft, and William Godwin." (*Norton Anthology*, p. 251)

London's Summer Morning

Who has not waked to list the busy sounds
Of summer's morning, in the sultry smoke
Of noisy London? On the pavement hot
The sooty chimney-boy, with dingy face
And tatter'd covering, shrilly bawls his trade,
Rousing the sleepy housemaid. At the door
The milk-pail rattles, and the tinkling bell
Proclaims the dustman's office; while the street
Is lost in clouds impervious. Now begins
The din of hackney-coaches, waggons, carts;
While tinmen's shops, and noisy trunk-makers,
Knife-grinders, coopers, squeaking cork-cutters,
Fruit barrows, and the hunger-giving cries
Of vegetable venders, fill the air.
Now every shop displays its varied trade,
And the fresh-sprinkled pavement cools the feet
Of early walkers. At the private door
The ruddy housemaid twirls the busy mop,
Annoying the smart 'prentice, or neat girl,

Analyze: "London's Summer Morning," Mary Darby Robinson; "The Rape of the Lock," Alexander Pope.

Reading Ahead: Review *Gulliver's Travels* and *Abolishing Christianity*, Jonathan Swift.

Guide Question: When is satire in good taste? When is it damaging?

Tripping with band-box lightly. Now the sun
Darts burning splendour on the glittering pane,
Save where the canvas awning throws a shade
On the day merchandize. Now, spruce and trim,
In shops (where beauty smiles with industry),
Sits the smart damsel; while the passenger
Peeps through the window, watching every charm.
Now pastry dainties catch the eye minute
Of humming insects, while the limy snare
Waits to enthral them. Now the lamp-lighter
Mounts the tall ladder, nimbly venturous,
To trim the half-fill'd lamp; while at his feet
The pot-boy yells discordant! All along
The sultry pavement, the old-clothes man cries
In tone monotonous, the side-long views
The area for his traffic: now the bag
Is slily open'd, and the half-worn suit
(Sometimes the pilfer'd treasure of the base
Domestic spoiler), for one half its worth,
Sinks in the green abyss. The porter now
Bears his huge load along the burning way;
And the poor poet wakes from busy dreams,
To paint the summer morning.
(*Norton Anthology of Literature by Women*, pp. 251-2)

CRITICAL THINKING

"London's Summer Morning" is prophetically modern in tone and substance. Explain.

In your essay include comments on Robinson's use of imagery.

97

Alexander Pope

BACKGROUND

The most accomplished male verse satirist in the English language, Alexander Pope, was born May 21, 1688. Pope's life, which he ironically described as "this long disease," was shaped by two great disadvantages: he was crippled from his earliest years by a deformity of the spine, and he was a member of the Roman Catholic Church, a fact which excluded him from the public life of his time and denied him a university education. Nevertheless, Pope was a gifted writer. Home-schooled, he wrote his earliest surviving poem when he was about twelve years old. Too sickly for boys' sports, he devoted his teenage years to literature. His most famous works were "An Essay on Criticism" (1711) and "The Rape of the Lock." Who can ever forget the tragic figure Miss Arabella Fermor, who lost a curl to the upstart young Baron Lord Petre!

CRITICAL THINKING

A. Read the first Canto of "Rape of the Lock" and paraphrase each stanza.

The Rape of the Lock

Canto I
What dire Offence from am'rous Causes springs,
What mighty Contests rise from trivial Things,
I sing-This verse to Caryl, Muse! is due;
This, ev'n Belinda may vouchsafe to view:
Slight is the Subject, but not so the Praise,
If She inspire, and He approve, my Lays.

Say what strange Motive, Goddess! cou'd compel
A well-bred Lord t'assault a gentle Belle?
Oh say what stranger Cause, yet unexplor'd,
Cou'd make a gentle Belle reject a Lord?
In tasks so bold, can little Men engage,
And in soft Bosoms, dwell such mighty Rage?

Sol through white Curtains shot a tim'rous Ray,
And ope'd those Eyes that must eclipse the Day:
Now Lap-dogs give themselves the rouzing Shake,
And sleepless Lovers, just at Twelve, awake:

Thrice rung the Bell, the Slipper knock'd the Ground,
And the press'd Watch return'd a silver sound,
Belinda still her downy Pillow prest,
Her guardian Sylph prolng'd the balmy rest.
'Twas he had summon'd to her silent Bed
The Morning Dream that hover'd o'er her Head.
A Youth more glitt'ring than a Birth-night Beau
(That ev'n in slumber caus'd her Cheek to glow)
Seem'd to her Ear his winning Lips to lay,
And thus in Whispers said, or seemed to say.

Fairest of Mortals, thou distinguish'd Care
Of thousand bright Inhabitants of Air!
If e'er one Vision touch'd thy infant Thought,
Of all the Nurse and all the Priest have taught,
Of airy Elves by Moonlight Shadows seen,
The silver Token, and the Circled Green,
Or Virgins visited by Angel-powers
With Golden Crowns and Wreaths of heav'nly Flow'rs;
Hear and believe! thy own Importance know,
Nor bound thy narrow Views to things below.
Some secret Truths, from Learned Pride conceal'd,
To Maids alone and Children are reveal'd:
What tho' no Credit doubting Wits may give?
The Fair and Innocent shall still believe.
Know then, unnumber'd Spirits round thee fly,
The light Militia of the lower sky:
These, tho' unseen, are ever on the Wing,
Hang o'er the Box, and hover round the Ring.
Think what an Equipage thou hast in Air,
And view with scorn Two-pages and a Chair.
As now your own, our Beings were of old,
And once inclos'd in Woman's beauteous Mold;
Thence, by a soft Transition, we repair
From earthly Vehicles to these of Air.
Think not, when Woman's transient Breath is fled,
That all her Vanities at once are dead.
Succeeding Vanities she still regards,
And tho' she plays no more, o'erlooks the Cards.
Her Joy in gilded Chariots, when alive,
And love of Ombre after Death survive.
For when the Fair in all their Pride expire,
To their first Elements the Souls retire:
The Sprites of fiery Termagants in Flame
Mount up, and take a Salamander's name.
Soft yielding Minds to Water glide away,
And sip, with Nymphs, their elemental Tea.
The graver Prude sinks downward to a Gnome,
In search of Mischief still on Earth to roam.
The light Coquettes in Sylphs aloft repair,
And sport and flutter in the Fields of Air.

Know further yet; Whoever fair and chaste
Rejects Mankind, is by some Sylph embrac'd:
For Spirits, freed from mortal Laws, with ease
Assume what Sexes and what Shapes they please.
What guards the Purity of melting Maids,
In Courtly Balls, and Midnight Masquerades,
Safe from the treach'rous Friend, the daring Spark,
The Glance by Day, the Whisper in the Dark;
When kind Occasion prompts their warm Desires,
When Music softens, and when Dancing fires?
'Tis but their Sylph, the wise Celestials know,
Tho' Honour is the Word with Men below.

Some Nymphs there are, too conscious of their Face,
For Life predestin'd to the Gnomes' Embrace.
Who swell their Prospects and exalt their Pride,
When Offers are disdain'd, and Love deny'd.
Then gay Ideas crowd the vacant Brain,
While Peers and Dukes, and all their sweeping Train,
And Garters, Stars, and Coronets appear,
And in soft sounds, Your Grace salutes their Ear.
'Tis these that early taint the Female Soul,
Instruct the eyes of young Coquettes to roll,
Teach Infant Cheeks a bidden Blush to know,
And little Hearts to flutter at a Beau.

Oft when the World imagine Women stray,
The Sylphs through Mystic mazes guide their Way.
Thro' all the giddy Circle they pursue,
And old Impertinence expel by new.
What tender Maid but must a Victim fall
To one Man's Treat, but for another's Ball?
When Florio speaks, what Virgin could withstand,
If gentle Damon did not squeeze her Hand?
With varying Vanities, from ev'ry Part,
They shift the moving Toyshop of their Heart;
Where Wigs with Wigs, with Sword-knots Sword-
    knots strive,
Beaux banish Beaux, and Coaches Coaches drive.
This erring Mortals Levity may call,
Oh blind to Truth! the Sylphs contrive it all.

Of these am I, who thy Protection claim,
A watchful Sprite, and Ariel is my name.
Late, as I rang'd the crystal Wilds of Air,
In the clear Mirror of thy ruling Star
I saw, alas! some dread Event impend,
Ere to the Main this morning's Sun descend,
But Heav'n reveals not what, or how, or where:
Warn'd by thy Sylph, oh pious Maid beware!
This to disclose is all thy Guardian can.

Beware of all, but most beware of Man!

He said: when Shock, who thought she slept too long,
Leap'd up, and wak'd his Mistress with his Tongue.
'Twas then, Belinda! if Report say true,
Thy Eyes first open'd on a Billet-doux;
Wounds, Charms, and Ardors, were no sooner read,
But all the Vision vanish'd from thy Head.

And now, unveil'd, the Toilet stands display'd,
Each Silver Vase in mystic Order laid.
First, rob'd in White, the Nymph intent adores
With Head uncover'd, the Cosmetic Pow'rs.
A heav'nly Image in the Glass appears,
To that she bends, to that her Eyes she rears;
Th' inferior Priestess, at her Altar's side,
Trembling, begins the sacred Rites of Pride.
Unnumber'd Treasures ope at once, and here
The various Off'rings of the World appear;
From each she nicely culls with curious Toil,
And decks the Goddess with the glitt'ring Spoil.
This casket India's glowing Gems unlocks,
And all Arabia breathes from yonder Box.
The Tortoise here and Elephant unite,
Transform'd to Combs, the speckled and the white.
Here Files of Pins extend their shining Rows,
Puffs, Powders, Patches, Bibles, Billet-doux.
Now awful Beauty puts on all its Arms;
The Fair each moment rises in her Charms,
Repairs her Smiles, awakens ev'ry Grace,
And calls forth all the Wonders of her Face;
Sees by Degrees a purer Blush arise,
And keener Lightnings quicken in her Eyes.
The busy Sylphs surround their darling Care;
These set the Head, and those divide the Hair,
Some fold the Sleeve, whilst others plait the Gown;
And Betty's prais'd for labours not her own.
(http://eir.library.utoronto.ca/rpo/display/poem1644.ht
    ml)

B. Compare Pope's satire with Chaucer's satire.

BIBLICAL APPLICATION

At the height of his career, Pope addressed questions of
metaphysics and ethics and wrote the didactic poem for
which he was best known in his time, *An Essay on Man*,
expressing eighteenth century perceptions of the universe and humanity's place in God's scheme. The work
surveys the nature and condition of man and declares
him a living paradox, a being caught somewhere
between order and chaos, "in doubt to deem himself a

God, or Beast." Weigh this perception of man against the biblical witness and write a three-page essay contrasting Pope's views with the Bible.

ENRICHMENT

Define the worldview deism and find evidence of this worldview in this section of *Essay on Man*.

Know then thyself, presume not God to scan,
The proper study of Mankind is Man.
Plac'd on this isthmus of a middle state,
A being darkly wise, and rudely great:
With too much knowledge for the Sceptic side,
With too much weakness for the Stoic's pride,
He hangs between; in doubt to act, or rest,
In doubt to deem himself a God, or Beast;

In doubt his Mind or Body to prefer;
Born but to die, and reas'ning but to err;
Alike in ignorance, his reason such,
Whether he thinks too little, or too much:
Chaos of Thought and Passion, all confus'd;
Still by himself abus'd, or disabus'd;
Created half to rise, and half to fall;
Great lord of all things, yet a prey to all;
Sole judge of Truth, in endless Error hurl'd:
The glory, jest, and riddle of the world!
(http://www.bartleby.com/40/2801.html)

FINAL PROJECT

Correct and rewrite all essays and place them in your Final Portfolio.

SUGGESTED
Weekly *Implementation*

DAY 1	DAY 2	DAY 3	DAY 4	DAY 5
Prayer journal.	**Prayer journal.**	**Prayer journal.**	**Prayer journal.**	**Prayer journal.**
Review required reading(s) *before* the assigned lesson begins.	Review reading(s) from next lesson.	Write rough drafts of all assigned essays.	Rewrite corrected copies of essays due tomorrow.	Essays are due.
Teacher may want to discuss assigned reading(s) with students.	Outline essays due at the end of the week.	The teacher and/or a peer evaluator may correct rough drafts.		Take Lesson 15 test.
Teacher and students will decide on required essays for this lesson, choosing two or three essays.	Per teacher instructions, students may answer orally in a group setting some of the essays that are not assigned as formal essays.			Reading Ahead: *Gulliver's Travels* and *Abolishing Christianity*, Jonathan Swift.
The rest of the essays can be outlined, answered with shorter answers, or skipped.				Guide: When is satire in good taste? When is it damaging?
Review all readings for Lesson 15.				

LESSON 16

EIGHTEENTH CENTURY *(Part 3)*

Gulliver's Travels

Jonathan Swift

BACKGROUND

The greatest satirist (parodist) England was to produce began as a poor beggar. His most famous book was *Gulliver's Travels*. It was an overnight success, a runaway best-seller. It had everything eighteenth-century England wanted: mystery and political/social scandal and remarkable humor. Since Swift poked fun at prominent political figures, he published the book anonymously. Most everyone knew, however, of Swift's authorship.

London buzzed with speculations, suggestions, and counter-suggestions regarding the author's identity, as well as those of some of his characters. In Part I, for example, the Lilliputian Emperor—tyrannical, cruel, corrupt, and obsessed with ceremony—though a timeless symbol of bad government, is also a biting satire of George I, King of England (from 1714 to 1727) during much of Swift's career. The Lilliputian Empress symbolizes Queen Anne, who blocked Swift's advancement in the Church of England. There are two political parties in Lilliput, the Low-Heels and the High-Heels. These correspond respectively to the Whigs and Tories, the two major British political parties. It didn't take long for people to grasp the author's symbolic representation of England in Lilliput, Brobdingnag, Laputa, and the land of the Houyhnhnms. It also didn't take long for the public to discover that the author was Jonathan Swift.

Swift was a clergyman, writer, and activist. Like many eighteenth-century clergy, Swift was caught up in the social milieu of his period. In 1729, when he was sixty-three, he wrote *A Modest Proposal*, considered by many to be the best satire ever written in English. Swift's last years were tormented by awful bouts of dizziness, nausea, deafness, and mental incapacity. His harshest critics tried to discredit the *Travels* on the grounds that the author was insane when he wrote it. However, *The Travels* was published in 1726—part IV,

> **Analyze:** *Gulliver's Travels* and *Abolishing Christianity*, Jonathan Swift.
>
> **Reading Ahead:** Review *The Vicar of Wakefield*, Oliver Goldsmith.
>
> **Guide Question:** Is the vicar a bumbling idiot or a wise, godly man?

which raised the most controversy, was written before part III—and Swift didn't enter a mental institution until 1742. He died in 1745. Reading the biting satire *Travels* with mature minds and hearts is a far different experience from reading it as a child.

CRITICAL THINKING

A. Gulliver is the most important character in this novel. He's also one of the most disconcerting characters in English literature. Discuss in great detail why Gulliver is such a difficult character for readers to enjoy.

B. Yahoos are some of the most colorful characters in English literature. Who are they, and what contemporary characters can you compare to Swift's Yahoos?

C. Compare Pope's "The Rape of the Lock" with Swift's *Gulliver's Travels*.

D. Examine in great detail the way in which Swift attacks his opponents.

ENRICHMENT

Read the following passage from Swift's essay entitled "An Argument to Prove That the Abolishing of Christianity in England, May as Things Now Stand, Be Attended with Some Inconveniencies, and Perhaps Not Produce Those Many Good Effects Proposed Thereby." The eighteenth-century spelling, syntax, and grammar rules have been maintained throughout the passage. Compare it to the style, tone, and theme of *Gulliver's Travels*.

I AM very sensible what Weakness and Presumption it is, to reason against the general Humour and Disposition of the World. I remember it was with great Justice, and a due regard to the Freedom both of the Publick and the Press, forbidden upon severe Penalties to Write, or Discourse, or lay Wagers against the Union, even before it was confirmed by Parliament, because that was look'd upon as a Design, to oppose the Current of the People, which besides the Folly of it, is a manifest Breach of the Fundamental Law that makes this Majority of Opinion the Voice of God. In like manner, and for the very same Reasons, it may perhaps be neither safe nor prudent to argue against the abolishing of Christianity: at a Juncture when all Parties seem so unanimously determined upon the Point, as we cannot but allow from their Actions, their Discourses, and their Writings. However, I know not how, whether from the Affectation of Singularity, or the Perverseness of Human Nature, but so it unhappily falls out, that I cannot be entirely of this Opinion. Nay, although I were sure, an Order were issued out for my immediate Prosecution by the Attorney General, I should still confess that in the present Posture of our Affairs at home or abroad, I do not yet see the absolute Necessity of extirpating the Christian Religion from among us.

THIS perhaps may appear too great a Paradox even for our wise and paradoxical Age to endure; therefore I shall handle it with all Tenderness, and with the utmost Deference to that great and profound Majority which is of another Sentiment.

AND yet the Curious may please to observe, how much the Genius of a Nation is liable to alter in half an Age. I have heard it affirmed for certain by some very old People, that the contrary Opinion was even in their Memories as much in Vogue as the other is now; And, that a Project for the abolishing Christianity would then have appeared as singular, and been thought as absurd, as it would be at this time to write or discourse in it's Defence.

Who are the Trinitarians?

THEREFORE I freely own that all Appearances are against me. The System of the Gospel after the Fate of other Systems is generally antiquated and exploded; and the Mass or Body of the common People, among whom it seems to have had it's latest Credit, are now grown as much ashamed of it as their Betters: Opinions like Fashions always descending from those of Quality to the middle sort, and thence to the Vulgar, where at length they are dropp'd and vanish.

BUT here I would not be mistaken, and must there-fore be so bold as to borrow a Distinction from the Writers on the other side, when they make a Difference between Nominal and Real Trinitarians. I hope no Reader imagines me so weak to stand up in the Defence of real Christianity, such as used in primitive Times (if we may believe the Authors of those Ages) to have an Influence upon Mens Belief and Actions: To offer at the restoring of That would indeed be a wild Project; It would be to dig up Foundations, to destroy at one Blow all the Wit, and half the Learning of the Kingdom; to break the entire Frame and Constitution of Things, to ruin Trade, extinguish Arts and Sciences with the Professors of them; In short, to turn our Courts, Exchanges, and shops into Deserts; and would be full as absurd as the Proposal of Horace, where he advises the Romans, all in a Body to leave their City, and seek a new Seat in some remote Part of the World, by way of a Cure for the Corruption of their Manners.

THEREFORE I think this Caution was in it self altogether unnecessary (which I have inserted only to prevent all Possibility of Caviling) since every candid Reader will easily understand my Discourse to be intended only in Defence of nominal Christianity, the other having been for some time wholly laid aside by general Consent, as utterly inconsistent with all our present Schemes of Wealth and Power.

BUT why we should therefore cast off the Name and Title of Christians, although the general Opinion and Resolution be so violent for it, I confess I cannot (with Submission) apprehend the Consequence necessary. However, since the Undertakers propose such wonderful Advantages to the Nation by this Project, and advance many plausible Objections against the System of Christianity, I shall briefly consider the Strength of both, fairly allow them their greatest Weight, and offer such Answers as I think most reasonable. After which I will beg leave to shew what Inconveniencies may possibly happen by such an Innovation, in the present Posture of our Affairs.

First, ONE great Advantage proposed by the abolishing of Christianity is, That it would very much enlarge and establish Liberty of Conscience, that great Bulwark of our Nation, and of the Protestant Religion, which is still too much limited by Priest-craft, notwithstanding all the good Intentions of the Legislature, as we have lately found by a severe Instance. For it is confidently reported, that two Young Gentlemen of great Hopes, bright Wit, and profound Judgment, who upon a thorough Examination of Causes and Effects, and by the meer Force of natural Abilities, without the least Tincture of Learning, having made a Discovery, that there was no God, and generously communicating their Thoughts for the good of the Publick; were some time ago by an unparalleled Severity, and upon I know not what obsolete Law, broke only for Blasphemy. And as it hath been wisely observed, if Persecution once begins no Man alive knows how far it may reach, or where it will end.

IN answer to all which, with deference to wiser Judgments, I think this rather shews the Necessity of a nominal Religion among us. Great Wits love to be free with the highest Objects, and if they cannot be allowed a God to revile or renounce; they will speak Evil of Dignities, abuse the Government, and reflect upon the Ministry, which I am sure few will deny to be of much more pernicious Consequence, according to the saying of Tiberius, DEORUM OFFENSA DIIS CURAE. As to the particular Fact related, I think it is not fair to argue from one Instance, perhaps another cannot be produced, yet (to the Comfort of all those who may be apprehensive of Persecution) Blasphemy we know is freely spoke a Million of times in every Coffee-House and Tavern, or wherever else good Company meet. It must be allowed indeed that to break an English Free-born Officer only for Blasphemy, was, to speak the gentlest of such an Action, a very high strain of absolute Power. Little can be said in Excuse for the General; Perhaps he was afraid it might give Offence to the Allies, among whom, for ought I know, it may be the Custom of the Country to believe a God. But if he argued, as some have done, upon a mistaken Principle, that an Officer who is guilty of speaking Blasphemy, may sometime or other proceed so far as to raise a Mutiny, the Consequence is by no means to be admitted; For, surely the Commander of an English Army is like to be but ill obey'd, whose Soldiers fear and reverence him as little as they do a Deity.

IT is further objected against the Gospel System, that it obliges men to the Belief of Things too difficult for free Thinkers, and such who have shook off the Prejudices that usually cling to a confin'd Education. To which I answer, that Men should be cautious how they raise Objections which reflect upon the Wisdom of the Nation. Is not every body freely allowed to believe whatever he pleaseth, and to publish his Belief to the World whenever he thinks fit, especially if it serve to strengthen the Party which is in the Right. Would any indifferent Foreigner, who should read the Trumpery lately written by Asgil, Tindall, Toland, Coward, and Forty more, imagine the Gospel to be our Rule of Faith, and to be confirmed by Parliaments. Does any Man either Believe, or say he believes, or desire to have it

thought that he says he Believes one Syllable of the Matter, and is any Man worse received upon that Score, or does he find his want of Nominal Faith a disadvantage to him in the Pursuit of any Civil or Military Employment? What if there be an old dormant Statute or two against him, are they not now obsolete, to a degree, that Empson and Dudley themselves if they were now alive, would find it impossible to put them in execution?

What are the tongue-in-cheek arguments that Swift is advancing?

IT is likewise urged, that there are by Computation in this Kingdom, above Ten Thousand Parsons, whose Revenues added to those of my Lords the Bishops, would suffice to maintain at least Two Hundred Young Gentlemen of Wit and Pleasure, and Free-thinking Enemies to Priest-Craft, narrow Principles, Pedantry, and Prejudices, who might be an Ornament to the Court and Town: And then, again, so great a Number of able (bodied) Divines might be a Recruit to our Fleet and Armies. This indeed appears to be a Consideration of some Weight: But then, on the other side, several Things deserve to be considered likewise: As, First, Whether it may not be thought necessary that in certain Tracts of Country, like what we call Parishes, there should be one Man at least, of Abilities to Read and Write. Then it seems a wrong Computation, that the Revenues of the Church throughout this Island would be large enough to maintain Two Hundred Young Gentlemen, or even half that Number, after the present refined Way of Living, that is, to allow each of them such a Rent, as in the modern Form of Speech, would make them easy. But still there is in this Project a greater Mischief behind; And we ought to beware of the Woman's Folly, who killed the Hen that every Morning laid her a Golden Egg. For, pray what would become of the Race of Men in the next Age, if we had nothing to trust to besides the Scrophulous consumptive Production furnished by our Men of Wit and Pleasure, when having squandered away their Vigour, Health, and Estates, they are forced by some disagreeable Marriage to piece up their broken Fortunes, and entail Rottenness and Politeness on their Posterity. Now, here are ten thousand Persons reduced by the wise Regulations of Henry the Eighth, to the Necessity of a low Dyet, and moderate Exercise, who are the only great Restorers of our Breed, without which the Nation would in an Age or two become but one great Hospital.

ANOTHER Advantage proposed by the Abolishing of Christianity, is the clear Gain of one Day in Seven, which is now entirely lost, and consequently the Kingdom one Seventh less considerable in Trade, Business, and Pleasure; beside the Loss to the Publick of so many Stately Structures now in the Hands of the Clergy, which might be converted into Theatres, Exchanges, Market-houses, common Dormitories, and other Publick Edifices.

I hope I shall be forgiven a hard Word if I call this a perfect Cavil. I readily own there hath been an old Custom time out of mind, for People to assemble in the Churches every Sunday, and that shops are still frequently shut, in order as it is conceived, to preserve the Memory of that antient Practice, but how this can prove a hindrance to Business or Pleasure, is hard to imagine. What if the Men of Pleasure are forced one Day in the Week to game at Home instead of the Chocolate-House. Are not the Taverns and Coffee-Houses open? Can there be a more convenient Season for taking a Dose of Physick? Are fewer Claps got upon Sundays than other Days? Is not that the chief Day for Traders to Sum up the Accounts of the Week, and for Lawyers to prepare their Briefs? But I would fain know how it can be pretended that the Churches are misapplied. Where are more Appointments and Rendezvouzes of Gallantry? Where more Care to appear in the foremost Box with greater Advantage of Dress? Where more Meetings for Business? Where more Bargains driven of all Sorts? And where so many Conveniences or Incitements to Sleep?

THERE is one Advantage greater than any of the foregoing, proposed by the Abolishing of Christianity, that it will utterly extinguish Parties among us, by removing those Factious Distinctions of High and Low Church, of Whig and Tory, Presbyterian and Church of England, which are now so many grievous Clogs upon Publick Proceedings, and dispose Men to prefer the gratifying themselves or depressing their Adversaries, before the most important Interest of the State. I confess, if it were certain that so great an Advantage would redound to the Nation by this Expedient, I would submit, and be silent: But, will any man say that if the Words, Drinking, Cheating, Lying, Stealing, were by Act of Parliament ejected out of the English Tongue and Dictionaries; We should all Awake next Morning Chast and Temperate, Honest and Just, and Lovers of Truth. Is this a fair Consequence? Or if the Physicians would forbid us to pronounce the Words Pox, Gout, Rheumatism and Stone, would that Expedient serve like so many Talismans to destroy the Diseases themselves. Are Party and Faction rooted in Mens Hearts no deeper than Phrases borrowed from Religion, or founded upon no firmer Principles? And is our Language so poor that we cannot find other Terms to express them? Are Envy, Pride, Avarice and Ambition such ill Nomenclators, that they cannot furnish Appellations for their Owners? Will not Heydukes and Mamalukes, Mandarins and Patshaws, or any other Words formed at Pleasure, serve to distinguish those who are in the Ministry from others who would be in it if they could? What, for instance, is easier than to vary the Form of Speech, and instead of the Word, Church, make it a Question in Politicks, Whether the Monument be in Danger? Because Religion was nearest at hand to furnish a few convenient Phrases, is our Invention so barren, we can find no other? Suppose for Argument sake, that the Tories favoured Margarita, the Whigs Mrs. Tofts, and the Trimmers Valentini, would not Margaritians, Toftians and Valentinians be very tolerable Marks of Distinction? The Prasini and Veneti, two most virulent Factions in Italy, began (if I remember right) by a Distinction of Colours in Ribbans, which we might do with as Good a Grace about the Dignity of the Blew and the Green, and would serve as properly to divide the Court, the Parliament, and the Kingdom between them, as any Terms of Art whatsoever, borrowed from Religion. Therefore I think there is little Force in this Objection against Christianity, or Prospect of so great an Advantage as is proposed in the abolishing of it.

IT is again objected as a very absurd ridiculous Custom, that a Set of Men should be suffered, much less employed and hired, to bawl one Day in Seven against the Lawfulness of those Methods most in use towards the Pursuit of Greatness, Riches and Pleasure, which are the constant Practice of all Men alive on the other Six. But this Objection is I think, a little unworthy so refined an Age as ours. Let us argue this Matter calmly; I appeal to the Breast of any polite Free Thinker, whether in the Pursuit of gratifying a predominant Passion, he hath not always felt a wonderful Incitement, by reflecting it was a Thing forbidden; And therefore we see, in order to cultivate this Taste, the Wisdom of the Nation hath taken special Care, that the Ladies should be furnished with Prohibited Silks, and the Men with Prohibited Wine; And indeed it were to be wisht, that some other Prohibitions were promoted, in order to improve the Pleasures of the Town, which for want of such Expedients begin already, as I am told, to flag and grow languid, giving way daily to cruel Inroads from the Spleen.

IT is likewise proposed as a great Advantage to the Publick, that if we once discard the System of the Gospel, all Religion will of course be banished for ever, and consequently along with it, those grievous Prejudices of Education, which under the Names of Virtue, Conscience, Honour, Justice, and the like, are so apt to disturb the Peace of human Minds, and the Notions whereof are so hard to be eradicated by Right Reason or Free Thinking, sometimes during the whole Course of our Lives.

HERE first I observe how difficult it is to get rid of a Phrase which the World is once grown fond of, although the Occasion that first produced it, be entirely taken away. For several Years past, if a Man had but an ill-favoured Nose, the deep Thinkers of the Age would some way or other contrive to impute the Cause to the Prejudice of his Education. From this Fountain are said to be derived all our foolish Notions of Justice, Piety, Love of our Country, all our Opinions of God or a Future State, Heaven, Hell and the like: And there might formerly perhaps have been some Pretence for this Charge. But so effectual Care hath been since taken to remove those Prejudices, by an entire Change in the Methods of Education, that (with Honour I mention it to our Polite Innovators) the Young Gentlemen, who are now on the Scene, seem to have not the least Tincture left of those Infusions, or String of those Weeds, and by consequence the Reason for abolishing Nominal Christianity upon that Pretext, is wholly ceast.

FOR the rest, it may perhaps admit a Controversy, whether the banishing all Notions of Religion whatsoever, would be convenient for the Vulgar. Not that I am in the least of Opinion with those who hold Religion to have been the Invention of Politicians, to keep the lower Part of the World in Awe by the fear of Invisible Powers; unless Mankind were then very different from what it is now: For I look upon the Mass or Body of our People here in England, to be as Free Thinkers, that is to say, as Stanch Unbelievers, as any of the highest Rank. But I conceive some scattered Notions about a Superior Power to be of singular Use for the Common People, as furnishing excellent Materials to keep Children quiet when they grow peevish, and providing Topicks of Amusement in a tedious Winter Night.

LASTLY, it is proposed as a singular Advantage, that the abolishing of Christianity will very much contribute to the uniting of Protestants, by enlarging the Terms of Communion so as to take in all sorts of Dissenters, who are now shut out of the Pale upon Account of a few Ceremonies which all Sides confess to be Things indifferent: That this alone will effectually answer the great Ends of a Scheme for Comprehension, by opening a large noble Gate, at which all Bodies may enter; whereas the chaffering with Dissenters, and

dodging about this or the other Ceremony, is but like opening a few Wickets, and leaving them at jar, by which no more than one can get in at a time, and that, not without stooping, and sideling, and squeezing his Body.

TO all this I answer; that there is one darling Inclination of Mankind, which usually affects to be a Retainer to Religion, though she be neither it's Parent, it's Godmother, or it's Friend; I mean the Spirit of Opposition, that lived long before Christianity, and can easily subsist without it. Let us for instance, examine wherein the Opposition of Sectaries among us consists. we shall find Christianity to have no hare in it at all. Does the Gospel any where prescribe a starcht squeezed Countenance, a Stiff formal Gate, a singularity of Manners and Habit, or any affected Modes of Speech different from the reasonable Part of Mankind. Yet, if Christianity did not lend it's name, to stand in the Gap, and to employ or divert these Humors, they must of necessity be spent in Contraventions to the Laws of the Land, and Disturbance of the Publick Peace. There is a Portion of Enthusiasm assigned to every Nation, which if it hath not proper Objects to work on, will burst out and set all in a Flame. If the Quiet of a State can be bought by only flinging Men a few Ceremonies to devour, it is a Purchase no Wise Man would refuse. Let the Mastiffs amuse themselves about a Sheepskin stufft with Hay, provided it will keep them from Worrying the Flock. The Institution of Convents abroad, seems in one Point a strain of great Wisdom, there being few Irregularities in human Passions, that may not have recourse to vent themselves in some of those Orders, which are so many Retreats for the Speculative, the Melancholy, the Proud, the Silent, the Politick and the Morose, to spend themselves, and evaporate the Noxious Particles; for each of whom we in this Island are forced to provide a several Sect of Religion, to keep them Quiet; and whenever Christianity shall be abolished, the Legislature must find some other Expedient to employ and entertain them. For what imports it how large a Gate you open, if there will be always left a Number who place a Pride and a Merit in refusing to enter?

HAVING thus consider'd the most important Objections against Christianity, and the chief Advantages proposed by the Abolishing thereof; I shall now with equal Deference and Submission to wiser Judgments as before, proceed to mention a few Inconveniencies that may happen, if the Gospel should be repealed; which perhaps the Projectors may not have sufficiently considered.

AND first, I am very sensible how much the Gentlemen of Wit and Pleasure are apt to murmur, and be choqued at the sight of so many daggled-tail Parsons, who happen to fall in their way, and offend their Eyes; but at the same Time these wise Reformers do not consider what an Advantage and Felicity it is, for great Wits to be always provided with Objects of Scorn and Contempt, in order to exercise and improve their Talents, and divert their Spleen from falling on each other or on themselves, especially when all this may be done without the least imaginable Danger to their Persons.

AND to urge another Argument of a parallel Nature. If Christianity were once abolished, how could the Free Thinkers, the Strong Reasoners, and the Men of profound Learning, be able to find another Subject so calculated in all Points whereon to display their Abilities. What wonderful Productions of Wit should we be deprived of, from those whose Genius by continual Practice hath been wholly turn'd upon Railery and Invectives against Religion, and would therefore never be able to shine or distinguish themselves upon any other Subject. We are daily complaining of the great decline of Wit among us, and would we take away the greatest, perhaps the only Topick we have left? Who would ever have suspected Asgil for a Wit, or Toland for a Philosopher, if the inexhaustible Stock of Christianity had not been at hand to provide them with Materials. What other Subject through all Art or Nature could have produced Tindall for a profound Author, or furnished him with Readers. It is the wise Choice of the Subject that alone adorns and distinguishes the Writer. For, had a Hundred such Pens as these been employed on the side of Religion, they would have immediately sunk into Silence and Oblivion.

NOR do I think it wholly groundless, or my Fears altogether imaginary, that the Abolishing of Christianity may perhaps bring the Church in Danger, or at least put the Senate to the Trouble of another Securing Vote. I desire I may not be mistaken; I am far from presuming to affirm or think that the Church is in Danger at present, or as Things now stand, but we know not how soon it may be so when the Christian Religion is repealed. As plausible as this Project seems, there may a dangerous Design lurk under it; Nothing can be more notorious, than that the Atheists, Deists, Socinians, Anti-Trinitarians, and other Subdivisions of Free Thinkers, are Persons of little Zeal for the present Ecclesiastical Establishment: Their declared Opinion is for repealing the Sacramental Test, they are very indif-ferent with regard to Ceremonies, nor do they hold the Jus Divinum of Episcopacy. Therefore this may be intended as one Politick step towards altering the Constitution of the Church Established, and setting up Presbytery in the stead, which I leave to be further considered by those at the Helm.

IN the last Place I think nothing can be more plain, than that by this Expedient, we shall run into the Evil we chiefly pretend to avoid; and that the Abolishment of the Christian Religion, will be the readiest Course we can take to introduce Popery. And I am the more inclined to this Opinion, because we know it has been the constant Practice of the Jesuits to send over Emissaries, with Instructions to personate themselves Members of the several prevailing Sects amongst us. So it is recorded, that they have at sundry Times appeared in the Guise of Presbyterians, Anabaptists, Independents, and Quakers, according as any of these were most in Credit; So, since the Fashion hath been taken up of exploding Religion, the Popish Missionaries have not been wanting to mix with the Free-Thinkers; among whom Toland the great Oracle of the Anti-Christians is an Irish Priest, the Son of an Irish Priest; and the most learned and ingenious Author of a Book called the Rights of the Christian Church, was in a proper Juncture reconciled to the Romish Faith, whose true Son, as appears by a hundred Passages in his Treatise, he still continues. Perhaps I could add some others to the Number; but the Fact is beyond Dispute, and the Reasoning they proceed by is right: For supposing Christianity to be extinguished, the People will never be at Ease till they find out some other Method of Worship; which will as infallibly produce Superstition, as this will end in Popery.

AND therefore, if notwithstanding all I have said, it still be thought necessary to have a Bill brought in for repealing Christianity; I would humbly offer an Amendment; That instead of the Word, Christianity, may be put Religion in general, which I conceive will much better answer all the good Ends proposed by the Projectors of it. For, as long as we leave in being, a God and his Providence, with all the necessary Consequences which curious and inquisitive Men will be apt to draw from such Premises, we do not strike at the Root of the Evil, though we should ever so effectually annihilate the present Scheme of the Gospel; For, of what Use is Freedom of Thought, if it will not produce Freedom of Action, which is the sole End, how remote soever in Appearance, of all Objections against Christianity; And therefore, the Free-Thinkers consider it as a Sort of Edifice, wherein all the Parts have such a mutual Dependence on each other, that if you happen to pull out one single Nail, the whole Fabrick must fall to the Ground. This was happily exprest by him who had heard of a Text brought for proof of the Trinity, which in an ancient Manuscript was differently read; He thereupon immediately took the Hint, and by a sudden Deduction of a long Sorites, most Logically concluded: Why, if it be as you say, I may safely Whore and Drink on, and defy the Parson. From which, and many the like Instances easy to be produced, I think nothing can be more manifest, than that the Quarrel is not against any particular Points of hard digestion in the Christian System, but against Religion in general, which, by laying Restraints on human Nature, is supposed the great Enemy to the Freedom of Thought and Action.

UPON the whole, if it shall still be thought for the Benefit of Church and State, that Christianity be abolished; I conceive however, it may be more convenient to defer the Execution to a Time of Peace, and not venture in this Conjuncture to disoblige our Allies, who as it falls out, are all Christians, and many of them, by the Prejudices of their Education, so bigotted, as to place a sort of Pride in the Appellation. If upon being rejected by them, we are to trust to an Alliance with the Turk, we shall find our selves much deceived: For, as he is too remote, and generally engaged in War with the Persian Emperor, so his People would be more Scandalized at our Infidelity, than our Christian Neighbours. Because the Turks are not only strict Observers of religious Worship; but what is worse, believe a God, which is more than is required of us, even while we preserve the Name of Christians.

TO conclude, Whatever some may think of the great Advantages to Trade by this favourite Scheme, I do very much apprehend, that in Six Months time after the Act is past for the Extirpation of the Gospel, the Bank, and East-India Stock, may fall at least One per Cent. And since that is Fifty times more than ever the Wisdom of our Age thought fit to venture for the Preservation of Christianity, there is no Reason we should be at so great a Loss meerly for the sake of destroying it. (http://etext.library.adelaide.edua.au/s/97ab/)

FINAL PROJECT

Correct and rewrite all essays and place them in your Final Portfolio.

SUGGESTED

Weekly *Implementation*

DAY 1	DAY 2	DAY 3	DAY 4	DAY 5
Prayer journal. Review required reading(s) *before* the assigned lesson begins. <u>Teacher and students will decide on required essays for this lesson, choosing two or three essays.</u> <u>The rest of the essays can be outlined, answered with shorter answers, or skipped.</u> Review all readings for Lesson 16.	**Prayer journal.** Review reading(s) from next lesson. Outline essays due at the end of the week. Per teacher instructions, students may answer orally in a group setting some of the essays that are not assigned as formal essays.	**Prayer journal.** Write rough drafts of all assigned essays. The teacher and/or a peer evaluator may correct rough drafts.	**Prayer journal.** Rewrite corrected copies of essays due tomorrow.	**Prayer journal.** Essays are due. Take Lesson 16 test. Reading Ahead: Review *The Vicar of Wakefield*, Oliver Goldsmith. Guide: Is the vicar a bumbling idiot or a wise, godly man?

LESSON 17

EIGHTEENTH CENTURY *(Part 4)*

The Vicar of Wakefield

Oliver Goldsmith

BACKGROUND

The Vicar of Wakefield, an early British novel, is about an eccentric pastor and his family. It became the prototype for a generation of novels written by Austen, Brontë, and others.

Irishman Oliver Goldsmith—born in Kilkenny West, Ireland, on November 10, 1730(?), died April 4, 1774. He first achieved literary success with "The Traveller" (1764), a poem making a social statement about British rule. Like Jonathan Swift, Goldsmith wrote social criticism, but unlike Swift, he did not use biting satire. Goldsmith's greatest poetic triumph, "The Deserted Village" (1770), lamented the passing of a simple rural life in the face of agricultural consolidation by the great landowners. Goldsmith championed the small town much like country music ballads today call their audience back to rural living. This same theme is developed in *The Vicar of Wakefield*. Goldsmith's most substantial work at that time was *The Citizen of the World* (1762), a collection of soft-satire essays on English life as viewed by an imaginary Chinese visitor. Goldsmith also wrote two successful plays, *The Good-Natured Man* (1768) and *She Stoops to Conquer* (1773), a witty attack on the sentimental drama of the day. *The Vicar of Wakefield* ranks as one of the truly great classics of the eighteenth century.

Analyze: *The Vicar of Wakefield*, Oliver Goldsmith.

Reading Ahead: Review "Mr. Johnson's Preface to His Edition of Shakespeare's Plays," Samuel Johnson.

Guide Question: What makes a good literary critic?

CRITICAL THINKING

A. What do you think about the ending to this novel? Defend your thoughts with quotations from the text.
B. Discuss Goldsmith's writing style.

BIBLICAL APPLICATION

Dr. Charles Primrose, the pastor presented in *Vicar*, is a complicated character. He clearly exhibits Christian tendencies, yet whether or not he was a committed Christian is debatable. What do you think? Defend your answer from the text.

ENRICHMENT

Some critics have criticized *Vicar of Wakefield* as being a silly, predictable book that presented a superficial study of human character. Why do you agree or disagree?

FINAL PROJECT

Correct and rewrite all essays and place them in your Final Portfolio.

SUGGESTED
Weekly *Implementation*

DAY 1	DAY 2	DAY 3	DAY 4	DAY 5
Prayer journal.	**Prayer journal.**	**Prayer journal.**	**Prayer journal.**	**Prayer journal.**
Review required reading(s) *before* the assigned lesson begins. Teacher and students will decide on required essays for this lesson, choosing two or three essays. The rest of the essays can be outlined, answered with shorter answers, or skipped. Review all readings for Lesson 17.	Review reading(s) from next lesson. Outline essays due at the end of the week. Per teacher instructions, students may answer orally in a group setting some of the essays that are not assigned as formal essays.	Write rough drafts of all assigned essays. The teacher and/or a peer evaluator may correct rough drafts.	Rewrite corrected copies of essays due tomorrow.	Essays are due. Take Lesson 17 test. Reading Ahead: Review "Mr. Johnson's Preface to His Edition of Shakespeare's Plays," Samuel Johnson. Guide: What makes a good literary critic?

LESSON 18

EIGHTEENTH CENTURY *(Part 5)*

Samuel Johnson

BACKGROUND

Samuel Johnson, essayist, poet, and critic, was the leading English writer of the second half of the eighteenth century. In recognition of his eminence the period is often called the Age of Johnson. He wrote the first English dictionary based on historical principles; he produced the first editorially intelligent edition of Shakespeare's plays; his literary criticism, after suffering a long period of disrepute, is now ranked with the finest in English; as a moral essayist he has always been admired. On September 18, 1709, Johnson was born in Lichfield, and on December 13, 1784, he died in London, which had become his home after 1737.

Typical English usage and punctuation of the eighteenth century has been preserved in the following essay by Johnson.

Preface to His Edition of Shakespeare's Plays

Samuel Johnson

THAT praises are without reason lavished on the dead, and that the honours due only to excellence are paid to antiquity, is a complaint likely to be always continued by those, who, being able to add nothing to truth, hope for eminence from the heresies of paradox; or those, who, being forced by disappointment upon consolatory expedients, are willing to hope from posterity what the present age refuses, and flatter themselves that the regard which is yet denied by envy, will be at last bestowed by time.

Analyze: "Mr. Johnson's Preface to His Edition of Shakespeare's Plays," Samuel Johnson.

Reading Ahead: *The Rivals*, Richard Brinsley Sheridan.

Guide Question: How does Sheridan create humor in this hilarious play?

Antiquity, like every other quality that attracts the notice of mankind, has undoubtedly votaries that reverence it, not from reason, but from prejudice. Some seem to admire indiscriminately what ever has been long preserved, without considering that time has sometimes co-operated with chance; all perhaps are more willing to honour past than present excellence; and the mind contemplates genius through the shades of age, as the eye surveys the sun through artificial opacity. The great contention of criticism is to find the faults of the moderns, and the beauties of the ancients. While an authour is yet living we estimate his powers by his worst performance, and when he is dead we rate them by his best.

To works, however, of which the excellence is not absolute and definite, but gradual and comparative; to works not raised upon principles demonstrative and scientifick, but appealing wholly to observation and experience, no other test can be applied than length of duration and continuance of esteem. What mankind have long possessed they have often examined and compared, and if they persist to value the possession, it is because frequent comparisons have confirmed opinion in its favour. As among the works of nature no man can properly call a river deep or a mountain high, without the knowledge of many mountains and many rivers; so in the productions of genius, nothing can be stiled excellent till it has been compared with other works of the same kind. Demonstration immediately displays its power, and has nothing to hope or fear from the flux of years; but works tentative and experimental must be estimated by their proportion to the general and collective ability of man, as it is discovered in a long succession of endeavours. Of the first building that was raised, it might be with certainty determined that it was round or square, but whether it was spacious or lofty must have been referred to time. The Pythagorean scale of numbers was at once discovered to be perfect; but the poems of Homer we yet know not to transcend the common limits of human intelligence, but by remarking, that nation after nation, and century after century, has been able to do little more than transpose his incidents, new name his characters, and paraphrase his sentiments.

The reverence due to writings that have long subsisted arises therefore not from any credulous confidence in the superior wisdom of past ages, or gloomy persuasion of the degeneracy of mankind, but is the consequence of acknowledged and indubitable positions, that what has been longest known has been most considered, and what is most considered is best understood.

The Poet, of whose works I have undertaken the revision, may now begin to assume the dignity of an ancient, and claim the privilege of established fame and prescriptive veneration. He has long outlived his century, the term commonly fixed as the test of literary merit. Whatever advantages he might once derive from personal allusions, local customs, or temporary opinions, have for many years been lost; and every topick of merriment or motive of sorrow, which the modes of artificial life afforded him, now only obscure the scenes which they once illuminated. The effects of favour and competition are at an end; the tradition of his friendships and his enmities has perished; his works support no opinion with arguments, nor supply any faction with invectives; they can neither indulge vanity nor gratify malignity, but are read without any other reason than the desire of pleasure, and are therefore praised only as pleasure is obtained; yet, thus unassisted by interest of passion, they have past through variations of taste and changes of manners, and, as they devolved from one generation to another, have received new honours at every transmission.

But because human judgment, though it be gradually gaining upon certainty, never becomes infallible; and approbation, though long continued, may yet be only the approbation of prejudice or fashion; it is proper to inquire, by what peculiarities of excellence Shakespeare has gained and kept the favour of his countrymen.

Nothing can please many, and please long, but just representations of general nature. Particular manners can be known to few, and therefore few only can judge how nearly they are copied. The irregular combinations of fanciful invention may delight a-while, by that novelty of which the common satiety of life sends us all in quest; but the pleasures of sudden wonder are soon exhausted, and the mind can only repose on the stability of truth.

Shakespeare is above all writers, at least above all modern writers, the poet of nature; the poet that holds up to his readers a faithful mirrour of manners and of life. His characters are not modified by the customs of particular places, unpractised by the rest of the world; by the peculiarities of studies or professions, which can operate but upon small numbers; or by the accidents of transient fashions or temporary opinions: they are the genuine progeny of common humanity, such as the world will always supply, and observation will always find. His persons act and speak by the influence of those general passions and principles by which all minds are agitated, and whole system of life is continued in motion. In the writings of other poets a character is too often an individual; in those of Shakespeare it is commonly a species.

It is from this wide extension of design that so much instruction is derived. It is this which fills the plays of Shakespeare with practical axioms and domestick wisdom. It was said of Euripides, that every verse was a precept; and it may be said of Shakespeare, that from his works may be collected a sys[t]em of civil and [e]conomical prudence. Yet his real power is not in the splendour of particular passages, but by the progress of his fable, and, the tenour of his dialogue; and he that tries to recommend him by select quotations, will succeed like the pedant in Hierocles, who, when he offered his house to sale, carried a brick in his pocket as a specimen.

It will not easily be imagined how much Shakespeare excells in accommodating his sentiments to real life, but by comparing him with other authours. It was observed of the ancient schools of declamation, that the more diligently they were frequented, the more was the student disquali[f]ed for the world, because he found nothing there which he should ever meet in any other place. The same remark may be applied to every stage but that of Shakespeare. The theatre, when it is under any other direction, is peopled by such characters as were never seen, conversing in a language which was never heard, upon topicks which will never arise in the commerce of mankind. But the dialogue of this authour is often so evidently determined by the incident which produces it, and is pursued with so much ease and simplicity, that it seems scarcely to claim the merit of fiction, but to have been gleaned by diligent selection out of common conversation, and common occurrences.

Upon every other stage the universal agent is love, by whose power all good and evil is distributed, and every action quickened or retarded. To bring a lover, a lady and a rival into the fable; to entangle them in contradictory obligations, perplex them with oppositions of interest, and harass them with violence of desires inconsistent with each other; to make them meet in rapture and part in agony; to fill their mouths with hyperbolical joy and outrageous sorrow; to distress them as nothing human ever was distressed; to deliver them as nothing human ever was delivered, is the business of the modern dramati[st]. For this probability is violated, life is misrepresented, and language is depraved. But love is only one of many passions, and as it has no great influence upon the sum of life, it has little operation in the dramas of a poet, who caught his ideas from the living world, and exhibited only what he saw before him. He knew, that any other passion, as it was regular or exorbitant, was a cause of happiness or calamity.

Characters thus ample and general were not easily discriminated and preserved, yet perhaps no poet ever kept his personages more distinct from each other. I will not say with Pope, that every speech may be assigned to the proper speaker, because many speeches there are which have nothing characteristical; but, perhaps, though some may be equally adapted to every person, it will be difficult to find, any that can be properly transferred from the present possessor to another claimant. The choice is right, when there is reason for choice.

Other dramatists can only gain attention by hyperbolical or aggravated characters, by fabulous and unexampled excellence or depravity, as the writers of barbarous romances invigorated the reader by a giant and a dwarf; and he that should form his expectations of human affairs from the play, or from the tale, would be equally deceived. Shakespeare has no heroes; his scenes are occupied only by men, who act and speak as the reader thinks that he should himself have spoken or acted on the same occasion: Even where the agency is supernatural the dialogue is level with life. Other writers disguise the most natural passions and most frequent incidents; so that he who contemplates them in the book will not know them in the world: Shakespeare approximates the remote, and familiarizes the wonderful; the event which he represents will not happen, but if it were possible, its effects would be probably such as he has assigned; and it may be said, that he has not only shewn human nature as it acts in real exigences, but as it would be found in trials, to which it cannot be

exposed.

This therefore is the praise of Shakespeare, that his drama is the mirrour of life; that he who has mazed his imagination, in following the phantoms which other writers raise up before him, may here be cured of his delirious extasies, by reading human sentiments in human language; by scenes from which a hermit may estimate the transactions of the world, and a confessor predict the progress of the passions.

His adherence to general nature has exposed him to the censure of criticks, who form their judgments upon narrower principles. Dennis and Rhymer think his Romans not sufficiently Roman; and Voltaire censures his kings as not completely royal. Dennis is offended, that Menenius, a senator of Rome, should play the buffoon; and Voltaire perhaps thinks decency violated when the Danish Usurper is represented as a drunkard. But Shakespeare always makes nature predominent over accident; and if he preserves the essential character, is not very careful of distinctions superinduced and adventitious. His story requires Romans and kings, but he thinks only on men. He knew that Rome, like every other city, had men of all dispositions; and wanting a buffoon, he went into the senate-house for that which the senate-house would certainly have afforded him. He was inclined to shew an usurper and a murderer not only odious but despicable, he therefore added drunkenness to his other qualities, knowing that kings love wine like other men, and that wine exerts its natural power upon kings. These are the petty cavils of petty minds; a poet overlooks the casual distinction of country and condition, as a painter, satisfied with the figure, neglects the drapery.

The censure which he has incurred by mixing comick and tragick scenes, as it extends to all his works, deserves more consideration. Let the fact be first stated, and then examined.

Shakespeare's plays are not in the rigorous or critical sense either tragedies or comedies, but compositions of a distinct kind; exhibiting the real state of sublunary nature, which partakes of good and evil, joy and sorrow, mingled with endless variety of proportion and innumerable modes of combination; and expressing the course of the world, in which the loss of one is the gain of another; in which, at the same time, the reveller is hasting to his wine, and the mourner burying his friend; in which the malignity of one is sometimes defeated by the frolick of another; and many mischiefs and many benefits are done and hindered without design.

Out of this chaos of mingled porposes [purposes] and casualties the ancient poets, according to the laws which custom had prescribed, selected some the crimes of men, and some of their absurdities; some the momentous vicissitudes of life, and some the lighter occurrences; some the terrours of distress, and some the gayeties of prosperity. Thus rose the two modes of imitation, known by the names of tragedy and comedy, compositions intended to promote different ends by contrary means, and considered as so little allied, that I do not recollect among the Greeks or Romans a single writer who attempted both.

Shakespeare has united the powers of exciting laughter and sorrow not only in one mind but in one composition. Almost all his plays are divided between serious and ludicrous characters, and, in the successive evolutions of the design, sometimes produce seriousness and sorrow, and sometimes levity and laughter.

That this is a practice contrary to the rules of criticism will be readily allowed; but there is always an appeal open from criticism to nature. The end of writing is to instruct; the end of poetry is to instruct by pleasing. That the mingled drama may convey all the instruction of tragedy or comedy cannot be denied, because it includes both in its alterations of exhibition, an[d] approaches nearer than either to the appearance of life, by shewing how great machinations and slender designs may promote or obviate one another, and the high and the low co-operate in the general system by unavoidable concatenation.

Shakespeare is above all writers, at least above all modern writers, the poet of nature; the poet that holds up to his readers a faithful mirrour of manners and of life.

(www.classicreader.com)

CRITICAL THINKING

A. Carefully read the excerpt above. Johnson seeks to know "by what peculiarities of excellence Shakespeare has gained and kept the favor of his countrymen." What answers does Johnson offer the reader?
B. Compare John Dryden's *An Essay on Dramatic Poesy* with Johnson's "Preface."
C. What does Johnson mean when he refers to Shakespeare as "the poet of nature"?
D. What does Johnson mean when he says that Shakespeare has no heroes?

BIBLICAL APPLICATION

Read Samuel Johnson's poem, "The Vanity of Human

Wishes." What does he tell us about human nature? Compare this view to the biblical witness (especially the book of *Ecclesiastes*).

The Vanity of Human Wishes
The Tenth Satire of Juvenal, Imitated
Let observation with extensive view,
Survey mankind, from China to Peru;
Remark each anxious toil, each eager strife,
And watch the busy scenes of crouded life;
Then say how hope and fear, desire and hate,
O'er spread with snares the clouded maze of fate,
Where wav'ring man, betray'd by vent'rous pride,
To tread the dreary paths without a guide,
As treach'rous phantoms in the mist delude,
Shuns fancied ills, or chases airy good.
How rarely reason guides the stubborn choice,
Rules the bold hand, or prompts the suppliant voice,
How nations sink, by darling schemes oppres'd,
When vengeance listens to the fool's request.
Fate wings with ev'ry wish th' afflictive dart,
Each gift of nature, and each grace of art,
With fatal heat impetuous courage glows,
With fatal sweetness elocution flows,
Impeachment stops the speaker's pow'rful breath,
And restless fire precipitates on death.

But scarce observ'd the knowing and the bold.
Fall in the gen'ral massacre of gold;
Wide-wasting pest! that rages unconfin'd,
And crouds with crimes the records of mankind,
For gold his sword the hireling ruffian draws,
For gold the hireling judge distorts the laws;
Wealth heap'd on wealth, nor truth nor safety buys,
The dangers gather as the treasures rise.

Let hist'ry tell where rival kings command,
And dubious title shakes the madded land,
When statutes glean the refuse of the sword,
How much more safe the vassal than the lord,
Low sculks the hind beneath the rage of pow'r,
And leaves the wealthy traytor in the Tow'r,
Untouch'd his cottage, and his slumbers sound,
Tho' confiscation's vulturs hover round.

The needy traveller, serene and gay,
Walks the wild heath, and sings his toil away.
Does envy seize thee? crush th' upbraiding joy,
Encrease his riches and his peace destroy,
New fears in dire vicissitude invade,
The rustling brake alarms, and quiv'ring shade,

Nor light nor darkness bring his pain relief,
One shews the plunder, and one hides the thief.

Yet still one gen'ral cry the skies assails,
And gain and grandeur load the tainted gales;
Few know the toiling statesman's fear or care,
Th' insidious rival and the gaping heir.
The vanquish'd hero leaves his broken bands,
And shews his miseries in distant lands;
Condemn'd a needy supplicant to wait,
While ladies interpose, and slaves debate.
But did not Chance at length her error mend?
Did no subverted empire mark his end?
Did rival monarchs give the fatal wound?
Or hostile millions press him to the ground?
His fall was destin'd to a barren strand,
A petty fortress, and a dubious hand;
He left the name, at which the world grew pale,
To point a moral, or adorn a tale.

All times their scenes of pompous woes afford,
From Persia's tyrant to Bavaria's lord.
In gay hostility, and barb'rous pride,
With half mankind embattled at his side,
Great Xerxes comes to seize the certain prey,
And starves exhausted regions in his way;
Attendant Flatt'ry counts his myriads o'er,
Till counted myriads sooth his pride no more;
Fresh praise is try'd till madness fires his mind,
The waves he lashes, and enchains the wind;
New pow'rs are claim'd, new pow'rs are still
    bestowed,
Till rude resistance lops the spreading god;
The daring Greeks deride the martial shew,
And heap their vallies with the gaudy foe;
Th' insulted sea with humbler thoughts he gains,
A single skiff to speed his flight remains;
Th' incumber'd oar scarce leaves the dreaded coast
Through purple billows and a floating host.

The bold Bavarian, in a luckless hour,
Tries the dread summits of Cesarean pow'r,
With unexpected legions bursts away,
And sees defenceless realms receive his sway;
Short sway! fair Austria spreads her mournful
    charms,
The queen, the beauty, sets the world in arms;
From hill to hill the beacons rousing blaze
Spreads wide the hope of plunder and of praise;
The fierce Croatian, and the wild Hussar,
And all the sons of ravage croud the war;

The baffled prince in honour's flatt'ring bloom
Of hasty greatness finds the fatal doom,
his foes derision, and his subjects blame,
And steals to death from anguish and from shame.

Enlarge my life with multitude of days,
In health, in sickness, thus the suppliant prays;
Hides from himself his state, and shuns to know,
That life protracted is protracted woe.
Time hovers o'er, impatient to destroy,
And shuts up all the passages of joy:
In vain their gifts the bounteous seasons pour,
The fruit autumnal, and the vernal flow'r,
With listless eyes the dotard views the store,
He views, and wonders that they please no more;
Now pall the tastless meats, and joyless wines,
And luxury with sighs her slave resigns.
Approach, ye minstrels, try the soothing strain,
And yield the tuneful lenitives of pain:
No sounds alas would touch th' impervious ear,
Though dancing mountains witness'd Orpheus near;
Nor lute nor lyre his feeble pow'rs attend,
Nor sweeter musick of a virtuous friend,
But everlasting dictates croud his tongue,
Perversely grave, or positively wrong.
The still returning tale, and ling'ring jest,
Perplex the fawning niece and pamper'd guest,
While growing hopes scarce awe the gath'ring sneer,
And scarce a legacy can bribe to hear;
The watchful guests still hint the last offence,
The daughter's petulance, the son's expence,
Improve his heady rage with treach'rous skill,
And mould his passions till they make his will.

Unnumber'd maladies his joints invade,
Lay siege to life and press the dire blockade;
But unextinguish'd Av'rice still remains,
And dreaded losses aggravate his pains;
He turns, with anxious heart and cripled hands,
His bonds of debt, and mortgages of lands;
Or views his coffers with suspicious eyes,
Unlocks his gold, and counts it till he dies.

But grant, the virtues of a temp'rate prime
Bless with an age exempt from scorn or crime;
An age that melts in unperceiv'd decay,
And glides in modest Innocence away;
Whose peaceful day Benevolence endears,
whose night congratulating Conscience cheers;
The gen'ral fav'rite as the gen'ral friend:
Such age there is, and who could wish its end?

Yet ev'n on this her load Misfortune flings,
To press the weary minutes flagging wings:
New sorrow rises as the day returns,
A sister sickens, or a daughter mourns.
Now kindred Merit fills the sable bier,
Now lacerated Friendship claims a tear.
Year chases year, decay pursues decay,
Still drops some joy from with'ring life away;
New forms arise, and diff'rent views engage,
Superfluous lags the vet'ran on the stage,
Till pitying nature signs the last release,
And bids afflicted worth retire to peace.

But few there are whom hours like these await,
Who set unclouded in the gulphs of fate.
From Lydia's monarch should the search descend,
By Solon caution'd to regard his end,
In life's last scene what prodigies surprise,
Fears of the brave, and follies of the wise?
From Marlb'rough's eyes the streams of dotage flow,
And Swift expires a driv'ler and a show.

The teeming mother, anxious for her race,
Begs for each birth the fortune of a face:
Yet Vane could tell what ills from beauty spring;
And Sedley curs'd the form that pleas'd a king.
Ye nymphs of rosy lips and radiant eyes,
Whom Pleasure keeps too busy to be wise,
Whom Joys with soft varieties invite,
By day the frolick, and the dance by night,
Who frown with vanity, who smile with art,
And ask the latest fashion of the heart,
What care, what rules your heedless charms shall
    save,
Each nymph your rival, and each youth your slave?
Against your fame with fondness hate combines,
The rival batters, and the lover mines.
With distant voice neglected Virtue calls,
Less heard, and less the faint remonstrance falls;
Tir'd with contempt, she quits the slipp'ry reign,

And Pride and Prudence take her seat in vain.
In croud at once, where none the pass defend,
The harmless Freedom, and the private Friend.
The guardians yield, by force superior ply'd;
By Int'rest, Prudence; and by Flatt'ry, Pride.
Now Beauty falls betray'd, despis'd, distress'd,
And hissing Infamy proclaims the rest.

Where then shall Hope and Fear their objects find?
Must dull Suspence corrupt the stagnant mind?
Must helpless man, in ignorance sedate,
Roll darkling down the torrent of his fate?
Must no dislike alarm, no wishes rise,
No cries attempt the mercies of the skies?
Enquirer, cease, petitions yet remain,
Which heav'n may hear, nor deem religion vain.
Still raise for good the supplicating voice,
But leave to heav'n the measure and the choice.
Safe in his pow'r, whose eyes discern afar
The secret ambush of a specious pray'r.
Implore his aid, in his decisions rest,
Secure whate'er he gives, he gives the best.
Yet when the sense of sacred presence fires,
And strong devotion to the skies aspires,
Pour forth thy fervours for a healthful mind,
Obedient passions, and a will resign'd;
For love, which scarce collective man can fill;
For patience sov'reign o'er transmuted ill;
For faith, that panting for a happier seat,
Counts death kind Nature's signal of retreat:
These goods for man the laws of heav'n ordain,
These goods he grants, who grants the pow'r to gain;
With these celestial wisdom calms the mind,
And makes the happiness she does not find.
(www.bartleby.com)

FINAL PROJECT

Correct and rewrite essays and place them in your Final
Portfolio.

SUGGESTED

Weekly *Implementation*

DAY 1	DAY 2	DAY 3	DAY 4	DAY 5
Prayer journal. Review required reading(s) *before* the assigned lesson begins. <u>Teacher and students will decide on required essays for this lesson, choosing two or three essays.</u> <u>The rest of the essays can be outlined, answered with shorter answers, or skipped.</u> Review all readings for Lesson 18.	**Prayer journal.** Review reading(s) from next lesson. Outline essays due at the end of the week. Per teacher instructions, students may answer orally in a group setting some of the essays that are not assigned as formal essays.	**Prayer journal.** Write rough drafts of all assigned essays. The teacher and/or a peer evaluator may correct rough drafts.	**Prayer journal.** Rewrite corrected copies of essays due tomorrow.	**Prayer journal.** Essays are due. Take Lesson 18 test. Reading Ahead: Review *The Rivals*, Richard Brinsley Sheridan. Guide: How does Sheridan create humor in this hilarious play?

The Rivals

Richard Brinsley Sheridan

BACKGROUND

The most highly regarded English playwright of the eighteenth century, Richard Brinsley Sheridan, was born in Dublin on October 31, 1751, and died in London on July 7, 1816. He grew up in a family with theatrical connections and received his formal education at Harrow. In 1772 he eloped to the Continent with Elizabeth Linley, a singer, and married her the following year. What a scandal! His first play, *The Rivals* (1775), a comedy mixing action and romantic sentimentality, was followed by *St. Patrick's Day*, a two-act farce, and *The Duenna*, a comic opera, both of which appeared later in 1775; all were milestones in British high comedy.

CRITICAL THINKING

A. *The Rivals* is a play about the mischievous, unexpected, and ever-present power of love. The two plots that form the structure of the play mirror each other and thereby amplify this thematic idea. In other words, Sheridan skillfully tells two stories at once. Where and when these two stories meet creates humor. Using this theme as a guide, identify the play's main plot and the various subplots as they have evolved by Act II.

B. Compare and contrast the love affair of Julia and Faulkland with the love affair of Lydia and Absolute.

C. Why does Bob Acres poorly represent a gentleman?

D. In *The Rivals* Sheridan gives names for his characters that are similar to the names Bunyan gives his characters in *Pilgrim's Progress*. One character is called Absolute. One lives in *Blunderbuss Hall*. What is an advantage of using this device? What are the disadvantages? Why is this device not used today?

E. Why are you satisfied or dissatisfied with the ending of the play? Are all the questions resolved?

F. What word did Sheridan's play *The Rivals* contribute to the English language?

FINAL PROJECT

Correct and rewrite essays and place them in your Final Portfolio.

Analyze: *The Rivals*, Richard Brinsley Sheridan.

Reading Ahead: Review "A Man's a Man for A' That," Robert Burns; "How Sweet I Roam'd from Field to Field," "And Did Those Feet in Ancient Time," "The Clod and the Pebble," "The Lamb," and "The Tyger," William Blake.

Guide Question: What is the Romantic vision of life that emerges in the early nineteenth century?

SUGGESTED

Weekly *Implementation*

DAY 1	DAY 2	DAY 3	DAY 4	DAY 5
Prayer journal.	**Prayer journal.**	**Prayer journal.**	**Prayer journal.**	**Prayer journal.**
Review required reading(s) *before* the assigned lesson begins.	Review reading(s) from next lesson.	Write rough drafts of all assigned essays.	Rewrite corrected copies of essays due tomorrow.	Essays are due.
<u>Teacher and students will decide on required essays for this lesson, choosing two or three essays.</u>	Outline essays due at the end of the week.	The teacher and/or a peer evaluator may correct rough drafts.		Take Lesson 19 test.
<u>The rest of the essays can be outlined, answered with shorter answers, or skipped.</u>	Per teacher instructions, students may answer orally in a group setting some of the essays that are not assigned as formal essays.			Reading Ahead: Review "A Man's a Man for A' That," Robert Burns; "How Sweet I Roam'd from Field to Field," "And Did Those Feet in Ancient Time," "The Clod and the Pebble," "The Lamb," and "The Tyger," William Blake.
Review all readings for Lesson 19.				Guide: What is the Romantic vision of life that emerges in the early nineteenth century?

Robert Burns

BACKGROUND

Robert Burns was born on January 25, 1759, into the family of a poor, subsistence farmer in the highlands of rural Scotland. His first published work was *Poems, Chiefly in the Scottish Dialect* (1786), printed in the small town of Kilmarnock. This work, which contains most of his poems, was expanded in 1787 and again in 1793. In 1789 he obtained the post of excise man, or inspector, but his heavy drinking had ruined his health, and he died July 21, 1796. Because of his indigenous writings, many Scottish people still revere Burns.

Analyze: "A Man's a Man for A' That," Robert Burns; "How Sweet I Roam'd from Field to Field," "And Did Those Feet in Ancient Time," "The Clod and the Pebble," "The Lamb," and "The Tyger," William Blake.

Reading Ahead: "A Song," Helen Maria Williams; "A Slumber Did My Spirit Seal," "To the Cuckoo," "London 1802," "My Heart Leaps Up When I Behold," "To a Sky-Lark," "Strange Fits of Passion Have I Known," "The Tables Turned," "Composed upon Westminster Bridge, September 3, 1802," and "Lines Written in Early Spring," William Wordsworth; from *The Grasmere Journals*, Dorothy Wordsworth.

Guide Question: Contrast Romantic poetry with Elizabethan poetry.

CRITICAL THINKING

Read these poems by Robert Burns and answer the questions that follow.

A Man's a Man for A' That

Is there for honest poverty
That hings his head, an a' that?
The coward slave, we pass him by —
We dare be poor for a' that!
For a' that, an a' that,
Our toils obscure, an a' that,
The rank is but the guinea's stamp,
The man's the gowd for a' that.

What though on hamely fare we dine,
Wear hoddin grey, an a' that?
Gie fools their silks, and knaves their wine —
A man's a man for a' that.
For a' that, an a' that.
Their tinsel show, an a' that,
The honest man, tho e'er sae poor,

Is king o' men for a' that.

Ye see you birkie ca'd a lord,
What struts, an stares, an a' that?
Tho hundreds worship at his word,
He's but a cuif for a' that.
For a' that, an a' that,
His ribband, star, an a' that,
The man o' independent mind,
He looks and laughs at a' that.

A prince can mak' a belted knight,
A marquis, duke, an' a' that;
But an honest man's aboon this might,
Guid faith he mauna fa' that!
For a' that, an' a' that,
Their dignities, an' a' that,
The pit o' sense, an' pride o' worth,
Are higher rank than a' that.

Then let us pray that come it may,

And come it will for a' that,
That sense and worth, o'er a' the earth,
May bear the gree, and a' that.
For a' that, an' a' that,
It's coming yet, for a' that,
That man to man, the warld o'er,
Shall brothers be for a' that.
(http://www.dgdclynx.plus.com/poetry/poets/man.html)

O, My Luve Is Like a Red, Red Rose

O, my luve is like a red, red rose,
That's newly sprung in June!
O, my luve is like a melodie,
That's sweetly play'd in tune.

As fair art thou, my bonie lass,
So deep in luve am I,
And I will luve thee still, my dear,
(http://www.bartleby.com/101/503.html)

Till a' the seas gang dry—

Till a' the seas gang dry, my dear,
And the rocks melt wi the sun!
And I will luve thee still, my dear,
While the sands o' life shall run.

And fare thee weel, my only luve!
And fare thee weel, a while!
And I will come again, my luve,
Tho it were ten thousand mile!
(http://www.bartleby.com/101/503.html)

To a Mouse

Wee sleekit, cow'rin, tim'rous beastie,
O, what a panic's in thy breastie!
Thou need na start awa sae hasty,
Wi' bickering brattle!
I wad be laith to rin an chase thee,
Wi' murdering pattle!

I'm truly sorry man's dominion
Has broken Nature's social union,
An' justifies that ill opinion,
Which makes thee startle
At me, thy poor, earth-born companion.
An' fellow mortal!

I doubt na, whyles, but thou may thieve:
What then? poor beastie, thou maun live!
A daimen icker in a thrave

'S a sma' request;
I'll get a blessin wi' the lave,
An' never miss't!

Thy wee-bit housie, too, in ruin!
Its silly wa's the win's are strewin!
An naething, now, to big a new ane,
O' foggage green!
An' bleak December's win's ensuin.
Baith snell an' keen!

Thou saw the fields laid bare an' waste,
An' weary winter comin fast.
An' cozie here, beneath the blast,
Thou thought to dwell—
Till crash! the cruel coulter past
Out thro' thy cell.

That wee bit heap o' leaves an stibble,
Has cost thee monie a weary nibble!
Now thou's turn'd out, for a' thy trouble.
But house or hald,
To thole the winter's sleety dribble,
An' cranreuch cauld!

But Mousie, thou art no thy lane,
In proving foresight may be vain:
The best-laid schemes o' mice an' men
Gang aft agley,
An' lea'e us nought but grief an' pain,
For promis'd joy!

Still thou art blest, compar'd wi' me!
The present only toucheth thee:
But, och! I backward cast my e'e,
On prospects drear!
An' forward, tho' I canna see,
I guess an' fear!
(http://www.electricscotland.com/burns/mouse.html)

A. Burns is quite an anomaly. He is difficult to place in
    any category. In a two-page essay, describe two or
    three salient points about Burns' poems. Compare
    Burns' poems with other eighteenth-century
    poems.
B. "A Man's a Man" was written in response to the
    French Revolution. What sort of political ideas
    does Burns challenge?

William Blake

In his writings and paintings, William Blake, a visionary English poet and artist, anticipated English Romanticism (a literary movement that emphasized the extraordinary and extolled Nature). He was born on November 28, 1757. A home-schooler, Blake at age ten was sent to an art school. Later he was apprenticed to an artist. He exhibited his first artwork in 1780, but his real gifts lay in writing poetry. He married Catherine Boucher in 1782 and published his first poems, *Poetical Sketches*, in 1783.

How Sweet I Roam'd from Field to Field

(http://eir.library.utoronto.ca/rpo/display/poem195.html)

How sweet I roam'd from field to field,
And tasted all the summer's pride,
'Till I the prince of love beheld,
Who in the sunny beams did glide!

He shew'd me lilies for my hair,
And blushing roses for my brow;
He led me through his gardens fair,
Where all his golden pleasures grow.

With sweet May dews my wings were wet,
And Phoebus fir'd my vocal rage;
He caught me in his silken net,
And shut me in his golden cage.

He loves to sit and hear me sing,
Then, laughing, sports and plays with me;
Then stretches out my golden wing,
And mocks my loss of liberty.

And Did Those Feet in Ancient Time?
(from the Preface to "Milton")

(http://eir.library.utoronto.ca/rpo/display/poem187.html)

And did those feet in ancient time
Walk upon England's mountains green?
And was the holy Lamb of God
On England's pleasant pastures seen?

And did the Countenance Divine
Shine forth upon our clouded hills?
And was Jerusalem builded here
Among these dark Satanic mills?

Bring me my bow of burning gold:
Bring me my arrows of desire:
Bring me my spear: O clouds unfold!
Bring me my chariot of fire.

I will not cease from mental fight,
Nor shall my sword sleep in my hand
Till we have built Jerusalem
In England's green and pleasant land.

The Clod and the Pebble

(http://eir.library.utoronto.ca/rpo/display/poem166.html)

"Love seeketh not itself to please,
Nor for itself hath any care,
But for another gives its ease,
And builds a Heaven in Hell's despair."

So sung a little Clod of Clay
Trodden with the cattle's feet,
But a Pebble of the brook
Warbled out these metres meet:

"Love seeketh only self to please,
To bind another to its delight,
Joys in another's loss of ease,
And builds a Hell in Heaven's despite."

The Lamb

(http://eir.library.utoronto.ca/rpo/display/poem181.html)
Little Lamb, who made thee?
Dost thou know who made thee?
Gave thee life, and bid thee feed
By the stream and o'er the mead;
Gave thee clothing of delight,
Softest clothing, woolly, bright;
Gave thee such a tender voice,
Making all the vales rejoice?
Little Lamb, who made thee?
Dost thou know who made thee?

Little Lamb, I'll tell thee,
Little Lamb, I'll tell thee:
He is called by thy name,
For he calls himself a Lamb.
He is meek, and he is mild;

He became a little child.
I a child, and thou a lamb.
We are called by his name.
Little Lamb, God bless thee!
Little Lamb, God bless thee!

The Tyger

(http://eir.library.utoronto.ca/rpo/display/poem198.html)

Tyger! Tyger! burning bright
In the forests of the night,
What immortal hand or eye
Could frame thy fearful symmetry?

In what distant deeps or skies
Burnt the fire of thine eyes?
On what wings dare he aspire?
What the hand dare seize the fire?

And what shoulder, and what art,
Could twist the sinews of thy heart,
And when thy heart began to beat,
What dread hand? and what dread feet?

What the hammer? what the chain?
In what furnace was thy brain?
What the anvil? what dread grasp
Dare its deadly terrors clasp?

When the stars threw down their spears,
And water'd heaven with their tears,
Did he smile his work to see?
Did he who made the Lamb make thee?

Tyger! Tyger! burning bright
In the forests of the night,
What immortal hand or eye,
Dare frame thy fearful symmetry?

BIBLICAL APPLICATION

A. Who is the speaker in "The Lamb"? Considering the fact that Blake clearly was not a Christian, what point is he making?

B. Blake created little unique mythology. He employed Christian narratives and metaphors without really understanding or believing them. As a result, William Blake exhibits a confused worldview. By identifying his worldview in his poetry, discover the real William Blake. In your opinion what is his faith?

CRITICAL THINKING

A. Compare the symbolism used in "The Lamb" and "The Tyger."

B. In "And Did Those Feet?" how well do the last two stanzas answer the first two stanzas?

C. Most likely, Blake did not fully comprehend Milton's Puritan vision. If he did, he could not have agreed with Milton because Blake and Milton had entirely opposite worldviews. Blake thought that man is basically good and was only the victim of bad judgment in the Garden of Eden. If anything, God was cruel for placing his creation in such a tempting place. The problem was not eating the fruit—but God's overreaction. Experiences—even bad ones—are inherently good to Blake. To Blake, then, Satan is not such a bad fellow. He was merely responding to a *natural* impulse to find *self-fulfillment*. Rebellion was a natural and inevitable human response to theistic authority. Milton labored under no such delusion. He openly embraced orthodox notions of good and evil. Identify some of Blake's views about human responsibility and about good and evil in his poems.

D. Write a comparison/contrast essay of Blake's poems presented in this lesson, focusing on tone, symbolism, and rhythm.

ENRICHMENT

Poetry in the nineteenth century wandered into areas where no writer had yet wandered: the whole Classical/Theistic worldview was under attack. As William Wordsworth wrote:

A sense sublime
Of something far more deeply interfused,
Whose dwelling is the light of setting suns,
And the round ocean and the living air,
And the blue sky, and in the mind of man.
(http://www.online-
literature.com/quotes/quotation_search.php?autho
r=William%20Wordsworth)

By its very nature, poetic imagery links human thoughts and emotions intimately with the external world. Poetry in English and American cultures has invited artists and writers to embrace various kinds of heresies (akin to contemporary New Age religions). Reading critically in current cultures is a necessity. Within Romanticism there is a tendency to believe that the soul pervades all matter. The full development of this feeling is a heresy called *pantheism*. Pantheism argues that deity is in everything and is everywhere. This belief became explicit among the Romantics and among various poets of other times. Examine the examples below for half-truths/lies and then state the truth.

William Blake (1757–1827)

God only Acts and Is, in existing beings or Men.
(in "The Marriage of Heaven and Hell" [1793])

The Lie:

The Truth:

William Wordsworth (1770–1850)

And I have felt
a presence that disturbs me with the joy
Of elevated thoughts; a sense sublime
Of something far more deeply interfused,
Whose dwelling is the light of setting suns,
And the round ocean and the living air,
And the blue sky, and in the mind of man:
A motion and a spirit, that impels
All thinking things, all objects of all thought,
And rolls through all things. Therefore am I still
A lover of the meadows and the woods,
And mountains; and of all that we behold
From this green earth. . . .
(from "Tintern Abbey," lines 93–105 [1798])

The Lie:

The Truth:

Samuel Taylor Coleridge (1772–1834)

At once the Soul of each, and God of all . . .
O! the one Life within us and abroad,
Which meets all motion and becomes its soul,
A light in sound, a sound-like power in light,
Rhythm in thought, and joyance everywhere –
Methinks, it should have been impossible
Not to love all things in a world so filled. . .
And what if all of animated nature
Be but organic harps diversely framed,
That tremble into thought, as o'er them sweeps
Plastic and vast, one intellectual breeze,
At once the Soul of each, and God of all.
(from "The Eoliean Harp" [1795–1817])

[To his baby sleeping in a cradle: Coleridge hopes for a better future for her than his own childhood in the city.]

But thou my babe! shalt wander like a breeze
By lakes and sandy shores, beneath the crags
Of ancient mountain, and beneath the clouds,
Which image in their bulk both lakes and shores
And mountain crags: so shalt thou see and hear
The lovely shapes and sounds intelligible
Of that eternal language, which thy God
Utters, who from eternity doth teach
Himself in all, and all things in himself.
(from "Frost at Midnight" [1798])

The Lie:

The Truth:

Alfred, Lord Tennyson (1809–1892)

The sun, the moon, the stars, the seas, the hills and the
    plains —
Are not these, O Soul, the Vision of Him who reigns?

Is not the Vision He? tho' He be not that which he
    seems?
Dreams are true while they last, and do we not live in
    dreams?

Earth, these solid stars, this weight of body and limb,
Are they not sign and symbol of thy division from
    Him?

Dark is the world to thee: thyself art the reason why;
For is He not all but that which has power to feel "I
    am I"?

Glory about thee, without thee; and thou fulfillest thy
    doom
Making him broken gleams, and a stifled splendour
    and gloom.

Speak to Him thou for He hears, and Spirit with
    Spirit can meet —
Closer is he than breathing, and nearer than hands
    and feet.

God is law, say the wise; O Soul, and let us rejoice,
For if he is thunder by law the thunder is yet his
    voice.
(from "The Higher Pantheism" [1870])

Flower in the crannied wall,
I pluck you out of the crannies,

I hold you here, root and all, in my hand,
Little flower - but if I could understand
What you are, root and all, and all in all,
I should know what God and man is.
(from "The Princess")

Hallowed be thy name—Halleluiah!—
Infinite ideality!
Immeasurable Reality!
Infinite Personality!
Hallowed be thy name—Halleluiah!
We feel we are nothing—for all is Thou and in Thee;
We feel we are something—that also has come from
    thee;
We know we are nothing—but Thou wilt help us to
    be.
Hallowed be thy name—Halleluiah!
(from "The Human Cry")

The Lie:

The Truth:

Oscar Wilde (1854–1900)

We are resolved into the supreme air,
We are made one with what we touch and see,
With our heart's blood each crimson sun is fair,
With our young lives each spring-impassioned tree
Flames into green, the wildest beasts that range
The moor our kinsmen are, all life is one, and all is
    change.

With beat of systole and of diastole
One grand great life throbs through earth's giant
    heart,
And mighty waves of single Being roll
From nerve-less germ to man, for we are part
Of every rock and bird and beast and hill,
One with the things that prey on us, and one with
    what we kill. . . .

One sacrament are consecrate, the earth
Not we alone hath passions hymeneal,
The yellow buttercups that shake for mirth

At daybreak know a pleasure not less real
Than we do, when in some fresh-blossoming wood
We draw the spring into our hearts, and feel that life
    is good. . . .

Is the light vanished from our golden sun,
Or is this daedal-fashioned earth less fair,
That we are nature's heritors, and one
With every pulse of life that beats the air?
Rather new suns across the sky shall pass,
New splendour come unto the flower, new glory to the
    grass.

And we two lovers shall not sit afar,
Critics of nature, but the joyous sea
Shall be our raiment, and the bearded star
Shoot arrows at our pleasure! We shall be
Part of the mighty universal whole,
And through all Aeons mix and mingle with the
    Kosmic Soul!

We shall be notes in that great Symphony
Whose cadence circles through the rhythmic spheres,
And all the live World's throbbing heart shall be
One with our heart, the stealthy creeping years
Have lost their terrors now, we shall not die,
The Universe itself shall be our Immortality!
(from "We Are Made One with What We Touch and
    See")

The Lie:

The Truth:

FINAL PROJECT

Correct and rewrite essays and place them in your Final
Portfolio.

SUGGESTED
Weekly *Implementation*

DAY 1	DAY 2	DAY 3	DAY 4	DAY 5
Prayer journal.	**Prayer journal.**	**Prayer journal.**	**Prayer journal.**	**Prayer journal.**
Review required reading(s) *before* the assigned lesson begins.	Review reading(s) from next lesson.	Write rough drafts of all assigned essays.	Rewrite corrected copies of essays due tomorrow.	Essays are due.
Teacher and students will decide on required essays for this lesson, choosing two or three essays.	Outline essays due at the end of the week.	The teacher and/or a peer evaluator may correct rough drafts.		Take Lesson 20 test.
The rest of the essays can be outlined, answered with shorter answers, or skipped.	Per teacher instructions, students may answer orally in a group setting some of the essays that are not assigned as formal essays.			Reading Ahead: "A Song," Helen Maria Williams; "A Slumber Did My Spirit Seal," "To the Cuckoo," "London 1802," "My Heart Leaps Up When I Behold," "To a Sky-Lark," "Strange Fits of Passion Have I Known," "The Tables Turned," "Composed upon Westminster Bridge, September 3, 1802," and "Lines Written in Early Spring," William Wordsworth; from *The Grasmere Journals*, Dorothy Wordsworth.
Review all readings for Lesson 20				Guide: Contrast Romantic poetry with Elizabethan poetry.

LESSON 21

NINETEENTH CENTURY *(Part 1)*

The Nineteenth Century

BACKGROUND

The nineteenth century in England was what Prime Minister Disraeli called a time of "two nations," meaning that it was a time of revolution and conflict. In the nineteenth century England was a very poor nation, exploited by the industrial revolution; however, it was also a very rich England, enriched by the industrial revolution. Meanwhile, Romanticism, begun by the writings of William Blake who had transfigured English literature, was already in evidence. In 1798, Samuel Taylor Coleridge and William Wordsworth rejected what they called the pretension of earlier eighteenth-century verse. As a young man, Wordsworth had been deeply stirred by a visit (1791–92) to revolutionary France. Human Nature, he felt, had been reborn; to be young was "very Heaven." The keynotes of Romantic poetry were its cult of youth and freedom, its reliance on the sovereign force of love, and its sense of a close relationship with Nature, which many eighteenth-century poets had tended to regard as merely a decorative background designed to enhance the activities of man. Now, the subject of English writing was Nature, not man.

Helen Maria Williams

Helen Maria Williams (1762-1827) was one of the best, if basically unknown, English poets of the early nineteenth century—arguably the greatest sonnet writer of the nineteenth century. Admired by William Wordsworth, her sonnets championed the anti-slavery movement. She is described as "an incisive observer, an astute commentator, and a sophisticated expatriate . . . a pioneering woman journalist who mediated between two cultures with subtlety and verve." (*Norton Anthology of Literature by Women*, p. 276). Williams was sympathetic to the principles of the French Revolution, and her letters "attracted attention because of their emotional immediacy and because of her personal engagement in political events." The following poem, "A

Analyze: "A Song," Helen Maria Williams; "A Slumber Did My Spirit Seal," "To the Cuckoo," "London 1802," "My Heart Leaps Up When I Behold," "To a Sky-Lark," "Strange Fits of Passion Have I Known," "The Tables Turned," "Composed upon Westminster Bridge, September 3, 1802," and "Lines Written in Early Spring," William Wordsworth; from *The Grasmere Journals*, Dorothy Wordsworth.

Reading Ahead: *Vindication of the Rights of Women*, Mary Wollstonecraft; "Don Juan" and "The Prisoner of Chillon," Lord Byron; "Kubla Khan" and "The Rime of the Ancient Mariner," Samuel Taylor Coleridge; "Ozymandias" and "To a Skylark," Percy Bysshe Shelley; "Bright Star," "Ode to a Nightingale," "Posthuma," and "Ode on a Grecian Urn," John Keats.

Guide Question: What nuances emerge from Romantic themes?

Song," represents her early poems, characterized by critic Mary Favret as "initial dependence on sentimental and romantic fictions" that eventually served as "registers for political rather than emotional turbulence. They become the instruments probing the inner workings of power structures." (p. 276)

A Song

I.

No riches from his scanty shore
My lover could impart;
He gave a boon I valued more — —
He gave me all his heart!

II.

His soul sincere, his gen'rous worth,
Might well this bosom move;
And when I ask'd for bliss on earth,
I only meant his love.

III.

127

But now for me, in search of gain
From shore to shore he flies:
Why wander riches to obtain,
When love is all I prize!

               IV.
The frugal meal, the lowly cot
If blest my love with thee!
That simple fare, that humble lot,
Were more than wealth to me.

               V.
While he the dang'rous ocean braves,
My tears but vainly flow:
Is pity in the faithless waves
To which I pour my woe?

               VI.
The night is dark, the waters deep,
Yet soft the billows roll;
Alas! at every breeze I weep——
The storm is in my soul.
(http://www.english.upenn.edu/~mgamer/Etexts/willia
ms.html)

CRITICAL THINKING

A. What is the central metaphor that Williams employs in this sonnet?
B. Find evidence in "A Song" that intimates the insights that would eventually bring Williams' works recognition in the political arena. Explain the modernity of this sonnet.

CRITICAL THINKING

A. Define these concepts: Romanticism, Victorian novel, Naturalism.
B. Compare and contrast the major themes of the eighteenth and nineteenth centuries.
C. Analyze the causes of the English urban crisis that Charles Dickens so powerfully portrayed in his novel *Oliver Twist*.

ENRICHMENT

"A Slumber Did My Spirit Seal" is the last of the so-called "Lucy poems," which center upon an imaginary girl in the English countryside. The poem is about death, but the last two lines redefine death altogether. How so?

William Wordsworth

BACKGROUND

Born at Cockermouth, Cumberland, April 7, 1770,
    William Wordsworth, perhaps the greatest of English Romantic poets, died April 23, 1850. He did much to restore simple language to English poetry and to establish Romanticism as the era's dominant literary move-ment. Romanticism was an intellectual movement that flourished in Europe between the mid-eighteenth and mid-nineteenth centuries. It celebrated the nationalistic movements that put the last nails into the coffins of European feudalism. The Enlightenment was urban-based, stressing the normative role of reason in the con-duct of social life and universal standards for excellence in the arts. Romanticism, a rural, country movement, may be considered as a counter-Enlightenment move-ment. The Enlightenment was grounded in difference rather than uniformity. Enlightenment scholars assumed that mankind is essentially similar across all ages and geographic origins. Romantics generally believed in the uniqueness of individual expression as it is constituted by life experience, an important dimension of which is fre-quently manifested as nationalism. Wordsworth's verse celebrates the moral influence exerted by Nature on human thought and feeling. He changed a great deal dur-ing his lifetime. A restless revolutionary in his younger days, Wordsworth died as a rigid ultra-conservative!

CRITICAL THINKING

Read the following poems by William Wordsworth.

London, 1802

(http://www.bartleby.com/145/ww219.html)

Milton! thou should'st be living at this hour:
England hath need of thee: she is a fen
Of stagnant waters: altar, sword, and pen,
Fireside, the heroic wealth of hall and bower,
Have forfeited their ancient English dower
Of inward happiness. We are selfish men;
Oh! raise us up, return to us again;

And give us manners, virtue, freedom, power.
Thy soul was like a Star, and dwelt apart:
Thou hadst a voice whose sound was like the sea:
Pure as the naked heavens, majestic, free,
So didst thou travel on life's common way,
In cheerful godliness; and yet thy heart
The lowliest duties on herself did lay.

A Slumber Did My Spirit Seal

(http://www.bartleby.com/145/ww150.html)

A slumber did my spirit seal;
I had no human fears:
She seemed a thing that could not feel
The touch of earthly years.

No motion has she now, no force;
She neither hears nor sees;
Rolled round in earth's diurnal course,
With rocks, and stones, and trees.

My heart Leaps Up when I Behold
My heart leaps up when I behold
A rainbow in the sky:
So was it when my life began;
So is it now I am a man;
So be it when I shall grow old,
Or let me die!
The Child is father of the Man;
I could wish my days to be
Bound each to each by natural piety.

To the Cuckoo

(http://www.bartleby.com/145/ww258.html)

O blithe New-comer! I have heard,
I hear thee and rejoice.
O Cuckoo! shall I call thee Bird,
Or but a wandering Voice?

While I am lying on the grass
Thy twofold shout I hear,
From hill to hill it seems to pass,
At once far off, and near.

Though babbling only to the Vale,
Of sunshine and of flowers,
Thou bringest unto me a tale
Of visionary hours.

Thrice welcome, darling of the Spring!
Even yet thou art to me
No bird, but an invisible thing,
A voice, a mystery;

The same whom in my school-boy days
I listened to; that Cry
Which made me look a thousand ways
In bush, and tree, and sky.

To seek thee did I often rove
Through woods and on the green;
And thou wert still a hope, a love;
Still longed for, never seen.

And I can listen to thee yet;
Can lie upon the plain
And listen, till I do beget
That golden time again.

O blessed Bird! the earth we pace
Again appears to be
An unsubstantial, faery place;
That is fit home for Thee!

To a Skylark

(http://www.bartleby.com/145/ww272.html)

Up with me! up with me into the clouds!
For thy song, Lark, is strong;
Up with me, up with me into the clouds!
Singing, singing,
With clouds and sky about thee ringing,
Lift me, guide me till I find
That spot which seems so to thy mind!

I have walked through wildernesses dreary
And to-day my heart is weary;
Had I now the wings of a Faery,
Up to thee would I fly.
There is madness about thee, and joy divine
In that song of thine;
Lift me, guide me high and high
To thy banqueting-place in the sky.

Joyous as morning
Thou art laughing and scorning;
Thou hast askest for thy love and thy rest,
And, though little troubled with sloth,
Drunken Lark! thou would'st be loth
To be such a traveller as I.

Happy, happy Liver,
With a soul as strong as a mountain river
Pouring out praise to the Almighty Giver,
Joy and jollity be with us both!

Alas! my journey, rugged and uneven,
Through prickly moors or dusty ways must wind;
But hearing thee, or others of thy kind,
As full of gladness and as free of heaven,
I, with my fate contented, will plod on,
And hope for higher raptures, when life's day is done.

Composed upon Westminster Bridge, Sept. 3, 1802

(http://www.bartleby.com/145/ww206.html)

Earth has not anything to show more fair:
Dull would he be of soul who could pass by
A sight so touching in its majesty:
This City now doth, like a garment, wear
The beauty of the morning; silent, bare,
Ships, towers, domes, theatres, and temples lie
Open unto the fields, and to the sky;
All bright and glittering in the smokeless air.
Never did sun more beautifully steep
In his first splendour, valley, rock, or hill;
Ne'er saw I, never felt, a calm so deep!
The river glideth at his own sweet will:
Dear God! the very houses seem asleep;
And all that mighty heart is lying still!

Strange Fits of Passion Have I Known

(http://www.bartleby.com/145/ww146.html)

Strange fits of passion have I known:
And I will dare to tell,
But in the Lover's ear alone,
What once to me befell.

When she I loved looked every day
Fresh as a rose in June,
I to her cottage bent my way,
Beneath an evening-moon.

Upon the moon I fixed my eye,
All over the wide lea;
With quickening pace my horse drew nigh
Those paths so dear to me.

And now we reached the orchard-plot;
And, as we climbed the hill,

The sinking moon to Lucy's cot
Came near, and nearer still.

In one of those sweet dreams I slept,
Kind Nature's gentlest boon!
And all the while my eyes I kept
On the descending moon.

My horse moved on; hoof after hoof
He raised, and never stopped:
When down behind the cottage roof,
At once, the bright moon dropped.

What fond and wayward thoughts will slide
Into a Lover's head!
"O mercy!" to myself I cried,
"If Lucy should be dead!"

The Tables Turned

(http://www.bartleby.com/145/ww134.html)

An Evening Scene on the Same Subject
Up! up! my Friend, and quit your books;
Or surely you'll grow double:
Up! up! my Friend, and clear your looks;
Why all this toil and trouble?

The sun, above the mountain's head,
A freshening lustre mellow
Through all the long green fields has spread,
His first sweet evening yellow.

Books! 'tis a dull and endless strife:
Come, hear the woodland linnet,
How sweet his music! on my life,
There's more of wisdom in it.

And hark! how blithe the throstle sings!
He, too, is no mean preacher:
Come forth into the light of things,
Let Nature be your teacher.

She has a world of ready wealth,
Our minds and hearts to bless —
Spontaneous wisdom breathed by health,
Truth breathed by cheerfulness.

One impulse from a vernal wood
May teach you more of man,
Of moral evil and of good,
Than all the sages can.

Sweet is the lore which Nature brings;
Our meddling intellect
Misshapes the beauteous forms of things:—
We murder to dissect.

Enough of Science and of Art;
Close up those barren leaves;
Come forth, and bring with you a heart
That watches and receives.

Lines Written in Early Spring

(http://www.bartleby.com/145/ww130.html)

I heard a thousand blended notes,
While in a grove I sate reclined,
In that sweet mood when pleasant thoughts
Bring sad thoughts to the mind.

To her fair works did Nature link
The human soul that through me ran;
And much it grieved my heart to think
What man has made of man.

Through primrose tufts, in that green bower,
The periwinkle trailed its wreaths;
And 'tis my faith that every flower
Enjoys the air it breathes.

The birds around me hopped and played,
Their thoughts I cannot measure:
But the least motion which they made
It seemed a thrill of pleasure.

The budding twigs spread out their fan,
To catch the breezy air;
And I must think, do all I can,
That there was pleasure there.

If this belief from heaven be sent,
If such be Nature's holy plan,
Have I not reason to lament
What man has made of man?

A. In "Lines Written in Early Spring," Wordsworth experiences several feelings. From the text give several examples of feelings.
B. When juxtaposed against Nature, how does mankind fare in this poem?
C. Among these poems, find as many expressions of positive emotion as you can. Write them down. What sort of pleasure does Wordsworth most enjoy?

D. "The Tables Turned" is a rebuttal to a critic's charge that Wordsworth was too abstract. What arguments does Wordsworth offer to rebuke his critic? What is most important to Wordsworth?
E. "London, 1802" was a moment of great disillusionment and distress for Wordsworth. His Romantic hero, Napoléon Bonaparte, had turned his back on libertarian values and proclaimed himself emperor. In his time of despair, why would Wordsworth turn to Milton?

BIBLICAL APPLICATION

Does "Composed upon Westminster Bridge" celebrate the human city or Nature?

Dorothy Wordsworth

Dorothy Wordsworth (1777-1855) was the younger sister of poet William Wordsworth, and she wrote prose with as much alacrity as her famous brother wrote poetry! Her most famous prose is to be found in her journals which she undertook to give her brother pleasure. Her journal entries capture the Wordsworths rural life intertwined with their literary world. Her brother considered that she "preserved me still a Poet" during times of personal crisis (*Norton Anthology of Literature by Women*, p. 318). From September 1795 until William's death in April 1850, Dorothy Wordsworth lived with her brother, where she became "a fond nurse to his children" and for whom "she wrote some accomplished verses" (p. 319). The following is one of her journal entry from *The Grasmere Journals*, Easter, 1802.

Oh William, William! You drive me to the very edge of distraction! How worthless it now seems, those agreements we had to adjourn Northward amid the rolling Grasmere greenhills, to start a New Life together away from all the hurly-burly of the literary set. In almost nine months thus far at Dove Cottage I have scarcely ventured further than Ambleside, even less up to where my heart truly lies—no races!—the steeps and summit ridges of Fairfield, Dollywagon Pike, Loughrigg Fell. Why, only recently I heard tell of a noble and fear-inducing ridge, one "Striding Edge", leading straight unto the summit cairn of high Helvellyn, yet I fear the day will never come to test myself against, its castellations.

All Wm. ever wishes is to write, write, write. Flowers and clouds, pastures and peasants, gods and goddesses... All well and good, I say, we need to earn a crust, but you promised... Promised to assist old Mister

Snape in repairing the roof, promised to refrain from partaking of substances with Southey, Coleridge and all the rest, promised to plant a few daffs in the garden rather than simply musing upon them. But no! Tomorrow, he says, tomorrow you may gird your skirts and venture forth. If only tomorrow would ever come!

And Coleridge! I fear he will not live to see the year's end. Only recently I hear his wanderings—which I envy greatly, though not so much as to wish to accompany his more risk-stricken jaunts—took him atop Sca Fell by a route most death-defying. By a slab named Broad Stand they say he returned, his mind quite addled by eastern intoxicants. He cannot surely cheat Death so often and so casually. At least my dear Wm stays tethered to his books and beloved Rydal Water.

But as for me... Our neighbour Beatrix tells of a town clerk in distant Kendal, Alfred Wheelwright or some such name, who has commenced compiling a "guide book" of the Lakeland heights. If only William would turn his gills to something similar, we could both perhaps find pleasure. But no, he will not listen. He has ears only for his Muse. Oft-times I despair of men. (http://bubl.ac.uk/org/tacit/tac/tac17/index.html) in The Angry Corrie, No. 17, Feb.-March 1994)

CRITICAL THINKING

Journals are highly personal, often sentimental recordings of ordinary events. However, Wordsworth's journal entries are different. What makes them different?

FINAL PORTFOLIO

Correct and rewrite essays and place them in your Final Portfolio.

SUGGESTED
Weekly *Implementation*

DAY 1	DAY 2	DAY 3	DAY 4	DAY 5
Prayer journal.	**Prayer journal.**	**Prayer journal.**	**Prayer journal.**	**Prayer journal.**
Review required reading(s) *before* the assigned lesson begins.	Review reading(s) from next lesson.	Write rough drafts of all assigned essays.	Rewrite corrected copies of essays due tomorrow.	Essays are due.
Teacher and students will decide on required essays for this lesson, choosing two or three essays.	Outline essays due at the end of the week.	The teacher and/or a peer evaluator may correct rough drafts.		Take Lesson 21 test.
The rest of the essays can be outlined, answered with shorter answers, or skipped.	Per teacher instructions, students may answer orally in a group setting some of the essays that are not assigned as formal essays.			Reading Ahead: *Vindication of the Rights of Women*, Mary Wollstonecraft; "Don Juan" and "The Prisoner of Chillon," Lord Byron; "Kubla Khan" and "The Rime of the Ancient Mariner," Samuel Taylor Coleridge; "Ozymandias" and "To a Skylark," Percy Bysshe Shelley; "Bright Star," "Ode to a Nightingale," "Posthuma," and "Ode on a Grecian Urn," John Keats.
Review all readings for Lesson 21.				Guide: What nuances emerge in Romantic themes?

Mary Wollstonecraft

Mary Wollstonecraft, 1759-1797, perhaps best known for being the mother of Mary Shelley, was an early proponent of the radical idea of educational equality between men and women. "Her fervent radicalism extended from a critique of private property and political oppression to a protest against the subjection of women." (*Norton Anthology of Literature by Women*, p. 255) Wollstonecraft's *Vindication of the Rights of Women* (1792) was a revolutionary social document and was roundly misunderstood by most of her contemporaries. "Her impassioned plea against the miseducation of women constituted a groundbreaking demonstration of how the very protection offered women confines them to the vices and virtues of an inferior class and thereby inhibits both women and men from establishing their common humanity." (p. 255) Wollstonecraft mightily objected to women being defined as male property and at the same time was "contemptuous of the reading habits of women, whose addiction to romance seemed to her to propagate only ignorance and further dependency."

CRITICAL THINKING

After reading *Vindication of the Rights of Women*, discuss in a two-page essay the reasons Wollstonecraft feels women are treated unfairly.

Chap. I. The Rights and Involved Duties of Mankind Considered. In the present state of society it appears necessary to go back to first principles in search of the most simple truths, and to dispute with some prevailing prejudice every inch of ground. To clear my way, I must be allowed to ask some plain questions, and the answers will probably appear as unequivocal as the axioms on which reasoning is built; though,

> **Analyze:** *Vindication of the Rights of Women,* Mary Wollstonecraft; "Don Juan" and "The Prisoner of Chillon," Lord Byron; "Kubla Khan" and "The Rime of the Ancient Mariner," Samuel Taylor Coleridge; "Ozymandias" and "To a Skylark," Percy Bysshe Shelley; "Bright Star," "Ode to a Nightingale," "Posthuma," and "Ode on a Grecian Urn," John Keats.
>
> **Reading Ahead:** *Jane Eyre,* Charlotte Brontë; *Frankenstein,* Mary Shelley.
>
> **Guide Question:** Is the monster Frankenstein a victim or a perpetrator of evil?

when entangled with various motives of action, they are formally contradicted, either by the words or conduct of men. In what does man's pre-eminence over the brute creation consist? The answer is as clear as that a half is less than the whole; in Reason. What acquirement exalts one being above another? Virtue; we spontaneously reply. For what purpose were the passions implanted? That man by struggling with them might attain a degree of knowledge denied to the brutes; whispers Experience. Consequently the perfection of our nature and capability of happiness, must be estimated by the degree of reason, virtue, and knowledge, that distinguish the individual, and direct the laws which bind society: and that from the exercise of reason, knowledge and virtue naturally flow, is equally undeniable, if mankind be viewed collectively. The rights and duties of man thus simplified, it seems almost impertinent to attempt to illustrate truths that appear so incontrovertible; yet such deeply rooted prejudices have clouded reason, and such spurious qualities have assumed the name of virtues, that it is necessary to pursue the course of reason as it has been perplexed and involved in error, by various adventitious circumstances, comparing the simple axiom with casual deviations. Men, in general, seem to employ their reason to justify prejudices, which they have imbibed, they cannot trace how, rather than to root them out. The mind must be strong that resolutely forms its own principles; for a kind of intellectual cowardice prevails which makes many men shrink from the task, or only do it by halves. Yet the imperfect conclusions thus drawn, are frequently very plausible, because they are built on partial experience, on just, though narrow, views. Going back to first principles, vice skulks, with all its native deformity, from close investigation; but a set of shallow reasoners are always exclaiming that these arguments prove too much, and that a measure rotten at the core may be expedient. Thus expediency is continually contrasted with simple principles, till truth is lost in a mist of words, virtue, in forms, and knowledge rendered a sounding nothing, by the specious prejudices that assume its name. That the society is formed in the wisest manner, whose constitution is founded on the nature of man, strikes, in the abstract, every thinking being so forcibly, that it looks like presumption to endeavour to bring forward proofs; though proof must be brought, or the strong hold of prescription will never be forced by reason; yet to urge prescription as an argument to justify the depriving men (or women) of their natural rights, is one of the absurd sophisms which daily insult common sense. The civilization of the bulk of the people of Europe is very partial; nay, it may be made a question, whether they have acquired any virtues in exchange for innocence, equivalent to the misery produced by the vices that have been plastered over unsightly ignorance, and the freedom which has been bartered for splendid slavery. The desire of dazzling by riches, the most certain pre-eminence that man can obtain, the pleasure of commanding flattering sycophants, and many other complicated low calculations of doting self-love, have all contributed to overwhelm the mass of mankind, and make liberty a convenient handle for mock patriotism. For whilst rank and titles are held of the utmost importance, before which Genius "must hide its diminished head," it is, with a few exceptions, very unfortunate for a nation when a man of abilities, without rank or property, pushes himself forward to notice.— —Alas! what unheard of misery have thousands suffered to purchase a cardinal's hat for an intriguing obscure adventurer, who longed to be ranked with princes, or lord it over them by seizing the triple crown! Such, indeed, has been the wretchedness that has flowed from hereditary honours, riches, and monarchy, that men of lively sensibility have almost uttered blasphemy in order to justify the dispensations of providence. Man has been held out as independent of his power who made him, or as a lawless planet darting from its orbit to steal the celestial fire of reason; and the

vengeance of heaven, lurking in the subtile flame, sufficiently punished his temerity, by introducing evil into the world. Impressed by this view of the misery and disorder which pervaded society, and fatigued with jostling against artificial fools, Rousseau became enamoured of solitude, and, being at the same time an optimist, he labours with uncommon eloquence to prove that man was naturally a solitary animal. Misled by his respect for the goodness of God, who certainly— —for what man of sense and feeling can doubt it!— —gave life only to communicate happiness, he considers evil as positive, and the work of man; not aware that he was exalting one attribute at the expense of another, equally necessary to divine perfection. Reared on a false hypothesis, his arguments in favour of a state of nature are plausible, but unsound. I say unsound; for to assert that a state of nature is preferable to civilization, in all its possible perfection, is, in other words, to arraign supreme wisdom; and the paradoxical exclamation, that God has made all things right, and that evil has been introduced by the creature, whom he formed, knowing what he formed, is as unphilosophical as impious. When that wise Being who created us and placed us here, saw the fair idea, he willed, by allowing it to be so, that the passions should unfold our reason, because he could see that present evil would produce future good. Could the helpless creature whom he called from nothing break loose from his providence, and boldly learn to know good by practising evil, without his permission? No.— —How could that energetic advocate for immortality argue so inconsistently? Had mankind remained for ever in the brutal state of nature, which even his magic pen cannot paint as a state in which a single virtue took root, it would have been clear, though not to the sensitive unreflecting wanderer, that man was born to run the circle of life and death, and adorn God's garden for some purpose which could not easily be reconciled with his attributes. But if, to crown the whole, there were to be rational creatures produced, allowed to rise in excellence by the exercise of powers implanted for that purpose; if benignity itself thought fit to call into existence a creature above the brutes, who could think and improve himself, why should that inestimable gift, for a gift it was, if man was so created as to have a capacity to rise above the state in which sensation produced brutal ease, be called, in direct terms, a curse? A curse it might be reckoned, if all our existence was bounded by our continuance in this world; for why should the gracious fountain of life give us passions, and the power of reflecting, only to imbitter our days and inspire us with mistaken notions of dignity? Why should he lead us from love of ourselves to the sublime emotions which the discovery of his wisdom and goodness excites, if these feelings were not set in motion to improve our nature, of which they make a part, and render us capable of enjoying a more godlike portion of happiness? Firmly persuaded that no evil exists in the world that God did not design to take place, I build my belief on the perfection of God. Rousseau exerts himself to prove that all *was* right originally: a crowd of authors that all *is* now right: and I, that all will *be* right. But, true to his first position, next to a state of nature, Rousseau celebrates barbarism, and, apostrophizing the shade of Fabricius, he forgets that, in conquering the world, the Romans never dreamed of establishing their own liberty on a firm basis, or of extending the reign of virtue. Eager to support his system, he stigmatizes, as vicious, every effort of genius; and, uttering the apotheosis of savage virtues, he exalts those to demi-gods, who were scarcely human — —the brutal Spartans, who, in defiance of justice and gratitude, sacrificed, in cold blood, the slaves who had shewn themselves men to rescue their oppressors. Disgusted with artificial manners and virtues, the citizen of Geneva, instead of properly sifting the subject, threw away the wheat with the chaff, without waiting to inquire whether the evils which his ardent soul turned from indignantly, were the consequence of civilization or the vestiges of barbarism. He saw vice trampling on virtue, and the semblance of goodness taking place of the reality; he saw talents bent by power to sinister purposes, and never thought of tracing the gigantic mischief up to arbitrary power, up to the hereditary distinctions that clash with the mental superiority that naturally raises a man above his fellows. He did not perceive that regal power, in a few generations, introduces idiotism into the noble stem, and holds out baits to render thousands idle and vicious. Nothing can set the regal character in a more contemptible point of view, than the various crimes that have elevated men to the supreme dignity. — —Vile intrigues, unnatural crimes, and every vice that degrades our nature, have been the steps to this distinguished eminence; yet millions of men have supinely allowed the nerveless limbs of the posterity of such rapacious prowlers to rest quietly on their ensanguined thrones. What but a pestilential vapour can hover over society when its chief director is only instructed in the invention of crimes, or the stupid routine of childish ceremonies? Will men never be wise? — —will they never cease to expect corn from tares, and figs from thistles? It is impossible for any man, when the most favourable circumstances concur, to acquire sufficient

knowledge and strength of mind to discharge the duties of a king, entrusted with uncontrouled power; how then must they be violated when his very elevation is an insuperable bar to the attainment of either wisdom or virtue; when all the feelings of a man are stifled by flattery, and reflection shut out by pleasure! Surely it is madness to make the fate of thousands depend on the caprice of a weak fellow creature, whose very station sinks him *necessarily* below the meanest of his subjects! But one power should not be thrown down to exalt another — —for all power intoxicates weak man; and its abuse proves, that the more equality there is established among men, the more virtue and happiness will reign in society. But this, and any similar maxim deduced from simple reason, raises an outcry — —the church or the state is in danger, if faith in the wisdom of antiquity is not implicit; and they who, roused by the sight of human calamity, dare to attack human authority, are reviled as despisers of God, and enemies of man. These are bitter calumnies, yet they reached one of the best of men, whose ashes still preach peace, and whose memory demands a respectful pause, when subjects are discussed that lay so near his heart. After attacking the sacred majesty of Kings, I shall scarcely excite surprise by adding my firm persuasion that every profession, in which great subordination of rank constitutes its power, is highly injurious to morality. A standing army, for instance, is incompatible with freedom; because subordination and rigour are the very sinews of military discipline; and despotism is necessary to give vigour to enterprizes that one will directs. A spirit inspired by romantic notions of honour, a kind of morality founded on the fashion of the age, can only be felt by a few officers, whilst the main body must be moved by command, like the waves of the sea; for the strong wind of authority pushes the crowd of subalterns forward, they scarcely know or care why, with headlong fury. Besides, nothing can be so prejudicial to the morals of the inhabitants of country towns as the occasional residence of a set of idle superficial young men, whose only occupation is gallantry, and whose polished manners render vice more dangerous, by concealing its deformity under gay ornamental drapery. An air of fashion, which is but a badge of slavery, and proves that the soul has not a strong individual character, awes simple country people into an imitation of the vices, when they cannot catch the slippery graces, of politeness. Every corps is a chain of despots, who, submitting and tyrannizing without exercising their reason, become dead weights of vice and folly on the community. A man of rank or fortune, sure of rising by interest, has nothing to do but to pursue some extravagant freak; whilst the needy *gentleman,* who is to rise, as the phrase turns, by his merit, becomes a servile parasite or vile pander. Sailors, the naval gentlemen, come under the same description, only their vices assume a different and a grosser cast. They are more positively indolent, when not discharging the ceremonials of their station; whilst the insignificant fluttering of soldiers may be termed active idleness. More confined to the society of men, the former acquire a fondness for humour and mischievous tricks; whilst the latter, mixing frequently with well-bred women, catch a sentimental cant.——But mind is equally out of the question, whether they indulge the horse-laugh, or polite simper. May I be allowed to extend the comparison to a profession where more mind is certainly to be found; for the clergy have superior opportunities of impovement, tho' subordination almost equally cramps their faculties? The blind submission imposed at college to forms of belief serves as a novitiate to the curate, who must obsequiously respect the opinion of his rector or patron, if he means to rise in his profession. Perhaps there cannot be a more forcible contrast than between the servile dependent gait of a poor curate and the courtly mien of a bishop. And the respect and contempt they inspire render the discharge of their separate functions equally useless. It is of great importance to observe that the character of every man is, in some degree, formed by his profession. A man of sense may only have a cast of countenance that wears off as you trace his individuality, whilst the weak, common man has scarcely ever any character, but what belongs to the body; at least, all his opinions have been so steeped in the vat consecrated by authority, that the faint spirit which the grape of his own vine yields cannot be distinguished. Society, therefore, as it becomes more enlightened, should be very careful not to establish bodies of men who must necessarily be made foolish or vicious by the very constitution of their profession. In the infancy of society, when men were just emerging out of barbarism, chiefs and priests, touching the most powerful springs of savage conduct, hope and fear, must have had unbounded sway. An aristocracy, of course, is naturally the first form of government. But, clashing interests soon losing their equipoise, a monarchy and hierarchy break out of the confusion of ambitious struggles, and the foundation of both is secured by feudal tenures. This appears to be the origin of monarchical and priestly power, and the dawn of civilization. But such combustible materials cannot long be pent up; and, getting vent in foreign wars and intestine insurrections, the people acquire

some power in the tumult, which obliges their rulers to gloss over their oppression with a shew of right. Thus, as wars, agriculture, commerce, and literature, expand the mind, despots are compelled, to make covert corruption hold fast the power which was formerly snatched by open force. And this baneful lurking gangrene is most quickly spread by luxury and superstition, the sure dregs of ambition. The indolent puppet of a court first becomes a luxurious monster, or fastidious sensualist, and then makes the contagion which his unnatural state spread, the instrument of tyranny. It is the pestiferous purple which renders the progress of civilization a curse, and warps the understanding, till men of sensibility doubt whether the expansion of intellect produces a greater portion of happiness or misery. But the nature of the poison points out the antidote; and had Rousseau mounted one step higher in his investigation, or could his eye have pierced through the foggy atmosphere, which he almost disdained to breathe, his active mind would have darted forward to contemplate the perfection of man in the establishment of true civilization, instead of taking his ferocious flight back to the night of sensual ignorance.

(http://www.bartleby.com/144/1.html)

George Gordon, Lord Byron

BACKGROUND

Lord Byron (1788–1824), an English poet, influenced Romantic literature as much with his colorful lifestyle and as he did with his powerful poetry. He fled England to avoid a scandal and died in the struggle for Greek Independence. His story was tragic and paralleled some of the other tragic stories of this century—James Dean and Ernest Hemingway, among others.

Romanticism is tied closely to republicanism and democracy—the much preferred governments for Romantics. Students will find evidence of these persuasions in the following Byron poems. (Note: Don Juan is pronounced Don Ju'an—two syllables with emphasis on the first syllable of Ju'an—because of the poem's rhyme scheme.)

Don Juan: Canto the First

I want a hero: an uncommon want,
When every year and month sends forth a new one,
Till, after cloying the gazettes with cant,
The age discovers he is not the true one;
Of such as these I should not care to vaunt,
I'll therefore take our ancient friend Don Juan,
We all have seen him, in the pantomime,
Sent to the Devil somewhat ere his time.

Vernon, the butcher Cumberland, Wolfe, Hawke,
Prince Ferdinand, Granby, Burgoyne, Keppel, Howe,
Evil and good, have had their tithe of talk,
And filled their sign-posts then, like Wellesley now;
Each in their turn like Banquo's monarchs stalk,
Followers of fame, "nine farrow" of that sow:
France, too, had Buonaparté and Dumourier
Recorded in the Moniteur and Courier.

Barnave, Brissot, Condorcet, Mirabeau,
Pétion, Clootz, Danton, Marat, La Fayette
Were French, and famous people, as we know;
And there were others, scarce forgotten yet,
Joubert, Hoche, Marceau, Lannes, Desaix, Moreau,
With many of the military set,
Exceedingly remarkable at times,
But not at all adapted to my rhymes.

Nelson was once Britannia's god of War,
And still should be so, but the tide is turn'd;
There's no more to be said of Trafalgar,
'Tis with our hero quietly inurn'd;
Because the army's grown more popular,
At which the naval people are concern'd;
Besides, the Prince is all for the land-service,
Forgetting Duncan, Nelson, Howe, and Jervis.

Brave men were living before Agamemnon
And since, exceeding valorous and sage,
A good deal like him too, though quite the same none;
But then they shone not on the poet's page,
And so have been forgotten: I condemn none,
But can't find any in the present age
Fit for my poem (that is, for my new one);
So, as I said, I'll take my friend Don Juan.
(http://eir.library.utoronto.ca/rpo/display/poem350.html)

The Prisoner of Chillon

My hair is grey, but not with years,
Nor grew it white

In a single night,
As men's have grown from sudden fears:
My limbs are bow'd, though not with toil,
But rusted with a vile repose,
For they have been a dungeon's spoil,
And mine has been the fate of those
To whom the goodly earth and air
Are bann'd, and barr'd—forbidden fare;
But this was for my father's faith
I suffer'd chains and courted death;
That father perish'd at the stake
For tenets he would not forsake;
And for the same his lineal race
In darkness found a dwelling place;
We were seven—who now are one,
Six in youth, and one in age,
Finish'd as they had begun,
Proud of Persecution's rage;
One in fire, and two in field,
Their belief with blood have seal'd,
Dying as their father died,
For the God their foes denied;—
Three were in a dungeon cast,
Of whom this wreck is left the last.

There are seven pillars of Gothic mould,
In Chillon's dungeons deep and old,
There are seven columns, massy and grey,
Dim with a dull imprison'd ray,
A sunbeam which hath lost its way,
And through the crevice and the cleft
Of the thick wall is fallen and left;
Creeping o'er the floor so damp,
Like a marsh's meteor lamp:
And in each pillar there is a ring,
And in each ring there is a chain;
That iron is a cankering thing,
For in these limbs its teeth remain,
With marks that will not wear away,
Till I have done with this new day,
Which now is painful to these eyes,
Which have not seen the sun so rise
For years—I cannot count them o'er,
I lost their long and heavy score
When my last brother droop'd and died,
And I lay living by his side.

They chain'd us each to a column stone,
And we were three—yet, each alone;
We could not move a single pace,
We could not see each other's face,

But with that pale and livid light
That made us strangers in our sight:
And thus together—yet apart,
Fetter'd in hand, but join'd in heart,
'Twas still some solace in the dearth
Of the pure elements of earth,
To hearken to each other's speech,
And each turn comforter to each
With some new hope, or legend old,
Or song heroically bold;
But even these at length grew cold.
Our voices took a dreary tone,
An echo of the dungeon stone,
A grating sound, not full and free,
As they of yore were wont to be:
It might be fancy—but to me
They never sounded like our own.

I was the eldest of the three
And to uphold and cheer the rest
I ought to do—and did my best—
And each did well in his degree.
The youngest, whom my father loved
Because our mother's brow was given
To him, with eyes as blue as heaven—
For him my soul was sorely moved:
And truly might it be distress'd
To see such bird in such a nest;
For he was beautiful as day—
(When day was beautiful to me
As to young eagles, being free)—
A polar day, which will not see
A sunset till its summer's gone,
Its sleepless summer of long light,
The snow-clad offspring of the sun:
And thus he was as pure and bright,
And in his natural spirit gay,
With tears for nought but others' ills,
And then they flow'd like mountain rills,
Unless he could assuage the woe
Which he abhorr'd to view below.

The other was as pure of mind,
But form'd to combat with his kind;
Strong in his frame, and of a mood
Which 'gainst the world in war had stood,
And perish'd in the foremost rank
With joy:—but not in chains to pine:
His spirit wither'd with their clank,
I saw it silently decline—
And so perchance in sooth did mine:

But yet I forced it on to cheer
Those relics of a home so dear.
He was a hunter of the hills,
Had followed there the deer and wolf;
To him this dungeon was a gulf,
And fetter'd feet the worst of ills.

Lake Leman lies by Chillon's walls:
A thousand feet in depth below
Its massy waters meet and flow;
Thus much the fathom-line was sent
From Chillon's snow-white battlement
Which round about the wave inthralls:
A double dungeon wall and wave
Have made—and like a living grave
Below the surface of the lake
The dark vault lies wherein we lay:
We heard it ripple night and day;
Sounding o'er our heads it knock'd;
And I have felt the winter's spray
Wash through the bars when winds were high
And wanton in the happy sky;
And then the very rock hath rock'd,
And I have felt it shake, unshock'd,
Because I could have smiled to see
The death that would have set me free.

I said my nearer brother pined,
I said his mighty heart declined,
He loathed and put away his food;
It was not that 'twas coarse and rude,
For we were used to hunter's fare,
And for the like had little care:
The milk drawn from the mountain goat
Was changed for water from the moat,
Our bread was such as captives' tears
Have moisten'd many a thousand years,
Since man first pent his fellow men
Like brutes within an iron den;
But what were these to us or him?
These wasted not his heart or limb;
My brother's soul was of that mould
Which in a palace had grown cold,
Had his free breathing been denied
The range of the steep mountain's side;
But why delay the truth?—he died.
I saw, and could not hold his head,
Nor reach his dying hand—nor dead,—
Though hard I strove, but strove in vain,
To rend and gnash my bonds in twain.
He died—and they unlock'd his chain,

And scoop'd for him a shallow grave
Even from the cold earth of our cave.
I begg'd them, as a boon, to lay
His corse in dust whereon the day
Might shine—it was a foolish thought,
But then within my brain it wrought,
That even in death his freeborn breast
In such a dungeon could not rest.
I might have spared my idle prayer—
They coldly laugh'd—and laid him there:
The flat and turfless earth above
The being we so much did love;
His empty chain above it leant,
Such Murder's fitting monument!

But he, the favourite and the flower,
Most cherish'd since his natal hour,
His mother's image in fair face
The infant love of all his race
His martyr'd father's dearest thought,
My latest care, for whom I sought
To hoard my life, that his might be
Less wretched now, and one day free;
He, too, who yet had held untired
A spirit natural or inspired—
He, too, was struck, and day by day
Was wither'd on the stalk away.
Oh, God! it is a fearful thing
To see the human soul take wing
In any shape, in any mood:
I've seen it rushing forth in blood,
I've seen it on the breaking ocean
Strive with a swoln convulsive motion,
I've seen the sick and ghastly bed
Of Sin delirious with its dread:
But these were horrors—this was woe
Unmix'd with such—but sure and slow:
He faded, and so calm and meek,
So softly worn, so sweetly weak,
So tearless, yet so tender—kind,
And grieved for those he left behind;
With all the while a cheek whose bloom
Was as a mockery of the tomb
Whose tints as gently sunk away
As a departing rainbow's ray;
An eye of most transparent light,
That almost made the dungeon bright;
And not a word of murmur—not
A groan o'er his untimely lot,—
A little talk of better days,
A little hope my own to raise,

For I was sunk in silence—lost
In this last loss, of all the most;
And then the sighs he would suppress
Of fainting Nature's feebleness,
More slowly drawn, grew less and less:
I listen'd, but I could not hear;
I call'd, for I was wild with fear;
I knew 'twas hopeless, but my dread
Would not be thus admonishèd;
I call'd, and thought I heard a sound—
I burst my chain with one strong bound,
And rushed to him:—
I found him not,
I only stirred in this black spot,
I only lived, I only drew
The accursed breath of dungeon-dew;
The last, the sole, the dearest link
Between me and the eternal brink,
Which bound me to my failing race
Was broken in this fatal place.
One on the earth, and one beneath—
My brothers—both had ceased to breathe:
I took that hand which lay so still,
Alas! my own was full as chill;
I had not strength to stir, or strive,
But felt that I was still alive—
A frantic feeling, when we know
That what we love shall ne'er be so.
I know not why
I could not die,
I had no earthly hope—but faith,
And that forbade a selfish death.
Why does the bird's song encourage the speaker?

What next befell me then and there
I know not well—I never knew—
First came the loss of light, and air,
And then of darkness too:
I had no thought, no feeling—none—
Among the stones I stood a state,
And was, scarce conscious what I wist,
As shrubless crags within the mist;
For all was blank, and bleak, and grey;
It was not night—it was not day;
It was not even the dungeon-light,
So hateful to my heavy sight,
But vacancy absorbing space,
And fixedness—without a place;
There were no stars, no earth, no time,
No check, no change, no good, no crime
But silence, and a stirless breath

Which neither was of life nor death;
A sea of stagnant idleness,
Blind, boundless, mute, and motionless!
A light broke in upon my brain,—
It was the carol of a bird;
It ceased, and then it came again,
The sweetest song ear ever heard,
And mine was thankful till my eyes
Ran over with the glad surprise,
And they that moment could not see
I was the mate of misery;
But then by dull degrees came back
My senses to their wonted track;
I saw the dungeon walls and floor
Close slowly round me as before,
I saw the glimmer of the sun
Creeping as it before had done,
But through the crevice where it came
That bird was perch'd, as fond and tame,
And tamer than upon the tree;
A lovely bird, with azure wings,
And song that said a thousand things,
And seemed to say them all for me!
I never saw its like before,
I ne'er shall see its likeness more:
It seem'd like me to want a mate,
But was not half so desolate,
And it was come to love me when
None lived to love me so again,
And cheering from my dungeon's brink,
Had brought me back to feel and think.
I know not if it late were free,
Or broke its cage to perch on mine,
But knowing well captivity,
Sweet bird! I could not wish for thine!
Or if it were, in wingèd guise,
A visitant from Paradise;
For—Heaven forgive that thought! the while
Which made me both to weep and smile—
I sometimes deem'd that it might be
My brother's soul come down to me;
Then at last away it flew,
And then 'twas mortal well I knew,
For he would never thus have flown—
And left me twice so doubly lone,—
Lone as the corse within its shroud,
Lone as a solitary cloud,
A single cloud on a sunny day,
While all the rest of heaven is clear,
A frown upon the atmosphere,
That hath no business to appear

When skies are blue, and earth is gay.

A kind of change came in my fate,
My keepers grew compassionate;
I know not what had made them so,
They were inured to sights of woe,
But so it was:—my broken chain
With links unfasten'd did remain,
And it was liberty to stride
Along my cell from side to side,
And up and down, and then athwart,
And tread it over every part;
And round the pillars one by one,
Returning where my walk begun,
Avoiding only, as I trod,
My brothers' graves without a sod;
For if I thought with heedless tread
My step profaned their lowly bed,
My breath came gaspingly and thick,
And my crush'd heart felt blind and sick.
I made a footing in the wall,
It was not therefrom to escape,
For I had buried one and all,
Who loved me in a human shape;
And the whole earth would henceforth be
A wider prison unto me:
No child, no sire, no kin had I,
No partner in my misery;
I thought of this, and I was glad,
For thought of them had made me mad;
But I was curious to ascend
To my barr'd windows, and to bend
Once more, upon the mountains high,
The quiet of a loving eye.

I saw them—and they were the same,
They were not changed like me in frame;
I saw their thousand years of snow
On high—their wide long lake below,
And the blue Rhone in fullest flow;
I heard the torrents leap and gush
O'er channell'd rock and broken bush;
I saw the white-wall'd distant town,
And whiter sails go skimming down;
And then there was a little isle,
Which in my very face did smile,
The only one in view;
A small green isle, it seem'd no more,
Scarce broader than my dungeon floor,
But in it there were three tall trees,
And o'er it blew the mountain breeze,

And by it there were waters flowing,
And on it there were young flowers growing,
Of gentle breath and hue.
The fish swam by the castle wall,
And they seem'd joyous each and all;
The eagle rode the rising blast,
Methought he never flew so fast
As then to me he seem'd to fly;
And then new tears came in my eye,
And I felt troubled—and would fain
I had not left my recent chain;
And when I did descend again,
The darkness of my dim abode
Fell on me as a heavy load;
It was as is a new-dug grave,
Closing o'er one we sought to save,—
And yet my glance, too much opprest,
Had almost need of such a rest.

It might be months, or years, or days—
I kept no count, I took no note—
I had no hope my eyes to raise,
And clear them of their dreary mote;
At last men came to set me free;
I ask'd not why, and reck'd not where;
It was at length the same to me,
Fetter'd or fetterless to be,
I learn'd to love despair.
And thus when they appear'd at last,
And all my bonds aside were cast,
These heavy walls to me had grown
A hermitage—and all my own!
And half I felt as they were come
To tear me from a second home:
With spiders I had friendship made
And watch'd them in their sullen trade,
Had seen the mice by moonlight play,
And why should I feel less than they?
We were all inmates of one place,
And I, the monarch of each race,
Had power to kill—yet, strange to tell!
In quiet we had learn'd to dwell;
My very chains and I grew friends,
So much a long communion tends
To make us what we are:—even I
Regain'd my freedom with a sigh.
(http://eir.library.utoronto.ca/rpo/display/poem363.html)

She Walks in Beauty

She walks in beauty, like the night

Of cloudless climes and starry skies;
And all that's best of dark and bright
Meet in her aspect and her eyes:
Thus mellow'd to that tender light
Which heaven to gaudy day denies.

One shade the more, one ray the less,
Had half impair'd the nameless grace
Which waves in every raven tress,
Or softly lightens o'er her face;
Where thoughts serenely sweet express
How pure, how dear their dwelling-place.

And on that cheek, and o'er that brow,
So soft, so calm, yet eloquent,
The smiles that win, the tints that glow,
But tell of days in goodness spent,
A mind at peace with all below,
A heart whose love is innocent!
(http://eir.library.utoronto.ca/rpo/display/poem365.html)

CRITICAL THINKING

A. Byron achieved a wide reputation as a poet and had a profound effect on the literature of Europe. He typified the romantic revolt and the cult of personal freedom that opposed the "stupid old system" of monarchical government and the repressive dictates of conservative society. Young French writers, such as Victor Hugo, were deeply indebted to his influence which extended through Germany and into Russia, where Aleksandr Pushkin held him in high esteem. Identify as many Romantic themes as possible in his poetry.
B. In "She Walks in Beauty," how thoroughly is the woman described? Identify different types of metaphors that Byron uses.
C. What is the basic paradox in "Chillon"? In an expository essay, identify how Byron makes his point.
D. "Don Juan" changes mood and theme regularly. Give two examples.

ENRICHMENT

Unlike most romantics, Byron admired Alexander Pope. Why didn't romantics like Pope? Compare Byron's poetry with Pope's.

Samuel Taylor Coleridge

Many of the Romantic poets are reminiscent of tragic rock singers systematically destroying their lives with loose living and drug abuse. One such figure is Samuel Taylor Coleridge (1772–1834) who wrote a great deal of his most promising poetry during six years of close friendship with William Wordsworth. Their collaboration resulted in the *Lyrical Ballads* (1798), a seminal work of the English Romantic movement.

Kubla Khan

In Xanadu did Kubla Khan
A stately pleasure-dome decree:
Where Alph, the sacred river, ran
Through caverns measureless to man
Down to a sunless sea.
So twice five miles of fertile ground
With walls and towers were girdled round:
And there were gardens bright with sinuous rills,
Where blossomed many an incense-bearing tree;
And here were forests ancient as the hills,
Enfolding sunny spots of greenery.

But O, that deep romantic chasm which slanted
Down the green hill athwart a cedarn cover!
A savage place! as holy and enchanted
As e'er beneath a waning moon was haunted
By woman wailing for her demon-lover!
And from this chasm, with ceaseless turmoil seething,
As if this earth in fast thick pants were breathing,
A mighty fountain momently was forced:
Amid whose swift half-intermitted burst
Huge fragments vaulted like rebounding hail,
Or chaffy grain beneath the thresher's flail:
And 'mid these dancing rocks at once and ever
It flung up momently the sacred river.
Five miles meandering with a mazy motion
Through wood and dale the sacred river ran,
Then reached the caverns measureless to man,
And sank in tumult to a lifeless ocean:
And 'mid this tumult Kubla heard from far
Ancestral voices prophesying war!

The shadow of the dome of pleasure
Floated midway on the waves;
Where was heard the mingled measure
From the fountain and the caves.
It was a miracle of rare device,
A sunny pleasure-dome with caves of ice!

In a vision once I saw:
It was an Abyssinian maid,
And on her dulcimer she played,
Singing of Mount Abora.
Could I revive within me
Her symphony and song,
To such a deep delight 'twould win me,
That with music loud and long,
I would build that dome in air,
That sunny dome! those caves of ice!
And all who heard should see them there,
And all should cry, Beware! Beware!
His flashing eyes, his floating hair!
Weave a circle round him thrice,
And close your eyes with holy dread,
For he on honey-dew hath fed,
And drunk the milk of Paradise.
(http://eir.library.utoronto.ca/rpo/display/poem524.html)

CRITICAL THINKING

A. Write an essay in which you describe the means Coleridge uses in "The Rime of the Ancient Mariner" to induce what he calls a "willing suspension of disbelief."

B. "Kubla Khan" is based upon a drug-induced dream. How does Coleridge create this effect?

C. Coleridge is famous for his use of sound. He frequently used the following devices:
   Internal rhyme: Rhyme that occurs within a line of poetry.
   Alliteration: The repetition of consonant sounds.
   Assonance: The repetition of vowel sounds.

   Find several examples of these literary devices in Coleridge's poems.

D. The story of the Wedding Guest's reactions in Parts I and VII in "Rime of the Ancient Mariner" functions as a frame for the narrative poem. How does the wedding guest enhance the reader's participation in the poem?

E. Most critics believe that Part VII contains the theme of the poem. What is it? Defend your answer.

BIBLICAL APPLICATION

Salvation is an important theme among Romantic writers. Most of them, however, reject an orthodox Christian understanding of the experience. Romantic poets can sound deceptively "Christian," very much like New Age authors today. As a theological statement, what is amiss with these verses from "The Rime of the Ancient Mariner"?

"Farewell, farewell; but this I tell
To thee, thou Wedding Guest!
He prayeth well, who loveth well
Both man and bird and beast.

"He prayeth best, who loveth best
All things both great and small;
For the dear God who loveth us.
He made and loveth all."
(www.bartleby.com)

Percy Bysshe Shelley

BACKGROUND

Note: Bysshe is pronounced "bish."

Percy Bysshe Shelley's life could make a good television movie. Shelley—who was born August 4, 1792, and died July 8, 1822—stands among Coleridge, Wordsworth, Keats, and Byron as great English Romantic poets. Shelley was educated at Eton and was expelled from Oxford for publishing an anti-Christian pamphlet called *The Necessity of Atheism* (1811). That same year he eloped to Ireland with sixteen-year-old Harriet Westbrook with whom he had a son and a daughter. Three years later Shelley eloped again, this time with Mary Wollstonecraft Godwin, whom he married in 1816, after Harriet had committed suicide. He and Mary had four children, only one of whom survived.

Ozymandias

I met a traveller from an antique land
Who said—"Two vast and trunkless legs of stone
Stand in the desert. Near them, on the sand,

Half sunk, a shattered visage lies, whose frown,
And wrinkled lip, and sneer of cold command,
Tell that its sculptor well those passions read
Which yet survive, stamped on these lifeless things,
The hand that mocked them and the heart that fed.
And on the pedestal these words appear —
'My name is Ozymandias, king of kings:
Look on my works, ye Mighty, and despair!'
Nothing beside remains. Round the decay
Of that colossal wreck, boundless and bare
The lone and level sands stretch far away."—
(http://eir.library.utoronto.ca/rpo/display/poem1904.html)

To a Skylark

Hail to thee, blithe Spirit!
Bird thou never wert,
That from Heaven, or near it,
Pourest thy full heart
In profuse strains of unpremeditated art.

Higher still and higher
From the earth thou springest
Like a cloud of fire;
The blue deep thou wingest,
And singing still dost soar, and soaring ever singest.

In the golden lightning
Of the sunken sun
O'er which clouds are bright'ning,
Thou dost float and run,
Like an unbodied joy whose race is just begun.

The pale purple even
Melts around thy flight;
Like a star of Heaven
In the broad daylight
Thou art unseen, but yet I hear thy shrill delight:

Keen as are the arrows
Of that silver sphere,
Whose intense lamp narrows
In the white dawn clear
Until we hardly see—we feel that it is there.

All the earth and air
With thy voice is loud.
As, when night is bare,
From one lonely cloud
The moon rains out her beams, and Heaven is over-
    flowed.

What thou art we know not;
What is most like thee?
From rainbow clouds there flow not
Drops so bright to see
As from thy presence showers a rain of melody.

Like a Poet hidden
In the light of thought,
Singing hymns unbidden,
Till the world is wrought
To sympathy with hopes and fears it heeded not:

Like a high-born maiden
In a palace tower,
Soothing her love-laden
Soul in secret hour
With music sweet as love, which overflows her bower:

Like a glow-worm golden
In a dell of dew,
Scattering unbeholden
Its aërial hue
Among the flowers and grass, which screen it from the
    view:

Like a rose embowered
In its own green leaves,
By warm winds deflowered,
Till the scent it gives
Makes faint with too much sweet these heavy-winged
    thieves.

Sound of vernal showers
On the twinkling grass,
Rain-awakened flowers,
All that ever was
Joyous, and clear, and fresh, thy music doth surpass.

Teach us, Sprite or Bird,
What sweet thoughts are thine:
I have never heard
Praise of love or wine
That panted forth a flood of rapture so divine.

Chorus Hymeneal
Or triumphal chaunt
Matched with thine, would be all
But an empty vaunt—
A thing wherein we feel there is some hidden want.

What objects are the fountains
Of thy happy strain?

What fields, or waves, or mountains?
What shapes of sky or plain?
What love of thine own kind? what ignorance of pain?

With thy clear keen joyance
Languor cannot be:
Shadow of annoyance
Never came near thee:
Thou lovest, but ne'er knew love's sad satiety.

Waking or asleep,
Thou of death must deem
Things more true and deep
Than we mortals dream,
Or how could thy notes flow in such a crystal stream?

We look before and after,
And pine for what is not:
Our sincerest laughter
With some pain is fraught;
Our sweetest songs are those that tell of saddest
    thought.

Yet if we could scorn
Hate, and pride, and fear;
If we were things born
Not to shed a tear,
I know not how thy joy we ever should come near.

Better than all measures
Of delightful sound,
Better than all treasures
That in books are found,
Thy skill to poet were, thou scorner of the ground!

Teach me half the gladness
That thy brain must know,
Such harmonious madness
From my lips would flow
The world should listen then, as I am listening now!
(http://eir.library.utoronto.ca/rpo/display/poem1915.ht
    ml)

CRITICAL THINKING

A. Explain what is ironic about "Ozymandias"?
B. Describe several things to which Shelley compares
    his skylark. What makes the skylark so appealing?
    What characteristics/qualities does the skylark
    manifest that a human being can never have?
C. Based on "Skylark," what does Shelley feel about
    his own poetry?

ENRICHMENT

Compare Wordsworth's "To a Skylark" with Shelley's "To a Skylark."

John Keats

BACKGROUND

Keats's short poetic life is unprecedented in English literature; between the ages of 18 and 24 he wrote poems of such power that they rank with the greatest in the language. Taking in all the senses, they lyrically render the totality of an experience and catch the complexity of life.

Bright Star

Bright star! would I were
steadfast as thou art—
Not in lone splendour hung
aloft the night,
And watching, with eternal lids
apart,
Like Nature's patient sleepless
Eremite,
The moving waters at their priestlike task
Of pure ablution round earth's human shores,
Or gazing on the new soft fallen mask
Of snow upon the mountains and the moors—
No—yet still steadfast, still unchangeable,
Pillow'd upon my fair love's ripening breast,
To feel for ever its soft fall and swell,
Awake for ever in a sweet unrest,
Still, still to hear her tender-taken breath,
And so live ever—or else swoon to death.
(http://eir.library.utoronto.ca/rpo/display/poem1119.ht
    ml)

Ode on a Grecian Urn

Thou still unravish'd bride of quietness,
Thou foster-child of silence and slow time,
Sylvan historian, who canst thus express
A flowery tale more sweetly than our rhyme:
What leaf-fring'd legend haunts about thy shape
Of deities or mortals, or of both,
In Tempe or the dales of Arcady?
What men or gods are these? What maidens loth?
What mad pursuit? What struggle to escape?
What pipes and timbrels? What wild ecstasy?

Heard melodies are sweet, but those unheard
Are sweeter; therefore, ye soft pipes, play on;
Not to the sensual ear, but, more endear'd,
Pipe to the spirit ditties of no tone:
Fair youth, beneath the trees, thou canst not leave
Thy song, nor ever can those trees be bare;
Bold Lover, never, never canst thou kiss,
Though winning near the goal—yet, do not grieve;
She cannot fade, though thou hast not thy bliss,
For ever wilt thou love, and she be fair!

Ah, happy, happy boughs! that cannot shed
Your leaves, nor ever bid the Spring adieu;
And, happy melodist, unwearied,
For ever piping songs for ever new;
More happy love! more happy, happy love!
For ever warm and still to be enjoy'd,
For ever panting, and for ever young;
All breathing human passion far above,
That leaves a heart high-sorrowful and cloy'd,
A burning forehead, and a parching tongue.

Who are these coming to the sacrifice?
To what green altar, O mysterious priest,
Lead'st thou that heifer lowing at the skies,
And all her silken flanks with garlands drest?
What little town by river or sea shore,
Or mountain-built with peaceful citadel,
Is emptied of this folk, this pious morn?
And, little town, thy streets for evermore
Will silent be; and not a soul to tell
Why thou art desolate, can e'er return.

O Attic shape! Fair attitude! with brede
Of marble men and maidens overwrought,
With forest branches and the trodden weed;
Thou, silent form, dost tease us out of thought
As doth eternity: Cold Pastoral!
When old age shall this generation waste,
Thou shalt remain, in midst of other woe
Than ours, a friend to man, to whom thou say'st,
"Beauty is truth, truth beauty,"—that is all
Ye know on earth, and all ye need to know.
(http://eir.library.utoronto.ca/rpo/display/poem1129.ht
    ml)

Ode to a Nightingale

My heart aches, and a drowsy numbness pains
My sense, as though of hemlock I had drunk,
Or emptied some dull opiate to the drains
One minute past, and Lethe-wards had sunk:

'Tis not through envy of thy happy lot,
But being too happy in thine happiness, —
That thou, light-winged Dryad of the trees,
In some melodious plot
Of beechen green, and shadows numberless,
Singest of summer in full-throated ease.

O, for a draught of vintage! that hath been
Cool'd a long age in the deep-delved earth,
Tasting of Flora and the country green,
Dance, and Provençal song, and sunburnt mirth!
O for a beaker full of the warm South,
Full of the true, the blushful Hippocrene,
With beaded bubbles winking at the brim,
And purple-stained mouth;
That I might drink, and leave the world unseen,
And with thee fade away into the forest dim:

Fade far away, dissolve, and quite forget
What thou among the leaves hast never known,
The weariness, the fever, and the fret
Here, where men sit and hear each other groan;
Where palsy shakes a few, sad, last gray hairs,
Where youth grows pale, and spectre-thin, and dies;
Where but to think is to be full of sorrow
And leaden-eyed despairs,
Where Beauty cannot keep her lustrous eyes,
Or new Love pine at them beyond to-morrow.

Away! away! for I will fly to thee,
Not charioted by Bacchus and his pards,
But on the viewless wings of Poesy,
Though the dull brain perplexes and retards:
Already with thee! tender is the night,
And haply the Queen-Moon is on her throne,
Cluster'd around by all her starry Fays;
But here there is no light,
Save what from heaven is with the breezes blown
Through verdurous glooms and winding mossy ways.

I cannot see what flowers are at my feet,
Nor what soft incense hangs upon the boughs,
But, in embalmed darkness, guess each sweet
Wherewith the seasonable month endows
The grass, the thicket, and the fruit-tree wild;
White hawthorn, and the pastoral eglantine;
Fast fading violets cover'd up in leaves;
And mid-May's eldest child,
The coming musk-rose, full of dewy wine,
The murmurous haunt of flies on summer eves.

Darkling I listen; and, for many a time
I have been half in love with easeful Death,
Call'd him soft names in many a mused rhyme,
To take into the air my quiet breath;
Now more than ever seems it rich to die,
To cease upon the midnight with no pain,
While thou art pouring forth thy soul abroad
In such an ecstasy!
Still wouldst thou sing, and I have ears in vain —
To thy high requiem become a sod.

Thou wast not born for death, immortal Bird!
No hungry generations tread thee down;
The voice I hear this passing night was heard
In ancient days by emperor and clown:
Perhaps the self-same song that found a path
Through the sad heart of Ruth, when, sick for home,
She stood in tears amid the alien corn;
The same that oft-times hath
Charm'd magic casements, opening on the foam
Of perilous seas, in faery lands forlorn.

Forlorn! the very word is like a bell
To toil me back from thee to my sole self!
Adieu! the fancy cannot cheat so well
As she is fam'd to do, deceiving elf.
Adieu! adieu! thy plaintive anthem fades
Past the near meadows, over the still stream,
Up the hill-side; and now 'tis buried deep
In the next valley-glades:
Was it a vision, or a waking dream?
Fled is that music:—Do I wake or sleep?
(http://eir.library.utoronto.ca/rpo/display/poem1131.ht
ml)

Posthuma

When I have fears that I may cease to be
Before my pen has glean'd my teeming brain,
Before high piled books, in charact'ry,
Hold like rich garners the full-ripen'd grain;
When I behold, upon the night's starr'd face,
Huge cloudy symbols of a high romance,
And think that I may never live to trace
Their shadows, with the magic hand of chance;
And when I feel, fair creature of an hour!
That I shall never look upon thee more,
Never have relish in the faery power
Of unreflecting love!—then on the shore
Of the wide world I stand alone, and think
Till Love and Fame to nothingness do sink.
(http://eir.library.utoronto.ca/rpo/display/poem1140.ht
ml)

CRITICAL THINKING

What is the theme of the poem "Ode on a Grecian Urn"?

FINAL PORTFOLIO

Correct and rewrite essays and place them in your Final Portfolio.

SUGGESTED
Weekly *Implementation*

DAY 1	DAY 2	DAY 3	DAY 4	DAY 5
Prayer journal. Review required reading(s) *before* the assigned lesson begins. Teacher and students will decide on required essays for this lesson, choosing two or three essays. The rest of the essays can be outlined, answered with shorter answers, or skipped. Review all readings for Lesson 22.	**Prayer journal.** Review reading(s) from next lesson. Outline essays due at the end of the week. Per teacher instructions, students may answer orally in a group setting some of the essays that are not assigned as formal essays.	**Prayer journal.** Write rough drafts of all assigned essays. The teacher and/or a peer evaluator may correct rough drafts.	**Prayer journal.** Rewrite corrected copies of essays due tomorrow.	**Prayer journal.** Essays are due. Take Lesson 22 test. Reading Ahead: *Jane Eyre*, Charlotte Bronte; *Frankenstein*, Mary Shelley. Guide: Is the monster Frankenstein a victim or a perpetrator of evil?

Jane Eyre

Charlotte Brontë

CRITICAL THINKING

Charlotte Brontë (1816-1854) was born into a devout Methodist family and was perhaps the most talented of the exceptionally talented Brontë family. Because women's works were not usually received seriously by reviewers, Charlotte and sisters Emily and Anne became Currer, Ellis, and Acton Bell, newly professional writers. *Jane Eyre*, Charlotte's most famous novel, came together as a powerful work of fiction where her difficulties as a governess and her unrequited love shaped the fictional autobiography of her heroine Jane. The novel was different from previous sentimental novels of manners popular in the early decades of the century. *Jane Eyre* includes a remarkable and unique character in the unflappable, plain, Jane, who refuses to be in the shadow of any man: "she spoke with surprising authority about a woman's desire for liberty—'for liberty I gasped; for liberty I uttered a prayer.'" (*Norton Anthology of Literature by Women*, p. 471). This novel thrust Charlotte Brontë into a dramatic public life, quite a change for the formerly shy, unsophisticated young woman. Read "Currer Bell's" novel and write an essay on several of the themes she develops.

> **Analyze:** *Jane Eyre*, Charlotte Brontë; *Frankenstein*, Mary Shelley.
>
> **Reading Ahead:** *A Tale of Two Cities*, Charles Dickens.
>
> **Guide Question:** Which best describes *A Tale of Two Cities*: a great literary work or a mediocre story with unoriginal characters and a plot infected with coincidence?

Frankenstein

Mary Shelley

BACKGROUND

Unlike most of her contemporaries, Mary Shelley foresaw the perils of the newly-born technological society, inherent in scientific research, and the exploitation of nature. Her novel, *Frankenstein*, was written during a particular period of crisis in Romanticism: the failure of the French Revolution. Like so many English authors, Shelley (like Wordsworth) loved the ideology of the French Revolution but struggled with its violent excesses.

Victor Frankenstein was a scientist who made himself *god* by creating a man-monster. There were disastrous results. The novel's premise allows the reader to hear the story not only from the perspective of the tragic, misguided Dr. Frankenstein but also from that of his listener, Captain Walton—who has entertained similar fascinations in the natural sciences. The book is divided into three sections: Shelley's preface, four letters from Walton to his sister back in England, and the twenty-four chapters that make up Dr. Frankenstein's story.

CRITICAL THINKING

A. Shelley uses Dr. Frankenstein as a vehicle to make a statement about Western culture. What is that statement?

B. Both Dr. Frankenstein and his monster are characters that develop over time. How do their developmental paths converge and diverge?

C. The women in *Frankenstein* are paradigms of social consciousness and moral guidance. They are passive creatures, not quick to criticize. In general, they are innocent victims of male waywardness. It is interesting that Mary Shelley, herself a strong, opinionated woman, creates so many fragile women in her novel: Elizabeth's mother dies in childbirth; Elizabeth herself indirectly suffers loneliness, and eventually death, through the hands of her fiancé Dr. Frankenstein; Caroline Frankenstein is powerless in the face of poverty and tragedy. Later, she dies nursing the scarlet-fever-stricken Elizabeth back to health. Justine was viciously and unjustly executed for the death of her murdered charge William Frankenstein. Finally, the gruesome Woman Creature Frankenstein, a dismembered potential partner of the Monster Frankenstein, is murdered by her creator, Dr. Frankenstein. Why does Shelley present women in this way?

BIBLICAL APPLICATION

In the tragic example of Saul, a whole nation and Saul's own family suffer terribly for his decisions, actions, and sin. Next, compare the demise of this family with the demise of Frankenstein's family.

ENRICHMENT

A. Compare Dr. Frankenstein with Aylmer in Nathaniel Hawthorne's short story "The Birthmark."

B. Who is a more "likeable" monster: Frankenstein or Hyde (in Robert Louis Stevenson's *Dr. Jekyll and Mr. Hyde*)? Why?

FINAL PORTFOLIO

Correct and rewrite essays and place them in your Final Portfolio.

SUGGESTED
Weekly *Implementation*

DAY 1	DAY 2	DAY 3	DAY 4	DAY 5
Prayer journal. Review required reading(s) *before* the assigned lesson begins. Teacher and students will decide on required essays for this lesson, choosing two or three essays. The rest of the essays can be outlined, answered with shorter answers, or skipped. Review all readings for Lesson 23.	**Prayer journal.** Review reading(s) from next lesson. Outline essays due at the end of the week. Per teacher instructions, students may answer orally in a group setting some of the essays that are not assigned as formal essays.	**Prayer journal.** Write rough drafts of all assigned essays. The teacher and/or a peer evaluator may correct rough drafts.	**Prayer journal.** Rewrite corrected copies of essays due tomorrow.	**Prayer journal.** Essays are due. Take Lesson 23 test. Reading Ahead: *A Tale of Two Cities*, Charles Dickens. Guide: Which best describes *A Tale of Two Cities:* a great literary work or a mediocre story with unoriginal characters and a plot infected with coincidence?

A Tale of Two Cities

Charles Dickens

BACKGROUND

When Charles Dickens was twelve, his father, John, was imprisoned for debt, an event that Dickens considered the most terrible experience of his life. Removed from school and put to work in a blacking (shoe-dye) factory, he lived alone, ashamed and frightened, in a lodging house in North London. It is from this experience that most of Dickens' novels arose.

During the eighteenth century, the novel had not ranked high as a form of literary expression; during the nineteenth century, thanks to the spread of circulating libraries and the growth of popular education, it became immensely powerful. Sir Walter Scott, who had begun his career in verse in 1805 with *The Lay of the Last Minstrel*, occupied himself between 1814 and 1823 with the Waverley novels, a series of historical romances that continued from *Waverley* to *Quentin Durward*. Sitting in her mother's living room and writing one novel after another, Jane Austen redefined the English novel. Her style was quite revolutionary—at times it approaches later Realism. The constellation of great Victorian novelists—Charles Dickens, Elizabeth Cleghorn Gaskell, William Makepeace Thackeray, and Anthony Trollope—were all, to some extent, committed writers who had a sense of grave responsibility for the welfare of their fellow human beings. Charles Dickens, in particular, took to heart the plight of his fellow Englishman.

CRITICAL THINKING

A. Evaluate Dickens' choice of title for his novel *A Tale of Two Cities*. Can you think of other names for this

> **Analyze:** *A Tale of Two Cities,* Charles Dickens.
> **Reading Ahead:** *Pride and Prejudice,* Jane Austen.
> **Guide Question:** How does Austen use the social party to develop characters and to advance action?

novel?

B. At the beginning of Book II, chapter 21, Dickens refers to Lucie as "ever busily winding the golden thread which bound her husband and her father, and herself . . . in a life of quiet bliss." Likewise, Madame Defarge is knitting a macabre shroud. What effect do these characters have on the novel? What was the golden thread?

C. Coincidence plays a rather large role in the story. What is its value to the novel?

D. Could *A Tale of Two Cities* be adapted for television? Which contemporary author(s) write(s) like Dickens? Explain your answer.

BIBLICAL APPLICATION

A. Does the end justify the means? Is there any justification for the Reign of Terror in France (1793–94)?

B. Which characters does Dickens like and dislike? What does this tell you about his values? How do his views fit biblical principles?

ENRICHMENT

Compare and contrast the American and French Revolutions.

FINAL PORTFOLIO

Correct and rewrite essays and place them in your Final Portfolio.

SUGGESTED
Weekly *Implementation*

DAY 1	DAY 2	DAY 3	DAY 4	DAY 5
Prayer journal.	**Prayer journal.**	**Prayer journal.**	**Prayer journal.**	**Prayer journal.**
Review required reading(s) *before* the assigned lesson begins.	Review reading(s) from next lesson.	Write rough drafts of all assigned essays.	Rewrite corrected copies of essays due tomorrow.	Essays are due.
<u>Teacher and students will decide on required essays for this lesson, choosing two or three essays.</u>	Outline essays due at the end of the week.	The teacher and/or a peer evaluator may correct rough drafts.		Take Lesson 24 test.
<u>The rest of the essays can be outlined, answered with shorter answers, or skipped.</u>	Per teacher instructions, students may answer orally in a group setting some of the essays that are not assigned as formal essays.			Reading Ahead: Review *Pride and Prejudice*, Jane Austen.
Review all readings for Lesson 24.				Guide: How does Austen use the social party to develop characters and to advance action?

LESSON 25

NINETEENTH CENTURY *(Part 5)*

Pride and Prejudice

Jane Austen

BACKGROUND

Jane Austen was one of the greatest novelist in British literature. Her insight into nineteenth-century English family life was unmatched. Many of her best works appeared before the beginning of the nineteenth century but found fame later. *Pride and Prejudice, Sense and Sensibility*, and *Northanger Abbey* had all been written and put aside before the eighteenth century ended. *Sense and Sensibility* appeared only in 1811; *Pride and Prejudice* and *Mansfield Park* were published in 1813 and 1814; and *Emma*, which many critics consider her most accomplished work, appeared in 1816. *Persuasion*, the last of her completed novels, was published posthumously in 1818. Jane Austen's range of subjects was limited, but she made a virtue of her limitations. Her characters are immutable and relevant to all time and to all generations.

Pride and Prejudice has consistently been Jane Austen's most popular novel. It portrayed life in the genteel rural society of the day and told of the initial misunderstandings and later mutual enlightenment between Elizabeth Bennett (whose liveliness and quick wit have often attracted readers) and the haughty Darcy. The title *Pride and Prejudice* referred (among other things) to the ways in which Elizabeth and Darcy first viewed each other. The original version of the novel was written in 1796–97 under the title *First Impressions* and was probably in the form of an exchange of letters.

> **Analyze:** *Pride and Prejudice*, Jane Austen.
>
> **Reading Ahead:** *Dr. Jekyll and Mr. Hyde*, Robert Louis Stevenson.
>
> **Guide Question:** Why must Dr. Jekyll destroy Mr. Hyde?

CRITICAL THINKING

A. The plot of *Pride and Prejudice* is partially based on a declining middle class, of which Jane Austen was a part. Discuss how this decline is evident in the novel.

B. Compare nineteenth-century marriages to contemporary marriages.

C. Who is Elizabeth Bennett, and why does Austen find her so attractive?

D. Austen's novel *Pride and Prejudice* is full of irony. Explain.

E. Evaluate the criticism suggesting that Jane Austen writes dull stories about ordinary people.

ENRICHMENT

Research Austen's life and discuss why *Pride and Prejudice* is autobiographical.

FINAL PORTFOLIO

Correct and rewrite essays and place them in your Final Portfolio.

SUGGESTED
Weekly *Implementation*

DAY 1	DAY 2	DAY 3	DAY 4	DAY 5
Prayer journal. Review required reading(s) *before* the assigned lesson begins. Teacher and students will decide on required essays for this lesson, choosing two or three essays. The rest of the essays can be outlined, answered with shorter answers, or skipped. Review all readings for Lesson 25.	**Prayer journal.** Review reading(s) from next lesson. Outline essays due at the end of the week. Per teacher instructions, students may answer orally in a group setting some of the essays that are not assigned as formal essays.	**Prayer journal.** Write rough drafts of all assigned essays. The teacher and/or a peer evaluator may correct rough drafts.	**Prayer journal.** Rewrite corrected copies of essays due tomorrow.	**Prayer journal.** Essays are due. Take Lesson 25 test. Reading Ahead: Review *Dr. Jekyll and Mr. Hyde*, Robert Louis Stevenson. Guide: Why must Dr. Jekyll destroy Mr. Hyde?

Dr. Jekyll and Mr. Hyde

Robert Louis Stevenson

BACKGROUND

The Scottish novelist, travel writer, poet, and essayist Robert Louis Stevenson, born at Edinburgh November 13, 1850, authored the enduringly popular romantic adventure stories *Treasure Island* and *Kidnapped* (1886) and the alarming psychological allegory *Dr. Jekyll and Mr. Hyde*. These works have become classics of juvenile literature, but Stevenson's writings are actually quite profound and have multiple layers of meaning. Although Stevenson struggled with agnosticism all his life, his vision is theistic.

CRITICAL THINKING

A. Consider whether *Dr. Jekyll and Mr. Hyde* is a horror story or a story of the reality of human sin.
B. How did Stevenson use setting to enhance the effect of his novel?
C. Compare and contrast the theme of *Frankenstein*, by Mary Shelley, and *Dr. Jekyll and Mr. Hyde*, by Stevenson.

Analyze: *Dr. Jekyll and Mr. Hyde*, Robert Louis Stevenson.

Reading Ahead: "The Witch," Mary Elizabeth Coleridge; "The Idea of a University," John Henry Newman; "The Charge of the Light Brigade," "Ulysses," and "Crossing the Bar," Alfred Lord Tennyson; "Prospice," "The Lost Leader," and "My Last Duchess Ferrara," Robert Browning; "Sonnet I," "Sonnet XIV," and "Sonnet XLIII," Elizabeth Barrett Browning.

Guide Question: What is a good university?

BIBLICAL APPLICATION

Why did Stevenson have Dr. Jekyll turn more and more frequently into Mr. Hyde without benefit of his chemical potion? Compare the plot of this book to the story of Samson.

FINAL PORTFOLIO

Correct and rewrite essays and place them in your Final Portfolio.

SUGGESTED
Weekly *Implementation*

DAY 1	DAY 2	DAY 3	DAY 4	DAY 5
Prayer journal.	**Prayer journal.**	**Prayer journal.**	**Prayer journal.**	**Prayer journal.**
Review required reading(s) *before* the assigned lesson begins.	Review reading(s) from next lesson.	Write rough drafts of all assigned essays.	Rewrite corrected copies of essays due tomorrow.	Essays are due.
Teacher and students will decide on required essays for this lesson, choosing two or three essays.	Outline essays due at the end of the week.	The teacher and/or a peer evaluator may correct rough drafts.		Take Lesson 26 test.
The rest of the essays can be outlined, answered with shorter answers, or skipped.	Per teacher instructions, students may answer orally in a group setting some of the essays that are not assigned as formal essays.			Reading Ahead: "The Witch," Mary Elizabeth Coleridge; "The Idea of a University," John Henry Newman; "The Charge of the Light Brigade," "Ulysses," and "Crossing the Bar," Alfred Lord Tennyson; "Prospice," "The Lost Leader," and "My Last Duchess Ferrara," Robert Browning; "Sonnet I," "Sonnet XIV," and "Sonnet XLIII," Elizabeth Barrett Browning.
Review all readings for Lesson 26.				Guide: What is a good university?

Mary Elizabeth Coleridge

Mary Elizabeth Coleridge (1861-1907) was born and lived her entire life in London, where, after 1890, she taught in College and contributed extensively to literary journals. Coleridge was the great-great-niece of the Romantic poet Samuel Taylor Coleridge. Her family often entertained such recognized poets as Tennyson and Browning. Raised to be a "dutiful nineteenth-centure English lady" Coleridge was well educated and "by the time she was nineteen she was well versed in [Hebrew], as well as in German, French, Italian; and a little later she became a keen reader of Greek." (*Norton Anthology of Literature by Women*, p. 1144). She also studied philosophy, and literature, participated in intellectual circles, traveled, and wrote stories and essays.

The Witch

I have walked a great while over the snow,
And I am not tall nor strong.
My clothes are wet, and my teeth are set,
And the way was hard and long.
I have wandered over the fruitful earth,
But I never came here before.
Oh, lift me over the threshold, and let me in
at the door!

The cutting wind is a cruel foe;
I dare not stand in the blast.
My hands are stone, and my voice a groan, And the
    worst of death is past.
I am but a little maiden still;
My little white feet are sore.
Oh, lift me over the threshold, and let me in
at the door!

Her voice was the voice that women have,
Who plead for their heart's desire.
She came-she came-and the quivering flame
Sank and died in the fire.
It never was lit again on my hearth
Since I hurried across the floor,
To lift her over the threshold, and let her in
at the door!
(*Norton Anthology*, p. 1147)

Analyze: "The Witch," Mary Elizabeth Coleridge; "The Idea of a University," John Henry Newman; "The Charge of the Light Brigade," "Ulysses," and "Crossing the Bar," Alfred Lord Tennyson; "Prospice," "The Lost Leader," and "My Last Duchess Ferrara," Robert Browning; "Sonnet I," "Sonnet XIV," and "Sonnet XLIII," Elizabeth Barrett Browning.

Reading Ahead: *The Mayor of Casterbridge,* Thomas Hardy.

Guide Question: How is this novel a reflection of Hardy's uneasiness with mid-nineteenth century British social change?

CRITICAL THINKING

Contrast the storyline with the deep feeling in this poem.

John Henry Newman

BACKGROUND

John Henry Newman was born in London, England, on February 21, 1801. He entered a private, exclusive school at Ealing in 1808, at the age of seven. Following  the failure of his father's bank in 1816, Newman, then in his final year at Ealing, underwent what he would later refer to as a "conversion." Like so many nineteenth-century Protestant evangelicals, his conversion left him with a hatred of the Roman Catholic Church and a personal conviction that the pope was the antichrist. This is an interesting fact because before the end of his life, Newman was a cardinal in the Roman Catholic Church. In the 1850s Newman lectured in Ireland and published *The Idea of a University*

(1852, 1854, 1858). In 1873 this presentation formed the basis for *The Idea of a University Defined and Illustrated*, a timeless compilation of his lectures on education written during the preceding two decades and still referenced by university scholars today. In 1878, Trinity College, Oxford, elected Newman as its first honorary fellow. John Henry Newman died at Edgbastion on August 11, 1890. Many Protestant Christians find Newman to be pedantic and subtle with a theistic vision.

CRITICAL THINKING

A. What stylistic strategies does Newman employ in the following first section of *The Idea of a University*? Examine his paragraph structure and organizational design.

A university may be considered with reference either to its students or to its studies; and the principle that all knowledge is a whole and the separate sciences parts of one, which I have hitherto been using in behalf of its studies, is equally important when we direct our attention to its students. Now, then, I turn to the students, and shall consider the education which, by virtue of this principle, a university will give them: and thus I shall be introduced, gentlemen, to the second question which I proposed to discuss, viz. whether and in what sense its teaching, viewed relatively to the taught, carries the attribute of utility along with it.

I have said that all branches of knowledge are connected together, because the subject-matter of knowledge is intimately united in itself as being the acts and the work of the Creator. Hence it is that the sciences, into which our knowledge may be said to be cast, have multiplied bearings one on another, and an internal sympathy, and admit, or rather demand, comparison and adjustment. They complete, correct, balance each other. This consideration, if well founded, must be taken into account, not only as regards the attainment of truth, which is their common end, but as regards the influence which they exercise upon those whose education consists in the study of them. I have said already that to give undue prominence to one is to be unjust to another; to neglect or supersede these is to divert those from their proper object. It is to unsettle the boundary lines between science and science, to disturb their action, to destroy the harmony which binds them together. Such a proceeding will have a corresponding effect when introduced into a place of education. There is no science but tells a different tale, when viewed as a portion of a whole, from what it is likely to suggest when taken by itself, without the safeguard, as I may call it, of others.

Let me make use of an illustration. In the combination of colours, very different effects are produced by a difference in their selection and juxtaposition; red, green, and white change their shades according to the contrast to which they are submitted. And, in like manner, the drift and meaning of a branch of knowledge varies with the company in which it is introduced to the student. If his reading is confined simply to one subject, however such division of labour may favour the advancement of a particular pursuit, a point into which I do not here enter, certainly it has a tendency to contract his mind. If it is incorporated with others, it depends on those others as to the kind of influence which it exerts upon him. Thus the classics, which in England are the means of refining the taste, have in France subserved the spread of revolutionary and deistical doctrines. In metaphysics, again, Butler's Analogy of Religion, which has had so much to do with the conversion to the Catholic faith of members of the University of Oxford, appeared to Pitt and others, who had received a different training, to operate only in the direction of infidelity. And so again, Watson Bishop of Llandaff, as I think he tells us in the narrative of his life, felt the science of mathematics to indispose the mind to religious belief, while others see in its investigations the best parallel, and thereby defence, of the Christian mysteries. In like manner, I suppose, Arcesilas would not have handled logic as Aristotle, nor Aristotle have criticized poets as Plato; yet reasoning and poetry are subject to scientific rules.

It is a great point then to enlarge the range of studies which a university professes, even for the sake of the students; and, though they cannot pursue every subject which is open to them, they will be the gainers by living among those and under those who represent the whole circle. This I conceive to be the advantage of a seat of universal learning, considered as a place of education. An assemblage of learned men, zealous for their own sciences, and rivals of each other, are brought, by familiar intercourse and for the sake of intellectual peace, to adjust together the claims and relations of their respective subjects of investigation. They learn to respect, to consult, to aid each other. Thus is created a pure and clear atmosphere of thought, which the student also breathes, though in his own case he only pursues a few sciences out of the multitude. He profits by an intellectual tradition which is independent of particular teachers, which guides him in his choice of subjects, and duly interprets for him those which he chooses. He apprehends the great outlines of knowledge, the principles on which it rests, the scale of its parts, its lights and its shades, its great points and its little, as he otherwise cannot apprehend them. Hence it is that his education is called "liberal." A habit of mind is formed which lasts through life, of which the attributes are freedom, equitableness, calmness, moderation, and wisdom; or what in a former discourse I have ventured to call a philosophical habit. This then I would assign as the special fruit of the education furnished at a university, as contrasted with other places of teaching or modes of teaching. This is the main purpose of a university in its treatment of its students.

And now the question is asked me, What is the use of it? And my answer will constitute the main subject of the discourses which are to follow.

Cautious and practical thinkers, I say, will ask of me, what, after all, is the gain of this philosophy of which I make such account and from which I promise so much. Even supposing it to enable us to exercise the degree of trust exactly due to every science respectively, and to estimate precisely the value of every truth which is anywhere to be found, how are we better for this master view of things, which I have been extolling? Does it not reverse the principle of the division of labour? Will practical objects be obtained better or worse by its cultivation? To what then does it lead? Where does it end? What does it do? How does it profit? What does it promise? Particular sciences are respectively the basis of definite arts, which carry on to results tangible and beneficial the truths which are the subjects of the knowledge attained; what is the art of this science of sciences? What is the fruit of such a philosophy? What are we proposing to effect, what inducements do we hold out to the Catholic community, when we set about the enterprise of founding a university?

I am asked what is the end of university education, and of the liberal or philosophical knowledge which I conceive it to impart: I answer that what I have already said has been sufficient to show that it has a very tangible, real, and sufficient end, though the end cannot be divided from that knowledge itself. Knowledge is capable of being its own end. If this is true of all knowledge, it is true also of that special philosophy which I have made to consist in a comprehensive view of truth in all its branches, of the relations of science to science, of their mutual bearings, and their respective values. . . . Knowledge, indeed, when thus exalted into a scientific form, is also power; not only is it excellent in itself, but whatever such excellence may be, it is something more,

it has a result beyond itself. Doubtless; but that is a further consideration with which I am not concerned. I only say that, prior to its being a power, it is a good; that it is not only an instrument, but an [also] end. I know well it may resolve itself into an art, and terminate in a mechanical process, and in tangible fruit; but it also may fall back upon that reason which informs it, and resolve itself into philosophy. In one case it is called useful knowledge, in the other liberal. The same person may cultivate it in both ways at once; but this again is a matter foreign to my subject; here I do but say that there are two ways of using knowledge, and in matter of fact those who use it in one way are not likely to use it in the other, or at least in a very limited measure.

Surely it is very intelligible to say that liberal education, viewed in itself, is simply the cultivation of the intellect, as such, and its object is nothing more or less than intellectual excellence. . . . To open the mind, to correct it, to refine it, to enable it to know, and to digest, master, rule, and use its knowledge, to give it power over its own faculties, application, flexibility, method, critical exactness, sagacity, resource, address, eloquent expression, is an object as intelligible (for here we are inquiring, not what the object of a liberal education is worth, nor what use the Church makes of it, but what it is in itself), I say, an object as intelligible as the cultivation of virtue, while, at the same time, it is absolutely distinct from it. (http://www.bartleby.com/28/2.html)

B. What is meant by liberal knowledge? Evaluate Newman's essay and present your conclusion. Defend your answer.

C. Evaluate Newman's "Definition of a Gentleman" in *The Idea of a University* and defend your position.

BIBLICAL APPLICATION

Contrast the education that Newman proposes with the education that occurs in most places today and with the education that Daniel received in the Bible.

Alfred Lord Tennyson

BACKGROUND

In the article "Tennyson" in the eleventh edition of the *Encyclopedia Britannica*, Edmond Gosse wrote:

We still look to the earlier masters for supreme excellence in particular directions: to Wordsworth for sublime philosophy, to Coleridge for ethereal magic, to Byron for passion, to Shelley for lyric intensity, to Keats for richness. Tennyson does not excel each of these in his own special field, but he is often nearer to the particular man in his particular mastery than anyone else can be said to be, and he has in addition his own special field of supremacy. What this is cannot be easily defined; it consists, perhaps, in the beauty of the atmosphere which Tennyson contrives to cast around his work, molding it in the blue mystery of twilight, in the opaline haze of sunset: this atmosphere, suffused over his poetry with inestimable skill and with a tact rarely at fault, produces an almost unfailing illusion or mirage of loveliness.

CRITICAL THINKING

Break, Break, Break

Break, break, break,
On thy cold gray stones, O Sea!
And I would that my tongue could utter
The thoughts that arise in me.

O, well for the fisherman's boy,
That he shouts with his sister at play!
O, well for the sailor lad,
That he sings in his boat on the bay!

And the stately ships go on
To their haven under the hill;
But O for the touch of a vanish'd hand,
And the sound of a voice that is still!

Break, break, break
At the foot of thy crags, O Sea!
But the tender grace of a day that is dead
Will never come back to me.
(http://eir.library.utoronto.ca/rpo/display/poem2115.html)

A. Tennyson's poems are deceptively simple. Their images are straightforward and ordinary. Describe several of the images that Tennyson offers in this poem, and compare these images with a Romantic poem that William Wordsworth might write.
B. Discuss Tennyson's use of personification in "The Charge of the Light Brigade."
C. It was common for poets to commemorate historical events by writing a poem. Research the charge of this light brigade. Did the poem accurately portray the historical event?

The Charge of the Light Brigade

Half a league, half a league,
Half a league onward,
All in the valley of Death
Rode the six hundred.
"Forward, the Light Brigade!
"Charge for the guns!" he said:
Into the valley of Death
Rode the six hundred.

"Forward, the Light Brigade!"
Was there a man dismay'd?
Not tho' the soldier knew
Someone had blunder'd:
Theirs not to make reply,
Theirs not to reason why,
Theirs but to do and die:
Into the valley of Death
Rode the six hundred.

Cannon to right of them,
Cannon to left of them,
Cannon in front of them
Volley'd and thunder'd;
Storm'd at with shot and shell,
Boldly they rode and well,
Into the jaws of Death,
Into the mouth of Hell
Rode the six hundred.

Flash'd all their sabres bare,
Flash'd as they turn'd in air,
Sabring the gunners there,
Charging an army, while
All the world wonder'd:
Plunged in the battery-smoke
Right thro' the line they broke;
Cossack and Russian
Reel'd from the sabre-stroke
Shatter'd and sunder'd.
Then they rode back, but not
Not the six hundred.

Cannon to right of them,
Cannon to left of them,
Cannon behind them
Volley'd and thunder'd;
Storm'd at with shot and shell,
While horse and hero fell,
They that had fought so well
Came thro' the jaws of Death,
Back from the mouth of Hell,
All that was left of them,
Left of six hundred.

When can their glory fade?
O the wild charge they made!
All the world wonder'd.
Honour the charge they made!
Honour the Light Brigade,
Noble six hundred!
(http://eir.library.utoronto.ca/rpo/display/poem2116.ht
    ml)

D. In "Ulysses" Tennyson draws on Homer's epic to
describe Ulysses many years after the fateful epic.
What is the theme of this poem?

Ulysses

It little profits that an idle king,
By this still hearth, among these barren crags,
Match'd with an aged wife, I mete and dole
Unequal laws unto a savage race,
That hoard, and sleep, and feed, and know not me.

I cannot rest from travel: I will drink
Life to the lees: All times I have enjoy'd
Greatly, have suffer'd greatly, both with those
That loved me, and alone, on shore, and when
Thro' scudding drifts the rainy Hyades
Vext the dim sea: I am become a name;
For always roaming with a hungry heart
Much have I seen and known; cities of men
And manners, climates, councils, governments,
Myself not least, but honour'd of them all;
And drunk delight of battle with my peers,
Far on the ringing plains of windy Troy.
I am a part of all that I have met;
Yet all experience is an arch wherethro'
Gleams that untravell'd world whose margin fades
For ever and forever when I move.
How dull it is to pause, to make an end,
To rust unburnish'd, not to shine in use!
As tho' to breathe were life! Life piled on life

Were all too little, and of one to me
Little remains: but every hour is saved
From that eternal silence, something more,
A bringer of new things; and vile it were
For some three suns to store and hoard myself,
And this gray spirit yearning in desire
To follow knowledge like a sinking star,
Beyond the utmost bound of human thought.

This is my son, mine own Telemachus,
To whom I leave the sceptre and the isle, —
Well-loved of me, discerning to fulfil
This labour, by slow prudence to make mild
A rugged people, and thro' soft degrees
Subdue them to the useful and the good.
Most blameless is he, centred in the sphere
Of common duties, decent not to fail
In offices of tenderness, and pay
Meet adoration to my household gods,
When I am gone. He works his work, I mine.

There lies the port; the vessel puffs her sail:
There gloom the dark, broad seas. My mariners,
Souls that have toil'd, and wrought, and thought with
    me—
That ever with a frolic welcome took
The thunder and the sunshine, and opposed
Free hearts, free foreheads—you and I are old;
Old age hath yet his honour and his toil;
Death closes all: but something ere the end,
Some work of noble note, may yet be done,
Not unbecoming men that strove with Gods.
The lights begin to twinkle from the rocks:
The long day wanes: the slow moon climbs: the deep
Moans round with many voices. Come, my friends,
'Tis not too late to seek a newer world.
Push off, and sitting well in order smite
The sounding furrows; for my purpose holds
To sail beyond the sunset, and the baths
Of all the western stars, until I die.
It may be that the gulfs will wash us down:
It may be we shall touch the Happy Isles,
And see the great Achilles, whom we knew.

Tho' much is taken, much abides; and tho'
We are not now that strength which in old days
Moved earth and heaven, that which we are, we are;
One equal temper of heroic hearts,
Made weak by time and fate, but strong in will
To strive, to seek, to find, and not to yield.
(http://eir.library.utoronto.ca/rpo/display/poem2191.html)

E. What is the theme of "Crossing the Bar"?

F. Is "Crossing the Bar" a religious poem? A Christian poem?

G. Every image in "Crossing the Bar" has a double meaning. Explain.

Crossing the Bar

Sunset and evening star,
And one clear call for me!
And may there be no moaning of the bar,
When I put out to sea,

But such a tide as moving seems asleep,
Too full for sound and foam,
When that which drew from out the boundless deep
Turns again home.

Twilight and evening bell,
And after that the dark!
And may there be no sadness of farewell,
When I embark;

For tho' from out our bourne of Time and Place
The flood may bear me far,
I hope to see my Pilot face to face
When I have crost the bar.
(http://eir.library.utoronto.ca/rpo/display/poem2118.ht
    ml)

BIBLICAL APPLICATION

Find evidence in Tennyson's poetry that helps you determine that he is or is not a born-again Christian.

Three queries for Biblical Application Question

What is of prime importance in the spiritual world?
ANSWER:

What makes man essentially unique?
ANSWER:

What characteristics of truth and goodness are objective?
ANSWER:

Robert Browning

BACKGROUND

Robert Browning was one of the greatest Victorian poets. He was also an incorrigible optimist. In that sense he was more a Renaissance artist than a nineteenth-century Romantic. One who examines Browning's work closely can observe that in his poetry evil often overcomes good. Born in London May 7, 1812, he derived from his parents a deep, if unconventional, faith and a love of books, music, and painting. His first published poem, "Pauline," (1833) was inspired by Percy Shelley; it was a series of musings on poetic sensibility. In 1846 Browning married Elizabeth Barrett, who became a poet of renown, also. They were one of the most celebrated married couples in English history. They settled in Casa Guidi in Florence, where he composed many more poems. Elizabeth died in 1861, breaking Browning's heart. He never fully recovered. In 1869, in his grief, he published "The Ring and the Book," which finally established his reputation as a major poet.

CRITICAL THINKING

A. Browning was endlessly resourceful in the invention of new stanza patterns and metrical combinations. He used harsh, rough images. Offer evidence from his poetry to support this statement.

B. In the first three lines, how do the images of fog, mist, and snow prepare the reader for the "fiend-voices" in line 23 of "Prospice"?

C. Contrast "Prospice" with "Crossing the Bar" (by Tennyson). Contrast "My Last Duchess" with "Ulysses."

Prospice

Fear death? — to feel the fog in my throat,
The mist in my face,
When the snows begin, and the blasts denote

I am nearing the place,
The power of the night, the press of the storm,
The post of the foe;
Where he stands, the Arch Fear in a visible form,
Yet the strong man must go:
For the journey is done and the summit attained,
And the barriers fall,
Though a battle's to fight ere the guerdon be gained,
The reward of it all.
I was ever a fighter, so—one fight more,
The best and the last!
I would hate that death bandaged my eyes and for-
bore,
And bade me creep past.
No! let me taste the whole of it, fare like my peers
The heroes of old,
Bear the brunt, in a minute pay glad life's arrears
Of pain, darkness and cold.
For sudden the worst turns the best to the brave,
The black minute's at end,
And the elements' rage, the fiend-voices that rave,
Shall dwindle, shall blend,
Shall change, shall become first a peace out of pain,
Then a light, then thy breast,
O thou soul of my soul! I shall clasp thee again,
And with God be the rest!
(http://eir.library.utoronto.ca/rpo/display/poem293.html)

D. Most scholars believe that "The Lost Leader" was
written about Wordsworth. Why was Browning so
critical of Wordsworth? How does he show his dis-
pleasure?

E. Explore two ways that "The Lost Leader" can be
read.

The Lost Leader

Just for a handful of silver he left us,
Just for a riband to stick in his coat—
Found the one gift of which fortune bereft us,
Lost all the others she lets us devote;
They, with the gold to give, doled him out silver,
So much was theirs who so little allowed:
How all our copper had gone for his service!
Rags—were they purple, his heart had been proud!
We that had loved him so, followed him, honoured
him,
Lived in his mild and magnificent eye,
Learned his great language, caught his clear accents,
Made him our pattern to live and to die!
Shakespeare was of us, Milton was for us,

Burns, Shelley, were with us,—they watch from their
graves!
He alone breaks from the van and the freemen,
He alone sinks to the rear and the slaves!

We shall march prospering,—not thro' his presence;
Songs may inspirit us,—not from his lyre;
Deeds will be done,—while he boasts his quiescence,
Still bidding crouch whom the rest bade aspire:
Blot out his name, then, record one lost soul more,
One task more declined, one more footpath untrod,
One more devils'-triumph and sorrow for angels,
One wrong more to man, one more insult to God!
Life's night begins: let him never come back to us!
There would be doubt, hesitation and pain,
Forced praise on our part—the glimmer of twilight,
Never glad confident morning again!
Best fight on well, for we taught him—strike gallantly,
Menace our heart ere we master his own;
Then let him receive the new knowledge and wait us,
Pardoned in heaven, the first by the throne!
(http://eir.library.utoronto.ca/rpo/display/poem282.html)

F. "My Last Duchess Ferrara" is the most popular of
Browning's poems (another dramatic monologue).
The scene is the castle of the Duke of Ferrara, an
arrogant Italian nobleman of the Renaissance
period. The duke is showing a painting of his first
wife to an envoy who has been sent to arrange the
details of a second marriage. What is the literary
purpose of this dramatic monologue?

G. What is the Duke's purpose in concluding his
speech by pointing out a bronze cast by the Duke
of Innsbruck?

H. What do you think really happened to the
Duchess? How does the text guide you to this conclusion?

My Last Duchess Ferrara

That's my last Duchess painted on the wall,
Looking as if she were alive. I call
That piece a wonder, now: Frà Pandolf's hands
Worked busily a day, and there she stands.
Will 't please you sit and look at her? I said
"Frà Pandolf" by design, for never read
Strangers like you that pictured countenance,
The depth and passion of its earnest glance,
But to myself they turned (since none puts by
The curtain I have drawn for you, but I)
And seemed as they would ask me, if they durst,

How such a glance came there; so, not the first
Are you to turn and ask thus. Sir, 'twas not
Her husband's presence only, called that spot
Of joy into the Duchess' cheek: perhaps
Frà Pandolf chanced to say, "Her mantle laps
Over my Lady's wrist too much," or "Paint
Must never hope to reproduce the faint
Half-flush that dies along her throat"; such stuff
Was courtesy, she thought, and cause enough
For calling up that spot of joy. She had
A heart . . . how shall I say? . . . too soon made glad,
Too easily impressed; she liked whate'er
She looked on, and her looks went everywhere.
Sir, 'twas all one! My favour at her breast,
The dropping of the daylight in the West,
The bough of cherries some officious fool
Broke in the orchard for her, the white mule
She rode with round the terrace—all and each
Would draw from her alike the approving speech,
Or blush, at least. She thanked men,—good; but
    thanked
Somehow . . . I know not how . . . as if she ranked
My gift of a nine-hundred-years-old name
With anybody's gift. Who'd stoop to blame
This sort of trifling? Even had you skill
In speech—(which I have not)—to make your will
Quite clear to such an one, and say, "Just this
Or that in you disgusts me; here you miss,
Or there exceed the mark"—and if she let
Herself be lessoned so, nor plainly set
Her wits to yours, forsooth, and made excuse,
—E'en then would be some stooping; and I chuse
Never to stoop. Oh, sir, she smiled, no doubt,
Whene'er I passed her; but who passed without
Much the same smile? This grew; I gave commands;
Then all smiles stopped together. There she stands
As if alive. Will 't please you rise? We'll meet
The company below, then. I repeat,
The Count your Master's known munificence
Is ample warrant that no just pretence
Of mine for dowry will be disallowed;
Though his fair daughter's self, as I avowed
At starting, is my object. Nay, we'll go
Together down, Sir! Notice Neptune, though,
Taming a sea-horse, thought a rarity,
Which Claus of Innsbruck cast in bronze for me.
(http://eir.library.utoronto.ca/rpo/display/poem282.html)

ENRICHMENT

How does Browning picture the Renaissance?

Elizabeth Barrett Browning

BACKGROUND

In her era Elizabeth Barrett Browning was a prolific, scholarly, and highly political poet and was considered a major author. She was an accomplished students and translator of Greek. According to *The Norton Anthology of Literature by Women*, "Nothing could be more misleading than the twentieth century image of 'Mrs. Browning' as a swooning Victorian invalid, languishing on a sofa, smelling salts in one hand and sentimental verses in the other." (p. 373) She suffered a spinal injury when she was fifteen, while saddling a pony, and then for ten years coped with chronic anxiety due that suffering and a lung ailment. Her writing offered escape from pain. Barrett Browning was known for her "Sonnets of the Portuguese," which introduced the "usually male-oriented genre of the sonnet cycle to female requirements, telling the story of a love affair from a woman's, instead of a man's, point of view." She also composed a translation of *Prometheus Bound* and *Poems of 1850*, which included a fierce political statement in *The Runaway Slave at Pilgrim's Point*, dramatizing the problem of slavery in the United States and the pain of impoverished children in England (*Anthology*, p. 375). Her epic-novel *Aurora Leigh* was published in 1857.

Elizabeth met Robert Browning in 1845, after he praised her poetry. He wrote to her, and Elizabeth responded by secretly writing love poems to him. At the age of forty, against the objections of her father, she married Robert Browning. Elizabeth continued writing poetry until she died June 29, 1861, in Florence, Italy.

CRITICAL THINKING

Carefully read the following poems and then respond to the questions:

A. What evidence do you have in these poems that Barrett Browning is very ill?

B. Notice the effect of repetition in Barrett Browning's poems. How do these repetitions affect the emotional impact of the poems?

C. Evaluate the literary criticism that the sonnets of

Elizabeth Barrett Browning are considered the most genuine expressions of love in the English language. Support your evaluation with three or four images from her poems.

D. Browning is emotional but never sentimental. How does she walk the narrow line between these two places?

Sonnet XIV

If thou must love me, let it be for nought
Except for love's sake only. Do not say
"I love her for her smile—her look—her way
Of speaking gently,—for a trick of thought
That falls in well with mine, and certes brought
A sense of pleasant ease on such a day"—
For these things in themselves, Beloved, may
Be changed, or change for thee,—and love, so
　　wrought,
May be unwrought so. Neither love me for
Thine own dear pity's wiping my cheeks dry,—
A creature might forget to weep, who bore
Thy comfort long, and lose thy love thereby!
But love me for love's sake, that evermore
Thou mayst love on, through love's eternity.

(http://eir.library.utoronto.ca/rpo/display/poem255.html)

Sonnet I

I thought once how Theocritus had sung
Of the sweet years, the dear and wished-for years,
Who each one in a gracious hand appears
To bear a gift for mortals, old or young:
And, as I mused it in his antique tongue,
I saw, in gradual vision through my tears,
The sweet, sad years, the melancholy years,

Those of my own life, who by turns had flung
A shadow across me. Straightway I was 'ware,
So weeping, how a mystic Shape did move
Behind me, and drew me backward by the hair:
And a voice said in mastery, while I strove,—
"Guess now who holds thee?"—"Death," I said. But,
　　there,
The silver answer rang,—"Not Death, but Love."

(http://eir.library.utoronto.ca/rpo/display/poem252.html)

Sonnet XLIII

How do I love thee? Let me count the ways.
I love thee to the depth and breadth and height
My soul can reach, when feeling out of sight
For the ends of Being and ideal Grace.
I love thee to the level of everyday's
Most quiet need, by sun and candle-light.
I love thee freely, as men strive for Right;
I love thee purely, as they turn from Praise.
I love thee with the passion put to use
In my old griefs, and with my childhood's faith.
I love thee with a love I seemed to lose
With my lost saints,—I love thee with the breath,
Smiles, tears, of all my life!—and, if God choose,
I shall but love thee better after death.

(http://eir.library.utoronto.ca/rpo/display/poem261.html)

FINAL PORTFOLIO

Correct and rewrite essays and place them in your Final Portfolio.

SUGGESTED
Weekly *Implementation*

DAY 1	DAY 2	DAY 3	DAY 4	DAY 5
Prayer journal.	**Prayer journal.**	**Prayer journal.**	**Prayer journal.**	**Prayer journal.**
Review required reading(s) *before* the assigned lesson begins.	Review reading(s) from next lesson.	Write rough drafts of all assigned essays.	Rewrite corrected copies of essays due tomorrow.	Essays are due.
<u>Teacher and students will decide on required essays for this lesson, choosing two or three.</u>	Outline essays due at the end of the week.	The teacher and/or a peer evaluator may correct rough drafts.		Take Lesson 27 test.
<u>The rest of the essays can be outlined, answered with shorter answers, or skipped.</u>	Per teacher instructions, students may answer orally in a group setting some of the essays that are not assigned as formal essays.			Reading Ahead: Review *The Mayor of Casterbridge*, Thomas Hardy.
Review all readings for Lesson 27.				Guide: How is this novel a reflection of Hardy's uneasiness with mid-nineteenth century British social change?

The Mayor of Casterbridge

Thomas Hardy

BACKGROUND

It is hard to believe that quiet Thomas Hardy could spark so much controversy: in his lifetime two of his books were banned! Today these books would not turn a head, but in Victorian England they were scandalous. *The Mayor of Casterbridge*, one of his books that escaped the banned list, has a powerful vision of goodness and forgiveness.

CRITICAL THINKING

A. Hardy observed the transformation of British society from a predominately agrarian, small town society into an industrial, urban society. Hardy did not like these changes. How are these concerns manifested in *The Mayor of Casterbridge*?

B. Like many Victorian writers, Hardy was troubled by a decline of Christian influence. He had carefully read the writings of Charles Darwin and other scientists and had lost some of his own belief that a controlling force governed the universe. This loss of faith is reflected in the bleakness of the landscape in Wessex and the harshness of the fate that plagues many of Hardy's major characters. In that sense,

Analyze: *The Mayor of Casterbridge*, Thomas Hardy.

Reading Ahead: *Lord Jim*, Joseph Conrad.

Guide Question: How does Conrad view evil?

Hardy is truly a modern writer. Find examples that support this loss of faith.

C. Divide *The Mayor of Casterbridge* into five distinct sections. Defend your answer.

BIBLICAL APPLICATION

In this novel Hardy retains a moral vision that was slowly disappearing from English novels. In a two-page essay explore what this moral vision is.

ENRICHMENT

A. Evaluate the criticism from most modern readers that Hardy's themes and characters seem contemporary. Support your evaluation and your conclusions.

B. Discuss in great detail the way Hardy develops his characters.

FINAL PORTFOLIO

Correct and rewrite essays and place them in your Final Portfolio.

SUGGESTED
Weekly *Implementation*

DAY 1	DAY 2	DAY 3	DAY 4	DAY 5
Prayer journal.	**Prayer journal.**	**Prayer journal.**	**Prayer journal.**	**Prayer journal.**
Review required reading(s) *before* the assigned lesson begins.	Review reading(s) from next lesson.	Write rough drafts of all assigned essays.	Rewrite corrected copies of essays due tomorrow.	Essays are due.
<u>Teacher and students will decide o required essays for this lesson, choosing two or three.</u>	Outline essays due at the end of the week.	The teacher and/or a peer evaluator may correct rough drafts.		Take Lesson 28 test.
<u>The rest of the essays can be outlined, answered with shorter answers, or skipped.</u>	Per teacher instructions, students may answer orally in a group setting some of the essays that are not assigned as formal essays.			Reading Ahead: *Lord Jim*, Joseph Conrad.
Review all readings for Lesson 28.				Guide: How does Conrad view evil?

The Twentieth Century

BACKGROUND

In British culture, no sharp dividing line separates the nineteenth from the twentieth century. Until the outbreak of World War I, fiction was still dominated by a group of novelists who had already achieved distinction during the Victorian Age—Thomas Hardy, the Anglo-American Henry James, George Moore, Joseph Conrad, Rudyard Kipling, H. G. Wells, John Galsworthy, and Arnold Bennett. Except for Hardy, who had abandoned the novel in disgust after the critics' unfriendly reception of *Jude the Obscure*, all remained extremely active writers.

CRITICAL THINKING

A. Define the following concepts: Surrealism, Realism, Absurdism, and Naturalism.
B. How did World War I affect English writing?
C. Evaluate the direction in general that English writing moves in the twentieth century and predict its future direction.

Joseph Conrad

BACKGROUND

Joseph Conrad, born in Poland but moved to England and was the first modern British writer. His themes emphasized the extraordinary, which put him in the Romantic/Victorian camp. Yet he also employed limited omniscient narration, only a step away from third-person objective narration, the narration of choice of many

> **Analyze:** *Lord Jim*, Joseph Conrad.
> **Reading Ahead:** "Not Waving but Drowning," Stevie Smith; Twentieth century short stories.
> **Guide Question:** Contrast these short stories to American and Russian short stories.

Naturalistic and Realistic writers. Conrad also employed psychological insights in character development. Like the American writer William Faulkner, he loved to utilize a stream of consciousness.

CRITICAL THINKING

A. Conrad's work was crucial to the development of the modern novel. He used the limited point of view, presenting a tale through a single consciousness (in the case of *Lord Jim*, through Marlow). Discuss this stylistic technique as it relates to *Lord Jim*.
B. Discuss three or four characters in *Lord Jim* and how they are used to advance the plot.
C. What is the theme of *Lord Jim*?

ENRICHMENT

The Heart of Darkness—a challenging but wonderful book, perhaps Conrad's best—is about human nature. What are the conclusions about human nature that Conrad posits?

FINAL PORTFOLIO

Correct and rewrite essays and place them in your Final Portfolio.

SUGGESTED
Weekly *Implementation*

DAY 1	DAY 2	DAY 3	DAY 4	DAY 5
Prayer journal.	**Prayer journal.**	**Prayer journal.**	**Prayer journal.**	**Prayer journal.**
Review required reading(s) *before* the assigned lesson begins.	Review reading(s) from next lesson.	Write rough drafts of all assigned essays.	Rewrite corrected copies of essays due tomorrow.	Essays are due.
Teacher and students will decide on required essays for this lesson, choosing two or three essays.	Outline essays due at the end of the week.	The teacher and/or a peer evaluator may correct rough drafts.		Take Lesson 29 test.
The rest of the essays can be outlined, answered with shorter answers, or skipped.	Per teacher instructions, students may answer orally in a group setting some of the essays that are not assigned as formal essays.			Reading Ahead: Twentieth century short stories (found in the text).
Review all readings for Lesson 29.				Guide: Contrast these short stories to American and Russian short stories.

LESSON 30
TWENIETH CENTURY (Part 2)

Stevie Smith
(Florence Margaret Smith)

Stevie Smith (1902-1972), born Florence Margaret Smith, has been compared to American poet-humorist Ogden Nash (*Norton Anthology of Literature by Women*, p. 1617), even though her poetry has a more "mordant and (occasionally) more morbid" tone than Nash. Her first volume of verse, *A Good Time Was Had by All* was followed by two novels and over ten collections of poetry. "Ranging from satiric melancholy to ferocious irony, Smith's work both celebrated and criticized the customs of a slowly declining British Empire" (p. 1618). Smith worked as a writer and broadcaster for the BBC and is noted for her alacrity and acid humor. Smith won the Queen's Gold Medal for poetry in 1969, two years before her death.

Read and reflect on the following sample of Smith's poetry. In a 1-2 page essay, compare and contrast it with other modern poetry.

Not Waving but Drowning

Nobody heard him, the dead man,
But still he lay moaning:
I was much further out than you thought
And not waving but drowning.

Poor chap, he always loved larking
And now he's dead
It must have been too cold for him his heart gave way,
They said.

Oh, no no no, it was too cold always
(Still the dead one lay moaning)
I was much too far out all my life
And not waving but drowning.
(*Norton Anthology*, p. 1621)

Analyze: "Not Waving but Drowning," Stevie Smith; "Miss Brill," Katherine Mansfield, "Araby," James Joyce, "The Selfish Giant," Oscar Wilde, "The Bag," Saki (H. H. Munro), "Without Benefit of Clergy," Rudyard Kipling, "Rocking-Horse Winner," D. H. Lawrence.

Reading Ahead: "Are Women Human?" Dorothy Sayers; "Terence, This is Stupid Stuff," "Loveliest of Trees," and "Be Still my Soul, A. E. Housman; World War I Poets: "Greater Love," Wilfred Owen, "The Fish," Rupert Brooke; "In Flanders Field," George McCrae; "An Irish Airman Forsees his Death," "When You are Old," "The Second Coming," "The White Swans at Coole," and "Byzantium," William Butler Yeats.

Guide Question: What worldviews emerge in these poems?

Short Stories

CRITICAL THINKING

A. Discuss the way Mansfield develops her protagonist. Include in your answer the narrative technique, the way that Mansfield uses foils, and the use of internal conflict.

Miss Brill
Katherine Mansfield

Although it was so brilliantly fine—the blue sky powdered with gold and great spots of light like white wine splashed over the Jardins Publiques—Miss Brill was glad that she had decided on her fur. The air was motionless, but when you opened your mouth there was just a faint chill, like a chill from a glass of iced water

before you sip, and now and again a leaf came drifting—from nowhere, from the sky. Miss Brill put up her hand and touched her fur. Dear little thing! It was nice to feel it again. She had taken it out of its box that afternoon, shaken out the moth powder, given it a good brush, and rubbed the life back into the dim little eyes. "What has been happening to me?" said the sad little eyes. Oh, how sweet it was to see them snap at her again from the red eiderdown!...but the nose, which was of some black composition, wasn't at all firm. It must have had a knock, somehow. Never mind—a little dab of black sealing wax when the time came—when it was absolutely necessary...Little rogue! Yes, she really felt like that about it. Little rogue biting its tail just by her left ear. She could have taken it off and laid it on her lap and stroked it. She felt a tingling in her hands and arms, but that came from walking, she supposed. And when she breathed, something light and sad—no, not sad, exactly—something gentle seemed to move in her bosom.

There were a number of people out this afternoon, far more than last Sunday. And the band sounded louder and gayer. That was because the Season had begun. For although he band played all the year round on Sundays, out of season it was never the same. It was like some one playing with only the family to listen; it didn't care how it played if there weren't any strangers present. Wasn't the conductor wearing a new coat, too? She was sure it was new. He scraped with his foot and flapped his arms like a rooster about to crow, and the bandsmen sitting in the green rotunda blew out their cheeks and glared at the music. Now there came a little "flutey" bit—very pretty!—a little chain of bright drops. She was sure it would be repeated. It was; she lifted her head and smiled.

Only two people shared her "special" seat; a fine old man in a velvet coat, his hands clasped over a huge carved walking stick, and a big old woman, sitting upright, with a roll of knitting on her embroidered apron. They did not speak. This was disappointing, for Miss Brill always looked forward to the conversation. She had become really quite expert, she thought, at listening as though she didn't listen, at sitting in other people's lives just for a minute while they talked round her.

She glanced, sideways, at the old couple. Perhaps they would go soon. Last Sunday, too, hadn't been as interesting as usual. An Englishman and his wife, he wearing a dreadful Panama hat and she button boots. And she'd gone on the whole time about how she ought to wear spectacles; she knew she needed them; but that it was no good getting any; they'd be sure to break and they'd never keep on. And he'd been so patient. He'd suggested everything—gold rims, the kind that curve round your ears, little pads inside the bridge. No nothing would please her. "They'll always be sliding down my nose!" Miss Brill had wanted to shake her.

The old people sat on a bench, still as statues. Never mind, there was always the crowd to watch. To and fro, in front of the flower beds and the band rotunda, the couples and groups paraded, stopped to talk, to greet, to buy a handful of flowers from the old beggar who had his tray fixed to the railings. Little children ran among them, swooping and laughing; little boys with big white silk bows under their chins, little girls, little French dolls, dressed up in velvet and lace. And sometimes a tiny staggerer came suddenly rocking into the open from under the trees, stopped, stated, as suddenly sat down "flop," until its small high-stepping mother, like a young hen, rushed scolding to its rescue. Other people sat on the benches and green chairs, but they were nearly always the same, Sunday after Sunday, and—Miss Brill had often noticed—there was something funny about nearly all of them. They were off, silent, nearly all old, and from the way they stared they looked as though they'd just come from dark little rooms or even—even cupboards!

Behind the rotunda the slender trees with yellow leaves down drooping, and through them just a line of sea, and beyond the blue sky with gold-veined clouds. Tum-tum-tum tittle-um! tiddle-um! tum tiddle-um tum ta! blew the band. Two young girls in red came by and two young soldiers in blue met them, and they laughed and paired and went off arm-in-arm. Two peasant women with funny straw hats passed, gravely, leading beautiful smoke-colored donkeys. A cold, pale nun hurried by. A beautiful woman came along and dropped her bunch of violets, and a little boy ran after to hand them to her, and she took them and threw them away as if they'd been poisoned. Dear me! Miss Brill didn't know whether to admire that or not! And now an ermine toque and a gentleman in gray met just in front of her. He was tall, stiff, dignified, and she was wearing the ermine toque she'd bought when her hair was yellow. Now everything, her hair, her face, even her eyes, was the same color as the shabby ermine, and her hand, in its cleaned glove, lifted to dab her lips, was a tiny yellowish paw. Oh, she was so pleased to see him—delighted! She rather thought they were going to meet that afternoon. She described where she'd been—everywhere, here, there, along by the sea. The day was so charming—didn't he agree? And wouldn't he, perhaps?...But he shook his head, lighted a cigarette, slowly breathed a great deep puff into her face, and even while she was still talking and laughing, flicked the match away and walked on. The ermine toque was alone; she smiled more brightly than ever. But even the band seemed to know what she was feeling and played more softly, played tenderly, and the drum beat, "The Brute! The Brute!" over and over. What would she do? What was going to happen now? But as Miss Brill wondered, the ermine toque turned, raised her hand as though she'd seen someone else, much nicer, just over there, and pattered away. And the band changed again and played more quickly, more gayly than ever, and the old couple on Miss Brill's seat got up and marched away, and such a funny old man with long whiskers hobbled along in time to the music and was nearly knocked over by four girls walking abreast.

Oh, how fascinating it was! How she enjoyed it! How she loved sitting here, watching it all! It was like a play. It was exactly like a play. Who could believe the sky at the back wasn't painted? But is wasn't till a little brown dog trotted on solemn and then slowly trotted off, like a little "theatre" dog, a little dog that had been drugged, that Miss Brill discovered what it was that made it so exciting. They were all on stage. They weren't only the audience, no only looking on; they were acting. Even she had a part and came every Sunday. No doubt somebody would have noticed if she hadn't been there; she was part of the performance after all. How strange she'd never thought of it like that before! And yet it explained why she made such point of starting from home at just the same time each week—so as not to be late for the performance—and it also explained why she had a queer, shy feeling at telling her English pupils how she spend her Sunday afternoons. No wonder! Miss Brill nearly laughed out loud. She was on the stage. She thought of the old invalid gentleman to whom she read the newspaper four afternoons a week awhile he slept in the garden. She had got quite used to the frail head on the cotton pillow, the hollowed eyes, the open mouth and the high pinched nose. If he'd been dead she mightn't have noticed for weeks; she wouldn't have minded. But suddenly he knew he was having the paper read to him by

an actress! "An actress!" The old head lifted; two points of light quivered in the old eyes. "An actress—are ye?" And Miss Brill smoothed the newspaper as though it were the manuscript of her part and said gently; "Yes, I have been an actress for a long time."

The band had been having a rest. Now they started again. And what they played was warm, sunny, yet there was just a faint chill—a something, what was it?—not sadness—no, not sadness—a something that made you want to sing. The tune lifted, lifted, the light shone; and it seemed to Miss Brill that in another moment all of them, all the whole company, would begin singing. The young ones, the laughing ones who were moving together, they would begin and the men's voices, very resolute and brave, would join them. And then she too, she too, and the others on the benches—they would come in with a kind of accompaniment—something low, that scarcely rose or fell, something so beautiful—moving...And Miss Brill's eyes filled with tears and she looked smiling at all the other members of the company. Yes, we understand, we understand she thought—though what they understood she didn't know.

Just at that moment a boy and girl came and sat down where the old couple had been. They were beautifully dressed; they were in love. The hero and heroine, of course, just arrived from his father's yacht. And still soundlessly singing, still with that trembling smile, Miss Brill prepared to listen.

"No, not now," said the girl. "Not here, I can't."

"But why? Because of that stupid old thing at the end there?" asked the boy. "Why does she come here at all—who wants her? Why doesn't she keep her silly old mug at home?"

"It's her fur which is so funny," giggled the girl. "It's exactly like a fried whiting."

"Ah, be off with you!" said the boy in an angry whisper. Then: "Tell me, ma petite chere—"

"No, not here," said the girl. "Not yet."

On her way home she usually bought a slice of honeycake at the baker's. It was her Sunday treat. Sometimes there was an almond in her slice, sometimes not. It made a great difference. If there was an almond it was like carrying home a tiny present—a surprise—something that might very well not have been there. She hurried on the almond Sundays and struck the match for the kettle in quite a dashing way. But today she passed the baker's by, climbed the stairs, went into the little dark room—her room like a cupboard—and sat down on the red eiderdown. She sat there for a long time. The box that the fur came out of was on the bed.

She unclasped the necklet quickly; quickly, without looking, laid it inside. But when she put the lid on she thought she heard something crying. (www.geocities.com/short-stories)

B. Discuss Joyce's use of stream of consciousness to tell this story. How reliable is the narrator?

Araby

James Joyce

North Richmond Street, being blind, was a quiet street except at the hour when the Christian Brothers' School set the boys free. An uninhabited house of two storeys stood at the blind end, detached from its neighbours in a square ground. The other houses of the street, conscious of decent lives within them, gazed at one another with brown imperturbable faces. The former tenant of our house, a priest, had died in the back drawing room. Air, musty from having been long enclosed, hung in all the rooms, and the waste room behind the kitchen was littered with old useless papers. Among these I found a few paper-covered books, the pages of which were curled and damp: *The Abbot*, by Walter Scott, *The Devout Communicant*, and *The Memoirs of Vidocq*. I liked the last best because its leaves were yellow. The wild garden behind the house contained a central apple tree and a few straggling bushes, under one of which I found the late tenant's rusty bicycle pump. He had been a very charitable priest; in his will he had left all his money to institutions and the furniture of his house to his sister.

When the short days of winter came, dusk fell before we had well eaten our dinners. When we met in the street the houses had grown sombre. The space of sky above us was the colour of ever-changing violet and towards it the lamps of the street lifted their feeble lanterns. The cold air stung us and we played till our bodies glowed. Our shouts echoed in the silent street. The career of our play brought us through the dark muddy lanes behind the houses, where we ran the gauntlet of the rough tribes from the cottages, to the back doors of the dark dripping gardens where odours arose from the ashpits, to the dark odorous stables where a coachman smoothed and combed the horse or shook music from the buckled harness. When we

returned to the street, light from the kitchen windows had filled the areas. If my uncle was seen turning the corner, we hid in the shadow until we had seen him safely housed. Or if Mangan's sister came out on the doorstep to call her brother in to his tea, we watched her from our shadow peer up and down the street. We waited to see whether she would remain or go in and, if she remained, we left our shadow and walked up to Mangan's steps resignedly. She was waiting for us, her figure defined by the light from the half-opened door. Her brother always teased her before he obeyed, and I stood by the railings looking at her. Her dress swung as she moved her body, and the soft rope of her hair tossed from side to side.

Every morning I lay on the floor in the front parlour watching her door. The blind was pulled down to within an inch of the sash so that I could not be seen. When she came out on the doorstep my heart leaped. I ran to the hall, seized my books and followed her. I kept her brown figure always in my eye and, when we came near the point at which our ways diverged, I quickened my pace and passed her. This happened morning after morning. I had never spoken to her, except for a few casual words, and yet her name was like a summons to all my foolish blood.

Her image accompanied me even in places the most hostile to romance. On Saturday evenings when my aunt went marketing I had to go to carry some of the parcels. We walked through the flaring streets, jostled by drunken men and bargaining women, amid the curses of labourers, the shrill litanies of shop-boys who stood on guard by the barrels of pigs' cheeks, the nasal chanting of street-singers, who sang a *come-all-you* about O'Donovan Rossa, or a ballad about the troubles in our native land. These noises converged in a single sensation of life for me: I imagined that I bore my chalice safely through a throng of foes. Her name sprang to my lips at moments in strange prayers and praises which I myself did not understand. My eyes were often full of tears (I could not tell why) and at times a flood from my heart seemed to pour itself out into my bosom. I thought little of the future. I did not know whether I would ever speak to her or not or, if I spoke to her, how I could tell her of my confused adoration. But my body was like a harp and her words and gestures were like fingers running upon the wires.

One evening I went into the back drawing-room in which the priest had died. It was a dark rainy evening and there was no sound in the house. Through one of the broken panes I heard the rain impinge upon the earth, the fine incessant needles of water playing in the sodden beds. Some distant lamp or lighted window gleamed below me. I was thankful that I could see so little. All my senses seemed to desire to veil themselves and, feeling that I was about to slip from them, I pressed the palms of my hands together until they trembled, murmuring: `O love! O love!' many times. At last she spoke to me. When she addressed the first words to me I was so confused that I did not know what to answer. She asked me was I going to *Araby*. I forgot whether I answered yes or no. It would be a splendid bazaar; she said she would love to go. 'And why can't you?' I asked.

While she spoke she turned a silver bracelet round and round her wrist. She could not go, she said, because there would be a retreat that week in her convent. Her brother and two other boys were fighting for their caps, and I was alone at the railings. She held one of the spikes, bowing her head towards me. The light from the lamp opposite our door caught the white curve of her neck, lit up her hair that rested there and, falling, lit up the hand upon the railing. It fell over one side of her dress and caught the white border of a petticoat, just visible as she stood at ease.

'It's well for you,' she said.

'If I go,' I said, 'I will bring you something.'

What innumerable follies laid waste my waking and sleeping thoughts after that evening! I wished to annihilate the tedious intervening days. I chafed against the work of school. At night in my bedroom and by day in the classroom her image came between me and the page I strove to read. The syllables of the word *Araby* were called to me through the silence in which my soul luxuriated and cast an Eastern enchantment over me. I asked for leave to go to the bazaar on Saturday night. My aunt was surprised, and hoped it was not some Freemason affair. I answered few questions in class. I watched my master's face pass from amiability to sternness; he hoped I was not beginning to idle. I could not call my wandering thoughts together. I had hardly any patience with the serious work of life which, now that it stood between me and my desire, seemed to me child's play, ugly monotonous child's play.

On Saturday morning I reminded my uncle that I wished to go to the bazaar in the evening. He was fussing at the hallstand, looking for the hat-brush, and answered me curtly:

'Yes, boy, I know.'

As he was in the hall I could not go into the front parlour and lie at the window. I felt the house in bad humour and walked slowly towards the school. The air was pitilessly raw and already my heart misgave me.

When I came home to dinner my uncle had not yet been home. Still it was early. I sat staring at the clock for some time and, when its ticking began to irritate me, I left the room. I mounted the staircase and gained the upper part of the house. The high, cold, empty, gloomy rooms liberated me and I went from room to room singing. From the front window I saw my companions playing below in the street. Their cries reached me weakened and indistinct and, leaning my forehead against the cool glass, I looked over at the dark house where she lived. I may have stood there for an hour, seeing nothing but the brown-clad figure cast by my imagination, touched discreetly by the lamplight at the curved neck, at the hand upon the railings and at the border below the dress.

When I came downstairs again I found Mrs. Mercer sitting at the fire. She was an old, garrulous woman, a pawnbroker's widow, who collected used stamps for some pious purpose. I had to endure the gossip of the tea-table. The meal was prolonged beyond an hour and still my uncle did not come. Mrs. Mercer stood up to go: she was sorry she couldn't wait any longer, but it was after eight o'clock and she did not like to be out late, as the night air was bad for her. When she had gone I began to walk up and down the room, clenching my fists. My aunt said: `I'm afraid you may put off your bazaar for this night of Our Lord.'

At nine o'clock I heard my uncle's latchkey in the hall door. I heard him talking to himself and heard the hallstand rocking when it had received the weight of his overcoat. I could interpret these signs. When he was midway through his dinner I asked him to give me the money to go to the bazaar. He had forgotten.

`The people are in bed and after their first sleep now,' he said.

I did not smile. My aunt said to him energetically:

`Can't you give him the money and let him go? You've kept him late enough as it is.'

My uncle said he was very sorry he had forgotten. He said he believed in the old saying: 'All work and no play makes Jack a dull boy.' He asked me where I was going and, when I told him a second time, he asked me did I know *The Arab's Farewell to his Steed*. When I left the kitchen he was about to recite the opening lines of the piece to my aunt.

I held a florin tightly in my hand as I strode down Buckingham Street towards the station. The sight of the streets thronged with buyers and glaring with gas recalled to me the purpose of my journey. I took my seat in a third-class carriage of a deserted train. After an intolerable delay the train moved out of the station slowly. It crept onward among ruinous houses and over the twinkling river. At Westland Row Station a crowd of people pressed to the carriage doors; but the porters moved them back, saying that it was a special train for the bazaar. I remained alone in the bare carriage. In a few minutes the train drew up beside an improvised wooden platform. I passed out on to the road and saw by the lighted dial of a clock that it was ten minutes to ten. In front of me was a large building which displayed the magical name. I could not find any sixpenny entrance and, fearing that the bazaar would be closed, I passed in quickly through a turnstile, handing a shilling to a weary-looking man. I found myself in a big hall girded at half its height by a gallery. Nearly all the stalls were closed and the greater part of the hall was in darkness. I recognized a silence like that which pervades a church after a service. I walked into the centre of the bazaar timidly. A few people were gathered about the stalls which were still open. Before a curtain, over which the words *Café Chantant* were written in coloured lamps, two men were counting money on a salver. I listened to the fall of the coins.

Remembering with difficulty why I had come, I went over to one of the stalls and examined porcelain vases and flowered tea-sets. At the door of the stall a young lady was talking and laughing with two young gentlemen. I remarked their English accents and listened vaguely to their conversation.

`O, I never said such a thing!'

`O, but you did!'

`O, but I didn't!'

`Didn't she say that?'

`Yes. I heard her.'

`O, there's a... fib!'

Observing me, the young lady came over and asked me did I wish to buy anything. The tone of her voice was not encouraging; she seemed to have spoken to me out of a sense of duty. I looked humbly at the great jars that stood like eastern guards at either side of the dark entrance to the stall and murmured:

`No, thank you.'

The young lady changed the position of one of the vases and went back to the two young men. They began to talk of the same subject. Once or twice the young lady glanced at me over her shoulder.

I lingered before her stall, though I knew my stay was useless, to make my interest in her wares seem the more real. Then I turned away slowly and walked down the middle of the bazaar. I allowed the two pennies to fall against the sixpence in my pocket. I heard a voice call from one end of the gallery that the light was out. The upper part of the hall was now completely dark.

Gazing up into the darkness I saw myself as a creature driven and derided by vanity; and my eyes burned with anguish and anger.

(http://www.classicreader.com/read.php/sid.6/book id.344/)

C. What thematic points is Wilde making through "The Selfish Giant"?

The Selfish Giant

Oscar Wilde

Every afternoon, as they were coming from school, the children used to go and play in the Giant's garden.

It was a large lovely garden, with soft green grass. Here and there over the grass stood beautiful flowers like stars, and there were twelve peach-trees that in the springtime broke out into delicate blossoms of pink and pearl, and in the autumn bore rich fruit. The birds sat on the trees and sang so sweetly that the children used to stop their games in order to listen to them. "How happy we are here!" they cried to each other.

One day the Giant came back. He had been to visit his friend the Cornish ogre, and had stayed with him for seven years. After the seven years were over he had said all that he had to say, for his conversation was limited, and he determined to return to his own castle. When he arrived he saw the children playing in the garden.

"What are you doing here?" he cried in a very gruff voice, and the children ran away.

"My own garden is my own garden," said the Giant; "any one can understand that, and I will allow nobody to play in it but myself." So he built a high wall all round it, and put up a notice-board.

TRESPASSERS WILL BE PROSECUTED

He was a very selfish Giant.

The poor children had now nowhere to play. They tried to play on the road, but the road was very dusty and full of hard stones, and they did not like it. They used to wander round the high wall when their lessons were over, and talk about the beautiful garden inside.

"How happy we were there," they said to each other.

Then the Spring came, and all over the country there were little blossoms and little birds. Only in the garden of the Selfish Giant it was still winter. The birds did not care to sing in it as there were no children, and the trees forgot to blossom. Once a beautiful flower put its head out from the grass, but when it saw the notice-board it was so sorry for the children that it slipped back into the ground again, and went off to sleep. The only people who were pleased were the Snow and the Frost. "Spring has forgotten this garden," they cried, "so we will live here all the year round." The Snow covered up the grass with her great white cloak, and the Frost painted all the trees silver. Then they invited the North Wind to stay with them, and he came. He was wrapped in furs, and he roared all day about the garden, and blew the chimney-pots down. "This is a delightful spot," he said, "we must ask the Hail on a visit." So the Hail came. Every day for three hours he rattled on the roof of the castle till he broke most of the slates, and then he ran round and round the garden as fast as he could go. He was dressed in grey, and his breath was like ice.

"I cannot understand why the Spring is so late in coming," said the Selfish Giant, as he sat at the window and looked out at his cold white garden; "I hope there will be a change in the weather."

But the Spring never came, nor the Summer. The Autumn gave golden fruit to every garden, but to the Giant's garden she gave none. "He is too selfish," she said. So it was always Winter there, and the North Wind, and the Hail, and the Frost, and the Snow danced about through the trees.

One morning the Giant was lying awake in bed when he heard some lovely music. It sounded so sweet to his ears that he thought it must be the King's musicians passing by. It was really only a little linnet singing outside his window, but it was so long since he had heard a bird sing in his garden that it seemed to him to be the most beautiful music in the world. Then the Hail stopped dancing over his head, and the North Wind ceased roaring, and a delicious perfume came to him through the open casement. "I believe the Spring has come at last," said the Giant; and he jumped out of bed and looked out.

What did he see?

He saw a most wonderful sight. Through a little hole in the wall the children had crept in, and they were sitting in the branches of the trees. In every tree that he could see there was a little child. And the trees were so glad to have the children back again that they had cov-

ered themselves with blossoms, and were waving their arms gently above the children's heads. The birds were flying about and twittering with delight, and the flowers were looking up through the green grass and laughing. It was a lovely scene, only in one corner it was still winter. It was the farthest corner of the garden, and in it was standing a little boy. He was so small that he could not reach up to the branches of the tree, and he was wandering all round it, crying bitterly. The poor tree was still quite covered with frost and snow, and the North Wind was blowing and roaring above it. "Climb up! little boy," said the Tree, and it bent its branches down as low as it could; but the boy was too tiny.

And the Giant's heart melted as he looked out. "How selfish I have been!" he said; "now I know why the Spring would not come here. I will put that poor little boy on the top of the tree, and then I will knock down the wall, and my garden shall be the children's playground for ever and ever." He was really very sorry for what he had done.

So he crept downstairs and opened the front door quite softly, and went out into the garden. But when the children saw him they were so frightened that they all ran away, and the garden became winter again. Only the little boy did not run, for his eyes were so full of tears that he did not see the Giant coming. And the Giant stole up behind him and took him gently in his hand, and put him up into the tree. And the tree broke at once into blossom, and the birds came and sang on it, and the little boy stretched out his two arms and flung them round the Giant's neck, and kissed him. And the other children, when they saw that the Giant was not wicked any longer, came running back, and with them came the Spring. "It is your garden now, little children," said the Giant, and he took a great axe and knocked down the wall. And when the people were going to market at twelve o'clock they found the Giant playing with the children in the most beautiful garden they had ever seen.

All day long they played, and in the evening they came to the Giant to bid him good-bye.

"But where is your little companion?" he said: "the boy I put into the tree." The Giant loved him the best because he had kissed him.

"We don't know," answered the children; "he has gone away."

"You must tell him to be sure and come here to-morrow," said the Giant. But the children said that they did not know where he lived, and had never seen him before; and the Giant felt very sad.

Every afternoon, when school was over, the children came and played with the Giant. But the little boy whom the Giant loved was never seen again. The Giant was very kind to all the children, yet he longed for his first little friend, and often spoke of him. "How I would like to see him!" he used to say.

Years went over, and the Giant grew very old and feeble. He could not play about any more, so he sat in a huge armchair, and watched the children at their games, and admired his garden. "I have many beautiful flowers," he said; "but the children are the most beautiful flowers of all."

One winter morning he looked out of his window as he was dressing. He did not hate the Winter now, for he knew that it was merely the Spring asleep, and that the flowers were resting.

Suddenly he rubbed his eyes in wonder, and looked and looked. It certainly was a marvellous sight. In the farthest corner of the garden was a tree quite covered with lovely white blossoms. Its branches were all golden, and silver fruit hung down from them, and underneath it stood the little boy he had loved.

Downstairs ran the Giant in great joy, and out into the garden. He hastened across the grass, and came near to the child. And when he came quite close his face grew red with anger, and he said, "Who hath dared to wound thee?" For on the palms of the child's hands were the prints of two nails, and the prints of two nails were on the little feet.

"Who hath dared to wound thee?" cried the Giant; "tell me, that I may take my big sword and slay him."

"Nay!" answered the child; "but these are the wounds of Love."

"Who art thou?" said the Giant, and a strange awe fell on him, and he knelt before the little child.

And the child smiled on the Giant, and said to him, "You let me play once in your garden, to-day you shall come with me to my garden, which is Paradise."

And when the children ran in that afternoon, they found the Giant lying dead under the tree, all covered with white blossoms.

((http://www.classicreader.com/read.php/sid.6/bookid.210/)

D. Discuss Saki's use of dialogue to advance the character development and plot development.

The Bag

Saki (H. H. Munro)

"The Major is coming in to tea," said Mrs. Hoopington to her niece. "He's just gone round to the stables with his horse. Be as bright and lively as you can; the poor man's got a fit of the glooms."

Major Pallaby was a victim of circumstances, over which he had no control, and of his temper, over which he had very little. He had taken on the Mastership of the Pexdale Hounds in succession to a highly popular man who had fallen foul of his committee, and the Major found himself confronted with the overt hostility of at least half the hunt, while his lack of tact and amiability had done much to alienate the remainder. Hence subscriptions were beginning to fall off, foxes grew provokingly scarcer, and wire obtruded itself with increasing frequency. The Major could plead reasonable excuse for his fit of the glooms.

In ranging herself as a partisan on the side of Major Pallaby Mrs. Hoopington had been largely influenced by the fact that she had made up her mind to marry him at an early date. Against his notorious bad temper she set his three thousand a year, and his prospective succession to a baronetcy gave a casting vote in his favour. The Major's plans on the subject of matrimony were not at present in such an advanced stage as Mrs. Hoopington's, but he was beginning to find his way over to Hoopington Hall with a frequency that was already being commented on.

"He had a wretchedly thin field out again yesterday," said Mrs. Hoopington. "Why you didn't bring one or two hunting men down with you, instead of that stupid Russian boy, I can't think."

"Vladimir isn't stupid," protested her niece; "he's one of the most amusing boys I ever met. Just compare him for a moment with some of your heavy hunting men—"

"Anyhow, my dear Norah, he can't ride."

"Russians never can; but he shoots."

"Yes; and what does he shoot? Yesterday he brought home a woodpecker in his game-bag."

"But he'd shot three pheasants and some rabbits as well."

"That's no excuse for including a woodpecker in his game-bag."

"Foreigners go in for mixed bags more than we do. A Grand Duke pots a vulture just as seriously as we should stalk a bustard. Anyhow, I've explained to Vladimir that certain birds are beneath his dignity as a sportsman. And as he's only nineteen, of course, his dignity is a sure thing to appeal to."

Mrs. Hoopington sniffed. Most people with whom Vladimir came in contact found his high spirits infectious, but his present hostess was guaranteed immune against infection of that sort.

"I hear him coming in now," she observed. "I shall

go and get ready for tea. We're going to have it here in the hall. Entertain the Major if he comes in before I'm down, and, above all, be bright."

Norah was dependent on her aunt's good graces for many little things that made life worth living, and she was conscious of a feeling of discomfiture because the Russian youth whom she had brought down as a welcome element of change in the country-house routine was not making a good impression. That young gentleman, however, was supremely unconscious of any shortcomings, and burst into the hall, tired, and less sprucely groomed than usual, but distinctly radiant. His game-bag looked comfortably full.

"Guess what I have shot," he demanded.

"Pheasants, woodpigeons, rabbits," hazarded Norah.

"No; a large beast; I don't know what you call it in English. Brown, with a darkish tail." Norah changed colour.

"Does it live in a tree and eat nuts?" she asked, hoping that the use of the adjective "large" might be an exaggeration.

Vladimir laughed.

"Oh no; not a biyelka."

"Does it swim and eat fish?" asked Norah, with a fervent prayer in her heart that it might turn out to be an otter.

"No," said Vladimir, busy with the straps of his game-bag; "it lives in the woods, and eats rabbits and chickens."

Norah sat down suddenly, and hid her face in her hands.

"Merciful Heaven!" she wailed; "he's shot a fox!"

Vladimir looked up at her in consternation. In a torrent of agitated words she tried to explain the horror of the situation. The boy understood nothing, but was thoroughly alarmed.

"Hide it, hide it!" said Norah frantically, pointing to the still unopened bag. "My aunt and the Major will be here in a moment. Throw it on the top of that chest; they won't see it there."

Vladimir swung the bag with fair aim; but the strap caught in its flight on the outstanding point of an antler fixed in the wall, and the bag, with its terrible burden, remained suspended just above the alcove where tea would presently be laid. At that moment Mrs. Hoopington and the Major entered the hall.

"The Major is going to draw our covers to-morrow," announced the lady, with a certain heavy satisfaction. "Smithers is confident that we'll be able to show him some sport; he swears he's seen a fox in the nut copse three times this week."

"I'm sure I hope so; I hope so," said the Major moodily. "I must break this sequence of blank days. One hears so often that a fox has settled down as a tenant for life in certain covers, and then when you go to turn him out there isn't a trace of him. I'm certain a fox was shot or trapped in Lady Widden's woods the very day before we drew them."

"Major, if any one tried that game on in my woods they'd get short shrift," said Mrs. Hoopington.

Norah found her way mechanically to the tea-table and made her fingers frantically busy in rearranging the parsley round the sandwich dish. On one side of her loomed the morose countenance of the Major, on the other she was conscious of the scared, miserable eyes of Vladimir. And above it all hung THAT. She dared not raise her eyes above the level of the tea-table, and she almost expected to see a spot of accusing vulpine blood drip down and stain the whiteness of the cloth. Her aunt's manner signalled to her the repeated message to "be bright"; for the present she was fully occupied in keeping her teeth from chattering.

"What did you shoot to-day?" asked Mrs. Hoopington suddenly of the unusually silent Vladimir.

"Nothing—nothing worth speaking of," said the boy.

Norah's heart, which had stood still for a space, made up for lost time with a most disturbing bound.

"I wish you'd find something that was worth speaking about," said the hostess; "every one seems to have lost their tongues."

"When did Smithers last see that fox?" said the Major.

"Yesterday morning; a fine dog-fox, with a dark brush," confided Mrs. Hoopington.

"Aha, we'll have a good gallop after that brush to-morrow," said the Major, with a transient gleam of good humour. And then gloomy silence settled again round the tea-table, a silence broken only by despondent munchings and the occasional feverish rattle of a tea-spoon in its saucer. A diversion was at last afforded by Mrs. Hoopington's fox-terrier, which had jumped on to a vacant chair, the better to survey the delicacies of the table, and was now sniffing in an upward direction at something apparently more interesting than cold tea-cake.

"What is exciting him?" asked his mistress, as the dog suddenly broke into short angry barks, with a running accompaniment of tremulous whines.

"Why," she continued, "it's your gamebag, Vladimir! What HAVE you got in it?"

"By Gad," said the Major, who was now standing up; "there's a pretty warm scent!"

And then a simultaneous idea flashed on himself and Mrs. Hoopington. Their faces flushed to distinct but harmonious tones of purple, and with one accusing voice they screamed, "You've shot the fox!"

Norah tried hastily to palliate Vladimir's misdeed in their eyes, but it is doubtful whether they heard her. The Major's fury clothed and reclothed itself in words as frantically as a woman up in town for one day's shopping tries on a succession of garments. He reviled and railed at fate and the general scheme of things, he pitied himself with a strong, deep pity too poignent for tears, he condemned every one with whom he had ever come in contact to endless and abnormal punishments. In fact, he conveyed the impression that if a destroying angel had been lent to him for a week it would have had very little time for private study. In the lulls of his outcry could be heard the querulous monotone of Mrs. Hoopington and the sharp staccato barking of the fox-terrier. Vladimir, who did not understand a tithe of what was being said, sat fondling a cigarette and repeating under his breath from time to time a vigorous English adjective which he had long ago taken affectionately into his vocabulary. His mind strayed back to the youth in the old Russian folk-tale who shot an enchanted bird with dramatic results. Meanwhile, the Major, roaming round the hall like an imprisoned cyclone, had caught sight of and joyfully pounced on the telephone apparatus, and lost no time in ringing up the hunt secretary and announcing his resignation of the Mastership. A servant had by this time brought his horse round to the door, and in a few seconds Mrs. Hoopington's shrill monotone had the field to itself. But after the Major's display her best efforts at vocal violence missed their full effect; it was as though one had come straight out from a Wagner opera into a rather tame thunderstorm. Realising, perhaps, that her tirades were something of an anticlimax, Mrs. Hoopington broke suddenly into some rather necessary tears and marched out of the room, leaving behind her a silence almost as terrible as the turmoil which had preceded it.

"What shall I do with — THAT?" asked Vladimir at last.

"Bury it," said Norah.

"Just plain burial?" said Vladimir, rather relieved. He had almost expected that some of the local clergy would have insisted on being present, or that a salute might have to be fired over the grave.

And thus it came to pass that in the dusk of a November evening the Russian boy, murmuring a few of the prayers of his Church for luck, gave hasty but decent burial to a large polecat under the lilac trees at Hoopington.

(http://www.classicreader.com/read.php/sid.6/book id.1627/)

E. Kipling is one of the best storytellers in history. Discuss Kipling's storytelling techniques in the following story. Identify the rising action, climax, and resolution.

Without Benefit of Clergy

Rudyard Kipling

Before my Spring I garnered Autumn's gain,
Out of her time my field was white with grain,
The year gave up her secrets to my woe.
Forced and deflowered each sick season lay,
In mystery of increase and decay;
I saw the sunset ere men saw the day,
Who am too wise in that I should not know.
　　　　　　　　　　　　　— —Bitter Waters.

I

"But if it be a girl?"

"Lord of my life, it cannot be. I have prayed for so many nights, and sent gifts to Sheikh Badl's shrine so often, that I know God will give us a son — —a man-child that shall grow into a man. Think of this and be glad. My mother shall be his mother till I can take him again, and the mullah of the Pattan mosque shall cast his nativity — — God send he be born in an auspicious hour! — —and then, and then thou wilt never weary of me, thy slave."

"Since when hast thou been a slave, my queen?"

"Since the beginning— —till this mercy came to me. How could I be sure of thy love when I knew that I had been bought with silver?"

"Nay, that was the dowry. I paid it to thy mother."

"And she has buried it, and sits upon it all day long like a hen. What talk is yours of dower! I was bought as though I had been a Lucknow dancing-girl instead of a child."

"Art thou sorry for the sale?"

"I have sorrowed; but to-day I am glad. Thou wilt never cease to love me now? — —answer, my king."

"Never— —never. No."

"Not even though the *mem-log*— —the white women of thy own blood— —love thee? And remember, I have watched them driving in the evening; they are very fair."

"I have seen fire-balloons by the hundred. I have seen the moon, and— —then I saw no more fire-balloons."

Ameera clapped her hands and laughed. "Very good talk," she said. Then with an assumption of great statelines, "It is enough. Thou hast my permission to depart, — —if thou wilt."

The man did not move. He was sitting on a low red-lacquered couch in a room furnished only with a blue and white floor-cloth, some rugs, and a very complete collection of native cushions. At his feet sat a woman of sixteen, and she was all but all the world in his eyes. By every rule and law she should have been otherwise, for he was an Englishman, and she a Mussulman's daughter bought two years before from her mother, who, being left without money, would have sold Ameera shrieking to the Prince of Darkness if the price had been sufficient.

It was a contract entered into with a light heart; but even before the girl had reached her bloom she came to fill the greater portion of John Holden's life. For her, and the withered hag her mother, he had taken a little house overlooking the great red-walled city, and found, — —when the marigolds had sprung up by the well in the court-yard, and Ameera had established herself according to her own ideas of comfort, and her mother had ceased grumbling at the inadequacy of the cooking-places, the distance from the daily market, and at matters of house-keeping in general, — —that the house was to him his home. Any one could enter his bachelor's bungalow by day or night, and the life that he led there was an unlovely one. In the house in the city his feet only could pass beyond the outer court-yard to the women's rooms; and when the big wooden gate was bolted behind him he was king in his own territory, with Ameera for queen. And there was going to be added to this kingdom a third person whose arrival Holden felt inclined to resent. It interfered with his perfect happiness. It disarranged the orderly peace of the house that was his own. But Ameera was wild with delight at the thought of it, and her mother not less so. The love of a man, and particularly a white man, was at the best an inconstant affair, but it might, both women argued, be held fast by a baby's hands. "And then," Ameera would always say, "then he will never care for the white *mem-log*. I hate them all— —I hate them all."

"He will go back to his own people in time," said the mother; "but by the blessing of God that time is yet afar off."

Holden sat silent on the couch thinking of the future, and his thoughts were not pleasant. The drawbacks of a double life are manifold. The Government, with singular care, had ordered him out of the station for a fortnight on special duty in the place of a man who was watching by the bedside of a sick wife. The verbal notification of the transfer had been edged by a cheerful remark that Holden ought to think himself lucky in being a bachelor and a free man. He came to break the news to Ameera.

"It is not good," she said slowly, "but it is not all bad. There is my mother here, and no harm will come to me— —unless indeed I die of pure joy. Go thou to thy work and think no troublesome thoughts. When the days are done I believe......nay, I am sure. And— —and then I shall lay *him* in thy arms, and thou wilt love me for ever. The train goes to-night, at midnight is it not? Go now, and do not let thy heart be heavy by cause of me. But thou wilt not delay in returning? Thou wilt not stay on the road to talk to the bold white *mem-log*. Come back to me swiftly, my life."

As he left the courtyard to reach his horse that was tethered to the gate-post, Holden spoke to the white-haired old watchman who guarded the house, and bade him under certain contingencies despatch the filled-up telegraph-form that Holden gave him. It was all that could be done, and with the sensations of a man who has attended his own funeral Holden went away by the night mail to his exile. Every hour of the day he dreaded the arrival of the telegram, and every hour of the night he pictured to himself the death of Ameera. In consequence his work for the State was not of first-rate quality, nor was his temper towards his colleagues of the most amiable. The fortnight ended without a sign from his home, and, torn to pieces by his anxieties, Holden returned to be swallowed up for two precious hours by a dinner at the club, wherein he heard, as a man hears in a swoon, voices telling him how execrably he had performed the other man's duties, and how he had endeared himself to all his associates. Then he fled on horseback through the night with his heart in his mouth. There was no answer at first to his blows on the gate, and he had just wheeled his horse round to kick it in when Pir Khan appeared with a lantern and held his stirrup.

"Has aught occurred?" said Holden.

"The news does not come from my mouth, Protector of the Poor, but— —" He held out his shaking hand as befitted the bearer of good news who is entitled to a reward.

Holden hurried through the courtyard. A light burned in the upper room. His horse neighed in the gateway, and he heard a shrill little wail that sent all the blood into the apple of his throat. It was a new voice, but it did not prove that Ameera was alive.

"Who is there?" he called up the narrow brick staircase.

There was a cry of delight from Ameera, and then the voice of the mother, tremulous with old age and pride — —"We be two women and — —the — —man — —thy — —son."

On the threshold of the room Holden stepped on a naked dagger, that was laid there to avert ill-luck, and it broke at the hilt under his impatient heel.

"God is great!" cooed Ameera in the half-light. "Thou hast taken his misfortunes on thy head."

"Ay, but how is it with thee, life of my life? Old woman, how is it with her?"

"She has forgotten her sufferings for joy that the child is born. There is no harm; but speak softly," said the mother.

"It only needed thy presence to make me all well," said Ameera. "My king, thou hast been very long away. What gifts hast thou for me? Ah, ah! It is I that bring gifts this time. Look, my life, look. Was there ever such a babe? Nay, I am too weak even to clear my arm from him."

"Rest then, and do not talk. I am here, *bachari* (little woman)."

"Well said, for there is a bond and a heel-rope (*peecharee*) between us now that nothing can break. Look——canst thou see in this light? He is without spot or blemish. Never was such a man-child. *Ya illah!* he shall be a pundit——no, a trooper of the Queen. And, my life, dost thou love me as well as ever, though I am faint and sick and worn? Answer truly."

"Yea. I love as I have loved, with all my soul. Lie still, pearl, and rest."

"Then do not go. Sit by my side here——so. Mother, the lord of this house needs a cushion. Bring it." There was an almost imperceptible movement on the part of the new life that lay in the hollow of Ameera"s arm. "Aho!" she said, her voice breaking with love. "The babe is a champion from his birth. He is kicking me in the side with mighty kicks. Was there ever such a babe! And he is ours to us——thine and mine. Put thy hand on his head, but carefully, for he is very young, and men are unskilled in such matters."

Very cautiously Holden touched with the tips of his fingers the downy head.

"He is of the Faith," said Ameera; "for lying here in the night-watches I whispered the call to prayer and the profession of faith into his ears. And it is most marvellous that he was born upon a Friday, as I was born. Be careful of him, my life; but he can almost grip with his hands."

Holden found one helpless little hand that closed feebly on his finger. And the clutch ran through his body till it settled about his heart. Till then his sole thought had been for Ameera. He began to realise that there was some one else in the world, but he could not feel that it was a veritable son with a soul. He sat down to think, and Ameera dozed lightly.

"Get hence, *sahib*," said her mother under her breath. "It is not good that she should find you here on waking. She must be still."

"I go," said Holden submissively. "Here be rupees. See that my *baba* gets fat and finds all that he needs."

The chink of the silver roused Ameera. "I am his mother, and no hireling," she said weakly. "Shall I look to him more or less for the sake of money? Mother, give it back. I have borne my lord a son."

The deep sleep of weakness came upon her almost before the sentence was completed. Holden went down to the courtyard very softly with his heart at ease. Pir Khan, the old watchman, was chuckling with delight. "This house is now complete," he said, and without further comment thrust into Holden"s hands the hilt of a sabre worn many years ago when he, Pir Khan, served the Queen in the police. The bleat of a tethered goat came from the well-kerb.

"There be two," said Pir Khan, "two goats of the best. I bought them, and they cost much money; and since there is no birth-party assembled their flesh will be all mine. Strike craftily, *sahib!* Tis an ill-balanced sabre at the best. Wait till they raise their heads from cropping the marigolds."

"And why?" said Holden, bewildered.

"For the birth-sacrifice. What else? Otherwise the child being unguarded from fate may die. The Protector of the Poor knows the fitting words to be said."

Holden had learned them once with little thought that he would ever speak them in earnest. The touch of the cold sabre-hilt in his palm turned suddenly to the clinging grip of the child up-stairs——the child that was his own son——and a dread of loss filled him.

"Strike!" said Pir Khan. "Never life came into the world but life was paid for it. See, the goats have raised their heads. Now! With a drawing cut!"

Hardly knowing what he did, Holden cut twice as he muttered the Mahomedan prayer that runs:

"Almighty! In place of this my son I offer life for life, blood for blood, head for head, bone for bone, hair for hair, skin for skin." The waiting horse snorted and bounded in his pickets at the smell of the raw blood that spirted over Holden"s riding-boots.

"Well smitten!" said Pir Khan wiping the sabre. "A swordsman was lost in thee. Go with a light heart, Heaven-born. I am thy servant, and the servant of thy son. May the Presence live a thousand years and......the flesh of the goats is all mine?" Pir Khan drew back richer by a month's pay. Holden swung himself into the saddle and rode off through the low-hanging wood-smoke of the evening. He was full of riotous exultation, alternating with a vast vague tenderness directed towards no particular object, that made him choke as he bent over the neck of his uneasy horse. "I never felt like this in my life," he thought. "I'll go to the club and pull myself together."

A game of pool was beginning, and the room was full of men. Holden entered, eager to get to the light and the company of his fellows, singing at the top of his voice——

In Baltimore a-walking, a lady I did meet!

"Did you?" said the club-secretary from his corner. "Did she happen to tell you that your boots were wringing wet? Great goodness, man, it's blood!"

"Bosh!" said Holden, picking his cue from the rack. "May I cut in? It's dew. I've been riding through high crops. My faith! my boots are in a mess though!

''And if it be a girl she shall wear a wedding-ring, And if it be a boy he shall fight for his king, With his dirk, and his cap, and his little jacket blue, He shall walk the quarter-deck——"

"Yellow on blue——green next player," said the marker monotonously.

"He shall walk the quarter-deck,——Am I green, marker? He shall walk the quarter-deck,——eh! that's a bad shot,——As his daddy used to do!"

"I don't see that you have anything to crow about," said a zealous junior civilian acidly. "The Government is not exactly pleased with your work when you relieved Sanders."

"Does that mean a wigging from headquarters?" said Holden with an abstracted smile. "I think I can stand it."

The talk beat up round the ever-fresh subject of each man's work, and steadied Holden till it was time to go to his dark empty bungalow, where his butler received him as one who knew all his affairs. Holden remained awake for the greater part of the night, and his dreams were pleasant ones.

II

"How old is he now?"

"Ya illah! What a man's question! He is all but six weeks old; and on this night I go up to the house-top with thee, my life, to count the stars. For that is auspicious. And he was born on a Friday under the sign of the Sun, and it has been told to me that he will outlive us both and get wealth. Can we wish for aught better, be-loved?"

"There is nothing better. Let us go up to the roof, and thou shalt count the stars——but a few only, for the sky is heavy with cloud."

"The winter rains are late, and maybe they come out of season. Come, before all the stars are hid. I have put on my richest jewels."

"Thou hast forgotten the best of all."

"Ai! Ours. He comes also. He has never yet seen the skies."

Ameera climbed the narrow staircase that led to the flat roof. The child, placid and unwinking, lay in the hollow of her right arm, gorgeous in silver-fringed muslin with a small skull-cap on his head. Ameera wore all that she valued most. The diamond nose-stud that takes the place of the Western patch in drawing attention to the curve of the nostril, the gold ornament in the centre of the forehead studded with tallow-drop emeralds and flawed rubies, the heavy circlet of beaten gold that was fastened round her neck by the softness of the pure metal, and the chinking curb-patterned silver anklets hanging low over the rosy ankle-bone. She was dressed in jade-green muslin as befitted a daughter of the Faith, and from shoulder to elbow and elbow to wrist ran bracelets of silver tied with floss silk, frail glass bangles slipped over the wrist in proof of the slenderness of the hand, and certain heavy gold bracelets that had no part in her country's ornaments, but, since they were Holden's gift and fastened with a cunning European snap, delighted her immensely.

They sat down by the low white parapet of the roof, overlooking the city and its lights.

"They are happy down there," said Ameera. "But I do not think that they are as happy as we. Nor do I think the white mem-log are as happy. And thou?"

"I know they are not."

"How dost thou know?"

"They give their children over to the nurses."

"I have never seen that," said Ameera with a sigh, "nor do I wish to see. Ahi!"——she dropped her head on Holden"s shoulder,——"I have counted forty stars, and I am tired. Look at the child, love of my life, he is counting too."

The baby was staring with round eyes at the dark of the heavens. Ameera placed him in Holden"s arms, and he lay there without a cry.

"What shall we call him among ourselves?" she said. "Look! Art thou ever tired of looking? He carries thy very eyes. But the mouth——"

"Is thine, most dear. Who should know better than I?"

"Tis such a feeble mouth. Oh, so small! And yet it holds my heart between its lips. Give him to me now. He has been too long away."

"Nay, let him lie; he has not yet begun to cry."

"When he cries thou wilt give him back——eh? What a man of mankind thou art! If he cried he were only the dearer to me. But, my life, what little name shall we give him?"

The small body lay close to Holden"s heart. It was utterly helpless and very soft. He scarcely dared to breathe for fear of crushing it. The caged green parrot that is regarded as a sort of guardian-spirit in most native households moved on its perch and fluttered a drowsy wing.

"There is the answer," said Holden. "Mian Mittu has spoken. He shall be the parrot. When he is ready he will talk mightily and run about. Mian Mittu is the parrot in thy——in the Mussulman tongue, is it not?"

"Why put me so far off?" said Ameera fretfully. "Let it be like unto some English name——but not wholly. For he is mine."

"Then call him Tota, for that is likest English."

"Ay, Tota, and that is still the parrot. Forgive me, my lord, for a minute ago, but in truth he is too little to wear all the weight of Mian Mittu for name. He shall be Tota——our Tota to us. Hearest thou, oh, small one? Littlest, thou art Tota." She touched the child's cheek, and he waking wailed, and it was necessary to return him to his mother, who soothed him with the wonderful rhyme of *Aréé koko, Faréé koko!* which says——

"Oh crow! Go crow! Baby's sleeping sound,

And the wild plums grow in the jungle, only a penny a pound. Only a penny a pound, baba, only a penny a pound."

Reassured many times as to the price of those plums, Tota cuddled himself down to sleep. The two sleek, white well-bullocks in the courtyard were steadily chewing the cud of their evening meal; old Pir Khan squatted at the head of Holden"s horse, his police sabre across his knees, pulling drowsily at a big water-pipe that croaked like a bull-frog in a pond. Ameera's mother sat spinning in the lower verandah, and the wooden gate was shut and barred. The music of a marriage-procession came to the roof above the gentle hum of the city, and a string of flying-foxes crossed the face of the low moon.

"I have prayed," said Ameera after a long pause, "I have prayed for two things. First, that I may die in thy stead if thy death is demanded, and in the second, that I may die in the place of the child. I have prayed to the Prophet and to Beebee Miriam (the Virgin Mary). Thinkest thou either will hear?"

"From thy lips who would not hear the lightest word?"

"I asked for straight talk, and thou hast given me sweet talk. Will my prayers be heard?"

"How can I say? God is very good."

"Of that I am not sure. Listen now. When I die, or the child dies, what is thy fate? Living, thou wilt return to the bold white *mem-log*, for kind calls to kind."

"Not always."

"With a woman, no; with a man it is otherwise. Thou wilt in this life, later on, go back to thine own folk. That I could almost endure, for I should be dead. But in thy very death thou wilt be taken away to a strange place and a paradise that I do not know."

"Will it be paradise?"

"Surely, for who would harm thee? But we two——I and the child——shall be elsewhere, and we cannot come to thee, nor canst thou come to us. In the old days, before the child was born, I did not think of these things; but now I think of them always. It is very hard talk."

"It will fall as it will fall. To-morrow we do not know, but to-day and love we know well. Surely we are happy now."

"So happy that it were well to make our happiness assured. And thy Beebee Miriam should listen to me; for she is also a woman. But then she would envy me! It is not seemly for men to worship a woman."

Holden laughed aloud at Ameera's little spasm of jealousy.

"Is it not seemly? Why didst thou not turn me from worship of thee, then?"

"Thou a worshipper! And of me? My king, for all thy sweet words, well I know that I am thy servant and thy slave, and the dust under thy feet. And I would not have it otherwise. See!"

Before Holden could prevent her she stooped forward and touched his feet; recovering herself with a little laugh hugged Tota closer to her bosom. Then, almost savagely——

"Is it true that the bold white *mem-log* live for three times the length of my life? Is it true that they make their marriages not before they are old women?"

"They marry as do others——when they are women."

"That I know, but they wed when they are twenty-five. Is that true?"

"That is true."

"*Ya illah!* At twenty-five! Who would of his own will take a wife even of eighteen? She is a woman——aging every hour. Twenty-five! I shall be an old woman at that age, and——Those *mem-log* remain young for ever. How I hate them!"

"What have they to do with us?"

"I cannot tell. I know only that there may now be alive on this earth a woman ten years older than I who may come to thee and take thy love ten years after I am an old woman, gray-headed, and the nurse of Tota's son. That is unjust and evil. They should die too."

"Now, for all thy years thou art a child, and shalt be picked up and carried down the staircase."

"Tota! Have a care for Tota, my lord! Thou at least art as foolish as any babe!" Ameera tucked Tota out of harm's way in the hollow of her neck, and was carried downstairs laughing in Holden's arms, while Tota opened his eyes and smiled after the manner of the lesser angels.

He was a silent infant, and, almost before Holden could realise that he was in the world, developed into a small gold-coloured little god and unquestioned despot of the house overlooking the city. Those were months of absolute happiness to Holden and Ameera——happiness withdrawn from the world, shut in behind the wooden gate that Pir Khan guarded. By day Holden did his work with an immense pity for such as were not so fortunate as himself, and a sympathy for small children that amazed and amused many mothers at the little station-gatherings. At nightfall he returned to Ameera,——Ameera, full of the wondrous doings of Tota; how he had been seen to clap his hands together and move his fingers with intention and purpose——which was manifestly a miracle——how later, he had of his own initiative crawled out of his low bedstead on to the floor and swayed on both feet for the space of three breaths.

"And they were long breaths, for my heart stood still with delight," said Ameera.

Then Tota took the beasts into his councils——the well-bullocks, the little gray squirrels, the mongoose that lived in a hole near the well, and especially Mian Mittu, the parrot, whose tail he grievously pulled, and Mian Mittu screamed till Ameera and Holden arrived.

"Oh villain! Child of strength! This to thy brother on the house-top! *Tobah, tobah!* Fie! Fie! But I know a charm to make him wise as Suleiman and Aflatoun (Solomon and Plato). Now look," said Ameera. She drew from an embroidered bag a handful of almonds. "See! we count seven. In the name of God!"

She placed Mian Mittu, very angry and rumpled, on the top of his cage, and seating herself between the babe and the bird she cracked and peeled an almond less white than her teeth. "This is a true charm, my life, and do not laugh. See! I give the parrot one-half and Tota the other." Mian Mittu with careful beak took his share from between Ameera's lips, and she kissed the other half into the mouth of the child, who ate it slowly with wondering eyes. "This I will do each day of seven, and without doubt he who is ours will be a bold speaker and wise. Eh, Tota, what wilt thou be when thou art a man and I am gray-headed?" Tota tucked his fat legs into adorable creases. He could crawl, but he was not going to waste the spring of his youth in idle speech. He wanted Mian Mittu"s tail to tweak.

When he was advanced to the dignity of a silver belt——which, with a magic square engraved on silver and hung round his neck, made up the greater part of his clothing——he staggered on a perilous journey down the garden to Pir Khan, and proffered him all his jewels in exchange for one little ride on Holden's horse, having seen his mother's mother chaffering with ped-lars in the verandah. Pir Khan wept and set the untried feet on his own gray head in sign of fealty, and brought the bold adventurer to his mother's arms, vowing that Tota would be a leader of men ere his beard was grown.

One hot evening, while he sat on the roof between his father and mother watching the never ending war-fare of the kites that the city boys flew, he demanded a kite of his own with Pir Khan to fly it, because he had a fear of dealing with anything larger than himself, and when Holden called him a "spark," he rose to his feet and answered slowly in defence of his new-found indi-viduality, "*Hum'park nahin hai. Hum admi hai* (I am no spark, but a man.)"

The protest made Holden choke and devote himself very seriously to a consideration of Tota's future. He need hardly have taken the trouble. The delight of that life was too perfect to endure. Therefore it was taken away as many things are taken away in India——sud-denly and without warning. The little lord of the house, as Pir Khan called him, grew sorrowful and complained of pains who had never known the meaning of pain. Ameera, wild with terror, watched him through the night, and in the dawning of the second day the life was shaken out of him by fever——the seasonal autumn fever. It seemed altogether impossible that he could die, and neither Ameera nor Holden at first believed the evidence of the little body on the bedstead. Then Ameera beat her head against the wall and would have flung herself down the well in the garden had Holden not restrained her by main force.

One mercy only was granted to Holden. He rode to his office in broad daylight and found waiting him an unusually heavy mail that demanded concentrated attention and hard work. He was not, however, alive to this kindness of the gods.

III

The first shock of a bullet is no more than a brisk pinch. The wrecked body does not send in its protest to the soul till ten or fifteen seconds later. Holden realised his pain slowly, exactly as he had realised his happiness, and with the same imperious necessity for hiding all trace of it. In the beginning he only felt that there had been a loss, and that Ameera needed comforting, where she sat with her head on her knees shivering as Mian Mittu from the house-top called, *Tota! Tota! Tota!* Later all his world and the daily life of it rose up to hurt him. It was an outrage that any one of the children at the band-stand in the evening should be alive and clamorous, when his own child lay dead. It was more than mere pain when one of them touched him, and stories told by over-fond fathers of their children's latest performances cut him to the quick. He could not declare his pain. He had neither help, comfort, nor sympathy; and Ameera at the end of each weary day would lead him through the Hell of self-questioning reproach which is reserved for those who have lost a child, and believe that with a little — — just a little more care — — it might have been saved.

"Perhaps," Ameera would say, "I did not take sufficient heed. Did I, or did I not? The sun on the roof that day when he played so long alone and I was — —*ahi!* braiding my hair — —it may be that the sun then bred the fever. If I had warned him from the sun he might have lived. But, oh my life, say that I am guiltless! Thou knowest that I loved him as I love thee. Say that there is no blame on me, or I shall die — —I shall die!"

"There is no blame, — —before God, none. It was written, and how could we do aught to save? What has been, has been. Let it go, beloved."

"He was all my heart to me. How can I let the thought go when my arm tells me every night that he is not here? *Ahi! Ahi!* Oh, Tota, come back to me — —come back again, and let us be all together as it was before!"

"Peace, peace! For thine own sake, and for mine also, if thou lovest me — —rest."

"By this I know thou dost not care; and how shouldst thou? The white men have hearts of stone and souls of iron. Oh, that I had married a man of mine own people — —though he beat me — —and had never eaten the bread of an alien!"

"Am I an alien — —mother of my son?"

"What else — —*Sahib?*......Oh, forgive me — —forgive! The death has driven me mad. Thou art the life of my heart, and the light of my eyes, and the breath of my life, and — —and I have put thee from me, though it was but for a moment. If thou goest away, to whom shall I look for help? Do not be angry. Indeed, it was the pain that spoke and not thy slave."

"I know, I know. We be two who were three. The greater need therefore that we should be one."

They were sitting on the roof as of custom. The night was a warm one in early spring, and sheet-lightning was dancing on the horizon to a broken tune played by far-off thunder. Ameera settled herself in Holden's arms.

"The dry earth is lowing like a cow for the rain, and I — —I am afraid. It was not like this when we counted the stars. But thou lovest me as much as before, though a bond is taken away? Answer!"

"I love more because a new bond has come out of the sorrow that we have eaten together, and that thou knowest."

"Yea, I knew," said Ameera in a very small whisper. "But it is good to hear thee say so, my life, who art so strong to help. I will be a child no more, but a woman and an aid to thee. Listen! Give me my *sitar* and I will sing bravely."

She took the light silver-studded *sitar* and began a song of the great hero Rajah Rasalu. The hand failed on the strings, the tune halted, checked, and at a low note turned off to the poor little nursery-rhyme about the wicked crow — —

"And the wild plums grow in the jungle, only a penny a pound. Only a penny a pound, baba — —only......"

Then came the tears, and the piteous rebellion against fate till she slept, moaning a little in her sleep, with the right arm thrown clear of the body as though it protected something that was not there. It was after this night that life became a little easier for Holden. The ever-present pain of loss drove him into his work, and the work repaid him by filling up his mind for nine or ten hours a day. Ameera sat alone in the house and brooded, but grew happier when she understood that Holden was more at ease, according to the custom of women. They touched happiness again, but this time with caution.

"It was because we loved Tota that he died. The jealousy of God was upon us," said Ameera. "I have hung up a large black jar before our window to turn the evil eye from us, and we must make no protestations of delight, but go softly underneath the stars, lest God find us out. Is that not good talk, worthless one?"

She had shifted the accent on the word that means "beloved," in proof of the sincerity of her purpose. But the kiss that followed the new christening was a thing that any deity might have envied. They went about henceforward saying, "It is naught, it is naught;" and hoping that all the Powers heard.

The Powers were busy on other things. They had allowed thirty million people four years of plenty, wherein men fed well and the crops were certain, and the birth-rate rose year by year; the districts reported a purely agricultural population varying from nine hundred to two thousand to the square mile of the over-burdened earth; and the Member for Lower Tooting, wandering about India in top-hat and frock-coat, talked largely of the benefits of British rule, and suggested as the one thing needful the establishment of a duly qualified electoral system and a general bestowal of the franchise. His long-suffering hosts smiled and made him welcome, and when he paused to admire, with pretty picked words, the blossom of the blood-red *dhak*-tree that had flowered untimely for a sign of what was coming, they smiled more than ever.

It was the Deputy Commissioner of Kot-Kumharsen, staying at the club for a day, who lightly told a tale that made Holden's blood run cold as he overheard the end.

"He won't bother any one any more. Never saw a man so astonished in my life. By Jove, I thought he meant to ask a question in the House about it. Fellow-passenger in his ship——dined next him——bowled over by cholera and died in eighteen hours. You needn't laugh, you fellows. The Member for Lower Tooting is awfully angry about it; but he's more scared. I think he's going to take his enlightened self out of India."

"I'd give a good deal if he were knocked over. It might keep a few vestrymen of his kidney to their own parish. But what's this about cholera? It's full early for anything of that kind," said the warden of an unprofitable salt-lick.

"Don't know," said the Deputy Commissioner reflectively. "We've got locusts with us. There's sporadic cholera all along the north——at least we're calling it sporadic for decency's sake. The spring crops are short in five districts, and nobody seems to know where the rains are. It's nearly March now. I don't want to scare anybody, but it seems to me that Nature's going to audit her accounts with a big red pencil this summer."

"Just when I wanted to take leave, too!" said a voice across the room.

"There won't be much leave this year, but there ought to be a great deal of promotion. I've come in to persuade the Government to put my pet canal on the list of famine-relief works. It's an ill-wind that blows no good. I shall get that canal finished at last."

"Is it the old programme then," said Holden; "famine, fever, and cholera?"

"Oh no. Only local scarcity and an unusual prevalence of seasonal sickness. You'll find it all in the reports if you live till next year. You're a lucky chap. *You* haven't got a wife to send out of harm's way. The hill-stations ought to be full of women this year."

"I think you're inclined to exaggerate the talk in the *bazars*," said a young civilian in the Secretariat. "Now I have observed——"

"I daresay you have," said the Deputy Commissioner, "but you've a great deal more to observe, my son. In the meantime, I wish to observe to you——" and he drew him aside to discuss the construction of the canal that was so dear to his heart. Holden went to his bungalow and began to understand that he was not alone in the world, and also that he was afraid for the sake of another,——which is the most soul-satisfying fear known to man.

Two months later, as the Deputy had foretold, Nature began to audit her accounts with a red pencil. On the heels of the spring-reapings came a cry for bread, and the Government, which had decreed that no man should die of want, sent wheat. Then came the cholera from all four quarters of the compass. It struck a pilgrim-gathering of half a million at a sacred shrine. Many died at the feet of their god; the others broke and ran over the face of the land carrying the pestilence with them. It smote a walled city and killed two hundred a day. The people crowded the trains, hanging on to the footboards and squatting on the roofs of the carriages, and the cholera followed them, for at each station they dragged out the dead and the dying. They died by the roadside, and the horses of the Englishmen shied at the corpses in the grass. The rains did not come, and the earth turned to iron lest man should escape death by hiding in her. The English sent their wives away to the hills and went about their work, coming forward as they were bidden to fill the gaps in the fighting-line. Holden, sick with fear of losing his chiefest treasure on earth, had done his best to persuade Ameera to go away with her mother to the Himalayas.

"Why should I go?" said she one evening on the roof.

"There is sickness, and people are dying, and all the white *mem-log* have gone."

"All of them?"

"All——unless perhaps there remain some old scald-head who vexes her husband's heart by running risk of death."

"Nay; who stays is my sister, and thou must not abuse her, for I will be a scald-head too. I am glad all the bold *mem-log* are gone."

"Do I speak to a woman or a babe? Go to the hills, and I will see to it that thou goest like a queen's daughter. Think, child. In a red-lacquered bullock cart, veiled and curtained, with brass peacocks upon the pole and red cloth hangings. I will send two orderlies for guard and——"

"Peace! Thou art the babe in speaking thus. What use are those toys to me? *He* would have patted the bullocks and played with the housings. For his sake, perhaps,——thou hast made me very English——I might have gone. Now, I will not. Let the *mem-log* run."

"Their husbands are sending them, beloved."

"Very good talk. Since when hast thou been my husband to tell me what to do? I have but borne thee a son. Thou art only all the desire of my soul to me. How shall I depart when I know that if evil befall thee by the breadth of so much as my littlest finger-nail——is that not small?——I should be aware of it though I were in paradise. And here, this summer thou mayest die——*ai, janee*, die! and in dying they might call to tend thee a white woman, and she would rob me in the last of thy love!"

"But love is not born in a moment or on a deathbed!"

"What dost thou know of love, stoneheart? She would take thy thanks at least and, by God and the Prophet and Beebee Miriam the mother of thy Prophet, that I will never endure. My lord and my love, let there be no more foolish talk of going away. Where thou art, I am. It is enough." She put an arm round his neck and a hand on his mouth.

There are not many happinesses so complete as those that are snatched under the shadow of the sword. They sat together and laughed, calling each other openly by every pet name that could move the wrath of the gods. The city below them was locked up in its own torments. Sulphur fires blazed in the streets; the conches in the Hindu temples screamed and bellowed, for the gods were inattentive in those days. There was a service in the great Mahomedan shrine, and the call to prayer from the minarets was almost unceasing. They heard the wailing in the houses of the dead, and once the shriek of a mother who had lost a child and was calling for its return. In the gray dawn they saw the dead borne out through the city gates, each litter with its own little knot of mourners. Wherefore they kissed each other and shivered.

It was a red and heavy audit, for the land was very sick and needed a little breathing-space ere the torrent of cheap life should flood it anew. The children of immature fathers and undeveloped mothers made no resistance. They were cowed and sat still, waiting till the sword should be sheathed in November if it were so willed. There were gaps among the English, but the gaps were filled. The work of superintending famine-relief, cholera-sheds, medicine-distribution, and what little sanitation was possible, went forward because it was so ordered.

Holden had been told to keep himself in readiness to move to replace the next man who should fall. There were twelve hours in each day when he could not see Ameera, and she might die in three. He was considering what his pain would be if he could not see her for three months, or if she died out of his sight. He was absolutely certain that her death would be demanded——so certain, that when he looked up from the telegram and saw Pir Khan breathless in the doorway, he laughed aloud. "And?" said he,——

"When there is a cry in the night and the spirit flutters into the throat, who has a charm that will restore? Come swiftly, Heaven-born! It is the black cholera."

Holden galloped to his home. The sky was heavy with clouds, for the long-deferred rains were near and the heat was stifling. Ameera"s mother met him in the courtyard, whimpering, "She is dying. She is nursing herself into death. She is all but dead. What shall I do, *sahib?*"

Ameera was lying in the room in which Tota had been born. She made no sign when Holden entered, because the human soul is a very lonely thing and, when it is getting ready to go away, hides itself in a misty borderland where the living may not follow. The black cholera does its work quietly and without explanation. Ameera was being thrust out of life as though the Angel of Death had himself put his hand upon her. The quick breathing seemed to show that she was either afraid or in pain, but neither eyes nor mouth gave any answer to Holden's kisses. There was nothing to be said or done. Holden could only wait and suffer. The first drops of the rain began to fall on the roof and he could hear shouts of joy in the parched city.

189

The soul came back a little and the lips moved. Holden bent down to listen. "Keep nothing of mine," said Ameera. "Take no hair from my head. *She* would make thee burn it later on. That flame I should feel. Lower! Stoop lower! Remember only that I was thine and bore thee a son. Though thou wed a white woman to-morrow, the pleasure of receiving in thy arms thy first son is taken from thee for ever. Remember me when thy son is born— —the one that shall carry thy name before all men. His misfortunes be on my head. I bear witness— —I bear witness"— —the lips were forming the words on his ear— —"that there is no God but— —thee, beloved!"

Then she died. Holden sat still, and all thought was taken from him,— —till he heard Ameera's mother lift the curtain.

"Is she dead, *sahib?*"

"She is dead."

"Then I will mourn, and afterwards take an inventory of the furniture in this house. For that will be mine. The *sahib* does not mean to resume it? It is so little, so very little, *sahib*, and I am an old woman. I would like to lie softly."

"For the mercy of God be silent a while. Go out and mourn where I cannot hear."

"*Sahib*, she will be buried in four hours."

"I know the custom. I shall go ere she is taken away. That matter is in thy hands. Look to it, that the bed on which— —on which she lies— —"

"Aha! That beautiful red-lacquered bed. I have long desired— —"

"That the bed is left here untouched for my disposal. All else in the house is thine. Hire a cart, take everything, go hence, and before sunrise let there be nothing in this house but that which I have ordered thee to respect."

"I am an old woman. I would stay at least for the days of mourning, and the rains have just broken. Whither shall I go?"

"What is that to me? My order is that there is a going. The house-gear is worth a thousand rupees and my orderly shall bring thee a hundred rupees to-night."

"That is very little. Think of the cart-hire."

"It shall be nothing unless thou goest, and with speed. O woman, get hence and leave me with my dead!"

The mother shuffled down the staircase, and in her anxiety to take stock of the house-fittings forgot to mourn. Holden stayed by Ameera's side and the rain roared on the roof. He could not think connectedly by reason of the noise, though he made many attempts to

do so. Then four sheeted ghosts glided dripping into the room and stared at him through their veils. They were the washers of the dead. Holden left the room and went out to his horse. He had come in a dead, stifling calm through ankle-deep dust. He found the courtyard a rain-lashed pond alive with frogs; a torrent of yellow water ran under the gate, and a roaring wind drove the bolts of the rain like buckshot against the mud-walls. Pir Khan was shivering in his little hut by the gate, and the horse was stamping uneasily in the water.

"I have been told the *sahib's* order," said Pir Khan. "It is well. This house is now desolate. I go also, for my monkey-face would be a reminder of that which has been. Concerning the bed, I will bring that to thy house yonder in the morning; but remember, *sahib*, it will be to thee a knife turning in a green wound. I go upon a pilgrimage, and I will take no money. I have grown fat in the protection of the Presence whose sorrow is my sorrow. For the last time I hold his stirrup."

He touched Holden's foot with both hands and the horse sprang out into the road, where the creaking bamboos were whipping the sky and all the frogs were chuckling. Holden could not see for the rain in his face. He put his hands before his eyes and muttered— —

"Oh you brute! You utter brute!"

The news of his trouble was already in his bungalow. He read the knowledge in his butler's eyes when Ahmed Khan brought in food, and for the first and last time in his life laid a hand upon his master's shoulder, saying, "Eat, *sahib*, eat. Meat is good against sorrow. I also have known. Moreover the shadows come and go, *sahib*; the shadows come and go. These be curried eggs."

Holden could neither eat nor sleep. The heavens sent down eight inches of rain in that night and washed the earth clean. The waters tore down walls, broke roads, and scoured open the shallow graves on the Mahomedan burying-ground. All next day it rained, and Holden sat still in his house considering his sorrow. On the morning of the third day he received a telegram which said only, "Ricketts, Myndonie. Dying. Holden relieve. Immediate." Then he thought that before he departed he would look at the house wherein he had been master and lord. There was a break in the weather, and the rank earth steamed with vapour.

He found that the rains had torn down the mud pillars of the gateway, and the heavy wooden gate that had guarded his life hung lazily from one hinge. There was grass three inches high in the courtyard; Pir Khan's lodge was empty, and the sodden thatch sagged between the beams. A gray squirrel was in possession

of the verandah, as if the house had been untenanted for thirty years instead of three days. Ameera's mother had removed everything except some mildewed matting. The *tick-tick* of the little scorpions as they hurried across the floor was the only sound in the house. Ameera's room and the other one where Tota had lived were heavy with mildew; and the narrow staircase leading to the roof was streaked and stained with rain-borne mud. Holden saw all these things, and came out again to meet in the road Durga Dass, his landlord,——portly, affable, clothed in white muslin, and driving a Cee-spring buggy. He was overlooking his property to see how the roofs stood the stress of the first rains.

"I have heard," said he, "you will not take this place any more, *sahib?*"

"What are you going to do with it?"

"Perhaps I shall let it again."

"Then I will keep it on while I am away."

Durga Dass was silent for some time. "You shall not take it on, *sahib,*" he said. "When I was a young man I also——, but to-day I am a member of the Municipality. Ho! Ho! No. When the birds have gone what need to keep the nest? I will have it pulled down——the timber will sell for something always. It shall be pulled down, and the Municipality shall make a road across, as they desire, from the burning-ghaut to the city wall, so that no man may say where this house stood."

(http://www.readbookonline.net/readOnlLine/2421/)

F. How does Lawrence build suspense in The Rocking-Horse Winner?

The Rocking-Horse Winner

D. H. Lawrence

There was a woman who was beautiful, who started with all the advantages, yet she had no luck. She married for love, and the love turned to dust. She had bonny children, yet she felt they had been thrust upon her, and she could not love them. They looked at her coldly, as if they were finding fault with her. And hurriedly she felt she must cover up some fault in herself. Yet what it was that she must cover up she never knew. Nevertheless, when her children were present, she always felt the center of her heart go hard. This troubled her, and in her manner she was all the more gentle and anxious for her children, as if she loved them very much. Only she herself knew that at the center of her heart was a hard little place that could not feel love, no, not for anybody. Everybody else said of her: "She is such a good mother. She adores her children." Only she herself, and her children themselves, knew it was not so. They read it in each other's eyes.

There were a boy and two little girls. They lived in a pleasant house, with a garden, and they had discreet servants, and felt themselves superior to anyone in the neighborhood.

Although they lived in style, they felt always an anxiety in the house. There was never enough money. The mother had a small income, and the father had a small income, but not nearly enough for the social position which they had to keep up. The father went into town to some office. But though he had good prospects, these prospects never materialized. There was always the grinding sense of the shortage of money, though the style was always kept up.

At last the mother said: "I will see if *I* can't make something." But she did not know where to begin. She racked her brains, and tried this thing and the other, but could not find anything successful. The failure made deep lines come into her face. Her children were growing up, they would have to go to school. There must be more money, there must be more money. The father, who was always very handsome and expensive in his tastes, seemed as if he never *would* be able to do anything worth doing. And the mother, who had a great belief in herself, did not succeed any better, and her tastes were just as expensive.

And so the house came to be haunted by the unspoken phrase: *There must be more money! There must be more money!* The children could hear it all the time though nobody said it aloud. They heard it at Christmas, when the expensive and splendid toys filled the nursery. Behind the shining modern rocking-horse, behind the smart doll's house, a voice would start whispering: "There *must* be more money! There *must* be more money!" And the children would stop playing, to listen for a moment. They would look into each other's eyes, to see if they had all heard. And each one saw in the eyes of the other two that they too had heard. "There *must* be more money! There *must* be more money!"

It came whispering from the springs of the still-swaying rocking-horse, and even the horse, bending his wooden, champing head, heard it. The big doll, sitting so pink and smirking in her new pram, could hear it quite plainly, and seemed to be smirking all the more self-consciously because of it. The foolish puppy, too, that took the place of the teddy-bear, he was looking so extraordinarily foolish for no other reason but that he heard the secret whisper all over the house: "There *must* be more money!"

Yet nobody ever said it aloud. The whisper was everywhere, and therefore no one spoke it. Just as no one ever says: "We are breathing!" in spite of the fact that breath is coming and going all the time.

"Mother," said the boy Paul one day, "why don't we keep a car of our own? Why do we always use uncle's, or else a taxi?"

"Because we're the poor members of the family," said the mother.

"But why *are* we, mother?"

"Well——I suppose," she said slowly and bitterly, "it's because your father has no luck."

The boy was silent for some time.

"Is luck money, mother?" he asked, rather timidly.

"No, Paul. Not quite. It's what causes you to have money."

"Oh!" said Paul vaguely. "I thought when Uncle Oscar said *filthy lucker,* it meant money."

"*Filthy lucre* does mean money," said the mother. "But it's lucre, not luck."

"Oh!" said the boy. "Then what *is* luck, mother?"

"It's what causes you to have money. If you're lucky you have money. That's why it's better to be born lucky than rich. If you're rich, you may lose your money. But if you're lucky, you will always get more money."

"Oh! Will you? And is father not lucky?"

"Very unlucky, I should say," she said bitterly.

The boy watched her with unsure eyes.

"Why?" he asked.

"I don't know. Nobody ever knows why one person is lucky and another unlucky."

"Don't they? Nobody at all? Does *nobody* know?"

"Perhaps God. But He never tells."

"He ought to, then. And aren't you lucky either, mother?"

"I can't be, if I married an unlucky husband."

"But by yourself, aren't you?"

"I used to think I was, before I married. Now I think I am very unlucky indeed."

"Why?"

"Well——never mind! Perhaps I'm not really," she said.

The child looked at her to see if she meant it. But he saw, by the lines of her mouth, that she was only trying to hide something from him.

"Well, anyhow," he said stoutly, "I'm a lucky person."

"Why?" said his mother, with a sudden laugh.

He stared at her. He didn't even know why he had said it.

"God told me," he asserted, brazening it out.

"I hope He did, dear!" she said, again with a laugh, but rather bitter.

"He did, mother!"

"Excellent!" said the mother.

The boy saw she did not believe him; or rather, that she paid no attention to his assertion. This angered him somewhat, and made him want to compel her attention.

He went off by himself, vaguely, in a childish way, seeking for the clue to "luck." Absorbed, taking no heed of other people, he went about with a sort of stealth, seeking inwardly for luck. He wanted luck, he wanted it, he wanted it. When the two girls were playing dolls in the nursery, he would sit on his big rocking-horse, charging madly into space, with a frenzy that made the little girls peer at him uneasily. Wildly the horse careered, the waving dark hair of the boy tossed, his eyes had a strange glare in them. The little girls dared not speak to him.

When he had ridden to the end of his mad little journey, he climbed down and stood in front of his rocking-horse, staring fixedly into its lowered face. Its red mouth was slightly open, its big eye was wide and glassy-bright.

Now! he would silently command the snorting steed. Now take me to where there is luck! Now take me!

And he would slash the horse on the neck with the little whip he had asked Uncle Oscar for. He *knew* the horse could take him to where there was luck, if only he forced it. So he would mount again and start on his furious ride, hoping at last to get there.

"You'll break your horse, Paul!" said the nurse.

"He's always riding like that! I wish he'd leave off!" said his elder sister Joan.

But he only glared down on them in silence. Nurse gave him up. She could make nothing of him. Anyhow, he was growing beyond her.

One day his mother and his Uncle Oscar came in when he was on one of his furious rides. He did not speak to them.

"Hallo, you young jockey! Riding a winner?" said his uncle.

"Aren't you growing too big for a rocking-horse? You're not a very little boy any longer, you know," said his mother.

But Paul only gave a blue glare from his big, rather close-set eyes. He would speak to nobody when he was in full tilt. His mother watched him with an anxious expression on her face.

At last he suddenly stopped forcing his horse into the mechanical gallop and slid down.

"Well, I got there!" he announced fiercely, his blue eyes still flaring, and his sturdy long legs straddling apart.

"Where did you get to?" asked his mother.

"Where I wanted to go," he flared back at her.

"That's right, son!" said Uncle Oscar. "Don't you stop till you get there. What's the horse's name?"

"He doesn't have a name," said the boy.

"Gets on without all right?" asked the uncle.

"Well, he has different names. He was called Sansovino last week."

"Sansovino, eh? Won the Ascot. How did you know his name?"

"He always talks about horse races with Bassett," said Joan.

The uncle was delighted to find that his small nephew was posted with all the racing news. Bassett, the young gardener, who had been wounded in the left foot in the war and had got his present job through Oscar Cresswell, whose batman he had been, was a perfect blade of the "turf." He lived in the racing events, and the small boy lived with him.

Oscar Cresswell got it all from Bassett.

"Master Paul comes and asks me, so I can't do more than tell him, sir," said Bassett, his face terribly serious, as if he were speaking of religious matters.

"And does he ever put anything on a horse he fancies?"

"Well——I don't want to give him away——he's a young sport, a fine sport, sir. Would you mind asking him himself? He sort of takes a pleasure in it, and perhaps he'd feel I was giving him away, sir, if you don't mind."

Bassett was serious as a church.

The uncle went back to his nephew and took him off for a ride in the car.

"Say, Paul, old man, do you ever put anything on a horse?" the uncle asked.

The boy watched the handsome man closely.

"Why, do you think I oughtn't to?" he parried.

"Not a bit of it! I thought perhaps you might give me a tip for the Lincoln."

The car sped on into the country, going down to Uncle Oscar's place in Hampshire.

"Honor bright?" said the nephew.

"Honor bright, son!" said the uncle.

"Well, then, Daffodil."

"Daffodil! I doubt it, sonny. What about Mirza?"

"I only know the winner," said the boy. "That's Daffodil."

"Daffodil, eh?"

There was a pause. Daffodil was an obscure horse comparatively.

"Uncle!"

"Yes, son?"

"You won't let it go any further, will you? I promised Bassett."

"Bassett be damned, old man! What's he got to do with it?"

"We're partners. We've been partners from the first. Uncle, he lent me my first five shillings, which I lost. I promised him, honor bright, it was only between me and him; only you gave me that ten-shilling note I started winning with, so I thought you were lucky. You won't let it go any further, will you?"

The boy gazed at his uncle from those big, hot, blue eyes, set rather close together. The uncle stirred and laughed uneasily.

"Right you are, son! I'll keep your tip private. Daffodil, eh? How much are you putting on him?"

"All except twenty pounds," said the boy. "I keep that in reserve."

The uncle thought it a good joke.

"You keep twenty pounds in reserve, do you, you young romancer? What are you betting, then?"

"I'm betting three hundred," said the boy gravely. "But it's between you and me, Uncle Oscar! Honor bright?"

The uncle burst into a roar of laughter.

"It's between you and me all right, you young Nat Gould," he said, laughing. "But where's your three hundred?"

"Bassett keeps it for me. We're partners."

"You are, are you! And what is Bassett putting on Daffodil?"

"He won't go quite as high as I do, I expect. Perhaps he'll go a hundred and fifty."

"What, pennies?" laughed the uncle.

"Pounds," said the child, with a surprised look at his uncle. "Bassett keeps a bigger reserve than I do."

Between wonder and amusement Uncle Oscar was silent. He pursued the matter no further, but he determined to take his nephew with him to the Lincoln races.

"Now, son," he said, "I'm putting twenty on Mirza, and I'll put five on for you on any horse you fancy. What's your pick?"

"Daffodil, uncle."

"No, not the fiver on Daffodil!"

"I should if it was my own fiver," said the child.

"Good! Good! Right you are! A fiver for me and a fiver for you on Daffodil."

The child had never been to a race meeting before, and his eyes were blue fire. He pursed his mouth tight and watched. A Frenchman just in front had put his money on Lancelot. Wild with excitement, he flayed his arms up and down, yelling *"Lancelot!, Lancelot!"* in his French accent.

Daffodil came in first, Lancelot second, Mirza third. The child, flushed and with eyes blazing, was curiously serene. His uncle brought him four five-pound notes, four to one.

"What am I to do with these?" he cried, waving them before the boys eyes.

"I suppose we'll talk to Bassett," said the boy. "I expect I have fifteen hundred now; and twenty in reserve; and this twenty."

His uncle studied him for some moments.

"Look here, son!" he said. "You're not serious about Bassett and that fifteen hundred, are you?"

"Yes, I am. But it's between you and me, uncle. Honor bright?"

"Honor bright all right, son! But I must talk to Bassett."

"If you'd like to be a partner, uncle, with Bassett and me, we could all be partners. Only, you'd have to promise, honor bright, uncle, not to let it go beyond us three. Bassett and I are lucky, and you must be lucky, because it was your ten shillings I started winning with...."

Uncle Oscar took both Bassett and Paul into Richmond Park for an afternoon, and there they talked.

"It's like this, you see, sir," Bassett said. "Master Paul would get me talking about racing events, spinning yarns, you know, sir. And he was always keen on knowing if I'd made or if I'd lost. It's about a year since, now, that I put five shillings on Blush of Dawn for him— —and we lost. Then the luck turned, with that ten shillings he had from you: that we put on Singhalese. And since then, it's been pretty steady, all things considering. What do you say, Master Paul?"

"We're all right when we're sure," said Paul. "It's when we're not quite sure that we go down."

"Oh, but we're careful then," said Bassett.

"But when are you *sure?*" Uncle Oscar smiled.

"It's Master Paul, sir," said Bassett in a secret, religious voice. "It's as if he had it from heaven. Like Daffodil, now, for the Lincoln. That was as sure as eggs."

"Did you put anything on Daffodil?" asked Oscar Cresswell.

"Yes, sir, I made my bit."

"And my nephew?"

Bassett was obstinately silent, looking at Paul.

"I made twelve hundred, didn't I, Bassett? I told uncle I was putting three hundred on Daffodil."

"That's right," said Bassett, nodding.

"But where's the money?" asked the uncle.

"I keep it safe locked up, sir. Master Paul he can have it any minute he likes to ask for it."

"What, fifteen hundred pounds?"

"And twenty! And *forty,* that is, with the twenty he made on the course."

"It's amazing!" said the uncle.

"If Master Paul offers you to be partners, sir, I would, if I were you; if you'll excuse me," said Bassett.

Oscar Cresswell thought about it.

"I'll see the money," he said.

They drove home again, and sure enough, Bassett came round to the garden house with fifteen hundred pounds in notes. The twenty pounds reserve was left with Joe Glee, in the Turf Commission deposit.

"You see, it's all right, uncle, when I'm *sure!* Then we go strong, for all we're worth, don't we, Bassett?"

"We do that, Master Paul."

"And when are you sure?" said the uncle, laughing.

"Oh, well, sometimes I'm *absolutely* sure, like about Daffodil," said the boy; "and sometimes I have an idea; and sometimes I haven't even an idea, have I, Bassett? Then we're careful, because we mostly go down."

"You do, do you! And when you're sure, like about Daffodil, what makes you sure, sonny?"

"Oh, well, I don't know," said the boy uneasily. "I'm sure, you know, uncle; that's all."

"It's as if he had it from heaven, sir," Bassett reiterated.

"I should say so!" said the uncle.

But he became a partner. And when the Leger was coming on, Paul was "sure" about Lively Spark, which was a quite inconsiderable horse. The boy insisted on putting a thousand on the horse, Bassett went for five hundred, and Oscar Cresswell two hundred. Lively Spark came in first, and the betting had been ten to one against him. Paul had made ten thousand.

"You see," he said. "I was absolutely sure of him."

Even Oscar Cresswell had cleared two thousand.

"Look here, son," he said, "this sort of thing makes me nervous."

"It needn't, uncle! Perhaps I shan't be sure again for a long time."

"But what are you going to do with your money?" asked the uncle.

"Of course," said the boy. "I started it for mother. She said she had no luck, because Father is unlucky, so I thought if *I* was lucky, it might stop whispering."

"What might stop whispering?"

"Our house. I *hate* our house for whispering."

"What does it whisper?"

"Why——why"——the boy fidgeted——"why, I don't know. But it's always short of money, you know, uncle."

"I know it, son, I know it."

"You know people send Mother writs, don't you, Uncle?"

"I'm afraid I do," said the uncle.

"And then the house whispers, like people laughing at you behind your back. It's awful, that is! I thought if I was lucky...."

"You might stop it," added the uncle.

The boy watched him with big blue eyes, that had an uncanny cold fire in them, and he said never a word.

"Well, then!" said the uncle. "What are we doing?"

"I shouldn't like Mother to know I was lucky," said the boy.

"Why not, son?"

"She'd stop me."

"I don't think she would."

"Oh!"——and the boy writhed in an odd way——"I *don't* want her to know, Uncle."

"All right, son! We'll manage it without her knowing."

They managed it very easily. Paul, at the other's suggestion, handed over five thousand pounds to his uncle, who deposited it with the family lawyer, who was then to inform Paul's mother that a relative had put five thousand pounds into his hands, which sum was to be paid out a thousand pounds at a time, on the mother's birthday, for the next five years.

"So she'll have a birthday present of a thousand pounds for five successive years," said Uncle Oscar. "I hope it won't make it all the harder for her later."

Paul's mother had her birthday in November. The house had been "whispering" worse than ever lately, and, even in spite of his luck, Paul could not bear up against it. He was very anxious to see the effect of the birthday letter, telling his mother about the thousand pounds.

When there were no visitors, Paul now took his meals with his parents, as he was beyond the nursery control. His mother went into town nearly every day. She had discovered that she had an odd knack of sketching furs and dress materials, so she worked secretly in the studio of a friend who was the chief artist for the leading drapers. She drew the figures of ladies in furs and ladies in silk and sequins for the newspaper advertisements. This young woman artist earned several thousand pounds a year, but Paul's mother only made several hundreds, and she was again dissatisfied. She so wanted to be first in something, and she did not succeed, even in making sketches for drapery advertisements.

She was down to breakfast on the morning of her birthday. Paul watched her face as she read her letters. He knew the lawyer's letter. As his mother read it, her face hardened and became more expressionless. Then a cold, determined look came on her mouth. She hid the letter under the pile of others, and said not a word about it.

"Didn't you have anything nice in the post for your birthday, mother?" said Paul.

"Quite moderately nice," she said, her voice cold and absent.

She went away to town without saying more.

But in the afternoon Uncle Oscar appeared. He said Paul's mother had had a long interview with the lawyer, asking if the whole five thousand could not be advanced at once, as she was in debt.

"What do you think, uncle?" said the boy.

"I leave it to you, son."

"Oh, let her have it, then! We can get some more with the other," said the boy.

"A bird in the hand is worth two in the bush, laddie!" said Uncle Oscar.

"But I'm sure to *know* for the Grand National; or the Lincolnshire; or else the Derby. I'm sure to know for *one* of them," said Paul.

So Uncle Oscar signed the agreement, and Paul's mother touched the whole five thousand.

Then something very curious happened. The voices in the house suddenly went mad, like a chorus of frogs on a spring evening. There were certain new furnishings, and Paul had a tutor. He was *really* going to Eton, his father's school, in the following autumn. There were flowers in the winter, and a blossoming of the luxury Paul's mother had been used to. And yet the voices in the house, behind the sprays of mimosa and almond-blossom, and from under the piles of iridescent cushions, simply trilled and screamed in a sort of ecstasy: "There *must* be more money! Oh-h-h; there *must* be more money. Oh, now, now-w! Now-w-w——there *must* be more money!——more than ever! More than ever!"

It frightened Paul terribly. He studied away at his Latin and Greek. But his intense hours were spent with Bassett. The Grand National had gone by: he had not "known," and had lost a hundred pounds. Summer was at hand. He was in agony for the Lincoln. But even for the Lincoln he didn't "know," and he lost fifty pounds. He became wild-eyed and strange, as if something were going to explode in him.

"Let it alone, son! Don't you bother about it!" urged Uncle Oscar. But it was as if the boy couldn't really hear what his uncle was saying.

"I've got to know for the Derby! I've got to know for the Derby!" the child reiterated, his big blue eyes blazing with a sort of madness.

His mother noticed how overwrought he was.

"You'd better go to the seaside. Wouldn't you like to go now to the seaside, instead of waiting? I think you'd better," she said, looking down at him anxiously, her heart curiously heavy because of him.

But the child lifted his uncanny blue eyes. "I couldn't possibly go before the Derby, mother!" he said. "I couldn't possibly!"

"Why not?" she said, her voice becoming heavy when she was opposed. "Why not? You can still go from the seaside to see the Derby with your Uncle Oscar, if that's what you wish. No need for you to wait here. Besides, I think you care too much about these races. It's a bad sign. My family has been a gambling family, and you won't know till you grow up how much damage it has done. But it has done damage. I shall have to send Bassett away, and ask Uncle Oscar not to talk racing to you, unless you promise to be reasonable about it; go away to the seaside and forget it. You're all nerves!"

"I'll do what you like, Mother, so long as you don't send me away till after the Derby," the boy said.

"Send you away from where? Just from this house?"

"Yes," he said, gazing at her.

"Why, you curious child, what makes you care about this house so much, suddenly? I never knew you loved it."

He gazed at her without speaking. He had a secret within a secret, something he had not divulged, even to Bassett or to his Uncle Oscar.

But his mother, after standing undecided and a little bit sullen for some moments, said:

"Very well, then! Don't go to the seaside till after the Derby, if you don't wish it. But promise me you won't let your nerves go to pieces. Promise you won't think so much about horse racing and *events*, as you call them!"

"Oh, no," said the boy casually. "I won't think much about them, Mother. You needn't worry. I wouldn't worry, Mother, if I were you."

"If you were me and I were you," said his mother,

"I wonder what we *should* do!"

"But you know you needn't worry, Mother, don't you?" the boy repeated.

"I should be awfully glad to know it," she said wearily.

"Oh, well, you *can*, you know. I mean, you *ought* to know you needn't worry," he insisted.

"Ought I? Then I'll see about it," she said.

Paul's secret of secrets was his wooden horse, that which had no name. Since he was emancipated from a nurse and a nursery governess, he had had his rocking-horse removed to his own bedroom at the top of the house.

"Surely, you're too big for a rocking-horse!" his mother had remonstrated.

"Well, you see, Mother, till I can have a *real* horse, I like to have *some* sort of animal about," had been his quaint answer.

"Do you feel he keeps you company?" She laughed.

"Oh yes! He's very good, he always keeps me company, when I'm there," said Paul.

So the horse, rather shabby, stood in an arrested prance in the boy's bedroom.

The Derby was drawing near, and the boy grew more and more tense. He hardly heard what was spoken to him, he was very frail, and his eyes were really uncanny. His mother had sudden strange seizures of uneasiness about him. Sometimes, for half an hour, she would feel a sudden anxiety about him that was almost anguish. She wanted to rush to him at once, and know he was safe.

Two nights before the Derby, she was at a big party in town, when one of her rushes of anxiety about her boy, her firstborn, gripped her heart till she could hardly speak. She fought with the feeling, might and main, for she believed in common sense. But it was too strong. She had to leave the dance and go downstairs to telephone to the country. The children's nursery governess was terribly surprised and startled at being rung up in the night.

"Are the children all right, Miss Wilmot?"

"Oh yes, they are quite all right."

"Master Paul? Is he all right?"

"He went to bed as right as a trivet. Shall I run up and look at him?"

"No," said Paul's mother reluctantly. "No! Don't trouble. It's all right. Don't sit up. We shall be home fairly soon." She did not want her son's privacy intruded upon.

"Very good," said the governess.

It was about one o'clock when Paul's mother and

father drove up to their house. All was still. Paul's mother went to her room and slipped off her white fur cloak. She had told her maid not to wait up for her. She heard her husband downstairs, mixing a whisky and soda.

And then, because of the strange anxiety at her heart, she stole upstairs to her son's room. Noiselessly she went along the upper corridor. Was there a faint noise? What was it?

She stood, with arrested muscles, outside his door, listening. There was a strange, heavy, and yet not loud noise. Her heart stood still. It was a soundless noise, yet rushing and powerful. Something huge, in violent, hushed motion. What was it? What in God's name was it? She ought to know. She felt that she knew the noise. She knew what it was.

Yet she could not place it. She couldn't say what it was. And on and on it went, like a madness.

Softly, frozen with anxiety and fear, she turned the door handle.

The room was dark. Yet in the space near the window, she heard and saw something plunging to and fro. She gazed in fear and amazement.

Then suddenly she switched on the light, and saw her son, in his green pajamas, madly surging on the rocking-horse. The blaze of light suddenly lit him up, as he urged the wooden horse, and lit her up, as she stood, blonde, in her dress of pale green and crystal, in the doorway.

"Paul!" she cried. "Whatever are you doing?"

"It's Malabar!" he screamed in a powerful, strange voice. "It's Malabar!"

His eyes blazed at her for one strange and senseless second, as he ceased urging his wooden horse. Then he fell with a crash to the ground, and she, all her tormented motherhood flooding upon her, rushed to gather him up.

But he was unconscious, and unconscious he remained, with some brain fever. He talked and tossed, and his mother sat stonily by his side.

"Malabar! It's Malabar! Bassett, Bassett, I *know*! It's Malabar!"

So the child cried, trying to get up and urge the rocking-horse that gave him his inspiration.

"What does he mean by Malabar?" asked the heart-frozen mother.

"I don't know," said the father stonily.

"What does he mean by Malabar?" she asked her brother Oscar.

"It's one of the horses running for the Derby," was the answer.

And, in spite of himself, Oscar Cresswell spoke to Bassett, and himself put a thousand on Malabar: at fourteen to one.

The third day of the illness was critical: they were waiting for a change. The boy, with his rather long, curly hair, was tossing ceaselessly on the pillow. He neither slept nor regained consciousness, and his eyes were like blue stones. His mother sat, feeling her heart had gone, turned actually into a stone.

In the evening Oscar Cresswell did not come, but Bassett sent a message, saying could he come up for one moment, just one moment? Paul's mother was very angry at the intrusion, but on second thoughts she agreed. The boy was the same. Perhaps Bassett might bring him to consciousness.

The gardener, a shortish fellow with a little brown moustache and sharp little brown eyes, tiptoed into the room, touched his imaginary cap to Paul's mother, and stole to the bedside, staring with glittering, smallish eyes at the tossing, dying child.

"Master Paul!" he whispered. "Master Paul! Malabar came in first all right, a clean win. I did as you told me. You've made over seventy thousand pounds, you have; you've got over eighty thousand. Malabar came in all right, Master Paul."

"Malabar! Malabar! Did I say Malabar, Mother? Did I say Malabar? Do you think I'm lucky, Mother? I knew Malabar, didn't I? Over eighty thousand pounds! I call that lucky, don't you, Mother? Over eighty thousand pounds! I knew, didn't I know I knew? Malabar came in all right. If I ride my horse till I'm sure, then I tell you, Bassett, you can go as high as you like. Did you go for all you were worth, Bassett?"

"I went a thousand on it, Master Paul."

"I never told you, Mother, that if I can ride my horse, and *get there*, then I'm absolutely sure——oh, absolutely! Mother, did I ever tell you? I *am* lucky!"

"No, you never did," said the mother.

But the boy died in the night.

And even as he lay dead, his mother heard her brother's voice saying to her: "My God, Hester, you're eighty-odd thousand to the good, and a poor devil of a son to the bad. But, poor devil, poor devil, he's best gone out of a life where he rides his rocking-horse to find a winner."

(http://mbhs.bergtraum.k12.ny.us/cybereng/shorts/rockwinr.html)

FINAL PORTFOLIO

Correct and rewrite essays and place them in your Final Portfolio.

SUGGESTED

Weekly *Implementation*

DAY 1	DAY 2	DAY 3	DAY 4	DAY 5
Prayer journal.	**Prayer journal.**	**Prayer journal.**	**Prayer journal.**	**Prayer journal.**
Review required reading(s) *before* the assigned lesson begins.	Review reading(s) from next lesson.	Write rough drafts of all assigned essays.	Rewrite corrected copies of essays due tomorrow.	Essays are due.
<u>Teacher and students will decide on required essays for this lesson, choosing tow or three essays.</u>	Outline essays due at the end of the week.	The teacher and/or a peer evaluator may correct rough drafts.		Take Lesson 30 test.
<u>The rest of the essays can be outlined, answered with shorter answers, or skipped.</u>	Per teacher instructions, students may answer orally in a group setting some of the essays that are not assigned as formal essays.			Reading Ahead: "Are Women Human?" Dorothy Sayers; "Terence, This is Stupid Stuff," "Loveliest of Trees," and "Be Still my Soul," A. E. Housman; World War I Poets: "Greater Love," Wilfred Owen, "The Fish," Rupert Brooke; "In Flanders Field," George McCrae; "An Irish Airman Forsees his Death," "When You are Old," "The Second Coming," "The White Swans at Coole," and "Byzantium," William Butler Yeats; "Do not go Gentle into the Night," Dylan Thomas.
Review all readings for Lesson 30.				Guide: What world-views emerge in these poems?

LESSON 31

TWENTIETH CENTURY (*Part 3*)

Dorothy Sayers

BACKGROUND

All the previous authors pale in substance and talent, in the author's opinion, when compared to Dorothy Sayers (1893-1957). She was one of the most famous Christian apologists of the 20th century. She was friends with T. S. Eliot and C. S. Lewis, both master apologists. Sayers believed, as she often said, "The only Christian work is good work, well done."

Sayers was born in Oxford, the only child of the Rev. Henry Sayers. Later, Sayers was to be the first woman to receive a degree from Oxford University. At the time, her father was headmaster of Christ Church Cathedral School, and she was born in the headmaster's house. Therefore, most of Sayers' young life was spent in a religious, educational setting that had a profound impact on her writing career.

In 1923 Sayers published her first novel, *Whose Body*, which introduced Lord Peter Wimsey, her hero for fourteen volumes of novels and short stories. Sayers also loved to write drama. Her most famous drama was *The Man Born to be King*, in which her decision to present Christ speaking in modern English raised an outcry of protest but revolutionized religious drama. Sayers would never compromise her values to accommodate public opinion. Later, before she died, Sayers translated Dante's *Inferno*.

CRITICAL THINKING

If not *the* most important, then *one* of the most important, of Sayers' short non-fiction works is *Are Women Human?* Peruse her two essays *Are Women Human?* and *The Human-Not-Quite-Human* in this short volume, reflect on her views, and write a response essay to her thoughts.

Analyze: "Are Women Human?" Dorothy Sayers; "Terence, This is Stupid Stuff," "Loveliest of Trees," and "Be Still my Soul," A. E. Housman; World War I Poets: "Greater Love," Wilfred Owen, "The Fish," Rupert Brooke; "In Flanders Field," George McCrae; "An Irish Airman Forsees his Death," "When You are Old," "The Second Coming," "The White Swans at Coole," and "Byzantium," William Butler Yeats.

Reading Ahead: *Mere Christianity*, C. S. Lewis.

Guide Question: What is Lewis' most persuasive argument for conversion?

A. E. Housman

BACKGROUND

Despite the small number of poems he published, A. E. Housman was a literary force in the late nineteenth and early twentieth centuries in England. He was a poet who loved to write about the country, and there was more than a hint of Naturalism in his writings. Read "Terence, This Is Stupid Stuff," "Loveliest of Trees," and "Be Still, My Soul."

CRITICAL THINKING

A. Housman was born in Burton-on-Trent, England, in 1865, just as the U.S. Civil War was ending. As a young child, he was disturbed by the news of slaughter from the former British colonies and was affected deeply. This turned him into a brooding, introverted teenager and a misanthropic, pessimistic adult. As a result, his outlook on life shows clearly in his poetry. Find examples of pessimism in his poems.

B. Evaluate the following literary criticism: Housman is considered a minor poet, primarily because of his use of rhyme and meter and his frequent and effective use of imagery and symbolism. It is generally accepted that major twentieth-century poetry must inevitably go beyond the strictures of late-nineteenth-century styles, so any poet using such styles can only be classed as minor.

C. How old is the speaker in "Loveliest of Trees"? What does the snow symbolize?

BIBLICAL APPLICATION

A. That Housman believed people were generally evil and life conspired against mankind is evident not only in his poetry, but also in his short stories. For example, his story, "The Child of Lancashire," published in 1893 in *The London Gazette*, is about a child who travels to London where his parents die, and he becomes a street urchin. The child becomes involved with a gang of similar youths, attacking affluent pedestrians and stealing their watches and gold coins. Eventually, he leaves the gang and becomes wealthy but is attacked by the same gang members (who don't recognize him). They throw him off London Bridge into the Thames, which unfortunately is frozen over, and he is killed on the hard ice below. Analyze pessimistic view of life according to a biblical perspective.

B. A few of Housman's poems show an uncharacteristic optimism and love of beauty. For example, his poem "Trees" begins:

Loveliest of trees, the cherry now
Hung low with bloom along the bow
Stands about the woodland side
A virgin in white for Eastertide.

and ends:

Poems are made by fools like me
But only God can make a tree.
(http://eir.library.utoronto.ca/rpo/display/poem1059.ht
ml)

Housman was no spiritual giant, though. He seems to have had trouble reconciling conventional Christianity with his deep clinical depression. Given these passages and other poems that you have read by Housman, what is his worldview?

World War I Poets

BACKGROUND

Never has a war so devastated a generation as World War I cruelly injured England. Author Tim Cross compiled an anthology entitled *The Lost Voices of World War I: An International Anthology of Writers, Poets and Playwrights*, with works by more than fifty authors who died in the four years of fighting in World War I. To read the works of these authors is unsettling, because the reader is constantly aware of how much talent was lost when these men died so young. The appendix to Cross's anthology is even more tragic in its implications, for it is a necrology (i.e., death list) of all the creative people who were killed from 1914 to 1918. As Cross says, "A complete list of all poets, playwrights, writers, artists, architects, and composers who died as a result of the First World War is an impossible task," but even so, he has compiled a list of about 750 names.

Cross's list includes only people who had already accomplished something of note in their fields. We are left to ponder how many of the nine million young men lost in the war might have gone on to do great things in the arts, sciences, medicine, and politics. Given the official number of military personnel killed between the years 1914 and 1918—over one million dead soldiers from the British Empire and the United States alone—a handful of artists might seem insignificant. A few survived—J. R. R. Tolkien, for instance.

The following is a list of a few poets who died in World War I:
Wilfred Owen,
Ropert Brooke, and
John McCrae.

Wilfred Edward Salter Owen

BACKGROUND

Wilfred Edward Salter Owen (1893-1918) was on the continent teaching until he visited a hospital for the wounded and then decided in September 1915 to return

to England and to enlist. "I came out in order to help these boys—directly by leading them as well as an officer can; indirectly, by watching their sufferings that I may speak of them as well as a pleader can. I have done the first" (October 1918). Owen was injured in March 1917 and sent home; he was fit for duty in August 1918 and returned to the front. November 4, just seven days before the Armistice, he was caught in a German machine-gun attack and was killed. He was twenty-five when he died. The bells were ringing on November 11, 1918, in Shrewsbury to celebrate the Armistice when the doorbell rang at his parent's home, bringing them the telegram about their son's death.

Greater Love

Red lips are not so red
As the stained stones kissed by the English dead.
Kindness of wooed and wooer
Seems shame to their love pure.
O Love, your eyes lose lure
When I behold eyes blinded in my stead!

Your slender attitude
Trembles not exquisite like limbs knife-skewed,
Rolling and rolling there
Where God seems not to care;
Till the fierce love they bear
Cramps them in death's extreme decrepitude.

Your voice sings not so soft,—
Though even as wind murmuring through raftered
　　　loft,—
Your dear voice is not dear,
Gentle, and evening clear,
As theirs whom none now hear,
Now earth has stopped their piteous mouths that
　　　coughed.

Heart, you were never hot
Nor large, nor full like hearts made great with shot;
And though your hand be pale,
Paler are all which trail
Your cross through flame and hail:
Weep, you may weep, for you may touch them not.
(http://www.anglik.net/ww1wilfredowen.htm)

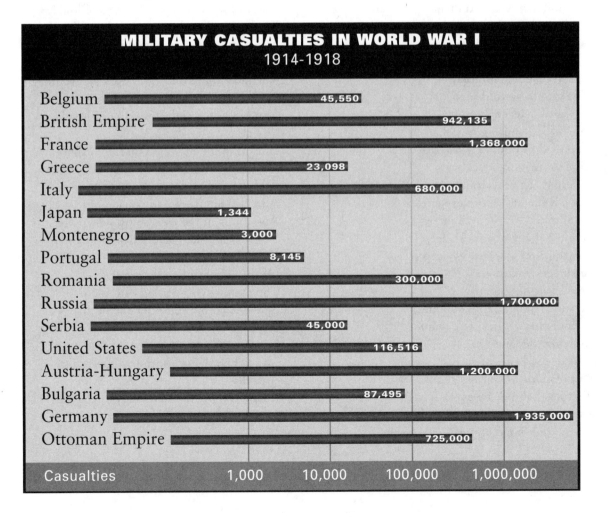

MILITARY CASUALTIES IN WORLD WAR I
1914-1918

Country	Casualties
Belgium	45,550
British Empire	942,135
France	1,368,000
Greece	23,098
Italy	680,000
Japan	1,344
Montenegro	3,000
Portugal	8,145
Romania	300,000
Russia	1,700,000
Serbia	45,000
United States	116,516
Austria-Hungary	1,200,000
Bulgaria	87,495
Germany	1,935,000
Ottoman Empire	725,000

Casualties　　1,000　　10,000　　100,000　　1,000,000

Rupert Brooke

BACKGROUND

Rupert Brooke(1887-1915) was a good student and athlete, and—in part because of his strikingly handsome looks—a popular young man who eventually numbered among his friends E. M. Forster and Virginia Woolf. Brooke actually saw little combat during the war; he contracted blood poisoning from a small neglected wound and died in April 1915.

The Fish

In a cool curving world he lies
And ripples with dark ecstasies.
The kind luxurious lapse and steal
Shapes all his universe to feel
And know and be; the clinging stream
Closes his memory, glooms his dream,
Who lips the roots o' the shore, and glides
Superb on unreturning tides.
Those silent waters weave for him
A fluctuant mutable world and dim,
Where wavering masses bulge and gape
Mysterious, and shape to shape
Dies momently through whorl and hollow,
And form and line and solid follow
Solid and line and form to dream
Fantastic down the eternal stream;
An obscure world, a shifting world,
Bulbous, or pulled to thin, or curled,
Or serpentine, or driving arrows,
Or serene slidings, or March narrows.
There slipping wave and shore are one,
And weed and mud. No ray of sun,
But glow to glow fades down the deep
(As dream to unknown dream in sleep);
Shaken translucency illumes
The hyaline of drifting glooms;
The strange soft-handed depth subdues
Drowned colour there, but black to hues,
As death to living, decomposes—
Red darkness of the heart of roses,
Blue brilliant from dead starless skies,
And gold that lies behind the eyes,
The unknown unnameable sightless white
That is the essential flame of night,

Lustreless purple, hooded green,
The myriad hues that lie between
Darkness and darkness! . . .

And all's one.
Gentle, embracing, quiet, dun,
The world he rests in, world he knows,
Perpetual curving. Only grows
An eddy in that ordered falling,
A knowledge from the gloom, a calling
Weed in the wave, gleam in the mud—
The dark fire leaps along his blood;
Dateless and deathless, blind and still,
The intricate impulse works its will;
His woven world drops back; and he,
Sans providence, sans memory,
Unconscious and directly driven,
Fades to some dank sufficient heaven.

O world of lips, O world of laughter,
Where hope is fleet and thought flies after,
Of lights in the clear night, of cries
That drift along the wave and rise
Thin to the glittering stars above,
You know the hands, the eyes of love!
The strife of limbs, the sightless clinging,
The infinite distance, and the singing
Blown by the wind, a flame of sound,
The gleam, the flowers, and vast around
The horizon, and the heights above
You know the sigh, the song of love!

But there the night is close, and there
Darkness is cold and strange and bare,
And the secret deeps are whisperless;
And rhythm is all deliciousness;
And joy is in the throbbing tide,
Whose intricate fingers beat and glide
In felt bewildering harmonies
Of trembling touch; and music is
The exquisite knocking of the blood.
Space is no more, under the mud;
His bliss is older than the sun.
Silent and straight the waters run.
The lights, the cries, the willows dim,
And the dark tide are one with him.
(http://www.emory.edu/ENGLISH/LostPoets/Fish.ht
    ml)

John McCrae

BACKGROUND

John McCrae (1872–1918) is remembered for what is probably the single best-known and popular poem from the war, "In Flanders Fields." He was a Canadian medical doctor and died of pneumonia while on active duty in 1918. His volume of poetry, *In Flanders Fields and Other Poems*, was published in 1919.

In Flanders Fields

In Flanders fields the poppies blow
Between the crosses, row on row
That mark our place; and in the sky
The larks, still bravely singing, fly
Scarce heard amid the guns below.

We are the Dead. Short days ago
We lived, felt dawn, saw sunset glow,
Loved and were loved, and now we lie
In Flanders fields.

Take up our quarrel with the foe:
To you from failing hands we throw
The torch; be yours to hold it high.
If ye break faith with us who die
We shall not sleep, though poppies grow
In Flanders fields.
(http://www.wsu.edu:8080/~wldciv/world_civ_reader/
   world_civ_reader_2/mccrae.html)

BIBLICAL APPLICATION

No one will disagree that World War I was a horrible war. Yet, some came out of the war without bitterness (e.g., J. R. R. Tolkien). Others were terribly bitter (e.g., Ernest Hemingway). How does one deal with bitterness and hardship that seems to surpass the ability to cope?

William Butler Yeats

BACKGROUND

(Note: Yeats is pronounced "Yates.")
In the May, 1938, *Atlantic Monthly* Louise Bogan wrote:

"William Butler Yeats, at the age of seventy-three, stands well within the company of the great poets. He is still writing, and the poems which now appear, usually embedded in short plays or set into the commentary and prefaces which have been another preoccupation of his later years, are, in many instances, as vigorous and as subtle as the poems written by him during the years ordinarily considered to be the period of a poet's maturity. Yeats has advanced into age with his art strengthened by a long battle which had as its object a literature written by Irishmen fit to take its place among the noble literatures of the world. The spectacle of a poet's work invigorated by his lifelong struggle against the artistic inertia of his nation is one that would shed strong light into any era.

The phenomenon of a poet who enjoys continued development into the beginning of old age is in itself rare. Goethe, Sophocles, and, in a lesser degree, Milton come to mind as men whose last works burned with the gathered fuel of their lives. More often development, in a poet, comes to a full stop; and it is frequently a negation of the ideals of his youth, as well as a declination of his powers, that throws a shadow across his final pages. In his middle years Yeats began to concern himself with the problem of the poet in age. We can trace, in Yeats, the continually enriched and undeviating course of an inspired man, from earliest youth to age. We can trace the rectitude of the spiritual line in his prose and poetry alike. And there is not a great deal of difference between the "lank, long-coated figure . . . who came and went as he pleased," dramatizing himself and his dreams in the streets of Dublin (the youth who had known William Morris and was to know Dowson and Wilde), and the man who, full of honors in our day, impresses us with his detachment and subtle modernity. Yeats, the fiery young Nationalist, rolling up with his own hands, the red carpet spread on a Dublin sidewalk "by some elderly Nationalist softened or weakened by time, to welcome Viceroyalty," is recognizable in the poet of advanced years who does not hesitate to satirize certain leaders of the new Ireland.

Yeats's faith in the development of his own powers has never failed. He wrote, in 1923, after receiving from the King of Sweden the medal symbolizing the Nobel Prize:

It shows a young man listening to a Muse, who stands young and beautiful with a great lyre in her hand, and I think as I examine it, 'I was good-looking once like that young man, but my unpractised verse was full of infirmity, my Muse old as it were, and now I am old and rheumatic and nothing to look at, but my Muse is young.' I am even persuaded that she is like those Angels in Swedenborg's vision, and moves perpetually 'towards the dayspring of her youth.'"

CRITICAL THINKING

A. Discuss Yeats's use of symbolism in his poetry.

B. Compare Keats' "Ode on a Grecian Urn" with "Byzantium."

FOR ENRICHMENT

Yeats and most twentieth-century writers were deeply affected by a movement called Surrealism. In literature and art, Surrealism is a movement whose effective life is generally assigned the years 1924–1945. In 1924, André Breton's first *Manifesto of Surrealism* appeared, defining the movement in philosophical and psychological terms. Its immediate predecessor was Dada, whose nihilistic reaction to Rationalism and the reigning "morality" that produced World War I cleared the way for Surrealism's positive message. Surrealism is often characterized only by its use of unusual, sometimes startling juxtapositions, by which it sought to transcend logic and habitual thinking to reveal deeper levels of meaning and unconscious associations. Why might a Christian have difficulty embracing Surrealism?

FINAL PORTFOLIO

Correct and rewrite essays and place them in your Final Portfolio.

SUGGESTED
Weekly *Implementation*

DAY 1	DAY 2	DAY 3	DAY 4	DAY 5
Prayer journal. Review required reading(s) *before* the assigned lesson begins. Teacher and students will decide on required essays for this lesson, choosing two or three essays. The rest of the essays can be outlined, answered with shorter answers, or skipped. Review all readings for Lesson 31.	**Prayer journal.** Review reading(s) from next lesson. Outline essays due at the end of the week. Per teacher instructions, students may answer orally in a group setting some of the essays that are not assigned as formal essays.	**Prayer journal.** Write rough drafts of all assigned essays. The teacher and/or a peer evaluator may correct rough drafts.	**Prayer journal.** Rewrite corrected copies of essays due tomorrow. Essays are due.	**Prayer journal.** Essays are due. Take Lesson 31 test. Reading Ahead: Review *Mere Christianity*, C. S. Lewis. Guide: What is Lewis' most persuasive argument for conversion?

LESSON 32

TWENTIETH CENTURY *(Part 4)*

C. S. Lewis

BACKGROUND

The English scholar and writer Clive Staples Lewis—November 29, 1898, to November 22, 1963—is one of the most famous Christian apologists of the twentieth century. By appealing to people of all ages, he has probably done more than any writer to bring people to a saving relationship with Jesus Christ. He is truly a remarkable phenomenon, a great asset to twentieth-century Christendom. *Mere Christianity*, Lewis's most popular book, is really three books in one: (1) "Right and Wrong as a Clue to the Meaning of the Universe," (2) "What Christians Believe," and (3) "Christian Behavior"—all adapted from a series of radio lectures. The book's title comes from Lewis's attempt to strip Christianity of all that is nonessential, getting down to the "mere" basics of what it means to be a Christian.

Analyze: *Mere Christianity*, C. S. Lewis.

Reading Ahead: *Lord of the Rings Trilogy*, J. R. R. Tolkien.

Guide Question: *Does Lord of the Rings advance a Theistic worldview?*

CRITICAL THINKING

A. Lewis states that if God is like the moral law, He is not soft or sentimental. Why is this shocking? Apart from the moral law, what else points to the existence of God? Complete this sentence: According to Lewis, Christianity will not make sense to anyone until they realize . . .

B. What does Lewis cite as the question of why God does not deal openly and decisively with the devil?

FINAL PORTFOLIO

Correct and rewrite essays and place them in your Final Portfolio.

SUGGESTED
Weekly *Implementation*

DAY 1	DAY 2	DAY 3	DAY 4	DAY 5
Prayer journal.	**Prayer journal.**	**Prayer journal.**	**Prayer journal.**	**Prayer journal.**
Review required reading(s) *before* the assigned lesson begins.	Review reading(s) from next lesson.	Write rough drafts of all assigned essays.	Rewrite corrected copies of essays due tomorrow.	Essays are due.
<u>Teacher and students will decide on required essays for this lesson, choosing two or three essays.</u>	Outline essays due at the end of the week.	The teacher and/or a peer evaluator may correct rough drafts.		Take Lesson 32 test.
<u>The rest of the essays can be outlined, answered with shorter answers, or skipped.</u>	Per teacher instructions, students may answer orally in a group setting some of the essays that are not assigned as formal essays.			Reading Ahead: Review *Lord of the Rings Trilogy*, J.R.R. Tolkien.
Review all readings for Lesson 32.				Guide: Does *Lord of the Rings* advance a Theistic worldview?

J.R.R. Tolkien

Tolkien's fertile mind inspired and blessed a generation of Englishmen. The horror of World War I affected him as it did other Englishmen. However, instead of turning inward and embracing existentialism, Tolkien reached outward to his faith and wrote some of the most powerful moral allegories of the twentieth century.

CRITICAL THINKING

A. Wastelands are often used in literature as a symbol of spiritual barrenness. Two good examples of this occur in F. Scott Fitzgerald's *The Great Gatsby* (1925) and T. S. Eliot's famous poem "The Waste Land" (1922). In *The Great Gatsby*, Nick, the narrator, passes through a wasteland of ashes on his way into New York City. How does the wasteland as a symbol of inner barrenness relate to Tolkien's concept of evil?

B. Discuss Tolkien's use of elves and fairies in his novels.

> **Analyze:** the *Lord of the Rings Trilogy*, J.R.R. Tolkien
>
> **Reading Ahead:** *Murder in the Cathedral*, C. S. Lewis.
>
> **Guide Question:** What is the purpose of the chorus in this play?

C. Evaluate the criticism against Tolkien for generally ignoring women in his novels.

D. Many of the characters in these three novels gain power through language. Give several examples.

E. Discuss Tolkien's use of song in his novels.

BIBLICAL APPLICATION

Discuss the unfolding power of good and evil in these three fantasies. Compare this power with orthodox Christianity.

FINAL PORTFOLIO

Correct and rewrite essays and place them in your Final Portfolio.

SUGGESTED
Weekly *Implementation*

DAY 1	DAY 2	DAY 3	DAY 4	DAY 5
Prayer journal.	**Prayer journal.**	**Prayer journal.**	**Prayer journal.**	**Prayer journal.**
Review required reading(s) *before* the assigned lesson begins. Teacher and students will decide on required essays for this lesson, choosing two or three essays. The rest of the essays can be outlined, answered with shorter answers, or skipped. Review all readings for Lesson 33.	Review reading(s) from next lesson. Outline essays due at the end of the week. Per teacher instructions, students may answer orally in a group setting some of the essays that are not assigned as formal essays.	Write rough drafts of all assigned essays. The teacher and/or a peer evaluator may correct rough drafts.	Rewrite corrected copies of essays due tomorrow.	Essays are due. Take Lesson 33 test. Reading Ahead: Review *Murder in the Cathedral*, C. S. Lewis. Guide: What is the purpose of the chorus in this play?

TWENTIETH CENTURY *(Part 6)*

Murder in the Cathedral

T.S. Eliot

BACKGROUND

An Anglo-American poet, critic, dramatist, and editor, Thomas Stearns Eliot was a major innovator in modern English poetry, famous above all for his revolutionary poem "The Waste Land" (1922). His seminal critical essays helped to usher in literary modernism by stressing tradition, continuity, and objective confessional Christianity over narcissistic egoism. In his lifetime, Eliot would move from self-centered cynicism to profound Christian spirituality. His journey, however, is an unusual one. In this period, modernism and absurdism captured many, or most, authors. Both movements expressed themselves in writings, music, and the arts. These movements embraced nihilism. They believed that there is nothing but chaos in the universe. To pretend that there is order and control is to live in a dream world. Everything is absurd, without meaning. There is no anchor on which a person can put his hat. A writer in the camp of absurdism—such as Kurt Vonnegut Jr.—would argue that theism, naturalism, realism are all bogus worldviews. However, God had other plans in mind for Eliot. Late in his life, he converted to Christianity and wrote this magnificent play, *Murder in the Cathedral*.

CRITICAL THINKING

A. Give the story line and historical background to *Murder in the Cathedral*.

<hr/>

Analyze: *Murder in the Cathedral*, T. S. Eliot

B. What is Eliot's universal concern which transcends all his prose and poetry?
C. Write a detailed analysis of the purpose of the choruses.
D. Illustrate Eliot's use of metaphor and symbolism to convey his message.

BIBLICAL APPLICATION

Evaluate Becket's decision to die as a martyr.

ENRICHMENT

Evaluate the following position:

This generation in North America is the first to graduate when murder is legal (i.e., abortion); the first generation to access 130 channels and at the same time access almost nothing of value; the first generation to see a nation and Congress refuse to remove a U.S. president for lying, infidelity, and perversion. Good news can be found in such authors as T. S. Eliot.

FINAL PORTFOLIO

Correct and rewrite essays and place them in your Final Portfolio.

SUGGESTED

Weekly *Implementation*

DAY 1	DAY 2	DAY 3	DAY 4	DAY 5
Prayer journal. Review required reading(s) *before* the assigned lesson begins. <u>Teacher and students will decide on required essays for this lesson, choosing two or three essays.</u> <u>The rest of the essays can be outlined, answered with shorter answers, or skipped.</u> Review all readings for Lesson 34.	**Prayer journal.** Review reading(s) from next lesson. Outline essays due at the end of the week. Per teacher instructions, students may answer orally in a group setting some of the essays that are not assigned as formal essays.	**Prayer journal.** Write rough drafts of all assigned essays. The teacher and/or a peer evaluator may correct rough drafts.	**Prayer journal.** Rewrite corrected copies of essays due tomorrow.	**Prayer journal.** Essays are due. Take Lesson 34 test. Final Portfolio is due next.

LESSON 35

BRITISH LITERATURE PORTFOLIO

SUBMIT THIS WEEK

This Final Portfolio is composed of what you have accomplished this year through *British Literature: Encouraging Thoughtful Christians to be World Changers.*

Consider this project a portfolio of your academic progress for this academic year. You should arrange to have an exhibition for peers, parents, and other academicians. You should keep your British Literature Portfolio as a record of your development as a writer, as a critical thinker, and as a British Literature scholar. It could also serve as a Biblical Application Journal if you have opted to complete the biblical application questions.

The **British Literature Portfolio** should contain the following in an attractive binder, clearly labeled with title, academic year, and your name:

BRITISH LITERATURE PORTFOLIO

Table of Contents
Corrected Literary Essays
Literary Reviews
Writing Journals
Pictures, (or paraphernalia, or travel journals) from field trips
Supplemental Material (or other Pertinent Information)
Vocabulary cards (in a separate pocket-type folder)

BRITISH LITERATURE

ENCOURAGING THOUGHTFUL CHRISTIANS
TO BE WORLD CHANGERS

APPENDICES

APPENDIX A

Writing Tips

How do students produce concise, well-written essays?

GENERAL STATEMENTS

• Essays should be written in the context of the other social sciences. This means that essays should be written on all topics: science topics, history topics, social science topics, etc.

• Some essays should be rewritten, depending on the assignment and the purpose of the writing; definitely those essays which are to be presented to various readers or a public audience should be rewritten for their best presentation. Parents and other educators should discuss with their students which and how many essays will be rewritten. Generally speaking, I suggest that students rewrite at least one essay per week.

• Students should write something every day and read something every day. Students will be prompted to read assigned whole books before they are due. It is imperative that students read ahead as they write present essays or they will not be able to read all the material. Remember this too: students tend to write what they read. Poor material—material that is too juvenile—will be echoed in the vocabulary and syntax of student essays.

• Students should begin writing assignments immediately after they are assigned. A suggested implementation schedule is provided. Generally speaking, students will write about one hour per day to accomplish the writing component of this course.

• Students should revise their papers as soon as they are evaluated. Follow the implementation schedule at the end of each course.

Every essay includes a *prewriting phase, an outlining phase,* a *writing phase,* a *revision phase,* and for the purposes of this course, *a publishing phase.*

PRE-WRITING THINKING CHALLENGE

ISSUE
State problem/issue in five sentences.

State problem/issue in two sentences.

State problem/issue in one sentence.

NAME THREE OR MORE SUBTOPICS OF PROBLEM.

NAME THREE OR MORE SUBTOPICS OF THE SUBTOPICS.

WHAT INFORMATION MUST BE KNOWN TO SOLVE THE PROBLEM OR TO ANSWER THE QUESTION?

STATE THE ANSWER TO THE QUESTION/
PROBLEM
—In five sentences.

—In two sentences.

—In one sentence.

STATED IN TERMS OF OUTCOMES, WHAT
EVIDENCES DO I SEE THAT CONFIRM THAT I
HAVE MADE THE RIGHT DECISION?

ONCE THE PROBLEM/QUESTION IS
ANSWERED/SOLVED, WHAT ONE OR TWO
NEW PROBLEMS/ANSWERS MAY ARISE?

ABBREVIATED PRE-WRITING THINKING CHALLENGE

What is the issue?
State problem/issue in five sentences.
State problem/issue in two sentences.
State problem/issue in one sentence.
Name three or more subtopics of problem.
Name three or more subtopics of the subtopics.
What information must be known to solve the problem
or to answer the question?
State the answer to the question/problem
—in five sentences —in two sentences —in one sen-
tence.
Stated in terms of outcomes, what evidences do I see
that confirms that I have made the right decision?

Once the problem or question is answered or solved,
what are one or two new problems or answers that
could arise?

PRE-WRITING PHASE

Often called the brainstorming phase, the pre-writing
phase is the time you decide on exactly what your topic
is. What questions must you answer? You should artic-

ulate a thesis (a one sentence statement of purpose for
why you are writing about this topic. The thesis typically has two to four specific points contained within
it). You should decide what sort of essay this is—for
instance, a definition, an exposition, a persuasive argument—and then design a strategy. For example, a
clearly persuasive essay will demand that you state the
issue and give your opinion in the opening paragraph.

Next, after a thesis statement, you will write an outline. *No matter what length the essay may be, 20 pages or one
paragraph, you should create an outline.*

Outline

<u>Thesis:</u> In his poem *The Raven*, Edgar Allan Poe
uses literary devices to describe such weighty topics as
death and *unrequited love*, which draw the reader to an
insightful and many times emotional moment. (Note
that this thesis informs the reader that the author will
be exploring *death* and *unrequited love*.)

   I.   Introduction (Opens to the reader the exploration of the writing and tells the reader what
to expect.)

   II.   Body (This particular essay will include two
main points developed in two main paragraphs, one paragraph about death and one
paragraph about emotions. The second paragraph will be introduced by means of a transition word or phrase or sentence.)
     A. Imagining Death
     B. Feeling Emotions

   III.   Conclusions (A paragraph which draws conclusions or solves the problem mentioned in
the thesis statement.)

One of the best ways to organize your thoughts is
to spend time in concentrated thinking, what some call
brainstorming. Thinking through what you want to
write is a way to narrow your topic.

Sample Outline:
Persuasive Paper with Three Major Points (Arguments)

I. Introduction: <u>Thesis statement</u> includes a listing or a summary of the three supportive arguments and introduces the paper.

II. Body
A. Argument 1
   Evidence
   (transition words or phrases or sentences to the next topic)
B. Argument 2
   Evidence
   (transition words or phrases or sentences to the next topic)
C. Argument 3
   Evidence
   (transition words or phrases or sentences to the conclusion)

III. Conclusion: Restatement of arguments and evidence used throughout the paper (do not use the words *in conclusion* — just conclude).

NOTE: For greater detail and explanation of outlining, refer to a composition handbook. Careful attention should be paid to parallel structure with words or phrases, to correct form with headings and subheadings, to punctuation, and to pairing of information. Correct outline structure will greatly enhance the writing of any paper.

Sample Outline:
Expository Essay with Four Major Points

I. Introduction: <u>Thesis statement</u> includes a listing or mention of four examples or supports and introduces the paper; use transitional words or phrases at the end of the paragraph.

II. Body
A. Example 1
   Application
   (transition words or phrases or sentences to the next topic)
B. Example 2
   Application
   (transition words or phrases or sentences to the next topic)
C. Example 3
   Application
   (transition words or phrases or sentences to the next topic)
D. Example 4
   Application
   (transition words or phrases or sentences to the conclusion)

III. Conclusion: Restatement of thesis, drawing from the evidence or applications used in the paper (do not use the words *in conclusion* — just conclude).

NOTE: For greater detail and explanation of outlining, refer to a composition handbook. Careful attention should be paid to parallel structure with words or phrases, to correct form with headings and subheadings, to punctuation, and to pairing of information. Correct outline structure will greatly enhance the writing of any paper.

The Thinking Challenge

The following is an example of a Thinking Challenge approach to Mark Twain's *The Adventures of Huckleberry Finn:*

The Problem or The Issue or The Question:

Should Huck turn in his escaped slave-friend Jim to the authorities?

State problem/issue in five sentences, then in two sentences, and, finally, in one sentence.

Five Sentences:
Huck runs away with Jim. He does so knowing that he is breaking the law. However, the lure of friendship overrides the perfidy he knows he is committing. As he floats down the Mississippi River, he finds it increasingly difficult to hide his friend from the authorities and to hide his feelings of ambivalence. Finally he manages to satisfy both ambiguities.

Two Sentences:
Huck intentionally helps his slave friend Jim escape from servitude. As Huck floats down the Mississippi River, he finds it increasingly difficult to hide his friend from the authorities and at the same time to hide his own feelings of ambivalence.

One Sentence:
After escaping with his slave-friend Jim and floating down the Mississippi River, Huck finds it increasingly difficult to hide his friend from the authorities and at the same time to hide his own feelings of ambivalence.

Name three or more subtopics of problem.
Are there times when we should disobey the law?
What responsibilities does Huck have to his family?
What should Huck do?

Name three or more subtopics of the subtopics.
Are there times when we should disobey the law?
Who determines what laws are unjust?
Should the law be disobeyed publicly?
Who is injured when we disobey the law?
What responsibilities does Huck have to his family?
Who is his family? Jim? His dad?

Is allegiance to them secondary to Jim's needs?
Should his family support his civil disobedience?
What should Huck do?
Turn in Jim?
Escape with Jim?
Both?

What information must be known?
Laws? Jim's character? If he is bad, then should Huck save him?

State the answer to the question/problem in five, two, and one sentence(s).

Five Sentences:
Huck can escape with Jim with profound feelings of guilt. After all, he is helping a slave escape. This is important because it shows that Huck is still a moral, if flawed, character. Jim's freedom does outweigh any other consideration—including the laws of the land and his family's wishes. As the story unfolds the reader sees that Huck is indeed a reluctant criminal, and the reader takes comfort in that fact.

Two Sentences:
Showing reluctance and ambivalence, Huck embarks on an arduous but moral adventure. Jim's freedom outweighs any other need or consideration.

One Sentence:
Putting Jim's freedom above all other considerations, Huck, the reluctant criminal, embarks on an arduous but moral adventure.

Once the Problem or Issue or Question is solved, what are one or two new problems that may arise? What if Huck is wrong? What consequences could Huck face?

Every essay has a beginning (introduction), a middle part (body), and an ending (conclusion). The introduction must draw the reader into the topic and usually presents the thesis to the reader. The body organizes the material and expounds on the thesis (a one sentence statement of purpose) in a cogent and inspiring way. The conclusion generally is a solution to the problem or issue or question or is sometimes a summary. Paragraphs in the body are connected with transitional words or phrases: *furthermore, therefore, in spite of.*

Another effective transition technique is to mention in the first sentence of a new paragraph a thought or word that occurs in the last sentence of the previous paragraph. In any event, the body should be intentionally organized to advance the purposes of the paper. A disciplined writer *always* writes a rough draft. Using the well-thought-out outline composed during the pre-writing phase is an excellent way to begin the actual writing. The paper has already been processed mentally and only lacks the writing.

WRITING PHASE

The writer must make the first paragraph grab the reader's attention enough that the reader will want to continue reading.

The writer should write naturally, but not colloquially. In other words, the writer should not use clichés and everyday coded language. *The football players blew it* is too colloquial.

The writer should use as much visual imagery and precise detail as possible, should assume nothing, and should explain everything.

REWRITING PHASE

Despite however many rewrites are necessary, when the writer has effectively communicated the subject and corrected grammar and usage problems, she is ready to write the final copy.

Top Ten Most Frequent Essay Problems

Agreement between the Subject and Verb: Use singular forms of verbs with singular subjects and use plural forms of verbs with plural subjects.
WRONG: Everyone finished their homework.
RIGHT: Everyone finished his homework (*Everyone* is an indefinite singular pronoun.)

Using the Second Person Pronoun—"you," "your" should rarely, if ever, be used in a formal essay.
WRONG: You know what I mean (Too informal).

Redundancy: Never use "I think" or "It seems to me"
WRONG: I think that is true.
RIGHT: That is true (We know you think it, or you would not write it!)

Tense consistency: Use the same tense (usually present) throughout the paper.
WRONG: I was ready to go, but my friend is tired.
RIGHT: I am ready to go but my friend is tired.

Misplaced Modifiers: Place the phrase or clause close to its modifier.
WRONG: The man drove the car with a bright smile into the garage.
RIGHT: The man with a bright smile drove the car into the garage.

Antecedent Pronoun Problems: Make sure pronouns match (agree) in number and gender with their antecedents.
WRONG: Mary and Susan both enjoyed her dinner.
RIGHT: Mary and Susan both enjoyed their dinners.

Parallelism: Make certain that your list/sentence includes similar phrase types.
WRONG: I like to take a walk and swimming.
RIGHT: I like walking and swimming

Affect vs. Effect: Affect is a verb; Effect is a noun unless it means to achieve.
WRONG: His mood effects me negatively.
RIGHT: His mood affects me negatively.
RIGHT: The effects of his mood are devastating.

Dangling Prepositions: Rarely end a sentence with an unmodified preposition.
WRONG: Who were you speaking to?
RIGHT: To whom were you speaking?

Transitions: Make certain that paragraphs are connected with transitions (e.g., furthermore, therefore, in spite of).
RIGHT: Furthermore, Jack London loves to describe animal behavior.

APPENDIX B

COMPOSITION EVALUATION EXAMPLE I

Based on 100 points: _____

I. Grammar and Syntax: Is the composition grammatically correct?
(25 points) 15/25
      Comments: See Corrections. Look up Subject/Verb Agreement, Fragments, Verb Tense, Parallel Structure, and Use of the Possessive, etc. in a comprehensive grammar text; read about them, write the grammar rules on the back of your essay, and then correct these parts of your essay.

II. Organization: Does this composition exhibit well-considered organization? Does it flow? Transitions? Introduction and a conclusion?
(25 points) 15/25
Comments: Good job with transitional phrases; introduction could be stronger. A clear thesis statement would provide the reader with a clear idea about the purpose of your paper. Your conclusion could better summarize your thesis.

III. Content: Does this composition answer the question, argue the point well, and/or persuade the reader?
(50 points) 30/50
Comments: Nice insights. Using quotes from the novel to support your argument would enhance your writing. Also, support your specific position regarding male and female writers.

Please revise your paper and then come discuss your thoughts and revisions with me.

*To be duplicated and placed on each essay.

COMPOSITION EVALUATION EXAMPLE 2

I. Organization
___ Is the writer's purpose stated clearly in the introduction? Is there a thesis sentence? What is it?
___ Does the writer answer the assignment?
___ Does the introduction grab the reader's attention?
___ Is the purpose advanced by each sentence and paragraph?
___ Does the body (middle) of the paper advance the purpose?
___ Does the conclusion accomplish its purpose?
Other helpful comments for the writer:

II. Mechanics
___ Does the writer use active voice?
___ Does the writer use the appropriate verb tense throughout the paper?
___ Is there agreement between all pronouns and antecedents?
___ Is there appropriately subject/verb agreement?
___ Are the transitions effective and appropriate?
Other mechanical trouble spots:

III. Argument
___ Are you persuaded by the arguments?
Other helpful comments for the writer:

COMPOSITION EVALUATION EXAMPLE 3

Peer Checklist
(May Prefer to Use Evaluation Technique Forms One or Two)

I. Organization
___ Is the writer's purpose clearly introduced? What is it?
___ Does the organization of the paper coincide with the outline?
___ Does the writer answer the assignment?
___ Does the introduction grab the reader's attention?
___ Is the purpose advanced by each sentence and paragraph? (Are there sentences which don't seem to belong in the paragraphs?)
___ Does the body (middle) of the paper advance the purpose?
___ Does the conclusion solve the purpose of the paper?

Comments regarding organization:

II. Mechanics
___ Does the writer use active voice?
___ Does the writer use the appropriate verb tense throughout the paper?
___ Is there agreement between all pronouns and antecedents?
___ Are there effective and appropriately used transitions?

Comments regarding other mechanical problems:

III. Argument

___ Are you persuaded by the arguments?
___ Does the author need stronger arguments? More arguments?

Other helpful comments:

APPENDIX C

NOVEL REVIEW

BOOK _____ STUDENT _____

AUTHOR _____ DATE OF READING _____

I. BRIEFLY DESCRIBE:
PROTAGONIST—

ANTAGONIST—

OTHER CHARACTERS USED TO DEVELOP PROTAGONIST—

IF APPLICABLE, STATE WHY ANY OF THE BOOK'S CHARACTERS REMIND YOU OF SPECIFIC BIBLE CHARACTERS.

II. SETTING:

III. POINT OF VIEW: (CIRCLE ONE) FIRST PERSON, THIRD PERSON, THIRD PERSON OMNISCIENT

IV. BRIEF SUMMARY OF THE PLOT:

V. THEME (THE QUINTESSENTIAL MEANING/PURPOSE OF THE BOOK IN ONE OR TWO SENTENCES):

VI. AUTHOR'S WORLDVIEW: HOW DO YOU KNOW? WHAT BEHAVIORS DO(ES) THE CHARACTER(S) MANIFEST THAT LEAD YOU TO THIS CONCLUSION?

VII. WHY DID YOU LIKE/DISLIKE THIS BOOK?

VIII. THE NEXT LITERARY WORK I READ WILL BE . . .

SHORT STORY REVIEW

SHORT STORY _____ STUDENT _____

AUTHOR _____ DATE OF READING _____

I. BRIEFLY DESCRIBE
PROTAGONIST—

ANTAGONIST—

OTHER CHARACTERS USED TO DEVELOP PROTAGONIST—

IF APPLICABLE, STATE WHY ANY OF THE STORY'S CHARACTERS REMIND YOU OF SPECIFIC BIBLE CHARACTERS.

II. SETTING

III. POINT OF VIEW: (CIRCLE ONE) FIRST PERSON, THIRD PERSON, THIRD PERSON OMNISCIENT

IV. BRIEF SUMMARY OF THE PLOT

IDENTIFY THE CLIMAX OF THE SHORT STORY.

V. THEME (THE QUINTESSENTIAL MEANING/PURPOSE OF THE STORY IN ONE OR TWO SENTENCES):

VI. AUTHOR'S WORLDVIEW:
HOW DO YOU KNOW THIS? WHAT BEHAVIORS DO(ES) THE CHARACTER(S) MANIFEST THAT LEAD YOU TO THIS CONCLUSION?

VII. WHY DID YOU LIKE/DISLIKE THIS SHORT STORY?

VIII. THE NEXT LITERARY WORK I READ WILL BE . . .

DRAMA REVIEW

PLAY _____ STUDENT _____

AUTHOR _____ DATE OF READING _____

I. BRIEFLY DESCRIBE
PROTAGONIST—

ANTAGONIST—

IF APPLICABLE, STATE WHY ANY OF THE PLAY'S CHARACTERS REMIND YOU OF SPECIFIC BIBLE
CHARACTERS.

II. SETTING

III. POINT OF VIEW: (CIRCLE ONE) FIRST PERSON, THIRD PERSON, THIRD PERSON OMNISCIENT

IV. BRIEF SUMMARY OF THE PLOT

IDENTIFY THE CLIMAX OF THE PLAY.

V. THEME (THE QUINTESSENTIAL MEANING/PURPOSE OF THE PLAY IN ONE OR TWO SENTENCES)

VI. AUTHOR'S WORLDVIEW
HOW DO YOU KNOW THIS? WHAT BEHAVIORS DO(ES) THE CHARACTER(S) MANIFEST THAT LEAD YOU TO THIS CONCLUSION?

VII. WHY DID YOU LIKE/DISLIKE THIS PLAY?

VIII. THE NEXT LITERARY WORK I WILL READ WILL BE . . .

NON-FICTION REVIEW

LITERARY WORK _____ STUDENT _____

AUTHOR _____ DATE OF READING _____

I. WRITE A PRÉCIS OF THIS BOOK. IN YOUR PRÉCIS, CLEARLY STATE THE AUTHOR'S THESIS AND SUPPORTING ARGUMENTS.

II. ARE YOU PERSUADED? WHY OR WHY NOT?

III. WHY DID YOU LIKE/DISLIKE THIS BOOK?

IV. THE NEXT LITERARY WORK I READ WILL BE . . .

APPENDIX D

PRAYER JOURNAL GUIDE

Journal Guide Questions
Bible Passage(s): _____
_____
_____

1. Centering Time (a list of those things that I must do later):

2. Discipline of Silence (remain absolutely still and quiet).

3. Reading Scripture Passage (with notes on text):

4. Living in Scripture:
A. How does the passage affect the person mentioned in the passage? How does he/she feel?

B. How does the passage affect my life? What is the Lord saying to me through this passage?

5. Prayers of Adoration and Thanksgiving, Intercession, and Future Prayer Targets:

6. Discipline of Silence

APPENDIX E

Book List for Supplemental Reading

Note:
Not all literature is suitable for all students; educators and students should choose literature appropriate to students' age, maturity, interests, and abilities.

Jane Austen, EMMA
Charlotte Brontë, JANE EYRE
Thomas Bulfinch, THE AGE OF FABLE
Pearl S. Buck, THE GOOD EARTH
John Bunyan, PILGRIM'S PROGRESS
Agatha Christie, AND THEN THERE WERE NONE
Samuel T. Coleridge, RIME OF THE ANCIENT MARINER
Jospeh Conrad, HEART OF DARKNESS, LORD JIM
James F. Cooper, THE LAST OF THE MOHICANS, DEERSLAYER
Stephen Crane, THE RED BADGE OF COURAGE
Clarence Day, LIFE WITH FATHER
Daniel Defoe, ROBINSON CRUSOE
Charles Dickens, GREAT EXPECTATIONS, A CHRISTMAS CAROL, A TALE OF TWO CITIES, OLIVER TWIST, NICHOLAS NICKLEBY
Arthur C. Doyle, THE ADVENTURES OF SHERLOCK HOLMES
Alexander Dumas, THE THREE MUSKETEERS
George Eliot, SILAS MARNER
T.S. Eliot, MURDER IN THE CATHEDRAL, SILAS MARNER
Anne Frank, THE DIARY OF ANNE FRANK
Oliver Goldsmith, THE VICAR OF WAKEFIELD
Edith Hamilton, MYTHOLOGY
Nathaniel Hawthorne, THE SCARLET LETTER, THE HOUSE OF THE SEVEN GABLES
Thor Heyerdahl, KON-TIKI
J. Hilton, LOST HORIZON, GOODBYE, MR. CHIPS
Homer, THE ODYSSEY, THE ILIAD

W. H. Hudson, GREEN MANSIONS
Victor Hugo, LES MISERABLES, THE HUNCHBACK OF NOTRE DAME
Zora Neale Hurston, THEIR EYES WERE WATCHING GOD
Washington Irving, THE SKETCH BOOK
Rudyard Kipling, CAPTAINS COURAGEOUS
Harper Lee, TO KILL A MOCKINGBIRD
Madeline L'Engle, A CIRCLE OF QUIET, THE SUMMER OF THE GREAT GRANDMOTHER, A WRINKLE IN TIME
C.S. Lewis, THE SCREWTAPE LETTERS, MERE CHRISTIANITY, CHRONICLES OF NARNIA
Jack London, THE CALL OF THE WILD, WHITE FANG
George MacDonald, CURATE'S AWAKENING, ETC.
Sir Thomas Malory, LE MORTE D'ARTHUR
Guy de Maupassant, SHORT STORIES
Herman Melville, BILLY BUDD, MOBY DICK
Monsarrat, THE CRUEL SEA
C. Nordhoff & Hall, MUTINY ON THE BOUNTY
Edgar Allen Poe, POEMS & SHORT STORIES
E. M. Remarque, ALL QUIET ON THE WESTERN FRONT
Anne Rinaldi, A BREAK WITH CHARITY: STORY OF THE SALEM WITCH TRIALS
Carl Sanburg, ABRAHAM LINCOLN
William Saroyan, THE HUMAN COMEDY
Sir Walter Scott, IVANHOE
William Shakespeare, HAMLET, MACBETH, JULIUS CAESAR, AS YOU LIKE IT, ROMEO AND JULIET, A MIDSUMMER NIGHT'S DREAM, ETC.
George Bernard Shaw, PYGMALION
Sophocles, ANTIGONE
Harriet Beecher Stowe, UNCLE TOM'S CABIN
John Steinbeck, OF MICE AND MEN, GRAPES OF WRATH
R. L. Stevenson, DR. JEKYLL AND MR. HYDE, TREASURE ISLAND, KIDNAPPED
Irving Stone, LUST FOR LIFE

Jonathan Swift, GULLIVER'S TRAVELS
Booth Tarkington, PENROD
J.R.R. Tolkien, THE LORD OF THE RINGS TRILOGY
Mark Twain, ADVENTURES OF HUCKLEBERRY FINN, THE ADVENTURES OF TOM SAWYER
Jules Verne, MASTER OF THE WORLD
Booker T. Washington, UP FROM SLAVERY
H. G. Wells, COLLECTED WORKS
Tennessee Williams, THE GLASS MENAGERIE

FOR OLDER STUDENTS

Chinua Achebe, THINGS FALL APART
Aristotle, POETICUS
Edward Bellamy, LOOKING BACKWARD
Jorge Luis Borges, VARIOUS SHORT STORIES
Stephen V. Benet, JOHN BROWN'S BODY
Charlotte Brontë, WUTHERING HEIGHTS
Camus, THE STRANGER
Chaucer, THE CANTERBURY TALES, BEOWULF
Willa Cather, MY ANTONIA
Miguel de Cervantes, DON QUIXOTE
Fyodor Dostovesky, CRIME AND PUNISHMENT, THE IDIOT, THE BROTHERS KARAMAZOV
William Faulkner, THE HAMLET TRIOLOGY
F. Scott Fitzgerald, THE GREAT GATSBY
John Galsworthy, THE FORSYTHE SAGA
Lorraine Hansberry, RAISIN IN THE SUN
Thomas Hardy, THE RETURN OF THE NATIVE, THE MAYOR OF CASTERBRIDGE

A. E. Housman, A SHROPSHIRE LAD
Henrik Ibsen, A DOLL'S HOUSE
Charles Lamb THE ESSAYS OF ELIA
Sinclair Lewis, BABBITT, ARROWSMITH
Kamala Markandaya, NECTAR IN A SIEVE
Gabriel Barcia Marquez, 100 YEARS OF SOLITUDE
John P. Marquand, THE LATE GEORGE APLEY
E. Lee Masters, A SPOON RIVER ANTHOLOGY
Somerset Maugham, OF HUMAN BONDAGE
Arthur Miller, THE CRUCIBLE, DEATH OF A SALESMAN
Eugene O'Neill, THE EMPEROR JONES
George Orwell, ANIMAL FARM, 1984
Thomas Paine, THE RIGHTS OF MAN
Alan Paton, CRY THE BELOVED COUNTRY
Plato, THE REPUBLIC
Plutarch, LIVES
O. E. Rolvaag, GIANTS IN THE EARTH
Edmund Rostand, CYRANO DE BERGERAC
Mary Shelley, FRANKENSTEIN
Sophocles, OEDIPUS REX
John Steinbeck, THE PEARL
Ivan Turgenev, FATHERS AND SONS
William Thackeray, VANITY FAIR
Leo Tolstoy, WAR AND PEACE
Edith Wharton, ETHAN FROME
Walt Whitman, LEAVES OF GRASS
Thornton Wilder, OUR TOWN
Thomas Wolfe, LOOK HOMEWARD ANGEL

APPENDIX F

GLOSSARY OF LITERARY TERMS

Allegory A story or tale with two or more levels of meaning—a literal level and one or more symbolic levels. The events, setting, and characters in an allegory are symbols for ideas or qualities.

Alliteration The repetition of initial consonant sounds. The repetition can be juxtaposed (side by side; e.g., simply sad). An example:

I conceive therefore, as to the business of being profound, that it is with writers, as with wells; a person with good eyes may see to the bottom of the deepest, provided any water be there; and that often, when there is nothing in the world at the bottom, besides dryness and dirt, though it be but a yard and a half under ground, it shall pass, however, for wondrous deep, upon no wiser a reason than because it is wondrous dark. (Jonathan Swift)

Allusion A casual and brief reference to a famous historical or literary figure or event:

You must borrow me Gargantua's mouth first. 'Tis a word too great for any mouth of this age's size. (Shakespeare)

Analogy The process by which new or less familiar words, constructions, or pronunciations conform to the pattern of older or more familiar (and often unrelated) ones; a comparison between two unlike things. The purpose of an analogy is to describe something unfamiliar by pointing out its similarities to something that is familiar.

Antagonist In a narrative, the character with whom the main character has the most conflict. In Jack London's "To Build a Fire" the antagonist is the extreme cold of the Yukon rather than a person or animal.

Archetype The original pattern or model from which all other things of the same kind are made; a perfect example of a type or group. (e.g. The biblical character Joseph is often considered an archetype of Jesus Christ.)

Argumentation The discourse in which the writer presents and logically supports a particular view or opinion; sometimes used interchangeably with *persuasion*.

Aside In a play an aside is a speech delivered by an actor in such a way that other characters on the stage are presumed not to hear it; an aside generally reveals a character's inner thoughts.

Autobiography A form of nonfiction in which a person tells his/her own life story. Notable examples of autobiography include those by Benjamin Franklin and Frederick Douglass.

Ballad A song or poem that tells a story in short stanzas and simple words with repetition, refrain, etc.

Biography A form of nonfiction in which a writer tells the life story of another person.

Character A person or an animal who takes part in the action of a literary work. The *main character* is the one on whom the work focuses. The person with whom the main character has the most conflict is the *antagonist*. He is the enemy of the main character (*protagonist*). For instance, in *The Scarlet Letter*, by Nathaniel Hawthorne, Chillingsworth is the antagonist. Hester is the protagonist. Characters who appear in the story may perform actions, speak to other characters, be described by the narrator, or be remembered. Characters introduced whose sole purpose is to develop the main character are called *foils*.

Classicism An approach to literature and the other arts that stresses reason, balance, clarity, ideal beauty, and orderly form in imitation of the arts of Greece and Rome.

Conflict A struggle between opposing forces; can be internal or external; when occurring within a character is called *internal conflict*. An example of this occurs in Mark Twain's *Adventures of Huckleberry Finn*. In this novel Huck is struggling in his mind about whether to return an escaped slave, his good friend Jim, to the authorities. An *external conflict* is normally an obvious conflict between the protagonist and antagonist(s). London's "To Build a Fire" illustrates conflict between a character and an outside force. Most plots develop from conflict, making conflict one of the primary elements of narrative literature.

Crisis or *Climax* The moment or event in the *plot* in which the conflict is most directly addressed: the main character "wins" or "loses"; the secret is revealed. After the climax, the *denouement* or falling action occurs.

Dialectic Examining opinions or ideas logically, often by the method of question and answer

Discourse, Forms of Various modes into which writing can be classified; traditionally, writing has been divided into the following modes:
Exposition Writing which presents information
Narration Writing which tells a story
Description Writing which portrays people, places, or things
Persuasion (sometimes also called *Argumentation*) Writing which attempts to convince people to think or act in a certain way

Drama A story written to be performed by actors; the playwright supplies dialogue for the characters to speak and stage directions that give information about costumes, lighting, scenery, properties, the setting, and the character's movements and ways of speaking.

Dramatic monologue A poem or speech in which an imaginary character speaks to a silent listener. Eliot's "The Love Song of J. Alfred Prufrock" is a dramatic monologue.

Elegy A solemn and formal lyric poem about death, often one that mourns the passing of some particular person; Whitman's "When Lilacs Last in the Dooryard Bloom'd" is an elegy lamenting the death of President Lincoln.

Essay A short, nonfiction work about a particular subject; *essay* comes from the Old French word *essai*, meaning "a trial or attempt"; meant to be explanatory, an essay is not meant to be an exhaustive treatment of a subject; can be classified as formal or informal, personal or impersonal; can also be classified according to purpose as either expository, argumentative, descriptive, persuasive, or narrative.

Figurative Language See *metaphor, simile, analogy*

Foil A character who provides a contrast to another character and whose purpose is to develop the main character.

Genre A division or type of literature; commonly divided into three major divisions, literature is either poetry, prose, or drama; each major genre can then be divided into smaller genres: poetry can be divided into lyric, concrete, dramatic, narrative, and epic poetry; prose can be divided into fiction (novels and short stories) and nonfiction (biography, autobiography, letters, essays, and reports); drama can be divided into serious drama, tragedy, comic drama, melodrama, and farce.

Gothic The use of primitive, medieval, wild, or mysterious elements in literature; Gothic elements offended 18th century classical writers but appealed to the Romantic writers who followed them. Gothic novels feature writers who use places like mysterious castles where horrifying supernatural events take place; Poe's "The Fall of the House of Usher" illustrates the influence of Gothic elements.

Harlem Renaissance Occurring during the 1920s, a time of African American artistic creativity centered in Harlem in New York City; Langston Hughes was a Harlem Renaissance writer.

Hyperbole A deliberate exaggeration or overstatement; in Mark Twain's "The Notorious Jumping From of Calaveras County," the claim that Jim Smiley would follow a bug as far as Mexico to win a bet is hyperbolic.

Idyll A poem or part of a poem that describes and idealizes country life; Whittier's "Snowbound" is an idyll.

Irony A method of humorous or subtly sarcastic expression in which the intended meanings of the words used is the direct opposite of their usual sense.

Journal A daily autobiographical account of events and personal reactions.

Kenning Indirect way of naming people or things; knowledge or recognition; in Old English poetry, a metaphorical name for something.

Literature All writings in prose or verse, especially those of an imaginative or critical character, without regard to their excellence and/or writings considered as having permanent value, excellence of form, great emotional effect, etc.

Metaphor (Figure of speech) A comparison which creatively identifies one thing with another dissimilar thing and transfers or ascribes to the first thing some of the qualities of the second. Unlike a *simile* or *analogy*, metaphor asserts that one thing is another thing—not just that one is like another. Very frequently a metaphor is invoked by the verb *to be*:

Affliction then is ours;
We are the trees whom shaking fastens more. (George Herbert)

Then Jesus declared, "I am the bread of life." (John 6:35)
Jesus answered, "I am the Way and the truth and the life." (John 14:6)

Meter A poem's rhythmical pattern, determined by the number and types of stresses, or beats, in each line; a certain number of *metrical feet* make up a *line* of verse; (pentameter denotes a line containing five metrical feet); the act of describing the meter of a poem is called *scanning* which involves marking the stressed and unstressed syllables, as follows:
iamb A foot with one unstressed syllable followed by one stressed syllable, as in the word *abound*.
trochee A foot with one stressed syllable followed by one unstressed syllable, as in the word *spoken*.
anapest A foot with two unstressed syllables followed by one stressed syllable, as in the word *interrupt*.

dactyl A foot with a stressed syllable followed by two unstressed syllables, as in the word *accident*.
spondee Two stressed feet: *quicksand, heartbeat*; occurs only occasionally in English.

Motif A main idea element, feature; a main theme or subject to be elaborated on.

Narration The way the author chooses to tell the story.
First Person Narration: A character and refers to himself or herself, using "I." Example: Huck Finn in *The Adventures of Huckleberry Finn* tells the story from his perspective. This is a creative way to bring humor into the plot.
Second Person Narration: Addresses the reader and/or the main character as "you" (and may also use first person narration, but not necessarily). One example is the opening of each of Rudyard Kipling's *Just So Stories*, in which the narrator refers to the child listener as "O Best Beloved."
Third Person Narration: Not a character in the story; refers to the story's characters as "he" and "she." This is probably the most common form of narration.
Limited Narration: Only able to tell what one person is thinking or feeling. Example: in *A Separate Peace*, by John Knowles, we only see the story from Gene's perspective.
Omniscient Narration: Charles Dickens employs this narration in most of his novels.
Reliable Narration: Everything this Narration says is true, and the Narrator knows everything that is necessary to the story.
Unreliable Narrator: May not know all the relevant information; may be intoxicated or mentally ill; may lie to the audience. Example: Edgar Allan Poe's narrators are frequently unreliable. Think of the delusions that the narrator of "The Tell-Tale Heart" has about the old man.

Narrative In story form.

Onomatopoeia. Use of words which, in their pronunciation, suggest their meaning. "Hiss," for example, when spoken is intended to resemble the sound of steam or of a snake. Other examples include these: *slam, buzz, screech, whirr, crush, sizzle, crunch, wring, wrench, gouge, grind, mangle, bang, blam, pow, zap, fizz, urp, roar, growl, blip, click, whimper*, and, of course, *snap, crackle, and pop*.

Parallelism Two or more balancing statements with phrases, clauses, or paragraphs of similar length and grammatical structure.

Plot Arrangement of the action in fiction or drama—events of the story in the order the story gives them. A typical plot has five parts: *Exposition, Rising Action, Crisis* or *Climax, Falling Action*, and *Resolution (*sometimes called *Denouement)*.

Précis Summary of the plot of a literary piece.

Protagonist The enemy of the main character (*antagonist*).

Rhetoric Using words effectively in writing and speaking.

Setting The place(s) and time(s) of a story, including the historical period, social milieu of the characters, geographical location, descriptions of indoor and outdoor locales.

Scop An Old English poet or bard.

Simile A figure of speech in which one thing is likened to another dissimilar thing by the use of *like, as*, etc.

Sonnet A poem normally of fourteen lines in any of several fixed verse and rhyme schemes, typically in rhymed iambic pentameter; sonnets characteristically express a single theme or idea.

Structure The arrangement of details and scenes that make up a literary work.

Style An author's characteristic arrangement of words. A style may be colloquial, formal, terse, wordy, theoretical, subdued, colorful, poetic, or highly individual. Style is the arrangement of words in groups and sentences; *diction* on the other hand refers to the choice of individual words; the arrangement of details and scenes make up the *structure* of a literary work; all combine to influence the tone of the work; thus, diction, style, and structure make up the *form* of the literary work.

Theme The one-sentence, major meaning of a literary piece, rarely stated but implied. The theme is not a moral, which is a statement of the author's didactic purpose of his literary piece. A thesis statement is very similar to the theme.

Tone The attitude the author takes toward his subject; author's attitude is revealed through choice of details, through diction and style, and through the emphasis and comments that are made; like theme and style, tone is sometimes difficult to describe with a single word or phrase; often it varies in the same literary piece to suit the moods of the characters and the situations. For instance, the tone or mood of Poe's "Annabel Lee" is very somber.

Credits, Permissions, and Sources

Efforts have been made to conform to US Copyright Law. Any infringement is unintentional, and any file which infringes copyright, and about which the copyright claimant informs me, will be removed pending resolution.

All graphics are copyrighted by Clipart.com unless otherwise noted.

Most of the literature cited in this book is in the public domain. Much of it is available on the Internet through the following sites:

Bartleby.com, Great Books Online
Aeschylus, *Oresteia*
Budda, *The Bhagavad-Gîtââ*
Confucius, *The Sayings of Confucius*
Epictetus, *The golden sayings of Epictetus*, with the Hymn of Cleanthes; translated and arranged by Hastings Crossley
Mohammed, *Koran*
Plato, *Apology*
Unknown, *The Song of Roland*

Susan Wise Bauer, *Writing The Short Story* (Charles City, VA)

Classical Short Stories: The Best of the Genre (http://www.geocities.com/short_stories_page/index.html)
Leo Tolstoy, The Death of Ivan Ilych, Translated by Louise and Aylmer Maude.

Early Christian Writings (http://www.earlychristianwritings.com/justin.html)
Writings, by Polycarp, Justin Martyr, and Clement

Enuma Elish translated by N. K. Sanders (http://www.piney.com/Enuma.html)

Everypoet.com
Dante, *Inferno*

Gilgamesh Epic, translated by E. A. Speiser, in *Ancient Near Eastern Texts* (Princeton, 1950), pp. 60-72, as reprinted in Isaac Mendelsohn (ed.), *Religions of the Ancient Near East*, Library of Religion paperbook series (New York, 1955). PP. 100-6; notes by Mendolenson (http://www-relg-studies.scu.edu/netcours/rs011/restrict/gilflood.htm).

Herodotus, *Histories*. Translated by Rawlinson. (http://www.concordance.com/)

Herodotus and the Bible, Wayne Jackson (http://www.christiancourier.com/archives/)

http://www.cyberhymnal.org/htm/m/i/mightyfo.htm
Martin Luther, *A Mighty Fortress is Our God*

Infomotions, Inc. The Alex Catalogue of Electronic Texts (http://www.infomotions.com/alex/).

Infoplease.com. 2002 Family Education Network. (http://aolsvc.aol.infoplease.com/ipa/A0874987.html)

The Internet Classics Archive (http://classics.mit.edu/Aristotle/poetics.1.1.html)

Aristotle, *Poetics*

Internet Applications Laboratory at the University of Evansville
Plato, *Symposium*

The Library of Congress Collection (http://www.loc.gov/exhibits/gadd/)

Lecture on Sor Juana Ines de la Cruz (http://www.latin_american.cam.ac.uk/SorJuana/)
Sor Juana Ines de la Cruz, "May Heaven Serve as Plate for the Engraving" and "Yet if, for Singing your Praise."

National Park Service (http://www.nps.gov/edal/index.htm)

The Pachomius Library (http://www.ocf.org/OrthodoxPage/reading/St.Pachomius/Liturgical/didache.html)
Unknown, *The Didache*, edited by Friar Martin Fontenot Gonzalez

Shinto Creation Stories (http://www.wsu.edu/~dee/ANCJAPAN/CREAT2.HTM)
The Creation of the gods (Translated by W.G. Aston, Nihongi (London: Kegan, Paul, Trench, Trüübner, 1896), 1-2

Stephane Theroux. Classic Reader (http://classicreader.com/)
Anton Chekov, *The Sea Gull*
Andrew Barton Paterson, The Man From Snowy River

University of Oregon. (http://www.uoregon.edu)
Iliad, Homer. Translated by Samuel Butler.

University of Pennsylvania (www.sas.upenn.edu/)
Author Unknown, *Ani Papyrus: Book of the Dead*

University of Virginia. Browse E-Books by Author (http://etext.lib.virginia.edu/ebooks/Wlist.html).

University of Wisconsin, Milwaukee. The Classic Text: Traditions and Interpretations (http://www.uwm.edu/Library/special/exhibits/clastext/clshome.htm)